DISCARDED

The American Exploration and Travel Series
(*Complete list on pages 422–24*)

The ADVENTURES *of*
Captain Bonneville

The ADVENTURES of
Captain Bonneville
U.S.A.

in the ROCKY MOUNTAINS and the FAR WEST

digested from his journal by
WASHINGTON IRVING

edited and with an introduction by
EDGELEY W. TODD

Norman : University of Oklahoma Press

by EDGELEY W. TODD

A Listener's Guide to Musical Form (Dubuque, 1949)
The Adventures of Captain Bonneville by Washington Irving (Editor) (Norman, 1961)

Library of Congress Catalog Card Number: 61-15144

New edition copyright 1961 by the University of Oklahoma Press, Publishing Division of the University. Composed and printed at Norman, Oklahoma, U. S. A., by the University of Oklahoma Press. First printing.

Editor's Foreword

THE ADVENTURES OF CAPTAIN BONNEVILLE has a double claim to recognition: it was written by one of America's foremost men of letters, and it accurately portrays the lives of roving bands of trappers in the years before the West became the goal of settlers and gold seekers. Although some literary historians have disparaged this book as a product of Irving's waning creativity, the fact remains that Irving wrote it with great interest and enthusiasm. He made every effort to be authentic, and he became, as a consequence of writing it and his two previous books, *A Tour on the Prairies* and *Astoria*, an authority on the fur trade and one of the best informed persons in the United States on the western frontier. Like its two predecessors, *The Adventures of Captain Bonneville* is still highly readable. Unaccountably, it has never previously been presented in an annotated edition.

This edition is not offered as a definitive treatment of Bonneville's role as a trader, explorer, or observer of Indian life. Undoubtedly there are documents that have not come to my attention that would enlarge our understanding of numerous circumstances connected with his expedition. There is only scanty knowledge, for example, of the financial aspects of Bonneville's expedition. But within such limitations, I have attempted with reasonable thoroughness to document the book to show Bonneville's activities in the larger context of the fur trade during the first half decade of the 1830's. I have tried, in addition, to relate his travels to the country which he traversed during a period of three years, and in this respect have been at some pains to detail his routes after following many of them myself. I hope that this effort plus close scrutiny of contemporary accounts of other men in the fur trade has clarified certain facts heretofore either confused or little understood. I have not hesitated where necessary to point out Irving's errors, which are surprisingly few considering when and where he wrote, or to add notes regarding details that he failed to touch upon.

Although it has been known since Irving published the book in 1837 that he had access to the manuscript journals of Nathaniel J. Wyeth, Bonneville's friend and contemporary in the fur trade, this edition for the first time shows the extent of Irving's dependence upon Wyeth as a supplement to Bonneville's own account. It also untangles a problem that has ensnared historians for too many years—the proper identification of Montero, one of Bonneville's men, as a personage distinct from Joseph R. Walker, with whom he has been confused. Although I have read every known account of the Walker expedition to California in 1833–34, I have not been able to add anything new to previous studies, such as that by Robert Glass Cleland in *This Reckless Breed of Men*. I have tried to assess the motives that gave rise to Bonneville's expedition, and, as will be evident in the Introduction, have taken a somewhat different view of it from that held by numerous other writers since Chittenden's *History of the American Fur Trade in the Far West* appeared in 1902. The Introduction also shows what resulted from Bonneville's overstaying his official army furlough by nearly two years. Although several writers have covered these events in a general way, I have tried to present in greater detail the efforts that Bonneville made to gain reinstatement and the considerations that finally restored him to his former rank. The pertinent documents in this connection cast a light on circumstances that have previously been obscure or unknown.

The text used here is that of the author's revised edition, which differs only slightly from the text of the first edition. Obvious errors have been silently corrected, and the original table of contents has been omitted. Irving's footnotes, however, have been retained as has his appendix, which appears here as Appendix A. Appendix B has been added. A special feature of this edition is the reprinting of the maps that appeared in the first edition. Photographs used as

Editor's Foreword

illustrations when not otherwise credited were made by the editor, Edgeley W. Todd.

In searching for information I have obligated myself to many people and institutions, more, indeed, than I can properly acknowledge: to the Henry E. Huntington Library and Art Gallery for grants-in-aid during three summers to enable me to continue my study of the fur trade and its cultural implications, and especially to the late Robert G. Cleland of that institution, warm and humane historian of the West, who freely shared his knowledge and enthusiasm; to the Newberry Library, the Colorado Historical Library, the Western Department of the Denver Public Library, and to the staff of the Colorado State University Library for many courtesies. Mr. Gilbert A. Cam and Mr. Robert W. Hill of the New York Public Library; Mr. Merle W. Wells of the Idaho Historical Society; Mrs. Dorothy Williams, Oklahoma Historical Society; Miss Barbara D. Simison, Yale University Library; Mr. James L. Harlan, Department of English, Colorado State University; Mr. James J. Heslin, New York Historical Society; Mr. Harry E. Lichter, Oregon Historical Society; Miss Mabel E. Deutrich, National Archives and Records Service; Dr. William A. Weber, Curator of the Herbarium, University of Colorado; Mrs. Frances H. Stadler, Missouri Historical Society; Mr. James Harrower of Pinedale, Wyoming; the late Perry Jenkins of Cora, Wyoming, and Salt Lake City; and numerous other persons have generously responded to my questions or have helped in other ways. To the Colorado State University Research Foundation I am also indebted for assistance in procuring needed documents.

Special thanks are due to Mrs. Margaret Lindsley of Drummond, Idaho, who showed me the site of Camp Henry west of the Tetons, and to Professor Ralph Wilson, Department of Forestry, Idaho State College, who kindly took of his time to guide me to the site of Fort Hall on the Snake River. Warm appreciation is extended to my good friends Mr. and Mrs. Floyd Spencer of Big Piney, Wyoming, who acquainted me years ago with the site of the several Green River rendezvous and who led me to the location of Fort Bonneville in Sublette County, Wyoming.

Finally to my wife, Lois, companion of many western trails, is due appreciation and affection for long-shared interest, help, and companionship in tramping over the dim traces of the faded past of America's historic West.

EDGELEY W. TODD

Contents

Editor's Foreword	*page* vii
Editor's Introduction	xvii
Introductory Notice	xlix
The Adventures of Captain Bonneville	3
Appendix A	374

    Mr. Wyeth, and the trade of the Far West
    Wreck of a Japanese junk on the Northwest coast
    Instructions to Captain Bonneville from the Major General commanding the Army of the United States

Appendix B	381

    Captain Bonneville's letter to Major General Macomb, July 29, 1833
    B. L. E. Bonneville's letter to the Secretary of War, Lewis Cass, September 30, 1835
    Captain Bonneville's Itinerary and Chronology

Editor's Bibliography	401
Index	409

List of Illustrations

Washington Irving	*facing page* xxxii
B. L. E. Bonneville	xxxiii
Jim Bridger	10
Joseph Reddeford Walker and His Squaw	11
"Buffalo Hunting"	74
"Buffalo Hunt, Under the White Wolf Skin"	75
Nathaniel Wyeth	106
South Pass	107
Fort Vancouver	202
Green River	203
Horse Creek	234
Letter from Captain Bonneville to David Adams	235
Site of Fort Bonneville	298
Old Fort Walla Walla	299
"Catching the Wild Horse"	330
Fort Hall Marker	331

List of Maps

The Plains and Rocky Mountains,
   1832–35 *page* 14
The Pacific Northwest 119
The Bonneville Map of the Sources of the
   Colorado and Big Salt Lake 154
The Bonneville Map of the Territory West
   of the Rocky Mountains 266
The Walker Expedition Country 291

Editor's Introduction

ON AUGUST 22, 1835, Captain Benjamin Bonneville and a procession of tattered, savage-looking trappers returned to Independence, Missouri, the westernmost settlement of the United States frontier, after nearly three and one-half years in the Rocky Mountains. By the end of August or early in September, Bonneville had journeyed on to New York, and at Hellgate, the country estate of John Jacob Astor, had the good fortune to meet Washington Irving, the man who would soon make him famous by publishing in 1837 a two-volume account of his expedition entitled *The Rocky Mountains,* later renamed *The Adventures of Captain Bonneville.*

Today many people who think of Irving chiefly as the author of the humorous Knickerbocker's *History of New York* or of the delightfully quaint stories of Rip Van Winkle and Ichabod Crane are surprised to learn that he was also the author of three highly interesting books on the early West. It was also a surprise to Irving's contemporaries that in 1832, after seventeen years of self-exile in the polite centers of Europe, he should almost at once vanish into the Indian country west of the Mississippi and after a few months of rough outdoor life with frontiersmen, trappers, Indians, and border soldiers publish an engrossing narrative of what he had seen and done. When *A Tour on the Prairies* came out in 1835, the year that Bonneville and Irving met in Astor's plush parlors, reviewers exclaimed over the unexpected light in which the famous, cosmopolitan writer now appeared. "What!" one of them in London could not but marvel, "Washington Irving a buffalo-hunter on the Prairies? . . . It was but as yesterday we saw this same Wash-

The ADVENTURES *of* CAPTAIN BONNEVILLE

ington Irving in London a quiet, gentlemanly, *douce*, little, middle-aged man."¹

By the time that readers were enjoying this unusual and latest product from Irving's pen, Irving had a second book on the Far West in preparation. This was *Astoria*, a history of Astor's fur-trading enterprise in the distant wilderness bordering the Columbia River over two decades before Irving found himself listening with eager attention to Bonneville's quiet account of his own experiences as an explorer and fur trader. In rapid succession Irving produced three substantial books devoted exclusively to the West. How can this seemingly new interest be explained in a writer whose reputation was built almost entirely on a concern with Old World culture?

Actually, this interest was neither new nor unpremeditated. It had, in fact, been thoroughly aroused when Irving was still a young man. At the age of twenty he had visited Montreal and there met the partners and clerks of the Northwest Company and the *voyageurs* from the interior of the fur-bearing wilderness. Seeing these "lords of the ascendant," he had "gazed with wondering and inexperienced eye at the baronial wassailing, and listened with astonished ear to their tales of hardships and adventures"² in uncivilized lands among savage tribes—a way of life far beyond the experience of a law clerk from New York.

In his introduction to *Astoria*, Irving commented:

> I was at an age when imagination lends its coloring to everything, and the stories of these Sinbads of the wilderness made the life of a trapper and fur trader perfect romance to me. I even meditated at one time a visit to the remote posts of the company in the boats which annually ascended the lakes and rivers, being thereto invited by one of the partners; and I have ever since regretted that I was prevented by circumstances from carrying my intention into effect. From these early impressions, the grand enterprise of the great fur companies, and the hazardous errantry of their associates in the wild parts of our vast continent, have always been themes of charmed interest to me; and I have felt anxious to get at the details of their adventurous

[1] Quoted by Stanley T. Williams, *The Life of Washington Irving*, II, 350 n.
[2] Washington Irving, *Astoria*, I, 25.

Editor's Introduction

expeditions among the savage tribes that peopled the depths of the wilderness.[3]

His visit to Canada took place in the summer of 1803, the year before Lewis and Clark set out on their momentous expedition to the mouth of the Columbia. That expedition and its report of rich fur-bearing streams in the mountain wilderness focused attention on the potential wealth to be reaped there by anyone with the capital and desire to promote a large-scale enterprise. John Jacob Astor had recognized that opportunity, and by 1811 his partners in the Pacific Fur Company had erected Fort Astoria on the south bank of the Columbia only a few miles from where Lewis and Clark had wintered at Fort Clatsop five years before.

When Irving had returned east from his tour in the Indian country in the autumn of 1832, Astor proposed to him that he write the history of the Astorian enterprise. "The suggestion struck upon the chord of early associations already vibrating in my mind," Irving later remarked;[4] and sensing the inherent interest of the subject as well as a means of preserving "a transient state of things fast passing into oblivion,"[5] he agreed to the undertaking.

In this way the book *Astoria* came into being. As stated earlier, Irving was working on it when he met Bonneville at Astor's home. In listening to Bonneville's story of his three years in the fur-trapping West, Irving was favorably impressed with the Captain and, he said, "addressed many questions to him." These were questions intended undoubtedly to elicit information pertinent to the writing of *Astoria*. But if anything was said about a future book about Bonneville's own expedition, no record has survived.

Within three or four months Irving called upon the Captain in his quarters in Washington, D. C. Bonneville had been dropped from the army in 1833 because he had overstayed his leave; and now, waiting for his superiors to consider his application for reinstatement, he was attempting to write a narrative of his expedition. Irving may have read portions of the manuscript during this visit,

[3] *Ibid.*, 3–4.
[4] *Ibid.*, 4.
[5] *Ibid.*, 25.

but of this we cannot be certain. Subsequently, we know he purchased it. All that he tells us in his introduction is that Bonneville put it "at my disposal"; but Pierre M. Irving, his nephew and future biographer, said later that Irving paid Bonneville one thousand dollars for it.[6] The circumstances of this purchase, which was made in March, 1836, will be detailed later.

Just what Irving bought at that time is a matter of speculation. The title page of the published book stated that it was "digested" from Bonneville's journal, and Bonneville subsequently referred to the book as "my journal." It seems likely that what Irving actually purchased was not the original journal that Bonnville had carried in the West but a manuscript based upon it. Since the original journal has not come to light, we can form no exact idea of what it was like; but if later Bonneville journals, for example his "Journal of a March from the Mouth of the Gallinas River to Fort Clark, Texas, in 1869,"[7] are typical, it consisted of tabulated data under such headings as "Date," "Weather," "Topography," and "Remarks." These tabulated field notes could best be worked into a connected narrative by the person who had compiled them; and what Irving eventually bought, it would appear, was the manuscript that he now found Bonneville working on—"rewriting and extending his travelling notes," as Irving tells us in his Introductory Notice. It was this second manuscript, not the original journal, for which Irving paid Bonneville one thousand dollars. The original journal had been turned over to the War Department as Bonneville's report of his observations of the western country and its inhabitants.

That the journal was submitted to the War Department is evident from a letter Irving wrote to Major General Alexander Macomb on September 20, 1835, not many days after Irving had met Bonneville at Hellgate. This letter, written in New York, reads in part:

> Capt Bonneville, who has recently returned from the Rocky Mountains has had the kindness to show me his journals in which are a few small maps of various parts of the mountains. As these maps throw a light on the topography of certain portions of the country

[6] Pierre M. Irving, *Life and Letters of Washington Irving*, III, 114.
[7] United States National Archives, Adjutant General's Office (Record Group 94).

Editor's Introduction

about which I feel some curiosity I am desirous of getting copies of two or three of them. Capt Bonneville tells me it is possible his journal may be deposited in your department.[8]

What Irving had seen at Hellgate was clearly the original journal that Bonneville immediately turned over to his superiors upon his arrival in Washington from New York. What Irving found Bonneville working on three or four months later, to repeat, was a second manuscript.

One may wonder why Irving early in September was interested in obtaining copies of Bonneville's maps at a time when he had no intention of writing a book devoted to Bonneville. The answer is that he wanted accurate information about the topography of the country involved in his narrative of Wilson Price Hunt's overland expedition to Astoria that was then taking shape as one of the central threads in the Astor book. This inference is clear from the following portion of Irving's letter to Macomb, ". . . I should take it as a great favor if you would have copied for me the map of the Wind River mountains, and another containing Henry[']s Fort and the upper branches of Snake river. There are two other maps illustrating the course of Snake river which I should likewise have."

No detailed maps of this country that Hunt and his men traversed were yet in existence in 1835. The country east along the Missouri was much better known and presented Irving with no special problem. But Hunt had come through the Wind River Mountains, and the Snake River country was where he and his party had met disaster owing to their ignorance of a treacherous and unnavigable river upon which they had confidently expected to sail safely to the Columbia. When Irving met Bonneville in Astor's home, therefore, he met a man who could help him—someone with a thorough, firsthand knowledge of the Wind River Mountains, of the entire course of Snake River, and also detailed maps of his own compilation.[9] A close

---

[8] Irving's manuscript letter is in the "Appointment, Commission and Personal Branch File relating to Benjamin L. E. Bonneville"; *ibid.* This file will hereafter be cited as Bonneville File (RG 94).

[9] If one can judge on the basis of the "Journal of a March from the Gallinas River to Fort Clark," the maps that Irving saw were small ones detailing hills,

comparison of the map published in the first edition of *Astoria* with the two appearing in *The Rocky Mountains* reveals so many similarities as to indicate that Irving—or whoever made the *Astoria* map for him—relied heavily upon the Bonneville maps. The knowledge that Bonneville brought with him to the East, consequently, contributed materially to Irving's preparation of *Astoria*.[10]

It is desirable now to shift attention to Bonneville's career in order to see the steps that led up to and qualified him for the expedition that he proposed to the government in 1831. Born in 1796 in Paris, France, where his family had been in sympathy with the Revolution, Bonneville had been brought as a child to New York, from which state he was appointed to the Military Academy at West Point in 1813 at the age of seventeen. When he graduated in 1815, he was assigned to duty in the Light Artillery in New England. Transferred to the Eighth Infantry and promoted to first lieutenant in 1819, he was ordered to duty in 1820 and assigned to construct a military road in Mississippi. This brought him to the frontier, with which most of his career from then on was connected, and provided the background leading to his expedition to the Far West.

During the ten years between 1821, when he was assigned to the Seventh Infantry, and 1831, when he obtained leave, he served at Fort Smith, Arkansas; at San Antonio, Texas; at Fort Gibson in Indian Territory; and at Jefferson Barracks in Missouri. By 1825 he had been promoted to the rank of captain.[11] At these various posts he was well located to observe events that signalized a rapidly changing West.

---

rivers, their branches, groves of trees, camp sites, distances, directions, and other features.

[10] It is noteworthy in this connection that the Appendix to *Astoria*, II, 275–79, contains an essay "Suggestions with respect to the Indian tribes, and the protection of our Trade," provided by Bonneville. Furthermore, Great Salt Lake on the *Astoria* map bears the name "Lake Bonneville."

[11] "Statement of the Military Service of Benjamin L. E. Bonneville," Bonneville File (RG 94).

Editor's Introduction

By 1820 only a relatively small portion of the Louisiana Territory and adjacent regions was officially known. Lewis and Clark and then Zebulon Pike had done their work prior to Bonneville's appearance in the West. But in 1820, Major Stephen Long led a government-sponsored exploration of the territory embraced within the limits of the Platte River, the east slopes of the Rocky Mountains, and the Arkansas River. From Fort Smith, which had been built only a few years before on a site selected by Major Long, Bonneville may have watched the historic trapping and trading party of Jacob Fowler and Colonel Hugh Glenn set out in September, 1821, for the upper Arkansas River and New Mexico. He undoubtedly was alert to the significance of William Becknell's trip from Missouri to Santa Fe on a successful trading venture in the same year, and he watched the subsequent rapid development of the Santa Fe trade. In 1822 and the years following, William H. Ashley and his men successfully opened up new beaver-trapping grounds west of the Continental Divide, and Jedediah Strong Smith and other Ashley men explored new territory as far as the Pacific Ocean for the first time. In 1824 the Hudson's Bay Company, having absorbed the Northwest Company in 1821, established a stronghold in the Northwest with the building of Fort Vancouver on the Columbia, thereby assuring themselves virtual control of the surrounding territory for many miles in every direction. The fur trade had become the dominant activity between the Mississippi River and the Pacific Ocean.

Bonneville could not have failed to notice these developments. He met many participants in the trade, men like Nathaniel Pryor, formerly of Lewis and Clark's expedition; A. P. Chouteau of the famous St. Louis family of fur traders; Hugh Glenn; Pierre Menard, associate of Manuel Lisa, who built the first trading post in Montana; and numerous others.[12] Possibly early in 1831 at Fort Gibson he met Joseph Reddeford Walker, one of Bonneville's important leaders during the three years in the mountains, and with him crystallized plans for forming his own expedition.[13] By this

---

[12] Grant Foreman, *Pioneer Days in the Early Southwest*, 244.

[13] See Douglas S. Watson, *West Wind; the Life Story of Joseph Reddeford Walker*, 19–24. Although this book is overly fictionalized and not always reliable,

time, Bonneville had had enough experience on the frontier and among Indians to make him feel confident that he could undertake such a venture.

For an army officer two primary obstacles stood in the way. He faced first the necessity of obtaining leave of absence. Since the United States was not at war and the Indian tribes along the border were quiet, he had no difficulty in achieving this object. The second obstacle was lack of money, for a captain's pay provided no capital for the sort of expedition Bonneville was planning. This requirement could be met, however, if he could interest New York businessmen in putting up the necessary capital in the expectation that the proposed trapping and trading would yield interest on their investment.

It does not appear, however, that Bonneville's purpose was primarily economic. First, he was motivated by a curiosity about a region that had not yet been visited by any official government exploring party since Lewis and Clark, who had entered only part of the country that Bonneville was to visit. Moreover, the drab life at frontier military posts undoubtedly failed to satisfy a certain adventurous element in his disposition. He desired also to add to official knowledge of a region known almost exclusively by Indians and trappers. He knew that the course of the nation was westward, and he may have had the foresight to recognize that within a few years this area was to be the scene of dramatic developments. In any case, the record does not show that Bonneville was motivated solely by the desire for personal financial gain. True, he needed capital, and the fur trade was the logical basis upon which to interest business sponsors in underwriting a private expedition. Congress not being particularly interested in 1831 in exploration of the trans-Mississippi country, into which emigration had not yet begun, it remained for an imaginative army captain to take the initiative. Some historians have advanced the theory that Bonneville's expedition may in reality have been a government spy mission, disguised as a private trading expedition, against the British in the Northwest and the

---

it provides the only account of the meeting between Walker and Bonneville. Unfortunately, it is undocumented.

Editor's Introduction

Mexicans in California.[14] But as interesting as such a hypothesis may be, the known records do not furnish conclusive support.

The steps that Bonneville took during the months of 1831 until he set out from Fort Osage in May, 1832, are readily followed. The following letter to Major General Macomb requests leave of absence and states Bonneville's proposed objectives. It is dated May 21, 1831, at Washington:

> Sir, Observing, that our country men are daily becoming more desirous of understanding the true situation and resources of that portion of our territories, lying to the north of Mexico and west of the Rocky-Mountains, has determined me, to offer my services for the advancement of that object.—I ask for no outfit, no presents for the indians, no command, wan't [sic] no protection, save passports from Our and the Mexican authorities at this place, and leave of absence for that purpose. Eleven years residence among the indians west of Arkansas Territory, has afforded me a good opportunity of becoming acquainted with the indian character, and the command of several distant [e]xpeditions into their country, some qualifications for the proposed enterprise. I would there, by observations, establish prominent points of that country, ascertain the general courses &c of the principal rivers, the location of the indian tribes and their habits, visit the American and British establishments, make myself acquainted with their manner of trade and intercourse with the Indians, finally, endevour to develop every advantage the country affords and by what means they may most readily be opened to the enterprise of our citisens [sic]. These, sir, are the objects I propose accomplishing. Early next spring, I would leave the United States, with some of the companies trading there, and on my arrival, immediately begin my labours. I have, for a long time, had this object in contemplation, anticipating with great pleasure the moment that would place it within my reach. I can conceive of no time more propitious than the present, while the attention of the Country, generally, is directed towards it. You will therefore, I trust, excuse me, if I indulge the hope of your approbation towards an enterprise, likely to prove, of so much importance. I am now on my way to New York, for the purpose of settling some private business, after

[14] See Isaac K. Russell and Howard R. Driggs, *Hidden Heroes of the Rockies*, 253-55; and Robert G. Cleland, *This Reckless Breed of Men*, 278-79.

which, if my application be favorably received, I shall earnestly turn my attention to such preparations, as may be necessary to ensure its complete success.

 I am Sir,
  Most respectfully,

       Your very obedient Servant.
       B.L.E. Bonneville
       Capt. 7th Regt. Infantry[15]

Before receiving official word that his request had been granted (see letter from Major General Macomb, July 29, 1831, Appendix A), Bonneville had left Washington and gone to New York to enlist the help of Alfred Seton, a member of a prominent mercantile family of that city and in 1831, it appears, the owner of a fur store. Years before, he had been one of the young clerks employed by Astor at Astoria. Irving explains in his Introductory Notice that Seton aided Bonneville in forming an association of businessmen, one of whom may have been Astor himself, although of this there is no direct proof. In addition to getting financial backing, Bonneville needed to assemble scientific instruments. To Major General Macomb on July 18, 1831, he wrote that he had obtained "a telescope, sextant & horizon, compass to determine the varieties of the needle, thermometer, microscope, pocket-compass case of instruments and—patent-lever time pieces to assist me in my observations. Barometers are so clumbsy [*sic*] and so easily broken, that I do not contemplate taking any."[16] Besides, he added, "I have also examined every work that was likely to yield me any information respecting that country—Humboldt's[,] MacKensie's and Clark's Journals."[17] This same letter requested passports again from both the United States and Mexican governments, possession of which would prevent "ground-

---

[15] Bonneville File (RG 94).
[16] *Ibid.*
[17] Baron Alexander von Humboldt (1769–1859), Prussian scientist, had advanced new theories of geography, meteorology, plant science, geology, and earth magnetism that probably interested Bonneville. Sir Alexander Mackenzie (1764–1820), of the Northwest Company, had been the first to cross the continent (1793); he published *Voyages . . . to the Frozen and Pacific Oceans* in 1801. Paul Allen edited the *History of the Expedition under . . . Lewis and Clark* in 1814.

Editor's Introduction

less suspicions," Bonneville wrote, should he by accident (or design) wander into Mexican territory. (These passports, it might be added here, were later carried into Mexican territory by the Walker expedition to California.) The next day, July 19, Bonneville went to West Point to practice taking astronomical observations.

Once he had completed the task of gaining financial sponsors, purchasing scientific instruments, and preparing himself for what lay ahead, Bonneville departed from New York for the frontier in August. Traveling west through Pittsburgh and Cincinnati, he arrived in St. Louis early in September. On the eleventh he left for Liberty, Missouri, near the Kansas River, and at this outfitting point probably joined Joseph R. Walker, who was helping to organize the outfit that would leave nearby Fort Osage in the coming spring. A month later he went up the Missouri some thirty miles to Fort Leavenworth for purposes that are not known, and by early December had gone below Liberty to Lexington, another outfitting point.[18] Although his permanent bachelor quarters were in St. Louis, he was moving from place to place as the assembling of his company and equipment dictated.

One of the main needs was to hire men. By May 1, when he left Fort Osage, Bonneville had 110 employees. Of these only a few are known. Since some deserted to rival traders once they reached the mountains and still others joined later, it is impossible to give an accurate list of the men he employed that winter.[19] But among them was one David Adams.

---

[18] Letters of September 10, October 10, and December 5, 1831, to Colonel Roger Jones, Bonneville File (RG 94).

[19] Not including those who joined at various times during Bonneville's stay in the mountains, the following men, besides Walker and Cerré, were among the original group (in some instances only last names are known): Matthieu; Benjamin Hardister (killed); David Adams; Jennings (killed by Indians at Sheep Rock); Le Roy (killed by Indians); Ross (killed by Indians); E [?] Hodgkiss, Bonneville's clerk. Antonio Montero and B. Bourdalone may have joined later. Eventually Zenas Leonard, Joseph Meek, Stephen Meek, George Nidever, Nathan Daily, William Craig, William S. Williams, Joseph Gale, Mark Head, Robert Mitchell, Alexis Godey, Antoine Janisse, and Robert Newell were at times employed by Bonneville. Rival traders complained of Bonneville's high wages; see Hiram M. Chittenden, *A History of the American Fur Trade of the Far West*, I, 405-406 n.

The ADVENTURES *of* CAPTAIN BONNEVILLE

The surviving contract between Adams and Bonneville shows the terms of employment for a man who was literate and sufficiently responsible to take charge of a trapping brigade, as Adams would once they reached the Green River. This contract was entered into on February 22, 1832, at the "counting room" in St. Louis of René Paul, who acted as witness. Since Bonneville's leave would expire in October, 1833, he hired Adams for a period of eighteen months as of March 1, 1832. Adams' pay was to be at the rate of two hundred dollars per year. He had to agree to be faithful to his employer, to "keep the secrets of my said principle," and not to purloin any furs, goods, or equipment. In case of riot or insubordination he was required to do all in his power to suppress it. Should he desert before the end of eighteen months, he would be penalized by the forfeiture of ninety dollars plus all wages due him. Wages—all of three hundred dollars for risking his life for a year and a half—were to be collected from Bonneville's agent at the counting room of René Paul at the expiration of his eighteen-month term of employment.[20] Probably the same contract, with varying wages, was used for all the men whom Bonneville signed up that winter.

By the end of April, all was in readiness. Men had been hired, horses, oxen, and cows had been bought, and wagons provided to carry the vast amount of supplies and trade goods necessary for a prolonged expedition. This meant the scientific instruments obtained in New York, rifles, shotguns, pistols, traps, knives, tomahawks, lead, powder, powder horns, bullet molds; it meant blankets, clothing, medicines, trade goods, trinkets and gifts for Indians; it meant coffee, sugar, flour, salt, liquor, and tobacco; axes, shovels, extra harnesses and saddles, hobbles and halters, horse shoes, and possibly some grain for the animals—in a word, sufficient equipment and supplies for animals and 110 men who were about to disappear into a great wilderness for at least a year and a half—so much, indeed, that Bonneville needed 20 substantial wagons to carry it all. The wagons would incidentally serve as useful barriers against the arrows of possible Indian attackers and would also alleviate the heavy chore of un-

[20] From a facsimile in the *Midwest Review,* Vol. VIII (July-August, 1927), frontispiece.

Editor's Introduction

loading pack animals each evening. Several months of planning, organizing, hiring, and buying had ended. On May 1, 1832, Bonneville gave the order for the huge outfit to begin moving.

Following the route that later became the road for thousands of emigrants on the Oregon Trail, Bonneville after nearly four months reached the Green River west of the Continental Divide. Then erecting a rude fortification on Green River near Horse Creek in early August, he dispatched two groups of trappers to widely separated points. One of these was headed by Matthieu. The other was under the leadership of David Adams, chosen presumably because of prior experience as a trapper and perhaps also because he was literate. A rare document from this period consists of the written orders that Bonneville handed to him:

Mouth of Horse River
August 17th, 1832

Mr. David Adams
  Sir,
    Your known intelligence and integrity warrants me in placing you at the head of our eastern Trapping party consisting of twenty one men and forty animals with their necessary equipment, and Sundry merchandise as per enclosed Invoice—

Your route will lay as marked out upon Mr Meldrum's map—round the foot of Wind River Mountains [at South Pass], down Wind River [Big Horn River] up Stinking [now Shoshone River] and upon the Small Streams keeping up the Yellowstone [to the west], crossing over the Galatin and Medicine [Madison] River from which you will cross over to Salmon River and descend to the forks [Salmon and Lemhi Rivers] where you will find a letter at the foot of the tree nearest the fork, instructing you where the main body will Winter, which it is believed will be there or very near it—

You Should consider trapping your business yet should an advantageous trade offer either for horses or Beaver you would of course improve it—but let nothing induce you to deviate your course for precarious trade—Nightly parks and close Staking you are aware are the only true methods of keeping your Animals in Security—

The Signals for our parties this fall are these—a blase upon the tree opposite the course pursued—One notch over it untill the 15th

Septr. two from that day untill the 25th October and three from that to the wintering ground; for distress blaze upon both Sides of the notches and first blaze—for loss of horses leave the Side blazes plain—for disperse [*sic*] hack the one of the Side blazes—for a Cache or Some writing hack both side blazes which would induce us to dig at the foot of the 2nd nearest tree for information.

Respectfully yours,

B.L.E. Bonneville & Co.[21]

How Adams' band fared on the journey here outlined, Irving relates in Chapter XIX.

Bonneville himself appears not to have devoted much if any of his own time to conducting trapping parties. Instead, he acted as planner and co-ordinator; he spent much time with various Indians, particularly the peaceful Nez Percés of Idaho; and he explored and made maps of the territory he covered. He made two ventures down the Snake River into Hudson's Bay Company territory on the Columbia but gained little in either attempt besides a knowledge of the country and the Indians. He did not visit Great Salt Lake, in which he professed much interest, but instead, mistakenly believing it to have been unexplored sent Joseph Walker and some fifty men there on their historic trek to California. Some historians have wondered why Bonneville, who was often conveniently near Great Salt Lake, did not explore it himself. The answer must be that he was more interested in something else. What this was can be inferred from his actions after Walker left the rendezvous at Green River on July 24, 1833, for Great Salt Lake and California.

The day after Walker left, Bonneville and Cerré started for the

---

[21] Adams Papers, Missouri Historical Society. The Meldrum to whom Bonneville refers in this letter was probably Robert Meldrum. He is mentioned by James Beckwourth, *The Life and Adventures of James P. Beckwourth*, 126, as being a Kentuckian, a trapper and blacksmith, and a onetime employee of the American Fur Company whom Beckwourth had met when Meldrum was living with the Crow Indians. Captain W. F. Raynolds in his exploration of the Yellowstone River in 1859 referred to Meldrum as "the best living authority in regard to the Crows ..., having spent over thirty years in their country, during that time visiting ... civilization but once, and on that occasion spending only 19 days in St. Louis." Quoted by J. Cecil Alter in *James Bridger*, 340. Bonneville may have met Meldrum in St. Louis and from him obtained maps and information about the Crow country.

Editor's Introduction

Big Horn River east of the Wind River Range. Cerré would conduct the year's small catch of beaver pelts by water to St. Louis, while Bonneville would go part way and then cross over to the upper Columbia. On July 29, 1833, he had escorted Cerré as far as the Wind River, and made camp.

Here he took time, before Cerré departed, to write his first report to Major General Macomb.[22] This report Cerré was to carry all the way to Washington, D. C., a responsibility he faithfully discharged. As a résumé of Bonneville's first year of activities, it is a most interesting document and also a valuable supplement to the book (see Appendix B, letter to Macomb dated Crow Country, Wind River, July 29, 1833). It contains Bonneville's explanation of why he thought he should remain in the mountains longer than he originally intended (his leave was to expire in three months), as well as some rather astonishing information and recommendations about the Hudson's Bay Company's posts strung out along the Columbia River and what the United States government had better do at once if it had any hopes of taking possession of the Oregon country, at that time held jointly by the United States and Great Britain under provision of the Treaty of Joint Occupation (1818; renewed 1827). The report comments perceptively on the cutthroat competition and the special economic advantages of the British company over the American traders; provides a history of the fur trade; gives detailed information about Indian tribes; offers an explanation of some of the technicalities of trapping parties, prices prevailing in the mountains, and the several kinds of trappers; furnishes a résumé of his own movements since leaving Missouri, plus a description of the geography, geology, and soils of the country he had observed; and enumerates the various losses sustained by his brigades sent out during this first year. It also explains his intentions for the immediate future.

Apparently not doubting that Cerré would bring from Major General Macomb the extension of his furlough which Bonneville explained was necessary if he was to collect all the information Ma-

[22] United States National Archives, files of the United States Senate relating to Captain Bonneville (Record Group 46). Hereafter cited as Bonneville File (RG 46).

comb desired, he briefly outlined his future movements. Upon separation from Cerré somewhere along the Big Horn (perhaps at the Yellowstone), "I will then proceed," he explained, "to the northwest towards the north of the Columbia." Later he added, "In the course of a few days I shall be on my rout to the Cottonais country [the Kutenai Indians in northern Idaho and northeastern Washington], and round to the south." These two statements were supplementary, however, to a very meaningful remark early in the report: "I hope I have not trespassed too much upon your goodness [in asking for additional leave], to explore the North of the Columbia in Cottonais Country and New Caledonia [British Columbia] to winter on the lower Columbia [perhaps at or near Fort Vancouver], and going to the South West towards Calefornia on my return, which will certainly be in the course of next fall."[23] This while Walker was on his way to California! Was Bonneville intending to meet him there?

These statements show that Bonneville intended to reconnoiter the Hudson's Bay Company territory by coming in from the east and north. The information gathered about this region and about the British posts included in his 1833 report to Macomb was secondhand information collected from whites and Indians during the preceding year. Now he would look into that country himself. Thus originated the first of his two difficult and fruitless journeys to the Columbia River.

Unfortunately for his purpose, the hostility of the Blackfeet along the Big Horn River blocked his further passage in that direction, and he was forced to adopt the Snake River route as an alternative. Regrettably he was unable to map the country lying along the route first selected, and he never did carry out his cherished scheme of visiting the Mexican-owned California. What he may have failed to realize in July of 1833 was just what obstacles he would confront in difficult terrain, which slowed his progress, and in the sharp refusal of the Hudson's Bay people to tolerate his threatened competition.

[23] See Chapter XVIII, note 1, for the bearing Nathaniel Wyeth had upon Bonneville's proposed California excursion.

Denver Public Library

WASHINGTON IRVING
Historian of the Bonneville Ventures

Denver Public Library

B. L. E. BONNEVILLE AS GENERAL
The Former Captain of the Rocky Mountain Adventures

Editor's Introduction

While Bonneville was attempting to fulfill these plans during that fall and winter (1833–34), Cerré had reached St. Louis with the furs and had traveled on to Washington to deliver Bonneville's report to Major General Macomb. By remaining in the West beyond October, 1833, Bonneville was jeopardizing his career in the army, but he confidently expected that the report would result in an extension of his leave, word of which Cerré was to bring when he rejoined Bonneville the following summer. Bonneville had closed his 1833 report by saying, ". . . if you shall have any instructions for me, [I] shall be glad to receive them; either to join any party that might be sent, to comply with any other commands in this Country, or to return to the States."

Cerré later wrote from St. Louis in December, 1835, at a time when Bonneville was attempting to get himself reinstated, that he had given the report to Macomb personally. Macomb read it that same day. In the evening Cerré returned to see him, and Macomb said the report "had given him great satisfaction." "He asked me," Cerré explained to Bonneville, "several questions relative to your expedition; such as, has Capt Bonneville taken any observations on his route, does he keep a minute of his travels, did he go into Oregon, where was he to go when you left [him] at the Big Horn, when will he return to the U. States & &. In answering the later [*sic*], I told him that it was impossible for you to return in due time to comply with your furlough; but you expected to be permitted to remain in the Mountains a longer space of time so as to comme [back] able to give a general Satisfaction."[24]

Cerré left Washington after Macomb interviewed him and went to New York, probably to report to Bonneville's financial backers, and then hurriedly returned to the frontier without first going back to Washington to obtain written orders extending his employer's leave. On July 28, 1834, he rejoined Bonneville at Bear Lake. "I stated to you . . . at the little Lake [Bear Lake]," he was to write in 1835, "that it was more than probable that Gen McComb should have written to you had I returned through Washington, & that a longer absence should have been granted to you. It may be that Gen

[24] Bonneville File (RG 94).

McComb told [me] that your furlough Should be continued for a longer time; but I cannot Say positively that he did. However I Confess that it was my impression at that time, as well as at present, that the Government wastisfied [was satisfied] that you Should remain some time in the Mountains for the sake of acquiring information—"[25]

But Cerré had hardly left the settlements when Macomb, on May 28, 1834, reported Bonneville absent without authority, and on May 31 the Adjutant General, Major General Roger Jones, signed Order No. 42 dropping him from the rolls of the army on order of the President on May 30.[26]

Bonneville, unaware of his new status and acting rather naïvely, it would seem, on the assumption that what Cerré had communicated to him at Bear Lake was reason for believing his leave had actually been extended, decided to continue his work. Before leaving Bear Lake, however, Bonneville prepared reports and letters for Major General McComb and other officials in Washington, and entrusted them to Cerré, who, although he had by now joined the American Fur Company, agreed to take them to Council Bluffs, from where they were to be forwarded. These reports never reached Washington, however, and what Bonneville had to communicate is forever lost.[27]

Five days after meeting Cerré, Bonneville left Bear Lake on his second expedition to the Columbia River. This journey, on which he was again repulsed by the Hudson's Bay factor at Fort Walla Walla, who rigidly refused even to furnish his men supplies, occupied him during the remainder of the summer and early autumn, and in November he was back once more on Bear River near the lake—driven from the Columbia by threat of winter and short rations.

Bonneville by now knew that he could not achieve all that he intended; and after wintering on Bear River, he prepared to return

[25] *Ibid.*
[26] *Ibid.*
[27] Bonneville to Secretary Cass, September 30, 1835, Bonneville File (RG 94). Reprinted in Appendix B.

Editor's Introduction

to the States. He met two bands of his trappers east of the Wind River Mountains in June, 1835, and leaving some men in the Crow country to continue trapping and trading, he raised camp at the mouth of the Popo Agie in late June and by August 22 led his ragged companions into Independence.

He reached Washington, as was shown earlier, in September and thereupon learned that he had been dropped from the army. Bonneville immediately wrote to Lewis Cass, secretary of war, requesting restoration of rank. This letter shows that it was not only Major General Macomb who was interested in his excursions to the Northwest. "I sat out on my tour," the former captain explained to Secretary Cass, "with the consent of the War Department, and was charged by General Eaton, then Secretary of War, with instructions to guide me in collecting information, with which he considered it advantageous for the Government to be possessed." His name was stricken from army rolls, he concluded, "at a time when a report of my death by the Indians received general credence."[28]

A report of Bonneville's case was immediately drawn up for Secretary Cass by the Acting Adjutant General on September 29 reviewing the circumstances of his absence and verifying that at the time Macomb reported Bonneville's absence a rumor of his death by Indians "was in circulation, and was generally accredited."[29] Bonneville at the same time prepared a long letter, dated September 30, to the Secretary of War in which he reviewed in some detail his actions during the previous four years. This letter is a valuable supplement to Bonneville's report of July 29, 1833, to Major General Macomb (see Appendix B for letter of September 30, 1835, to Secretary Cass).

Whatever his superior officers in Washington may have thought of his petitions for reinstatement, his fellow officers of the Seventh Infantry at Fort Gibson were strongly opposed. Seventeen of them, with the concurrence of Brevet Brigadier General Matthew Arbuckle, commanding officer, forwarded their protest to the Secretary

---

[28] Bonneville to Secretary Cass, September 26, 1835, Bonneville File (RG 46).
[29] "Report in the Case of Capt. Bonneville," dated September 26, 1835, Bonneville File (RG 94).

of War, alleging that Bonneville's expedition was solely commercial and that he could have returned prior to the expiration of his furlough. They charged him with deliberate neglect of military duty in order to advance his private interests. Probably their real concern, however, was not so much these matters of principle as it was that their advancement in rank would be delayed should Bonneville's former rank of captain be restored. Their effort in the long run was without effect.[30]

Major General Macomb appears from the beginning to have been sympathetic to Bonneville's cause. In a report to Secretary Cass, November 17, 1835, he cleared the way for Bonneville's reinstatement by recognizing the value of his accomplishments in the West and by pointing out that he could be restored to rank "by a renomination to the Senate, before the eldest Lieutenant last promoted, should be nominated to that Body."[31]

Although the machinery now moved slowly, the Adjutant General on January 4, 1836, finally submitted Bonneville's name to the Secretary of War for reappointment, the resignation of another officer of the Seventh Infantry on December 31 making a place for Bonneville without need to revise the list of promotions then pending before the Senate. The next day, January 5, Secretary Cass placed his recommendation in the hands of the President, adding his opinion "now the facts are all known, that the penalty is greater than the public service requires." Without delay, President Andrew Jackson, on January 6, sent his nomination to the Senate.[32]

There the matter rested in the hands of the Military Committee until April. In the meantime Bonneville waited "the slow adjustment of his affairs with the War Department," as Irving tactfully expressed it, by writing an account of his expedition; and it was while Bonneville was engaged in this task that Irving, as stated earlier, visited him in his Washington quarters in either November

---

[30] See letter of November 3 from the officers of Fort Gibson and the letter of November 4 from Brigadier General Arbuckle. Bonneville rebutted their protest in a letter to Secretary Cass, December 7, 1835, Bonneville File (RG 94).

[31] Bonneville File (RG 94).

[32] *Ibid.*

Editor's Introduction

or December, 1835. It may be assumed that Bonneville had written only a portion of his manuscript at that time, but by early March the manuscript was finished. Bonneville now wrote to Secretary Cass explaining why he had to be absent briefly from Washington, "Under the impression, that a temporary absence from the metropolis, will not prejudice my interests now in the hands of the Senate, I have thought it adviseable to publish my Journal immediately and with that intention proceed to New-York tomorrow."[33]

He made the rounds of the publishers; but not meeting with the success he hoped for, he asked for an interview with Irving. This meeting took place on March 25. Irving described the interview in a letter written two days later to Bonneville's friend Major James Harvey Hook, in whose quarters Bonneville had written the manuscript and to whom it was dedicated. Irving wrote:

> He appeared desirous that I should take the work in hand. I glanced over the Mss: and observing there were materials on which I thought I could found a work that would be acceptable to the public I purchased the Mss of him for a price [$1000] which I conceived to be above what he could procure from any Bookseller.
>
> I shall proceed to construct a work out of these materials, to the best of my abilities, and shall take care to do every thing that shall place the captain's talents and services in the fairest point of view, and contribute to his reputation, as he is a gentleman for whom I have already conceived a high regard.[34]

Almost immediately after this visit with Irving, Bonneville left the East for Missouri without waiting to learn the action of the Senate. General Order No. 25 from the Adjutant General's Office, dated April 22, 1836, reinstating him with orders to report for immediate duty at Fort Gibson, was forwarded to him at Fort Leavenworth. But by the time it arrived there, Bonneville could not be reached. He did not receive it until August 6, and for an interesting reason. He had returned to the mountains.

---

[33] Bonneville to Secretary Cass, March 11, 1836, *ibid*.

[34] The full letter is quoted by John F. McDermott, "Washington Irving and the Journal of Captain Bonneville," *Mississippi Valley Historical Review*, Vol. XLIII (December, 1956), 465–66.

Probably he went only as far as the Powder River in Wyoming. Remaining but a short time, he returned to Fort Leavenworth and from there, on August 7, 1836, wrote to the Adjutant General: "I have now been absent from the settlements since May 8 last, at which time not being able to hear of any decision being had, I proceeded to the far West to make a final close of my interests there,— and now have the pleasure to say, I shall proceed immediately to the post Fort Gibson. . . ."[35] A somewhat different reason for his summer in the West appears in a letter dated October 20, 1836, at Fort Gibson. To Brigadier General Arbuckle, commander of the South Western Frontier, he explained his earlier apprehension over the possible outcome of action by the Senate and the efforts to prevent his reappointment. These considerations, he wrote, "forced me to keep in view my former habits of life, and to prevent wasting the small means yet within my reach; induced me to improve the liberty granted me by the Honorable Senator T. H. Benton, who as chairman of the military comm. etc., assured me my presence was entirely unnecessary. . . . I therefore turned my personal efforts to sustain myself in case of failure."[36] Had Bonneville not regained his rank, it is interesting to speculate what his future role in the West might have been.

Once returned to Fort Gibson, Bonneville settled back into the routine of a frontier military post. Perhaps he was content to do this; but his mind must often have reverted to his uncommon life of the past few years. "Although I am far from the Voyageurs," he wrote in 1837 to his friend David Adams at St. Louis, "yet I take great interest in knowing all about them—let me hear how things go on with the Rocky Mts. companies—and their men and in fine every thing about the Mts. the companies and the hands."[37]

Bonneville's subsequent career may be briefly summarized. He participated in the second Seminole war in Florida; saw service in the Mexican War, when he was wounded and advanced to the rank of Brevet Lieutenant Colonel "for gallantry and meritorious con-

[35] Bonneville File (RG 94).
[36] *Ibid.*
[37] June 23, 1837. Adams Papers, Missouri Historical Society.

Editor's Introduction

duct in the battles of Contreras and Churubusco"; and later served at Fort Kearny and at other posts in Wisconsin, New York, and California. The United States military reservation at Fort Vancouver, which he had aspired to visit during his years as an erstwhile fur trader and which after the treaty of 1846 with Great Britain was located in American territory, came under Bonneville's command between 1853 and 1855, and from this position he must have watched with unusual satisfaction the influx of American settlers into a region about which he had written some twenty years earlier, "if our Government ever intend taking possession of Oregon the sooner it shall be done the better."[38]

Subsequently, Bonneville was commander of the Department of New Mexico. Between 1855 and 1866 he was variously stationed at Fort Fillmore and Fort Marcy in New Mexico; at Fort Clark, Texas, and Benton Barracks and Jefferson Barracks, Missouri, in a variety of capacities. He retired in 1861, but immediately came out of retirement to serve during the Civil War in recruiting service for two years and as chief mustering and disbursing officer in Missouri for an additional two years. In 1865 he was promoted to the rank of Brevet Brigadier General "for long and faithful service in the Army." When he died on June 12, 1878, at the age of eighty-two, at Fort Smith, Arkansas, he was the oldest officer on the retired list.[39]

Something remains to be said now in assessing the importance of Bonneville's expedition as well as Irving's book devoted to it. The most valuable attempt in this effort

---

[38] Letter to Major General Macomb, July 29, 1833, Appendix B.

[39] Details of Bonneville's army career are from a "Statement of the Military Service of Benjamin L. E. Bonneville," compiled by the Adjutant General's Office, June 25, 1926, in the Bonneville File (RG 94). In this file is a letter written on June 16, 1878, by his friend from fur-trading days, Robert Campbell. Addressed to the Adjutant General on behalf of Bonneville's widow, the letter reads:

"I have the honor to communicate the sad news of the death of Genl B. L. E. Bonneville of the U.S. Army at his residence near the City of Fort Smith Ark on the morning of the 12th instant at 10 O'clock A.M. Will you be kind enough to inform me the necessary steps to be taken by the Genl's wife, Mrs Sue Bonneville, so as to receive the pay due the Genl for the 12 days in this month, & oblige."

was made in 1902 by Hiram M. Chittenden in his *History of the American Fur Trade of the Far West*. Chittenden deals very severely with Bonneville, owing, perhaps, to a possible prejudice regarding a fellow army officer who, in Chittenden's eyes, seemed to have flouted military etiquette, and also to lack of knowledge of certain documents which otherwise would have caused him to alter certain judgments.

Chittenden interpreted Bonneville's enterprise as being primarily commercial, and on this basis condemned him as an unqualified failure. Failure he certainly was from this standpoint. But the fact remains that the existing documents contain more evidence that the expedition was primarily noncommercial than that it was solely commercial in purpose. Too little is actually known about Bonneville's financial tie-up with his New York sponsors to enable anyone to speak with finality about it. It has, however, been the view taken here that trapping and trading were the means by which Bonneville attempted to finance his expedition. This view is supported by the following passage from a letter Bonneville addressed to Secretary Cass on December 7, 1835, defending himself against the charges made by the officers of Fort Gibson that the expedition had been conducted purely for selfish economic gain. To this charge Bonneville replied:

> That I started as a trader and acted as such, is what I never attempted to conceal. Genl. Scott Eustis and even Genl. Macomb assisted me to become one, as their letters now in my possession will show. The whole army knew it. It was deemed more proper for me to go as such, and with out expense to the Government [and] furnish them with such information as they believed useful and interesting to the Country; than for the Government to be at the expense of hiring men for that purpose, and of making presents to every Indian nation they should meet.[40]

His superior officers would have denied this statement had there been reason to do so.

Chittenden also charges Bonneville with having failed in his

[40] Bonneville File (RG 94).

Editor's Introduction

scientific aims. "The Captain never made any report of his work to the Department," he stated, "and it is probable that he had nothing of value to report."[41] Bonneville, as has already been pointed out, made several reports, the first from the Crow country to Major General Macomb on July 29, 1833, and delivered to him by Cerré. There were other reports, including those which Cerré later carried to Council Bluffs but which never reached Washington. Commenting on this misfortune in his letter of September 30, 1835, to Secretary Cass, Bonneville remarked, "These letters owing to causes impossible for me to explain, I regret to state, never reached their destination, which appears to have been the fate of most of the communications made to the States, and which it was next to an impossibility to accomplish without employing persons expressly for that purpose." Furthermore, the journal that Bonneville kept for three years was turned over to the War Department upon his return in 1835 and constituted an extensive report of his observations. Of these various reports, Major General Macomb stated in a communication to Secretary Cass on November 17, 1835, "Captain Bonneville has now returned to Washington . . . [and] brought with him interesting and important accounts of what he has seen and fulfilled satisfactorily the objects of the instructions given him on his departure." Clearly his superior officers were satisfied with the information Bonneville obtained. It is also possible that Bonneville's journal contained information never made public, Irving's book being, admittedly, only a digest, as he stated on the title page; and in the absence of the original journal, we can never know fully what possible additional data prompted Macomb to declare it to be "important."

Chittenden on the positive side acknowledges the worth of Bonneville's maps by saying they were "the one really valuable result" of the expedition, but he immediately tempers this statement by saying that they won for Bonneville "a degree of credit for promoting geographical discovery to which he is in no sense entitled."[42] Chittenden further remarks that Bonneville was indebted to Gallatin's

[41] Chittenden, *American Fur Trade*, I, 429.
[42] *Ibid.*, I, 429.

The ADVENTURES *of* CAPTAIN BONNEVILLE

map of 1836 without acknowledging his indebtedness. It is true that there are features on his maps concerning country he never personally visited. Some of this information, however, could well have come from his men, in which case Bonneville need not have seen Gallatin's map. The question of Gallatin's priority is not so certain, moreover, when one considers that Bonneville supplied information for the map in *Astoria,* and the completed manuscript for this book was in the publisher's hands by May, 1836. A recent authority, cartographer Carl I. Wheat, referring to the first of the two maps in the first edition of *The Rocky Mountains,* declares it not only excellent but superior to any previously published.[43] Lieutenant Gouverneur Warren in his *Memoir* of the 1850's had high praise for Bonneville's maps, stating that they were "the first to correctly represent the hydrography" of the country west of the Rocky Mountains.[44]

Bonneville, gratified for Warren's commendation (first expressed in a letter to him), wrote to Warren on August 24, 1857:

> I thank you for your desire to do me justice as regards my map and explorations in the Rocky Mountains. . . . On all the maps of those days the Great Salt Lake had two great outlets to the Pacific ocean. . . . It was from my explorations and those of my party alone that it was ascertained that this lake had no outlet; that the California range *basined* all the waters of its eastern slope without further outlet; that the Buenaventura and all other California streams drained only the western slope.[45] The Great Lava plain was never known as such; until my report drew attention to its character, it was confidently asserted that there was [*sic*] no prismatic basalt columns in that region. I saw it perfectly formed once only, and this

---

[43] Carl I. Wheat, *Mapping the Transmississippi West,* II, 158.

[44] For Warren's examination of Bonneville's map, see his *Memoir* in *Reports of Explorations and Surveys,* 36 Cong., 2 sess., *Sen. Exec. Doc.* [unnumbered] (Washington, 1861), XI, 33–34. Chittenden counters Warren's statement by pointing out that Warren had not seen Gallatin's map and that if he had, he would not have praised Bonneville so highly.

[45] If Bonneville sincerely thought he had reason for these claims, he was obviously ignorant of the explorations of Jedediah Smith and other Ashley men. But even Frémont on his second expedition was still looking for the mythical Buenaventura, which a reading of Irving's book would have made unnecessary.

Editor's Introduction

on Snake river, below Gun creek [Powder River, Oregon]. The Three Buttes [in the Snake River Plain] have often been my camping ground. ... It was from my observations and plotting that the headwaters of Snake river, of the Columbia, Muscle [*sic*] Shell, and Yellowstone; headwaters of the Missouri and Sweetwater, of the Platte, and those of the Colorado of the West, were brought together in one view, as reported in my journal.[46]

Chittenden declares, finally, that Bonneville as a leader of men was an unqualified success, and he gives him due credit for being the first to prove the feasibility of taking loaded wagons across South Pass. But Bonneville's greatest service to his country, Chittenden concludes, was his chance meeting with Washington Irving. The resulting book represented the fur trade during its "best days." "*Captain Bonneville* . . . is a true and living picture of those early scenes, and taken with *Astoria* will ever remain our highest authority upon the events to which they relate."[47] Chittenden's judgment here is correct. In *The Adventures of Captain Bonneville*, Irving made the first attempt at writing a history of the fur trade in the post-Ashley period of the 1830's, and as the first book of its kind, it still remains an important and engrossing account of that era.

Even before Irving finished it, the press had made the prospect of the new work a matter of widespread interest. Not many days after Bonneville returned to the settlements from his summer excursion of 1836, *Niles Register*, which was read throughout the nation, reprinted the following news item from the *St. Louis Observor*:

> Captain B. L. E. Bonneville . . . returned to this city on Sunday morning from a tour to the Rocky Mountains, where he has been (with the exception of a few months) for the last five [*sic*] years. We are happy to learn that the captain, in connection with Washington Irving, esq. contemplates compiling a narrative of his travels, together with an account of the various tribes among which he sojourned, and a geographical account of the country through which he passed. We await with impatience the appearance of this work.[48]

---

[46] Reprinted in Warren, *Memoir, loc. cit.*, XI, 33.
[47] Chittenden, *American Fur Trade*, II, 432.
[48] *Niles Register*, Vol. LI (September 3, 1836), 16.

This news item serves to remind the modern reader of something he may overlook, namely, that for readers in the 1830's *The Adventures of Captain Bonneville* had current interest. The events were recent, and many people in the book were still active in the fur trade. Others were prominent figures in Missouri or in the East. We read the book today as a historic record of events long vanished; Irving's readers in 1837 read it as an absorbing account of events having only recently occurred.

Just how important this book was in the impact it made upon its readers at that time and in the years immediately following is extremely difficult to determine. But anyone who reads the old files of magazines and newspapers of that period cannot but observe that the frequency of news items, statistical records, essays, and reviews about the West was symptomatic of widespread public interest in a country where many people felt the westward course of empire was soon to take its way. Irving was fortunately able to take advantage of this interest. His name alone meant a certain success, especially after *A Tour on the Prairies* and *Astoria*. But his name plus the subject of the book guaranteed that it would have wide appeal.[49]

Just what that appeal was can be glimpsed through the reactions of reviewers. One of these may be quoted here as perhaps indicative of the general reaction in America:

> Through these scenes of the Far West the graces of [Irving's] pen have literally made the solitary wilderness blossom like a garden. . . . But little was known before the appearance of Astoria of the great Western region. We heard there were hunters and trappers employed in gaining a dangerous and difficult livelihood from the

[49] The title page of the first American edition reads: "*The Rocky Mountains: or, Scenes, Incidents, and Adventures in the Far West; digested from the Journal of Captain B. L. E. Bonneville of the Army of the United States, and Illustrated from Various other Sources*. By Washington Irving. In Two Volumes. Philadelphia. Carey, Lea, & Blanchard, 1837." With one exception, subsequent American editions were entitled *The Adventures of Captain Bonneville*. The first English edition, brought out in London by Richard Bentley, was entitled *Adventures of Captain Bonneville, or Scenes Beyond the Rocky Mountains of the Far West*. Translations appeared in Dutch, French, and German (William R. Langfeld, *Washington Irving, a Bibliography*, 77). Irving's American publisher paid him $3,000, his English publisher 900 pounds (P. Irving, *Life and Letters*, III, 114).

Editor's Introduction

peltries of the Columbia and Far Pacific . . . ; we saw the rich furs collected in the warehouses . . . ; but we knew nothing of the life of adventure and excitement associated with that distant region. But Irving has thrown a better light on the land for young and old. He has shown us that here, in these worn-out times of the world, there is a last foothold left for a remnant of chivalry in the wild life of the Far West. . . . Whether in fact or fable, may Irving continue to send forth more such delightful volumes. . . .[50]

His success must have given a tremendous impetus to the exploitation of the West as a literary resource. But who can estimate what such a book must have contributed to a knowledge of the country it depicted and what part it may have played in the imminent migration into Oregon Territory? Though he buried his most relevant remarks on this latter subject in the Appendix, he urged the immediate settlement of the territorial dispute between the United States and Great Britain and encouraged his readers to think of the Pacific Northwest as a region to be settled by Americans. With sure foresightedness, Irving pointed to the valleys of that distant region, which at that time, he said, lay "waste and uninhabited, and to the eyes of the trader and trappers, present but barren wastes," as an area that "would in the hands of skilful agriculturists and husbandmen, soon assume a different aspect, and teem with waving crops, or be covered with flocks and herds."[51] Irving played a part, however uncertain its extent, in helping to propagandize America's right to a rich domain.

Any close study of *The Adventures of Captain Bonneville* astonishes one with one of its strongest merits—its accuracy. Its least dependable portion is the account of Walker's California expedition, but since Bonneville was not present on this expedition and could not report it at firsthand, this weakness is understandable. There are also small errors of detail. But the surprising thing is how infrequent

[50] *New York Review*, Vol. I (October, 1837), 439–40.
[51] Such information might well have come from Nathaniel J. Wyeth, who had not only established a farm in the Willamette Valley but had also observed the agricultural success of the Hudson's Bay Company in that area. Irving corresponded with Wyeth during the writing of *Bonneville*, but this correspondence, unfortunately, has not come to light.

The ADVENTURES *of* CAPTAIN BONNEVILLE

they are considering the fact that Irving was writing about places he had not seen and about events in which he had not participated. It is possible for any one familiar with the geography and terrain of the West to retrace Bonneville's routes with exactness in all but a few places, as this writer has done. The descriptions of terrain are faithful to the land. The rivers flow in the right directions, and the passes and the mountains are where Irving says they are. At countless points one knows where Bonneville was and on what date he was there. Collateral accounts of other trappers, such as Ferris's *Life in the Rocky Mountains,* the *Narrative of the Adventures of Zenas Leonard,* Wyeth's *Correspondence and Journals,* to name but three such sources, substantiate much of what Irving says. In some cases Irving is better than his critics. This writer has learned that when Irving makes a statement he should be heeded until certain evidence proves the contrary.

What does all of this mean? For one thing, it means that Bonneville was an accurate observer of what he saw and an accurate recorder of what he did. It means that he provided Irving with data that could be depended upon. It means, furthermore, that Irving approached his own task with a careful respect for the facts as he knew them and wrote the book in the spirit of a careful historian. He supplemented Bonneville in matters that Bonneville left untouched, inserting details that add much to the completeness and interest of the text. The book is not just a narrative of Bonneville's actions; it is, as Irving said, "a party-colored web." We also know that after returning from his own tour west of the Mississippi, Irving read widely in whatever he could find pertaining to the Far West and kept notes on his reading.[52] He studied carefully before writing *Astoria,* and the preparation for that book added greatly to his knowledge. He talked to and corresponded with the participants in events narrated in both *Astoria* and the Bonneville book. He sought out such men; he read their diaries and letters; he read the newspapers closely. In a word, Irving knew his subject.

It is surprising, then, that both *Astoria* and *The Adventures of*

[52] Edgeley W. Todd, "Washington Irving Discovers the Frontier," *Western Humanities Review,* Vol. XI (Winter, 1957), 27–39.

Editor's Introduction

Captain Bonneville have suffered, in the words of Bernard DeVoto, a "curious decline in reputation."[53] Partly this decline is owing to erroneous opinions formed by people who have never read either book. Partly it is owing to a widespread conviction that Irving was writing fiction. Partly, also, it is owing to a certain prejudice that Irving, renowned for his European writing, was somehow demeaning himself by writing about Western subjects. One of his biographers, for example, ignoring the spirit and the care with which Irving wrote these books, considered them to be mere hack work. Some of it, finally, is owing to ignorance and some of it to unexplainable maliciousness. Probably no more savage attack was ever made upon Bonneville personally and upon Irving indirectly than by H. H. Bancroft, who wrote of Bonneville as "being in his course way *bon-vivant* and voluptuary" with "every fortnight a new unmarried wife.... To shoot buffalo was rare fun; but men were the nobler game, whom to search out in their retreat and slaughter and scalp was glorious. What were the far-off natives ... doing that this restless, reckless, blood-thirsty, and cruel Frenchman should be permitted to kill them?" And as if this were not enough, Bancroft must close by saying that "this French butcher finds among our first writers a man to heroify him and to set up his dastardly deeds as models for the young."[54] Considering the extensive distribution of Bancroft's *Works* and their presence in many libraries, much of the source for the decline can be attributed to such irresponsible writing of history.

Since Irving wrote, the number of books on the fur trade in the trans-Mississippi West has increased tremendously. The next few decades after 1837 saw numerous personal narratives published by men who had been trappers themselves. In time historians, novelists, and poets endeavored to interpret the fur trade as a unique part of the American experience. Some of these books have been best sellers and have informed modern readers about a colorful and important

[53] Bernard DeVoto, *Across the Wide Missouri*, 426–27.

[54] Hubert Howe Bancroft, *History of the Northwest Coast*, II; *Works*, XXVIII, 568–70. See Chittenden, *American Fur Trade*, I, 432–33 n., for a proper rejoinder. Bonneville never killed a single Indian and took every measure he could to promote peace among the Indians themselves.

era in American history. In short, a literary tradition devoted to the fur trade extends from the time of the fur trade itself to the present. It has enriched our literature and awakened many Americans to our pre-pioneer past. In the creation of that tradition, Washington Irving, who desired to help preserve "a transient state of things fast passing into oblivion" contributed one of the lasting records of a segment of the American heritage.

Introductory Notice

WHILE ENGAGED in writing an account of the grand enterprise of Astoria, it was my practice to seek all kinds of oral information connected with the subject. Nowhere did I pick up more interesting particulars than at the table of Mr. John Jacob Astor;[1] who, being the patriarch of the fur trade in the United States, was accustomed to have at his board various persons of adventurous turn, some of whom had been engaged in his own great undertaking; others, on their own account, had made expeditions to the Rocky Mountains and the waters of the Columbia.

Among these personages, one who peculiarly took my fancy was Captain Bonneville, of the United States army; who, in a rambling kind of enterprise, had strangely ingrafted the trapper and hunter upon the soldier. As his expeditions and adventures will form the leading theme of the following pages, a few biographical particulars concerning him may not be unacceptable.

Captain Bonneville is of French parentage.[2] His father was a

---

[1] Born in Germany in 1763, Astor came to the United States in 1783 and entered the fur trade, exporting his furs to Europe at a great profit. He soon amassed a large fortune. He incorporated the American Fur Company in 1808 and the Pacific Fur Company in 1810. Astoria was founded as a fur-trading post of the latter organization at the mouth of the Columbia River in the following year, but was lost as a consequence of the War of 1812. Its history is recorded in Irving's *Astoria*. The American Fur Company eventually developed a virtual monopoly of the fur trade on the Upper Missouri. Astor sold his interests in this company in 1834 when he foresaw that the trade was soon to decline. During his career he accumulated such vast wealth as to be able to lend money to the United States government. He died in 1848. Irving was a warm, personal friend of Astor, in whose home he was a frequent guest. At Astor's funeral Irving was one of the pallbearers. See James Parton, "John Jacob Astor," *Harper's Monthly*, Vol. XXX (February, 1865), 308–23; and Kenneth W. Porter, *John Jacob Astor, Business Man*.

[2] See Editor's Introduction.

worthy old emigrant, who came to this country many years since, and took up his abode in New-York. He is represented as a man not much calculated for the sordid struggle of a money-making world, but possessed of a happy temperament, a festivity of imagination, and a simplicity of heart, that made him proof against its rubs and trials. He was an excellent scholar; well acquainted with Latin and Greek, and fond of the modern classics. His book was his elysium; once immersed in the pages of Voltaire, Corneille, or Racine, or of his favorite English author, Shakespeare, he forgot the world and all its concerns. Often would he be seen in summer weather, seated under one of the trees on the Battery, or the portico of St. Paul's church in Broadway, his bald head uncovered, his hat lying by his side, his eyes riveted to the page of his book, and his whole soul so engaged, as to lose all consciousness of the passing throng or the passing hour.

Captain Bonneville, it will be found, inherited something of his father's *bonhommie*, and his excitable imagination; though the latter was somewhat disciplined in early years, by mathematical studies. He was educated at our national Military Academy at West Point, where he acquitted himself very creditably; thence, he entered the army, in which he has ever since continued.

The nature of our military service took him to the frontier, where, for a number of years, he was stationed at various posts in the Far West. Here he was brought into frequent intercourse with Indian traders, mountain trappers, and other pioneers of the wilderness; and became so excited by their tales of wild scenes and wild adventures, and their accounts of vast and magnificent regions as yet unexplored, that an expedition to the Rocky Mountains became the ardent desire of his heart, and an enterprise to explore untrodden tracts, the leading object of his ambition.

By degrees he shaped his vague day-dream into a practical reality. Having made himself acquainted with all the requisites for a trading enterprise beyond the mountains, he determined to undertake it. A leave of absence, and a sanction of his expedition, was obtained from the major general in chief, on his offering to combine public utility with his private projects, and to collect statistical information

Introductory Notice

for the War Department concerning the wild countries and wild tribes he might visit in the course of his journeyings.

Nothing now was wanting to the darling project of the captain, but the ways and means. The expedition would require an outfit of many thousand dollars; a staggering obstacle to a soldier, whose capital is seldom any thing more than his sword. Full of that buoyant hope, however, which belongs to the sanguine temperament, he repaired to New-York, the great focus of American enterprise, where there are always funds ready for any scheme, however chimerical or romantic. Here he had the good fortune to meet with a gentleman of high respectability and influence, who had been his associate in boyhood, and who cherished a schoolfellow friendship for him. He took a general interest in the scheme of the captain; introduced him to commercial men of his acquaintance, and in a little while an association was formed, and the necessary funds were raised to carry the proposed measure into effect. One of the most efficient persons in this association was Mr. Alfred Seton,[3] who, when quite a youth, had accompanied one of the expeditions sent out by Mr. Astor to his commercial establishments on the Columbia, and had distinguished himself by his activity and courage at one of the interior posts. Mr. Seton was one of the American youths who were at Astoria at the time of its surrender to the British, and who manifested such grief and indignation at seeing the flag of their country hauled down. The hope of seeing that flag once more planted on the shores of the Columbia, may have entered into his motives for engaging in the present enterprise.

[3] Seton as a young man went to Astoria by sea in the spring of 1812 and remained there until April, 1814. He returned to New York only after great difficulties, including capture at sea and imprisonment by the Spanish. While Irving was preparing to write *Astoria*, Seton published in the *American Monthly Magazine* for May and July, 1835, an account of his experiences in the Pacific Northwest entitled "Life on the Oregon," which Irving undoubtedly read. It has been reprinted in the *Oregon Historical Quarterly*, Vol. XXXVI (June, 1935), 185–204. Seton appears at several points in *Astoria*, most prominently in Chapter 53. In New York, subsequent to his return there, he entered the insurance business and in 1854 was vice-president of the Sun Mutual Insurance Company. See Fred S. Perrine, "Early Days on the Willamette," *Oregon Hist. Quarterly*, Vol. XXV, (December, 1924), 305 n.

The ADVENTURES *of* CAPTAIN BONNEVILLE

Thus backed and provided, Captain Bonneville undertook his expedition into the Far West, and was soon beyond the Rocky Mountains. Year after year elapsed without his return. The term of his leave of absence expired, yet no report was made of him at head quarters at Washington. He was considered virtually dead or lost, and his name was stricken from the army list.

It was in the autumn of 1835, at the country seat of Mr. John Jacob Astor, at Hellgate, that I first met with Captain Bonneville. He was then just returned from a residence of upwards of three years among the mountains, and was on his way to report himself at head quarters, in the hopes of being reinstated in the service. From all that I could learn, his wanderings in the wilderness, though they had gratified his curiosity and his love of adventure, had not much benefited his fortunes. Like Corporal Trim[4] in his campaigns, he had "satisfied the sentiment," and that was all. In fact, he was too much of the frank, freehearted soldier, and had inherited too much of his father's temperament, to make a scheming trapper, or a thrifty bargainer. There was something in the whole appearance of the captain that prepossessed me in his favor. He was of the middle size, well made and well set; and a military frock of foreign cut, that had seen service, gave him a look of compactness. His countenance was frank, open, and engaging; well browned by the sun, and had something of a French expression. He had a pleasant black eye, a high forehead, and, while he kept his hat on, the look of a man in the jocund prime of his days; but the moment his head was uncovered, a bald crown gained him credit for a few more years than he was really entitled to.

Being extremely curious, at the time, about every thing connected with the Far West, I addressed numerous questions to him.[5] They drew from him a number of extremely striking details, which were given with mingled modesty and frankness; and in a gentleness of manner, and a soft tone of voice, contrasting singularly with the wild and often startling nature of his themes. It was difficult to

[4] A character in Laurence Sterne's *Tristram Shandy*.
[5] Irving had begun the writing of *Astoria* in August, 1835.

Introductory Notice

conceive the mild, quiet-looking personage before you, the actual hero of the stirring scenes related.

In the course of three or four months, happening to be at the city of Washington, I again came upon the captain, who was attending the slow adjustment of his affairs with the War Department. I found him quartered with a worthy brother in arms, a major in the army. Here he was writing at a table, covered with maps and papers, in the centre of a large barrack room, fancifully decorated with Indian arms, and trophies, and war dresses, and the skins of various wild animals, and hung round with pictures of Indian games and ceremonies, and scenes of war and hunting. In a word, the captain was beguiling the tediousness of attendance at court, by an attempt at authorship; and was rewriting and extending his travelling notes, and making maps of the regions he had explored. As he sat at the table, in this curious apartment, with his high bald head of somewhat foreign cast, he reminded me of some of those antique pictures of authors that I have seen in old Spanish volumes.

The result of his labors was a mass of manuscript, which he subsequently put at my disposal, to fit it for publication and bring it before the world. I found it full of interesting details of life among the mountains, and of the singular castes and races, both white men and red men, among whom he had sojourned. It bore, too, throughout, the impress of his character, his *bonhommie*, his kindliness of spirit, and his susceptibility to the grand and beautiful.

That manuscript has formed the staple of the following work. I have occasionally interwoven facts and details, gathered from various sources, especially from the conversations and journals of some of the captain's contemporaries, who were actors in the scenes he describes. I have also given it a tone and coloring drawn from my own observation, during an excursion into the Indian country beyond the bounds of civilization; as I before observed, however, the work is substantially the narrative of the worthy captain, and many of its most graphic passages are but little varied from his own language.

I shall conclude this notice by a dedication which he had made of his manuscript to his hospitable brother in arms, in whose quarters I found him occupied in his literary labors; it is a dedication which, I believe, possesses the qualities, not always found in complimentary documents of the kind, of being sincere, and being merited.

To JAMES HARVEY HOOK,
    Major, U. S. A.,

    whose jealousy of its honor, whose anxiety for
    its interests, and whose sensibility for its wants,
    have endeared him to the service as
    The Soldier's Friend;

    and whose general amenity, constant cheerfulness,
    disinterested hospitality, and unwearied
    benevolence, entitle him to the still loftier title of
    The Friend of Man,

    this work is inscribed, etc.

New-York, 1843.   WASHINGTON IRVING

The ADVENTURES *of*
Captain Bonneville

I.

State of the fur trade of the Rocky Mountains—American enterprises—General Ashley and his associates—Sublette, a famous leader—Yearly rendezvous among the mountains—Stratagems and dangers of the trade—Bands of trappers—Indian banditti—Crows and Blackfeet—Mountaineers—Traders of the Far West—Character and habits of the trapper

IN A RECENT WORK[1] we have given an account of the grand enterprise of Mr. John Jacob Astor to establish an American emporium for the fur trade at the mouth of the Columbia, or Oregon River; of the failure of that enterprise through the capture of Astoria by the British, in 1814; and of the way in which the control of the trade of the Columbia and its dependencies fell into the hands of the Northwest Company. We have stated, likewise, the unfortunate supineness of the American government in neglecting the application of Mr. Astor for the protection of the American flag, and a small military force, to enable him to reinstate himself in the possession of Astoria at the return of peace; when the post was formally given up by the British government, though still occupied by the Northwest Company. By that supineness the sovereignty in the country has been virtually lost to the United States; and it will cost both governments much trouble and difficulty to settle matters on that just and rightful footing on which they would readily have been placed had the proposition of Mr. Astor been attended to. We shall now state a few particulars

---

[1] This was Irving's *Astoria, or Anecdotes of an Enterprise beyond the Rocky Mountains.*

of subsequent events, so as to lead the reader up to the period of which we are about to treat, and to prepare him for the circumstances of our narrative.

In consequence of the apathy and neglect of the American government, Mr. Astor abandoned all thoughts of regaining Astoria, and made no further attempt to extend his enterprises beyond the Rocky Mountains; and the Northwest Company considered themselves the lords of the country. They did not long enjoy unmolested the sway which they had somewhat surreptitiously attained. A fierce competition ensued between them and their old rivals, the Hudson's Bay Company; which was carried on at great cost and sacrifice, and occasionally with the loss of life. It ended in the ruin of most of the partners of the Northwest Company; and the merging of the relics of that establishment, in 1821, in the rival association. From that time, the Hudson's Bay Company enjoyed a monopoly of the Indian trade from the coast of the Pacific to the Rocky Mountains, and for a considerable extent north and south. They removed their emporium from Astoria to Fort Vancouver, a strong post on the left bank of the Columbia River, about sixty miles from its mouth;[2] whence they furnished their interior posts, and sent forth their brigades of trappers.

The Rocky Mountains formed a vast barrier between them and the United States, and their stern and awful defiles, their rugged valleys, and the great western plains watered by their rivers, remained almost a terra incognita to the American trapper. The difficulties experienced in 1808, by Mr. Henry[3] of the Missouri

---

[2] This fort was built in 1824 on the north bank of the Columbia River by the Hudson's Bay Company; it was abandoned in 1846 with the settlement of the boundary dispute between England and the United States. Dr. John McLoughlin (1784–1857) was in charge for the 22 years of its existence. Its distance from the mouth of the Columbia was closer to 115 miles.

[3] This was Andrew Henry, who in 1808 was one of the organizers of the St. Louis Missouri Fur Company. He helped build Fort Lisa at the junction of the Big Horn River and the Yellowstone in 1809, and in 1810, with Pierre Menard and John Colter, built a stockade at Three Forks that was shortly abandoned, owing to the hostility of the Blackfeet. Henry then moved with a group of men across the Continental Divide into the Snake River country and explored its tributaries west of the Teton Range for the first time. Several remarkable stones, one inscribed

The ADVENTURES *of* CAPTAIN BONNEVILLE

Company, the first American who trapped upon the head-waters of the Columbia; and the frightful hardships sustained by Wilson P. Hunt, Ramsay Crooks, Robert Stuart,[4] and other intrepid Astorians, in their ill-fated expeditions across the mountains, appeared for a time to check all further enterprise in that direction. The American traders contented themselves with following up the head branches of the Missouri, the Yellowstone, and other rivers and streams on the Atlantic side of the mountains, but forbore to attempt those great snow-crowned sierras.

One of the first to revive these tramontane expeditions was General Ashley,[5] of Missouri, a man whose courage and achievements

"Camp Henry Sept 1810," attest to the location of at least one of Henry's camps near Drummond, Idaho. Another stone bears the names A. Henry, J. Hoback, P. McBride, B. Jackson, and L. Cather. See Margaret Hawkes Lindsley, "Major Andrew Henry," *Scenic Idaho*, Vol. X (1955), 6 ff.

[4] See Irving's *Astoria* for an account of these participants in the overland trek to Astoria in 1811. Wilson Price Hunt (1782?–1842), one of the partners in the Pacific Fur Company, was the leader of the overland Astorians. Ramsay Crooks (1787–1859) had been in the Canadian fur trade before entering the Pacific Fur Company. Eventually he became president of the American Fur Company. Robert Stuart (1785–1848), besides being a partner in the Astorian enterprise and eventually head of the Northern Department of the American Fur Company in the Great Lakes region, is best remembered for his courageous leadership of the returning Astorians, who crossed the continent from Astoria to St. Louis in 1812–13. This heroic trek is recorded in Robert Stuart's *The Discovery of the Oregon Trail: Robert Stuart's Narratives* (ed. by Phillip Ashton Rollins) and *On the Oregon Trail: Robert Stuart's Journey of Discovery* (ed. by Kenneth A. Spaulding). Irving's account of Stuart's journeys is in *Astoria*, Chapters 43–50.

[5] William H. Ashley (c.1778–1838), after serving as lieutenant-governor of Missouri, entered the fur trade in 1822 in partnership with Andrew Henry. He brought into the business such men as James Bridger, Thomas Fitzpatrick, Jedediah S. Smith, James Beckwourth, William Sublette, Hugh Glass, David Jackson, Robert Campbell, Mike Fink, and others, all of whom became not only important in the history of the fur trade but also the subjects of western legend. It was Ashley men who rediscovered South Pass, which a few years later Bonneville would be the first to cross with a wagon; it was Ashley men who found the rich fur-bearing waters of the Green River valley and much of the country beyond and who thus guaranteed Ashley a fortune; and it was Ashley who introduced the rendezvous system, which Irving describes on p. 154 ff., as a substitute for permanent trading posts and thereby changed the character of the fur trade. When he retired from the fur trade in 1826, he did so as a wealthy man. Subsequently he served in Congress from 1831 to 1837. Ashley's diary as a fur trader has been edited by Dale

in the prosecution of his enterprises have rendered him famous in the Far West. In conjunction with Mr. Henry, already mentioned, he established a post on the banks of the Yellowstone River in 1822, and in the following year pushed a resolute band of trappers across the mountains to the banks of the Green River or Colorado of the West, often known by the Indian name of the Seeds-ke-dee Agie.[6] This attempt was followed up and sustained by others, until in 1825 a footing was secured, and a complete system of trapping organized beyond the mountains.[7]

It is difficult to do justice to the courage, fortitude, and perseverance of the pioneers of the fur trade, who conducted these early expeditions, and first broke their way through a wilderness where everything was calculated to deter and dismay them. They had to traverse the most dreary and desolate mountains, and barren and trackless wastes, uninhabited by man, or occasionally infested by predatory and cruel savages. They knew nothing of the country beyond the verge of their horizon, and had to gather information as they wandered. They beheld volcanic plains stretching around them, and ranges of mountains piled up to the clouds, and glistening with eternal frost: but knew nothing of their defiles, nor how they were to be penetrated or traversed. They launched themselves in frail canoes on rivers, without knowing whither their swift currents would carry them, or what rocks and shoals and rapids they might encounter in their course. They had to be continually on the alert, too, against the mountain tribes, who beset every defile, laid ambuscades in their path, or attacked them in their night encampments; so that, of the hardy bands of trappers that first entered into these regions, three-fifths are said to have fallen by the hands of savage foes.

Morgan in the *Bulletin of the Missouri Historical Society*, Vol. XI (1954-55), 9-40, 158-86, 279-302.

[6] *i. e.* the Prairie Hen River. Agie in the Crow language signifies river (Irving's note).

[7] Ashley's fur trading is well covered in Harrison C. Dale's *The Ashley-Smith Explorations and the Discovery of a Central Route to the Pacific;* Donald McKay Frost's *Notes on General Ashley, the Overland Trail, and South Pass;* and Dale Morgan's *Jedediah Smith and the Opening of the West.*

The Adventures of Captain Bonneville

In this wild and warlike school a number of leaders have sprung up, originally in the employ, subsequently partners of Ashley; among these we may mention Smith, Fitzpatrick, Bridger, Robert Campbell, and William Sublette;[8] whose adventures and exploits partake of the wildest spirit of romance. The association commenced by General Ashley underwent various modifications. That gentleman having acquired sufficient fortune, sold out his interest and retired; and the leading spirit that succeeded him was Captain William Sublette; a man worthy of note, as his name has become renowned in frontier story. He is a native of Kentucky, and of game descent; his maternal grandfather, Colonel Wheatley,[9] a companion of Boon, having been one of the pioneers of the West, celebrated in Indian warfare, and killed in one of the contests of the "Bloody Ground." We shall frequently have occasion to speak of this Sublette, and always to the credit of his game qualities. In 1830, the association took the name of the Rocky Mountain Fur Company, of which Captain Sublette and Robert Campbell were prominent members.[10]

In the meantime, the success of this company attracted the attention and excited the emulation of the American Fur Company, and brought them once more into the field of their ancient enterprise. Mr. Astor, the founder of the association, had retired from busy life, and the concerns of the company were ably managed by Mr.

---

[8] For biographies of these men, see Morgan, *Jedediah Smith*; LeRoy Hafen and W. J. Ghent, *Broken Hand, the Life Story of Thomas Fitzpatrick*; Alter, *James Bridger*; and John E. Sunder, *Bill Sublette, Mountain Man*. No biography of Campbell has been written, but his correspondence appears in *Glimpses of the Past*, ed. by Stella M. Drumm and Isaac H. Lionberger, Vol. VIII (1941), 3-65, and in *The Rocky Mountain Letters of Robert Campbell*.

[9] Colonel William Whitley. See Sunder, *Bill Sublette*, 5-7.

[10] The Rocky Mountain Fur Company was formed in 1830 when Jedediah Smith, David Jackson, and William Sublette sold their interests to Thomas Fitzpatrick, Milton Sublette, James Bridger, Henry Fraeb, and Jean Baptiste Gervais. Irving confused William Sublette with his younger brother Milton in this transaction. In 1832, the year of Bonneville's appearance in the fur trade, William Sublette and Robert Campbell formed a partnership that lasted for ten years. They built Fort Laramie in 1834 and, as Irving states in the next paragraph, opposed the American Fur Company on the Upper Missouri with the building of Fort William.

Ramsay Crooks, of Snake River renown, who still officiates as its president. A competition immediately ensued between the two companies for the trade with the mountain tribes and the trapping of the head-waters of the Columbia and the other great tributaries of the Pacific. Beside the regular operations of these formidable rivals, there have been from time to time desultory enterprises, or rather experiments, of minor associations, or of adventurous individuals, beside roving bands of independent trappers, who either hunt for themselves, or engage for a single season, in the service of one or other of the main companies.

The consequence is that the Rocky Mountains and the ulterior regions, from the Russian possessions in the north down to the Spanish settlements of California, have been traversed and ransacked in every direction by bands of hunters and Indian traders; so that there is scarcely a mountain pass, or defile, that is not known and threaded in their restless migrations, nor a nameless stream that is not haunted by the lonely trapper.

The American fur companies keep no established posts beyond the mountains. Everything there is regulated by resident partners; that is to say, partners who reside in the tramontane country, but who move about from place to place, either with Indian tribes, whose traffic they wish to monopolize, or with main bodies of their own men, whom they employ in trading and trapping. In the meantime, they detach bands, or "brigades" as they are termed, of trappers in various directions, assigning to each a portion of country as a hunting or trapping ground. In the months of June and July, when there is an interval between the hunting seasons, a general rendezvous is held, at some designated place in the mountains, where the affairs of the past year are settled by the resident partners, and the plans for the following year arranged.

To this rendezvous repair the various brigades of trappers from their widely separated hunting grounds, bringing in the products of their year's campaign. Hither also repair the Indian tribes accustomed to traffic their peltries with the company. Bands of free trappers resort hither also, to sell the furs they have collected; or to engage their services for the next hunting season.

To this rendezvous the company sends annually a convoy of supplies from its establishment on the Atlantic frontier,[11] under the guidance of some experienced partner or officer. On the arrival of this convoy, the resident partner at the rendezvous depends to set all his next year's machinery in motion.

Now as the rival companies keep a vigilant eye upon each other, and are anxious to discover each other's plans and movements, they generally contrive to hold their annual assemblages at no great distance apart. An eager competition exists also between their respective convoys of supplies, which shall first reach its place of rendezvous. For this purpose, they set off with the first appearance of grass on the Atlantic frontier and push with all diligence for the mountains. The company that can first open its tempting supplies of coffee, tobacco, ammunition, scarlet cloth, blankets, bright shawls, and glittering trinkets has the greatest chance to get all the peltries and furs of the Indians and free trappers, and to engage their services for the next season. It is able, also, to fit out and dispatch its own trappers the soonest, so as to get the start of its competitors, and to have the first dash into the hunting and trapping grounds.

A new species of strategy has sprung out of this hunting and trapping competition. The constant study of the rival bands is to forestall and outwit each other; to supplant each other in the good will and custom of the Indian tribes; to cross each other's plans; to mislead each other as to routes; in a word, next to his own advantage, the study of the Indian trader is the disadvantage of his competitor.

The influx of this wandering trade has had its effects on the habits of the mountain tribes. They have found the trapping of the beaver their most profitable species of hunting; and the traffic with the white man has opened to them sources of luxury of which they previously had no idea. The introduction of firearms has rendered them more successful hunters, but at the same time, more formidable foes; some of them, incorrigibly savage and warlike in their

---

[11] Irving's phrase is misleading. St. Louis was the business and main supply center of the Rocky Mountain fur trade. Supply trains assembled goods, animals, equipment, and men near Independence, Missouri, in the spring.

nature, have found the expeditions of the fur traders grand objects of profitable adventure. To waylay and harass a band of trappers with their pack-horses, when embarrassed in the rugged defiles of the mountains, has become as favorite an exploit with these Indians as the plunder of a caravan to the Arab of the desert. The Crows and Blackfeet, who were such terrors in the path of the early adventurers to Astoria, still continue their predatory habits, but seem to have brought them to greater system. They know the routes and resorts of the trappers; where to waylay them on their journeys; where to find them in the hunting seasons, and where to hover about them in winter quarters. The life of a trapper, therefore, is a perpetual state militant, and he must sleep with his weapons in his hands.

A new order of trappers and traders, also, has grown out of this system of things. In the old times of the great Northwest Company, when the trade in furs was pursued chiefly about the lakes and rivers, the expeditions were carried on in batteaux and canoes. The voyageurs or boatmen were the rank and file in the service of the trader, and even the hardy "men of the north," those great rufflers and game birds, were fain to be paddled from point to point of their migrations.

A totally different class has now sprung up:—"the Mountaineers," the traders and trappers that scale the vast mountain chains, and pursue their hazardous vocations amidst their wild recesses. They move from place to place on horseback. The equestrian exercises, therefore, in which they are engaged, the nature of the countries they traverse, vast plains and mountains, pure and exhilarating in atmospheric qualities, seem to make them physically and mentally a more lively and mercurial race than the fur traders and trappers of former days, the self-vaunting "men of the north." A man who bestrides a horse must be essentially different from a man who cowers in a canoe. We find them, accordingly, hardy, lithe, vigorous, and active; extravagant in word, and thought, and deed; heedless of hardship; daring of danger; prodigal of the present, and thoughtless of the future.

A difference is to be perceived even between these mountain

Kansas State Historical Society

JIM BRIDGER
The Incomparable Mountain Man

Walters Art Gallery, Baltimore

JOSEPH REDDEFORD WALKER AND HIS SQUAW
From a Painting by Alfred Jacob Miller, 1837

hunters and those of the lower regions along the waters of the Missouri. The latter, generally French creoles, live comfortably in cabins and log-huts, well sheltered from the inclemencies of the seasons. They are within the reach of frequent supplies from the settlements; their life is comparatively free from danger, and from most of the vicissitudes of the upper wilderness. The consequence is that they are less hardy, self-dependent and game-spirited than the mountaineer. If the latter by chance comes among them on his way to and from the settlements, he is like a game-cock among the common roosters of the poultry-yard. Accustomed to live in tents, or to bivouac in the open air, he despises the comforts and is impatient of the confinement of the log-house. If his meal is not ready in season, he takes his rifle, hies to the forest or prairie, shoots his own game, lights his fire, and cooks his repast. With his horse and his rifle, he is independent of the world, and spurns at all its restraints. The very superintendents at the lower posts will not put him to mess with the common men, the hirelings of the establishment, but treat him as something superior.

There is, perhaps, no class of men on the face of the earth, says Captain Bonneville, who lead a life of more continued exertion, peril, and excitement, and who are more enamored of their occupations, than the free trappers of the West. No toil, no danger, no privation can turn the trapper from his pursuit. His passionate excitement at times resembles a mania. In vain may the most vigilant and cruel savages beset his path; in vain may rocks and precipices and wintry torrents oppose his progress; let but a single track of a beaver meet his eye, and he forgets all dangers and defies all difficulties. At times, he may be seen with his traps on his shoulder, buffeting his way across rapid streams, amidst floating blocks of ice: at other times, he is to be found with his traps swung on his back clambering the most rugged mountains, scaling or descending the most frightful precipices, searching, by routes inaccessible to the horse, and never before trodden by white man, for springs and lakes unknown to his comrades, and where he may meet with his favorite game. Such is the mountaineer, the hardy trapper of the West; and such, as we have slightly sketched it, is the wild, Robin Hood kind of life, with all its strange and motley populace, now existing in full vigor among the Rocky Mountains.

Having thus given the reader some idea of the actual state of the fur trade in the interior of our vast continent, and made him acquainted with the wild chivalry of the mountains, we will no longer delay the introduction of Captain Bonneville and his band into this field of their enterprise, but launch them at once upon the perilous plains of the Far West.

2.

Departure from Fort Osage—Modes of transportation—Pack-horses—Wagons—Walker and Cerré; their characters—Buoyant feelings on launching upon the prairies—Wild equipments of the trappers—Their gambols and antics—Difference of character between the American and French trappers—Agency of the Kansas—General Clarke—White Plume, the Kansas chief—Night scene in a trader's camp—Colloquy between White Plume and the captain—Bee-hunters—Their expeditions—Their feuds with the Indians—Bargaining talent of White Plume

It was on the first of May, 1832, that Captain Bonneville took his departure from the frontier post of Fort Osage,[1] on the Missouri. He had enlisted a party of

[1] Built in 1808 under the supervision of General William Clark far from any white settlement, Fort Osage served as a frontier garrison and government trading post until 1822, when the United States factory system of Indian trading was discontinued. It was located on a high bluff of the south bank of the Missouri River about fourteen miles northeast of Independence. Writing in 1836, Alphonso Wetmore stated:

"Fort Osage, formerly a frontier military post, was dismantled many years ago. The United States factory was located here. It was a point where the Osages and Kanzas resorted to trade, when the United States bartered powder, traps, and scalping-knives for furs and peltries. . . . The site is now the property of Mr. Archibald Gamble, who has laid off a town, to which he has given the name of Sibley. The gentleman [George C. Sibley] whose name is given to this town-site was the United States factor for Indian trade there, and [his] hospitable mansion and amiable family, at an early period, robbed the wilderness of its terrors and crude aspect, and imposed agreeable surprise on the weary and necessitous traveller. . . . It has already been made a point of landing for Santa Fe goods, and it will probably share largely in the increasing advantages of that trade. The landing

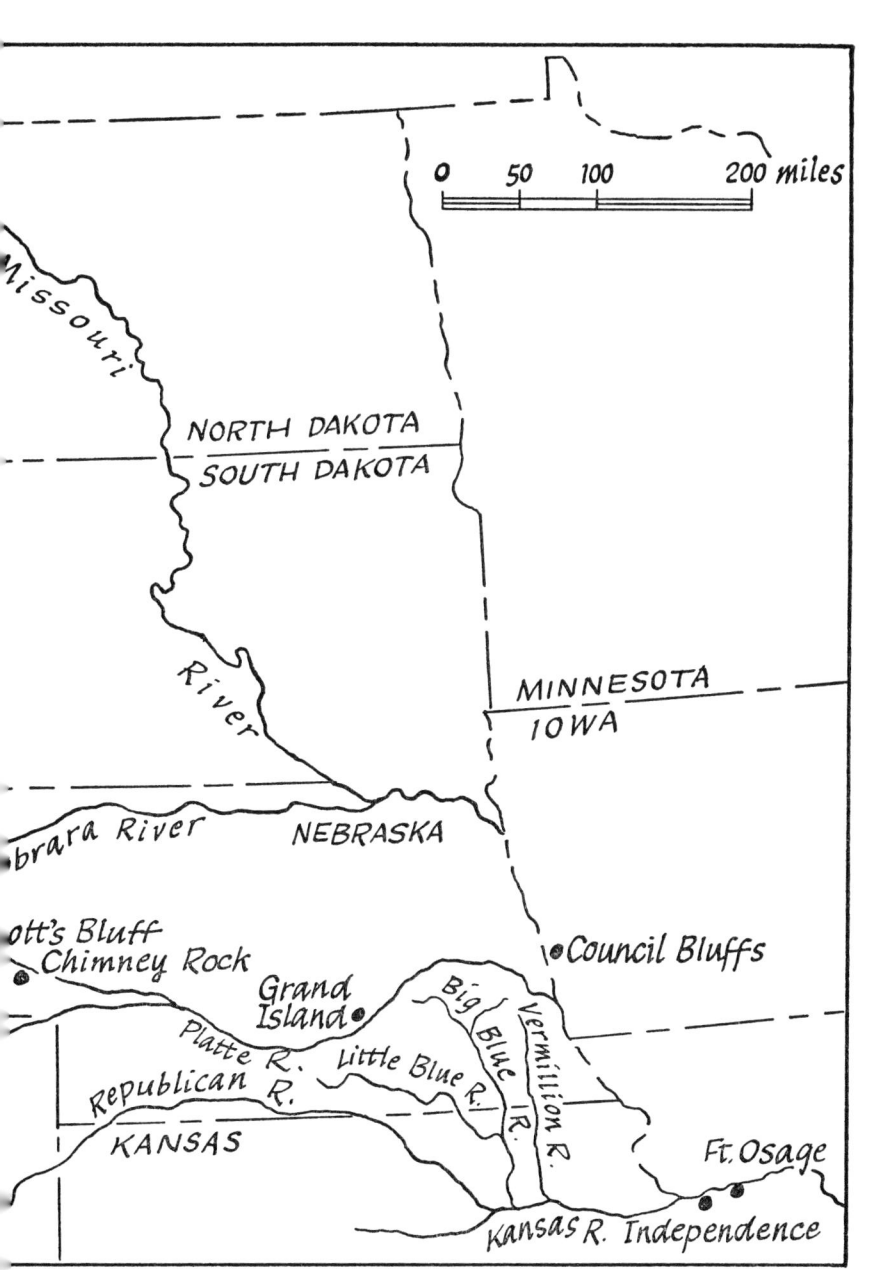

The Plains and Rocky Mountains, 1832–35

one hundred and ten men, most of whom had been in the Indian country, and some of whom were experienced hunters and trappers. Fort Osage, and other places on the borders of the western wilderness, abound with characters of the kind, ready for any expedition.

The ordinary mode of transportation in these great inland expeditions of the fur traders is on mules and pack-horses; but Captain Bonneville substituted wagons.[2] Though he was to travel through a trackless wilderness, yet the greater part of his route would lie across open plains, destitute of forests, and where wheel carriages can pass in every direction. The chief difficulty occurs in passing the deep ravines cut through the prairies by streams and winter torrents. Here it is often necessary to dig a road down the banks, and to make bridges for the wagons.

In transporting his baggage in vehicles of this kind, Captain Bonneville thought he would save the great delay caused every morning by packing the horses, and the labor of unpacking in the evening. Fewer horses also would be required, and less risk incurred of their wandering away, or being frightened or carried off by the Indians. The wagons, also, would be more easily defended, and might form a kind of fortification in case of attack in the open prairies. A train of twenty wagons, drawn by oxen, or by four mules or horses each, and laden with merchandise, ammunition, and provisions, were disposed in two columns in the center of the party, which was equally divided into a van and a rear-guard. As sub-leaders or lieutenants in his expedition, Captain Bonneville had made choice of Mr. I. R. Walker[3] and Mr. M. S. Cerré.[4] The

---

and harbour of Sibley are excellent, made so by the eddy-water at the base of the bluff." *Gazetteer of the State of Missouri* (St. Louis, 1837), 97–98.

For reasons which are not clear, Bonneville found it more advantageous to assemble his company and equipment here than at Lexington or Independence.

[2] Although not the first to use wagons to transport goods to the mountains, Bonneville became the first to take them over historic South Pass to Green River, where he built his fort. He thus proved the feasibility of a wagon route across the Continental Divide which thousands of emigrants would use in the next decade and years to follow. Besides wagons, he had oxen, a cow, and a calf.

[3] This was Joseph Reddeford Walker (1798–1876), who figures prominently in several later chapters as the leader of an expedition to Great Salt Lake and Califor-

The ADVENTURES of CAPTAIN BONNEVILLE

former was a native of Tennessee, about six feet high, strong built, dark complexioned, brave in spirit, though mild in manners. He had resided for many years in Missouri, on the frontier; had been among the earliest adventurers to Santa Fé, where he went to trap beaver, and was taken by the Spaniards. Being liberated, he engaged with the Spaniards and Sioux Indians in a war against the Pawnees; then returned to Missouri, and had acted by turns as sheriff, trader, trapper, until he was enlisted as a leader by Captain Bonneville.

Cerré, his other leader, had likewise been in expeditions to Santa Fé, in which he had endured much hardship. He was of the middle size, light complexioned, and though but about twenty-five years of age, was considered an experienced Indian trader. It was a great object with Captain Bonneville to get to the mountains before the summer heats and summer flies should render the travelling across the prairies distressing; and before the annual assemblages of people connected with the fur trade should have broken up, and dispersed to the hunting grounds.

The two rival associations already mentioned, the American Fur Company and the Rocky Mountain Fur Company, had their several places of rendezvous for the present year at no great distance apart,

---

nia. Walker was born in Tennessee and before being engaged by Bonneville had lived and traded near Independence, had been with William Becknell in the first trading expedition to Santa Fe in 1821, and had served as sheriff of Jackson County, Missouri. He was thus an experienced, well-qualified frontiersman when he met Bonneville at Fort Gibson in 1831. Zenas Leonard, a member of Walker's party to California, spoke of him as being "well hardened to the hardships of the wilderness—understood the character of the Indians very well—and to explore unknown regions was his chief delight." Zenas Leonard, *Adventures of Zenas Leonard, Fur Trader* (ed. by John C. Ewers), 64.

Walker's biography has been written by Watson in *West Wind*. See also Daniel E. Conner, *Joseph Reddeford Walker and the Arizona Adventure* (ed. by Donald J. Berthrong and Odessa Davenport).

[4] Michel (or Michael) Sylvestre Cerré (1804–60). He was from a family of well-known French fur traders and as a young man had engaged in the Santa Fe trade and had also been in charge of a trading post. He was, like Walker, a valuable addition to Bonneville's company, and Bonneville later entrusted him with the responsibility of transporting the harvest of beaver skins to St. Louis and bringing back to the mountains the annual supplies for continued operations. His name appears frequently in fur-trade literature.

The ADVENTURES *of* CAPTAIN BONNEVILLE

in Pierre's Hole,[5] a deep valley in the heart of the mountains, and thither Captain Bonneville intended to shape his course.

It is not easy to do justice to the exulting feelings of the worthy captain at finding himself at the head of a stout band of hunters, trappers, and woodmen; fairly launched on the broad prairies, with his face to the boundless West. The tamest inhabitant of cities, the veriest spoiled child of civilization, feels his heart dilate and his pulse beat high on finding himself on horseback in the glorious wilderness; what then must be the excitement of one whose imagination had been stimulated by a residence on the frontier, and to whom the wilderness was a region of romance!

His hardy followers partook of his excitement. Most of them had already experienced the wild freedom of savage life, and looked forward to a renewal of past scenes of adventure and exploit. Their very appearance and equipment exhibited a piebald mixture, half civilized and half savage. Many of them looked more like Indians than white men in their garbs and accoutrements, and their very horses were caparisoned in barbaric style, with fantastic trappings. The outset of a band of adventurers on one of these expeditions is always animated and joyous. The welkin rang with their shouts and yelps, after the manner of the savages; and with boisterous jokes and light-hearted laughter. As they passed the straggling hamlets and solitary cabins that fringe the skirts of the frontier, they would startle their inmates by Indian yells and war-whoops, or regale them with grotesque feats of horsemanship, well suited to their half-savage appearance. Most of these abodes were inhabited by men who had themselves been in similar expeditions; they welcomed the travellers, therefore, as brother trappers, treated them with a hunter's hospitality, and cheered them with an honest God speed at parting.

[5] Now known as Teton Basin, Pierre's Hole lies immediately west of the Teton Range. The scene of the 1832 rendezvous, it was approached from the east by way of Jackson Hole and Teton Pass. It is a broad flat area, and in the period of the fur trade was well provided with game and forage. The rendezvous site was located a few miles south of modern Driggs, Idaho, in Teton County. Here occurred in 1832 the famous battle of Pierre's Hole between the trappers and a band of Blackfeet Indians. See Chapter VI for Irving's account of this conflict.

And here we would remark a great difference, in point of character and quality, between the two classes of trappers, the "American" and "French," as they are called in contradistinction. The latter is meant to designate the French creole of Canada or Louisiana; the former, the trapper of the old American stock, from Kentucky, Tennessee, and others of the western States. The French trapper is represented as a lighter, softer, more self-indulgent kind of man. He must have his Indian wife, his lodge, and his petty conveniences. He is gay and thoughtless, takes little heed of landmarks, depends upon his leaders and companions to think for the common weal, and, if left to himself, is easily perplexed and lost.

The American trapper stands by himself, and is peerless for the service of the wilderness. Drop him in the midst of a prairie, or in the heart of the mountains, and he is never at a loss. He notices every landmark; can retrace his route through the most monotonous plains, or the most perplexed labyrinths of the mountains; no danger nor difficulty can appal him, and he scorns to complain under any privation. In equipping the two kinds of trappers, the Creole and Canadian are apt to prefer the light fusee; the American always grasps his rifle; he despises what he calls the "shot-gun." We give these estimates on the authority of a trader of long experience, and a foreigner by birth. "I consider one American," said he, "equal to three Canadians in point of sagacity, aptness at resources, self-dependence, and fearlessness of spirit. In fact, no one can cope with him as a stark tramper of the wilderness."

Beside the two classes of trappers just mentioned, Captain Bonneville had enlisted several Delaware Indians in his employ, on whose hunting qualifications he placed great reliance.

On the 6th of May the travellers passed the last border habitation,[6] and bade a long farewell to the ease and security of civiliza-

---

[6] This was Independence, Missouri, founded in 1827. Irving spent three days here in September, 1832, on the journey he narrates in *A Tour on the Prairies*. Charles Latrobe, one of his travelling companions, described Independence as consisting at that time "of nothing but a ragged congeries of five or six rough log-huts, two or three clapboard houses, two or three so-called hotels, alias grogshops; a few stores, a bank, printing office, and barn-looking church. It lacked at the time I commemorate, the three last edifices, but was nevertheless a thriving and aspiring

tion. The buoyant and clamorous spirits with which they had commenced their march gradually subsided as they entered upon its difficulties. They found the prairies saturated with the heavy cold rains, prevalent in certain seasons of the year in this part of the country, the wagon wheels sank deep in the mire, the horses were often to the fetlock, and both steed and rider were completely jaded by the evening of the 12th, when they reached the Kansas River;[7] a fine stream about three hundred yards wide, entering the Missouri from the south. Though fordable in almost every part at the end of summer and during the autumn, yet it was necessary to construct a raft for the transportation of the wagons and effects. All this was done in the course of the following day, and by evening, the whole party arrived at the agency of the Kansas tribe. This was under the superintendence of General Clarke, brother of the celebrated traveller of the same name, who, with Lewis, made the first expedition down the waters of the Columbia. He was living like a patriarch, surrounded by laborers and interpreters, all snugly housed, and provided with excellent farms. The functionary next in consequence to the agent was the blacksmith, a most important, and, indeed, indispensable personage in a frontier community. The Kansas resemble the Osages in features, dress, and language; they raise corn and hunt the buffalo, ranging the Kansas River, and its tributary streams; at the time of the captain's visit, they were at war with the Pawnees of the Nebraska, or Platte River.

The unusual sight of a train of wagons caused quite a sensation among these savages; who thronged about the caravan, examining everything minutely, and asking a thousand questions: exhibiting a

---

place, in its way. . . . A little beyond this point, all carriage roads ceased, and one deep black trail alone, which might be seen tending to the south-west, was that of the Santa Fe trappers and traders." Charles J. Latrobe, *The Rambler in North America*, I, 104–105.

[7] The Kansas River flows easterly, joining the Missouri at Kansas City. Bonneville probably followed the trail used by the Santa Fe traders angling off toward the southwest and then left it to approach the river in the neighborhood of modern Topeka, where he forded it. North of the river the trail pointed northwest toward the Platte River.

degree of excitability, and a lively curiosity totally opposite to that apathy with which their race is so often reproached.

The personage who most attracted the captain's attention at this place was "White Plume," the Kansas chief, and they soon became good friends.[8] White Plume (we are pleased with his chivalrous *soubriquet*) inhabited a large stone house, built for him by order of the American government: but the establishment had not been carried out in corresponding style. It might be palace without, but it was wigwam within; so that, between the stateliness of his mansion and the squalidness of his furniture, the gallant White Plume presented some such whimsical incongruity as we see in the gala equipments of an Indian chief on a treaty-making embassy at Washington, who has been generously decked out in cocked hat and military coat, in contrast to his breech-clout and leathern leggins; being grand officer at top, and ragged Indian at bottom.

White Plume was so taken with the courtesy of the captain, and pleased with one or two presents received from him, that he accompanied him a day's journey on his march, and passed a night in his camp, on the margin of a small stream. The method of encamping generally observed by the captain was as follows: The twenty wagons were disposed in a square, at the distance of thirty-three feet from each other. In every interval there was a mess stationed; and each mess had its fire, where the men cooked, ate, gossiped, and slept. The horses were placed in the centre of the square, with a guard stationed over them at night.

The horses were "side lined," as it is termed: that is to say, the fore and hind foot on the same side of the animal were tied together, so as to be within eighteen inches of each other. A horse thus fettered is for a time sadly embarrassed, but soon becomes sufficiently accustomed to the restraint to move about slowly. It prevents his wandering; and his being easily carried off at night by lurking Indians. When a horse that is "foot free" is tied to one thus secured, the latter forms, as it were, a pivot, round which the other runs and curvets, in case of alarm.

[8] A portrait of White Plume by Alfred Jacob Miller appears in *The West of Alfred Jacob Miller* (ed. by Marvin C. Ross), 17.

The ADVENTURES *of* CAPTAIN BONNEVILLE

The encampment of which we are speaking presented a striking scene. The various mess-fires were surrounded by picturesque groups, standing, sitting, and reclining; some busied in cooking, others in cleaning their weapons: while the frequent laugh told that the rough joke or merry story was going on. In the middle of the camp, before the principal lodge, sat the two chieftains, Captain Bonneville and White Plume, in soldier-like communion, the captain delighted with the opportunity of meeting on social terms with one of the red warriors of the wilderness, the unsophisticated children of nature. The latter was squatted on his buffalo robe, his strong features and red skin glaring in the broad light of a blazing fire, while he recounted astounding tales of the bloody exploits of his tribe and himself in their wars with the Pawnees; for there are no old soldiers more given to long campaigning stories than Indian "braves."

The feuds of White Plume, however, had not been confined to the red men; he had much to say of brushes with bee hunters,[9] a class of offenders for whom he seemed to cherish a particular abhorrence. As the species of hunting prosecuted by these worthies is not laid down in any of the ancient books of venerie, and is, in fact, peculiar to our western frontier, a word or two on the subject may not be unacceptable to the reader.

The bee hunter is generally some settler on the verge of the prairies; a long, lank fellow, of fever and ague complexion, acquired from living on new soil, and in a hut built of green logs. In the autumn, when the harvest is over, these frontier settlers form parties of two or three, and prepare for a bee hunt. Having provided themselves with a wagon, and a number of empty casks, they sally off, armed with their rifles, into the wilderness, directing their course east, west, north, or south, without any regard to the ordinance of

[9] Bee hunters appear frequently in frontier literature of this period, and Irving himself had devoted Chapter 9 in *A Tour on the Prairie* to narrating a bee hunt in which he had participated in 1832. His notebooks for this tour also contain observations of bee hunters and bee hunting; see Washington Irving, *Western Journals* (ed. by John F. McDermott), 92, 119–20. A comparison of Chapter 9 in *A Tour*, entries in the *Western Journals*, and the present passage in *Bonneville* shows that Irving's description here was based upon firsthand observation.

the American government, which strictly forbids all trespass upon the lands belonging to the Indian tribes.

The belts of woodland that traverse the lower prairies and border the rivers are peopled by innumerable swarms of wild bees, which make their hives in hollow trees and fill them with honey tolled from the rich flowers of the prairies. The bees, according to popular assertion, are migrating like the settlers, to the west. An Indian trader, well experienced in the country, informs us that within ten years that he has passed in the Far West, the bee has advanced westward above a hundred miles. It is said on the Missouri, that the wild turkey and the wild bee go up the river together: neither is found in the upper regions. It is but recently that the wild turkey has been killed on the Nebraska, or Platte; and his travelling competitor, the wild bee, appeared there about the same time.

Be all this as it may: the course of our party of bee hunters is to make a wide circuit through the woody river bottoms, and the patches of forest on the prairies, marking, as they go out, every tree in which they have detected a hive. These marks are generally respected by any other bee hunter that should come upon their track. When they have marked sufficient to fill all their casks, they turn their faces homeward, cut down the trees as they proceed, and having loaded their wagon with honey and wax, return well pleased to the settlements.

Now it so happens that the Indians relish wild honey as highly as do the white men, and are the more delighted with this natural luxury from its having, in many instances, but recently made its appearance in their lands. The consequence is numberless disputes and conflicts between them and the bee hunters: and often a party of the latter, returning, laden with rich spoil, from one of their forays, are apt to be waylaid by the native lords of the soil; their honey to be seized, their harness cut to pieces, and themselves left to find their way home the best way they can, happy to escape with no greater personal harm than a sound rib-roasting.

Such were the marauders of whose offences the gallant White Plume made the most bitter complaint. They were chiefly the settlers of the western part of Missouri, who are the most famous bee hunters on the frontier, and whose favorite hunting ground lies within the lands of the Kansas tribe. According to the account of White Plume, however, matters were pretty fairly balanced between him and the offenders; he having as often treated them to a taste of the bitter, as they had robbed him of the sweets.

It is but justice to this gallant chief to say that he gave proofs of having acquired some of the lights of civilization from his proximity to the whites, as was evinced in his knowledge of driving a bargain. He required hard cash in return for some corn with which he supplied the worthy captain, and left the latter at a loss which most to admire, his native chivalry as a brave, or his acquired adroitness as a trader.

3·

Wide prairies—Vegetable productions—Tabular hills—
Slabs of sandstone—Nebraska or Platte River—Scanty
fare—Buffalo skulls—Wagons turned into boats—
Herds of buffalo—Cliffs resembling castles—The
chimney—Scott's Bluffs—Story connected with
them—The bighorn or ahsahta—Its nature and
habits—Difference between that and the "woolly
sheep," or goat of the mountains

FROM THE MIDDLE to the end of May, Captain Bonneville pursued a western course over vast undulating plains, destitute of tree or shrub, rendered miry by occasional rain, and cut up by deep water-courses where they had to dig roads for their wagons down the soft crumbling banks and to throw bridges across the streams. The weather had attained the summer heat; the thermometer standing about fifty-seven degrees in the morning, early, but rising to about ninety degrees at noon. The incessant breezes, however, which sweep these vast plains render the heats endurable. Game was scanty, and they had to eke out their scanty fare with wild roots and vegetables, such as the Indian potato, the wild onion, and the prairie tomato, and they met with quantities of "red root," from which the hunters make a very palatable beverage.[1] The only human being that crossed their path was a Kansas warrior, returning from some solitary expedition of bravado or revenge, bearing a Pawnee scalp as a trophy.

The country gradually rose as they proceeded westward, and

---

[1] Indian potato *(Ipomoea leptophylla)*, wild onion *(Allium textile)*, prairie tomato *(Solanum triflorum)*. Identification of "red root" is uncertain.

their route took them over high ridges, commanding wide and beautiful prospects. The vast plain was studded on the west with innumerable hills of conical shape, such as are seen north of the Arkansas River. These hills have their summits apparently cut off about the same elevation, so as to leave flat surfaces at top. It is conjectured by some that the whole country may originally have been of the altitude of these tabular hills; but through some process of nature may have sunk to its present level; these insulated eminences being protected by broad foundations of solid rock.

Captain Bonneville mentions another geological phenomenon north of Red River,[2] where the surface of the earth, in considerable tracts of country, is covered with broad slabs of sandstone, having the form and position of grave-stones, and looking as if they had been forced up by some subterranean agitation. "The resemblance," says he, "which these very remarkable spots have in many places to old church-yards is curious in the extreme. One might almost fancy himself among the tombs of the pre-Adamites."

On the 2d of June, they arrived on the main stream of the Nebraska or Platte River; twenty-five miles below the head of the Great Island.[3] The low banks of this river give it an appearance of

---

[2] The Vermillion River. Lieutenant John C. Frémont in 1842 also noted the sandstone formations of this area. "Many large boulders," he wrote, "of a very compact sandstone, of various shades of red, some of them of four or five tons in weight, were scattered along the hills." John C. Frémont, *The Exploring Expedition to the Rocky Mountains, Oregon and California*, 12. His maps and other early maps show Little Vermillion River and further west Big (or Red) Vermillion River.

[3] Irving does not specify Bonneville's route, but Bonneville in a letter to Major General Alexander Macomb, July 29, 1833, written from the Wind River, stated: "On the 12th May crossed the Kansas, Kept up the left [north] bank, move[d] up the Republican, which I headed, having at first gone through a rolling country on the Republican. I marched upon an elevated plain, then struck it a little west and in one day fell on the Platte, the 2d June . . . and I [then] marched to the forks 130 miles. . . ." See Appendix B. This statement presents certain difficulties. Bonneville could not have traveled to the head of the Republican because by doing so he would have marched actually west of the forks of the Platte. Furthermore, his distance of 130 miles east of the forks indicates Grand Island, which Irving denotes Great Island, between 40 and 50 miles long, formed by two channels of the Platte. But had Bonneville followed the Republican he would have been led

great width. Captain Bonneville measured it in one place, and found it twenty-two hundred yards from bank to bank. Its depth was from three to six feet, the bottom full of quicksands. The Nebraska is studded with islands covered with that species of poplar called the cotton-wood tree. Keeping up along the course of this river for several days, they were obliged, from the scarcity of game, to put themselves upon short allowance, and, occasionally, to kill a steer. They bore their daily labors and privations, however, with great good humor, taking their tone, in all probability, from the buoyant spirit of their leader. "If the weather was inclement," said the captain, "we watched the clouds, and hoped for a sight of the blue sky and the merry sun. If food was scanty, we regaled ourselves with the hope of soon falling in with herds of buffalo, and having nothing to do but slay and eat." We doubt whether the genial captain is not describing the cheeriness of his own breast, which gave a cheery aspect to everything around him.

There certainly were evidences, however, that the country was not always equally destitute of game. At one place, they observed a field decorated with buffalo skulls, arranged in circles, curves, and other mathematical figures, as if for some mystic rite or ceremony. They were almost innumerable, and seemed to have been a vast hecatomb offered up in thanksgiving to the Great Spirit for some signal success in the chase.

On the 11th of June, they came to the fork of the Nebraska,[4] where it divides itself into two equal and beautiful streams. One of these branches rises in the west-southwest, near the headwaters of the Arkansas. Up the course of this branch, as Captain Bonneville was well aware, lay the route to the Camanche and Kioway

more than a day's journey south of Grand Island. After he left the Vermillion, the first stream he met had to be the Blue River. It seems likely, therefore, that Bonneville may have mistaken the Blue for the Republican. By ascending the Little Blue he would have been led near its head to a distance of one day's march directly below Grand Island.

[4] At this point, near modern North Platte, Nebraska, the South and North Platte rivers converge. Bonneville had been traveling along the south bank of the Platte, and it now became necessary to ford the South Platte and cross the intervening divide separating it from the North Platte.

The ADVENTURES *of* CAPTAIN BONNEVILLE

Indians, and to the northern Mexican settlements;[5] of the other branch he knew nothing. Its sources might lie among wild and inaccessible cliffs, and tumble and foam down rugged defiles and over craggy precipices; but its direction was in the true course, and up this stream he determined to prosecute his route to the Rocky Mountains. Finding it impossible, from quicksands and other dangerous impediments, to cross the river in this neighborhood, he kept up along the south fork for two days, merely seeking a safe fording place. At length he encamped, caused the bodies of the wagons to be dislodged from the wheels, covered with buffalo hides, and besmeared with a compound of tallow and ashes; thus forming rude boats. In these, they ferried their effects across the stream, which was six hundred yards wide, with a swift and strong current. Three men were in each boat, to manage it; others waded across, pushing the barks before them. Thus all crossed in safety. A march of nine miles took them over high rolling prairies to the north fork; their eyes being regaled with the welcome sight of herds of buffalo at a distance, some careering the plain, others grazing and reposing in the natural meadows.

Skirting along the north fork for a day or two, excessively annoyed by musquitoes and buffalo gnats, they reached, in the evening of the 17th, a small but beautiful grove, from which issued the confused notes of singing birds, the first they had heard since crossing the boundary of Missouri. After so many days of weary travelling through a naked, monotonous and silent country, it was delightful once more to hear the song of the bird, and to behold the verdure of the grove. It was a beautiful sunset, and a sight of the glowing rays, mantling the tree-tops and rustling branches, gladdened every heart. They pitched their camp in the grove, kindled their fires, partook merrily of their rude fare, and resigned themselves to the sweetest sleep they had enjoyed since their outset upon the prairies.

[5] These were Taos and Santa Fe in New Mexico, both of them frequented by trappers. They were also objectives in the Santa Fe trade, which was well established by 1832.

The ADVENTURES *of* CAPTAIN BONNEVILLE

The country now became rugged and broken. High bluffs advanced upon the river, and forced the travellers occasionally to leave its banks and wind their course into the interior. In one of the wild and solitary passes they were startled by the trail of four or five pedestrians, whom they supposed to be spies from some predatory camp of either Arickara or Crow Indians. This obliged them to redouble their vigilance at night, and to keep especial watch upon their horses. In these rugged and elevated regions they began to see the black-tailed deer, a species larger than the ordinary kind, and chiefly found in rocky and mountainous countries. They had reached also a great buffalo range; Captain Bonneville ascended a high bluff, commanding an extensive view of the surrounding plains. As far as his eye could reach, the country seemed absolutely blackened by innumerable herds. No language, he says, could convey an adequate idea of the vast living mass thus presented to his eye. He remarked that the bulls and cows generally congregated in separate herds.

Opposite to the camp at this place was a singular phenomenon, which is among the curiosities of the country. It is called the chimney.[6] The lower part is a conical mound, rising out of the naked plain; from the summit shoots up a shaft or column, about one hundred and twenty feet in height, from which it derives its name. The height of the whole, according to Captain Bonneville, is a hundred and seventy-five yards. It is composed of indurated clay, with alternate layers of red and white sandstone, and may be seen at the distance of upward of thirty miles.

On the 21st, they encamped amidst high and beetling cliffs of indurated clay and sandstone, bearing the semblance of towers, castles, churches, and fortified cities. At a distance, it was scarcely possible to persuade one's self that the works of art were not mingled with these fantastic freaks of nature. They have received the name of Scott's Bluffs, from a melancholy circumstance. A number of years since, a party were descending the upper part of the river in canoes,

---

[6] Chimney Rock, a landmark and curiosity for all travellers along the future Oregon Trail. It is located in Nebraska near the western edge of Morrill County.

when their frail barks were overturned and all their powder spoiled. Their rifles being thus rendered useless, they were unable to procure food by hunting and had to depend upon roots and wild fruits for subsistence. After suffering extremely from hunger, they arrived at Laramie's Fork, a small tributary of the north branch of the Nebraska, about sixty miles above the cliffs just mentioned. Here one of the party, by the name of Scott, was taken ill; and his companions came to a halt, until he should recover health and strength sufficient to proceed. While they were searching round in quest of edible roots, they discovered a fresh trail of white men, who had evidently but recently preceded them. What was to be done? By a forced march they might overtake this party, and thus be able to reach the settlements in safety. Should they linger, they might all perish of famine and exhaustion. Scott, however, was incapable of moving; they were too feeble to aid him forward, and dreaded that such a clog would prevent their coming up with the advance party. They determined, therefore, to abandon him to his fate. Accordingly, under pretence of seeking food, and such simples as might be efficacious in his malady, they deserted him and hastened forward upon the trail. They succeeded in overtaking the party of which they were in quest, but concealed their faithless desertion of Scott; alleging that he had died of disease.

On the ensuing summer, these very individuals visiting these parts in company with others, came suddenly upon the bleached bones and grinning skull of a human skeleton, which, by certain signs they recognized for the remains of Scott. This was sixty long miles from the place where they had abandoned him; and it appeared that the wretched man had crawled that immense distance before death put an end to his miseries. The wild and picturesque bluffs in the neighborhood of his lonely grave have ever since borne his name.[7]

[7] Irving was the first to publish the story of Hiram Scott, whose tragic death occurred presumably in 1828. Apparently the story was orally reported to Bonneville by the trappers in his party. Rapidly it became a legend and part of the folklore of the early West. Numerous versions appear in diaries and travel narratives subsequent to *Bonneville*. Little is known about Scott, a trapper employed by Wil-

Amidst this wild and striking scenery, Captain Bonneville, for the first time, beheld flocks of the ahsahta or bighorn, an animal which frequents these cliffs in great numbers. They accord with the nature of such scenery, and add much to its romantic effect; bounding like goats from crag to crag, often trooping along the lofty shelves of the mountains, under the guidance of some venerable patriarch with horns twisted lower than his muzzle, and sometimes peering over the edge of a precipice, so high that they appear scarce bigger than crows; indeed, it seems a pleasure to them to seek the most rugged and frightful situations, doubtless from a feeling of security.

This animal is commonly called the mountain sheep, and is often confounded with another animal, the "woolly sheep," found more to the northward, about the country of the Flatheads. The latter likewise inhabits cliffs in summer, but descends into the valleys in the winter. It has white wool, like a sheep, mingled with a thin growth of long hair; but it has short legs, a deep belly, and a beard like a goat. Its horns are about five inches long, slightly curved backwards, black as jet, and beautifully polished. Its hoofs are of the same color. This animal is by no means so active as the bighorn; it does not bound much, but sits a good deal upon its haunches. It is not so plentiful either; rarely more than two or three are seen at a time. Its wool alone gives a resemblance to the sheep; it is more properly of the goat genus. The flesh is said to have a musty flavor; some have thought the fleece might be valuable, as it is said to be as fine as that of the goat of Cashmere, but it is not to be procured in sufficient quantities.

The ahsahta, argali, or bighorn, on the contrary, has short hair like a deer, and resembles it in shape, but has the head and horns of a sheep, and its flesh is said to be delicious mutton. The Indians consider it more sweet and delicate than any other kind of venison. It abounds in the Rocky Mountains, from the fiftieth degree of north latitude, quite down to California; generally in the highest regions capable of vegetation; sometimes it ventures into the val-

---

liam Ashley, and his deserters have never been identified. For an excellent study of the legend, see Merrill J. Mattes, "Hiram Scott, Fur Trader," *Nebraska History*, Vol. XXVI (September, 1945), 127–62.

The ADVENTURES of CAPTAIN BONNEVILLE

leys, but on the least alarm, regains its favorite cliffs and precipices, where it is perilous, if not impossible for the hunter to follow.[8]

[8] Dimensions of a male of this species, from the nose to the base of the tail, five feet; length of tail, four inches; girth of the body, four feet; height, three feet eight inches; the horn, three feet six inches long; one foot three inches in circumference at base (Irving's note).

4.

An alarm—Crow Indians—Their appearance—
Mode of approach—Their vengeful errand—Their
curiosity—Hostility between the Crows and Blackfeet—
Loving conduct of the Crows—Laramie's Fork—
First navigation of the Nebraska—Great elevation of
the country—Rarity of the atmosphere—Its effect on
the wood-work of wagons—Black Hills—Their wild
and broken scenery—Indian dogs—Crow trophies—
Sterile and dreary country—Banks of the Sweet
Water—Buffalo hunting—Adventure of Tom Cain,
the Irish cook

WHEN ON THE MARCH, Captain Bonneville always sent some of his best hunters in the advance to reconnoitre the country, as well as to look out for game. On the 24th of May,[1] as the caravan was slowly journeying up the banks of the Nebraska, the hunters came galloping back, waving their caps, and giving the alarm cry, Indians! Indians!

The captain immediately ordered a halt: the hunters now came up and announced that a large war-party of Crow Indians were just above, on the river. The captain knew the character of these savages; one of the most roving, warlike, crafty, and predatory tribes of the mountains; horse-stealers of the first order, and easily provoked to acts of sanguinary violence. Orders were accordingly given to prepare for action, and every one promptly took the post that had been

[1] An error for June 24. The same error also appears in the first edition. Bonneville had reached the Platte (the Nebraska) on June 2 and the North Platte on June 13 or 14. His statement later in this chapter that his position was 41° 7' would confirm the date of June 24, and also indicate that he was still in the vicinity of Chimney Rock on the south side of the North Platte.

assigned him in the general order of the march, in all cases of warlike emergency.

Everything being put in battle array, the captain took the lead of his little band, and moved on slowly and warily. In a little while he beheld the Crow warriors emerging from among the bluffs. There were about sixty of them; fine martial-looking fellows, painted and arrayed for war, and mounted on horses decked out with all kinds of wild trappings. They came prancing along in gallant style, with many wild and dexterous evolutions, for none can surpass them in horsemanship; and their bright colors, and flaunting and fantastic embellishments, glaring and sparkling in the morning sunshine, gave them really a striking appearance.

Their mode of approach, to one not acquainted with the tactics and ceremonies of this rude chivalry of the wilderness, had an air of direct hostility. They came galloping forward in a body, as if about to make a furious charge, but, when close at hand, opened to the right and left, and wheeled in wide circles round the travellers, whooping and yelling like maniacs.

This done, their mock fury sank into a calm, and the chief, approaching the captain, who had remained warily drawn up, though informed of the pacific nature of the maneuver, extended to him the hand of friendship. The pipe of peace was smoked, and now all was good fellowship.

The Crows were in pursuit of a band of Cheyennes, who had attacked their village in the night and killed one of their people. They had already been five and twenty days on the track of the marauders, and were determined not to return home until they had sated their revenge.

A few days previously, some of their scouts, who were ranging the country at a distance from the main body, had discovered the party of Captain Bonneville. They had dogged it for a time in secret, astonished at the long train of wagons and oxen, and especially struck with the sight of a cow and calf, quietly following the caravan; supposing them to be some kind of tame buffalo. Having satisfied their curiosity, they carried back to their chief intelligence of all that they had seen. He had, in consequence, diverged from his pursuit of vengeance to behold the wonders described to him. "Now that we have met you," said he to Captain Bonneville, "and have seen these marvels with our own eyes, our hearts are glad." In fact, nothing could exceed the curiosity evinced by these people as to the objects before them. Wagons had never been seen by them before, and they examined them with the greatest minuteness; but the calf was the peculiar object of their admiration. They watched it with intense interest as it licked the hands accustomed to feed it, and were struck with the mild expression of its countenance, and its perfect docility.

After much sage consultation, they at length determined that it must be the "great medicine" of the white party; an appellation given by the Indians to anything of supernatural and mysterious power that is guarded as a talisman. They were completely thrown out in their conjecture, however, by an offer of the white men to exchange the calf for a horse; their estimation of the great medicine sank in an instant, and they declined the bargain.

At the request of the Crow chieftain the two parties encamped together, and passed the residue of the day in company. The captain was well pleased with every opportunity to gain a knowledge of the "unsophisticated sons of nature," who had so long been objects of his poetic speculations; and indeed this wild, horse-stealing tribe is one of the most notorious of the mountains. The chief, of course, had his scalps to show and his battles to recount. The Blackfoot is the hereditary enemy of the Crow, toward whom hostility is like a cherished principle of religion; for every tribe, besides its casual antagonists, has some enduring foe with whom there can be no permanent reconciliation. The Crows and Blackfeet, upon the whole, are enemies worthy of each other, being rogues and ruffians of the first water. As their predatory excursions extend over the same regions, they often come in contact with each other, and these casual conflicts serve to keep their wits awake and their passions alive.

The present party of Crows, however, evinced nothing of the invidious character for which they are renowned. During the day and night that they were encamped in company with the travellers,

The ADVENTURES of CAPTAIN BONNEVILLE

their conduct was friendly in the extreme. They were, in fact, quite irksome in their attentions, and had a caressing manner at times quite importunate. It was not until after separation on the following morning that the captain and his men ascertained the secret of all this loving-kindness. In the course of their fraternal caresses, the Crows had contrived to empty the pockets of their white brothers; to abstract the very buttons from their coats, and, above all, to make free with their hunting knives.

By equal altitudes of the sun, taken at this last encampment, Captain Bonneville ascertained his latitude to be 41° 47′ north. The thermometer, at six o'clock in the morning, stood at fifty-nine degrees; at two o'clock, P. M., at ninety-two degrees; and at six o'clock in the evening, at seventy degrees.

The Black Hills,[2] or Mountains, now began to be seen at a distance, printing the horizon with their rugged and broken outlines; and threatening to oppose a difficult barrier in the way of the travellers.

On the 26th of May,[3] the travellers encamped at Laramie's Fork,[4] a clear and beautiful stream, rising in the west-southwest, maintaining an average width of twenty yards, and winding through broad meadows abounding in currants and gooseberries, and adorned with groves and clumps of trees.

By an observation of Jupiter's satellites, with a Dolland reflecting telescope, Captain Bonneville ascertained the longitude to be 102° 57′ west of Greenwich.

We will here step ahead of our narrative to observe that about

[2] Not the present Black Hills of South Dakota but the first range of the Rocky Mountains of Wyoming, now known as the Laramie Mountains. It was customary at this time to refer to the foothills of the Rockies as the Black Hills.

[3] An error for June 26.

[4] The Laramie River flows into the North Platte in eastern Wyoming. Near the junction of the two rivers, William Sublette and Robert Campbell in 1834 (not 1835, as Irving states in the next paragraph) built a trading post named Fort William (although more commonly referred to as Fort Laramie). It dominated the area for many miles around. Later it was bought by the United States Government as a military post and was of great importance to travelers on the Oregon Trail. It is today in process of reconstruction. See LeRoy R. Hafen and Francis M. Young, *Fort Laramie and the Pageant of the West, 1834–1890.*

three years after the time of which we are treating, Mr. Robert Campbell, formerly of the Rocky Mountain Fur Company, descended the Platte from this fork, in skin canoes, thus proving, what had always been discredited, that the river was navigable. About the same time, he built a fort or trading post at Laramie's Fork, which he named Fort William, after his friend and partner, Mr. William Sublette. Since that time, the Platte has become a highway for the fur traders.

For some days past, Captain Bonneville had been made sensible of the great elevation of country into which he was gradually ascending by the effect of the dryness and rarefaction of the atmosphere upon his wagons. The wood-work shrunk; the paint boxes of the wheels were continually working out, and it was necessary to support the spokes by stout props to prevent their falling asunder. The travellers were now entering one of those great steppes of the Far West, where the prevalent aridity of the atmosphere renders the country unfit for cultivation. In these regions there is a fresh sweet growth of grass in the spring, but it is scanty and short, and parches up in the course of the summer, so that there is none for the hunters to set fire to in the autumn. It is a common observation that "above the forks of the Platte the grass does not burn." All attempts at agriculture and gardening in the neighborhood of Fort William have been attended with very little success. The grain and vegetables raised there have been scanty in quantity and poor in quality. The great elevation of these plains, and the dryness of the atmosphere, will tend to retain these immense regions in a state of pristine wildness.

In the course of a day or two more, the travellers entered that wild and broken tract of the Crow country called the Black Hills, and here their journey became toilsome in the extreme. Rugged steeps and deep ravines incessantly obstructed their progress, so that a great part of the day was spent in the painful toil of digging through banks, filling up ravines, forcing the wagons up the most forbidding ascents, or swinging them with ropes down the face of dangerous precipices. The shoes of their horses were worn out, and their feet injured by the rugged and stony roads. The travellers were annoyed also by frequent but brief storms, which would come hurrying over the hills, or through the mountain defiles, rage with great fury for a short time, and then pass off, leaving everything calm and serene again.

For several nights the camp had been infested by vagabond Indian dogs, prowling about in quest of food. They were about the size of a large pointer; with ears short and erect, and a long bushy tail—altogether, they bore a striking resemblance to a wolf. These skulking visitors would keep about the purlieus of the camp until daylight; when, on the first stir of life among the sleepers, they would scamper off until they reached some rising ground, where they would take their seats, and keep a sharp and hungry watch upon every movement. The moment the travellers were fairly on the march, and the camp was abandoned, these starving hangers-on would hasten to the deserted fires, to seize upon the half-picked bones, the offal and garbage that lay about; and, having made a hasty meal, with many a snap and snarl and growl, would follow leisurely on the trail of the caravan. Many attempts were made to coax or catch them, but in vain. Their quick and suspicious eyes caught the slightest sinister movement, and they turned and scampered off. At length one was taken. He was terribly alarmed, and crouched and trembled as if expecting instant death. Soothed, however, by caresses, he began after a time to gather confidence and wag his tail, and at length was brought to follow close at the heels of his captors, still, however, darting around furtive and suspicious glances, and evincing a disposition to scamper off upon the least alarm.

On the first of July the band of Crow warriors again crossed their path. They came in vaunting and vainglorious style; displaying five Cheyenne scalps, the trophies of their vengeance. They were now bound homewards, to appease the manes of their comrade by these proofs that his death had been revenged, and intended to have scalp-dances and other triumphant rejoicings. Captain Bonneville and his men, however, were by no means disposed to renew their confiding intimacy with these crafty savages, and above all, took care to avoid their pilfering caresses. They remarked one precaution of the Crows with respect to their horses; to protect their hoofs from the sharp and jagged rocks among which they had to pass, they had covered them with shoes of buffalo hide.

The route of the travellers lay generally along the course of the Nebraska or Platte, but occasionally, where steep promontories advanced to the margin of the stream, they were obliged to make inland circuits. One of these took them through a bold and stern country, bordered by a range of low mountains, running east and west.[5] Everything around bore traces of some fearful convulsion of nature in times long past. Hitherto the various strata of rock had exhibited a gentle elevation toward the southwest, but here everything appeared to have been subverted, and thrown out of place. In many places there were heavy beds of white sandstone resting upon red. Immense strata of rocks jutted up into crags and cliffs; and sometimes formed perpendicular walls and overhanging precipices. An air of sterility prevailed over these savage wastes. The valleys were destitute of herbage, and scantily clothed with a stunted species of wormwood, generally known among traders and trappers by the name of sage. From an elevated point of their march through this region, the travellers caught a beautiful view of the Powder River Mountains[6] away to the north, stretching along the very verge of the horizon, and seeming, from the snow with which they were mantled, to be a chain of small white clouds, connecting sky and earth.

Though the thermometer at mid-day ranged from eighty to ninety, and even sometimes rose to ninety-three degrees, yet occasional spots of snow were to be seen on the tops of the low mountains, among which the travellers were journeying; proofs of the great elevation of the whole region.

The Nebraska, in its passage through the Black Hills, is confined to a much narrower channel than that through which it flows in the plains below; but it is deeper and clearer, and rushes with a

[5] The description of the terrain suggests that Bonneville was now in the vicinity of modern Casper, Wyoming, passing the northern extremity of the Laramie Mountains.

[6] The Big Horn Mountains, the eastern slopes of which are drained by the Powder River and its tributaries.

stronger current. The scenery, also, is more varied and beautiful. Sometimes it glides rapidly but smoothly through a picturesque valley, between wooded banks; then, forcing its way into the bosom of rugged mountains, it rushes impetuously through narrow defiles, roaring and foaming down rocks and rapids, until it is again soothed to rest in some peaceful valley.

On the 12th of July, Captain Bonneville abandoned the main stream of the Nebraska,[7] which was continually shouldered by rugged promontories, and making a bend to the southwest, for a couple of days, part of the time over plains of loose sand, encamped on the 14th on the banks of the Sweet Water, a stream about twenty yards in breadth, and four or five feet deep, flowing between low banks over a sandy soil, and forming one of the forks or upper branches of the Nebraska. Up this stream they now shaped their course for several successive days, tending, generally, to the west.[8] The soil was light and sandy; the country much diversified. Frequently the plains were studded with isolated blocks of rock, sometimes in the shape of a half globe, and from three to four hundred feet high. These singular masses had occasionally a very imposing, and even sublime appearance, rising from the midst of a savage and lonely landscape.

As the travellers continued to advance, they became more and more sensible of the elevation of the country. The hills around were more generally capped with snow. The men complained of cramps and colics, sore lips and mouths, and violent headaches. The wood-work of the wagons also shrank so much that it was with difficulty the wheels were kept from falling to pieces. The country bordering upon the river was frequently gashed with deep ravines,

[7] He probably left the North Platte near modern Alcova, Wyoming. By traveling slightly south of west, he would strike an elbow of the Sweetwater River, which he came to within two days. The certainty with which Bonneville was moving through country unknown to him shows that he was guided by veteran trappers thoroughly familiar with it. He was still following the route which later became the Oregon Trail.

[8] The Sweetwater River, which originates at the south tip of the Wind River Mountains, provided a natural and easily traversed route to South Pass and the Green River valley beyond.

or traversed by high bluffs, to avoid which, the travellers were obliged to make wide circuits through the plains. In the course of these, they came upon immense herds of buffalo, which kept scouring off in the van, like a retreating army.

Among the motley retainers of the camp was Tom Cain, a raw Irishman, who officiated as cook, whose various blunders and expedients in his novel situation, and in the wild scenes and wild kind of life into which he had suddenly been thrown, had made him a kind of butt or droll of the camp. Tom, however, began to discover an ambition superior to his station; and the conversation of the hunters, and their stories of their exploits, inspired him with a desire to elevate himself to the dignity of their order. The buffalo in such immense droves presented a tempting opportunity for making his first essay. He rode, in the line of march, all prepared for action: his powder-flask and shot-pouch knowingly slung at the pommel of his saddle, to be at hand; his rifle balanced on his shoulder. While in this plight, a troop of buffalo came trotting by in great alarm. In an instant, Tom sprang from his horse and gave chase on foot. Finding they were leaving him behind, he levelled his rifle and pulled [the] trigger. His shot produced no other effect than to increase the speed of the buffalo, and to frighten his own horse, who took to his heels, and scampered off with all the ammunition. Tom scampered after him, hallooing with might and main, and the wild horse and wild Irishman soon disappeared among the ravines of the prairie. Captain Bonneville, who was at the head of the line, and had seen the transaction at a distance, detached a party in pursuit of Tom. After a long interval they returned, leading the frightened horse; but though they had scoured the country, and looked out and shouted from every height, they had seen nothing of his rider.

As Captain Bonneville knew Tom's utter awkwardness and inexperience, and the dangers of a bewildered Irishman in the midst of a prairie, he halted and encamped at an early hour, that there might be a regular hunt for him in the morning.

At early dawn on the following day scouts were sent off in every direction, while the main body, after breakfast, proceeded slowly on its course. It was not until the middle of the afternoon that the hunters returned, with honest Tom mounted behind one of them. They had found him in a complete state of perplexity and amazement. His appearance caused shouts of merriment in the camp,—but Tom for once could not join in the mirth raised at his expense: he was completely chapfallen, and apparently cured of the hunting mania for the rest of his life.

5.

Magnificent scenery—Wind River Mountains—
Treasury of waters—A stray horse—An Indian trail—
Trout streams—The Great Green River Valley—
An alarm—A band of trappers—Fontenelle, his
information—Sufferings of thirst—Encampment on
the Seeds-ke-dee—Strategy of rival traders—
Fortification of the camp—The Blackfeet—Banditti
of the mountains—Their character and habits

IT WAS ON THE 20TH of July that Captain Bonneville first came in sight of the grand region of his hopes and anticipations, the Rocky Mountains. He had been making a bend to the south, to avoid some obstacles along the river, and had attained a high, rocky ridge, when a magnificent prospect burst upon his sight. To the west rose the Wind River Mountains, with their bleached and snowy summits towering into the clouds. These stretched far to the north-northwest, until they melted away into what appeared to be faint clouds, but which the experienced eyes of the veteran hunters of the party recognized for the rugged mountains of the Yellowstone; at the feet of which extended the wild Crow country: a perilous, though profitable region for the trapper.

To the southwest, the eye ranged over an immense extent of wilderness, with what appeared to be a snowy vapor resting upon its horizon. This, however, was pointed out as another branch of the Great Chippewyan, or Rocky chain; being the Eutaw Mountains,[1] at whose basis the wandering tribe of hunters of the same name pitch their tents.

[1] The "high rocky ridge" that Irving refers to in the preceding paragraph is the Antelope Hills. Only by climbing these could he have seen the Eutaw Mountains,

We can imagine the enthusiasm of the worthy captain when he beheld the vast and mountainous scene of his adventurous enterprise thus suddenly unveiled before him. We can imagine with what feelings of awe and admiration he must have contemplated the Wind River Sierra, or bed of mountains; that great fountain-head from whose springs, and lakes, and melted snows some of those mighty rivers take their rise, which wander over hundreds of miles of varied country and clime, and find their way to the opposite waves of the Atlantic and the Pacific.

The Wind River Mountains are, in fact, among the most remarkable of the whole Rocky chain; and would appear to be among the loftiest. They form, as it were, a great bed of mountains, about eighty miles in length, and from twenty to thirty in breadth; with rugged peaks, covered with eternal snows, and deep, narrow valleys, full of springs, and brooks, and rock-bound lakes. From this great treasury of waters issue forth limpid streams, which, augmenting as they descend, become main tributaries of the Missouri on the one side, and the Columbia on the other; and give rise to the Seeds-ke-dee Agie,[2] or Green River, the great Colorado of the West, that empties its current into the Gulf of California.

The Wind River Mountains are notorious in hunters' and trappers' stories: their rugged defiles, and the rough tracts about their neighborhood, having been lurking places for the predatory hordes of the mountains, and scenes of rough encounter with Crows and Blackfeet. It was to the west of these mountains, in the valley of the Seeds-ke-dee Agie, or Green River, that Captain Bonneville intended to make a halt for the purpose of giving repose to his people and his horses after their weary journeying; and of collecting information as to his future course. This Green River valley, and its immediate neighborhood, as we have already observed,

---

today known as the Uinta Mountains, lying about two hundred miles to the south. The streams there were in rich trapping country.

[2] Seeds-ke-dee Agie in the Crow language means Prairie Chicken River. Many miles of this river still flow through desert country covered with sagebrush, where prairie chickens are numerous even today. The tributaries of the Green were rich with beaver in the 1820's.

formed the main point of rendezvous, for the present year, of the rival fur companies, and the motley populace, civilized and savage, connected with them. Several days of rugged travel, however, yet remained for the captain and his men before they should encamp in this desired resting-place.

On the 21st of July, as they were pursuing their course through one of the meadows of the Sweet Water, they beheld a horse grazing at a little distance. He showed no alarm at their approach, but suffered himself quietly to be taken, evincing a perfect state of tameness. The scouts of the party were instantly on the look-out for the owners of this animal; lest some dangerous band of savages might be lurking in the vicinity. After a narrow search, they discovered the trail of an Indian party, which had evidently passed through that neighborhood but recently. The horse was accordingly taken possession of, as an estray; but a more vigilant watch than usual was kept round the camp at nights, lest his former owners should be upon the prowl.

The travellers had now attained so high an elevation that on the 23d of July, at daybreak, there was considerable ice in the water-buckets, and the thermometer stood at twenty-two degrees. The rarety of the atmosphere continued to affect the wood-work of the wagons, and the wheels were incessantly falling to pieces. A remedy was at length devised. The tire of each wheel was taken off; a band of wood was nailed round the exterior of the felloes, the tire was then made red hot, replaced round the wheel, and suddenly cooled with water. By this means, the whole was bound together with great compactness.

The extreme elevation of these great steppes, which range along the feet of the Rocky Mountains, takes away from the seeming height of their peaks, which yield to few in the known world in point of altitude above the level of the sea.

On the 24th, the travellers took final leave of the Sweet Water,[3] and keeping westwardly, over a low and very rocky ridge, one of the most southern spurs of the Wind River Mountains, they encamped, after a march of seven hours and a half, on the banks of a

[3] Leaving the Sweetwater they would cross South Pass, elevation 7,550 feet.

The Adventures of Captain Bonneville

small clear stream,[4] running to the south, in which they caught a number of fine trout.

The sight of these fish was hailed with pleasure, as a sign that they had reached the waters which flow into the Pacific; for it is only on the western streams of the Rocky Mountains that trout are to be taken. The stream on which they had thus encamped proved, in effect, to be tributary to the Seeds-ke-dee Agie, or Green River, into which it flowed at some distance to the south.

Captain Bonneville now considered himself as having fairly passed the crest of the Rocky Mountains; and felt some degree of exultation in being the first individual that had crossed, north of the settled provinces of Mexico, from the waters of the Atlantic to those of the Pacific, with wagons. Mr. William Sublette, the enterprising leader of the Rocky Mountain Fur Company, had, two or three years previously, reached the valley of the Wind River, which lies on the northeast of the mountains; but had proceeded with them no further.[5]

A vast valley now spread itself before the travellers, bounded on one side by the Wind River Mountains, and to the west, by a long range of high hills.[6] This, Captain Bonneville was assured by a veteran hunter in his company, was the great valley of the Seeds-ke-dee; and the same informant would have fain persuaded him that a small stream, three feet deep, which he came to on the 25th, was that river. The captain was convinced, however, that the stream was too insignificant to drain so wide a valley and the adjacent mountains: he encamped, therefore, at an early hour, on its borders, that he might take the whole of the next day to reach the main river; which he presumed to flow between him and the distant range of western hills.

On the 26th of July, he commenced his march at an early hour,

---

[4] Probably Little Sandy Creek, a tributary of Sandy Creek, which flows into Green River.

[5] In 1830, Sublette had taken ten wagons and two dearborns to the rendezvous held that year on the Popo Agie near its junction with Wind River; therefore, there was no reason for him to cross the Continental Divide.

[6] The Salt Range and Commissary Ridge lying along the western border of Wyoming.

making directly across the valley, toward the hills in the west; proceeding at as brisk a rate as the jaded condition of his horses would permit. About eleven o'clock in the morning, a great cloud of dust was descried in the rear, advancing directly on the trail of the party. The alarm was given; they all came to a halt, and held a council of war. Some conjectured that the band of Indians, whose trail they had discovered in the neighborhood of the stray horse, had been lying in wait for them in some secret fastness of the mountains; and were about to attack them on the open plain, where they would have no shelter. Preparations were immediately made for defence; and a scouting party sent off to reconnoitre. They soon came galloping back, making signals that all was well. The cloud of dust was made by a band of fifty or sixty mounted trappers, belonging to the American Fur Company, who soon came up, leading their pack-horses. They were headed by Mr. Fontenelle,[7] an experienced leader, or "partisan," as a chief of a party is called in the technical language of the trappers.

Mr. Fontenelle informed Captain Bonneville that he was on his way from the company's trading post[8] on the Yellowstone to the yearly rendezvous, with reinforcements and supplies for their hunting and trading parties beyond the mountains; and that he expected to meet, by appointment, with a band of free trappers in that very neighborhood. He had fallen upon the trail of Captain Bonneville's party, just after leaving the Nebraska; and, finding that they had frightened off all the game, had been obliged to push on, by forced marches, to avoid famine: both men and horses were, therefore, much travel-worn; but this was no place to halt; the plain before them he said was destitute of grass and water, neither of which would be met with short of the Green River, which was

[7] Lucien Fontenelle, born around 1807 in New Orleans, was orphaned at an early age, went to St. Louis and entered the fur trade, and eventually became associated with Andrew Dripps in the American Fur Company. Fontenelle Creek, a small tributary of Green River below La Barge, Wyoming, is named for him. A reference in W. A. Ferris, *Life in the Rocky Mountains* (ed. by Paul C. Phillips), 158, indicates that Etienne Provot was with him.

[8] Fort Union, built in 1829 on the Missouri River near the mouth of the Yellowstone.

yet at a considerable distance. He hoped, he added, as his party were all on horseback, to reach the river, with hard travelling, by nightfall: but he doubted the possibility of Captain Bonneville's arrival there with his wagons before the day following. Having imparted this information, he pushed forward with all speed.

Captain Bonneville followed on as fast as circumstances would permit. The ground was firm and gravelly; but the horses were too much fatigued to move rapidly. After a long and harassing day's march, without pausing for a noontide meal, they were compelled, at nine o'clock at night, to encamp in an open plain, destitute of water or pasturage. On the following morning, the horses were turned loose at the peep of day; to slake their thirst, if possible, from the dew collected on the sparse grass, here and there springing up among dry sand-banks. The soil of a great part of this Green River valley is a whitish clay, into which the rain cannot penetrate, but which dries and cracks with the sun. In some places it produces a salt weed, and grass along the margins of the streams; but the wider expanses of it are desolate and barren. It was not until noon that Captain Bonneville reached the banks of the Seeds-ke-dee, or Colorado of the West; in the meantime, the sufferings of both men and horses had been excessive, and it was with almost frantic eagerness that they hurried to allay their burning thirst in the limpid current of the river.

Fontenelle and his party had not fared much better; the chief part had managed to reach the river by nightfall, but were nearly knocked up by the exertion; the horses of others sank under them, and they were obliged to pass the night upon the road.

On the following morning, July 27th,[9] Fontenelle moved his camp across the river; while Captain Bonneville proceeded some little distance below, where there was a small but fresh meadow, yielding abundant pasturage. Here the poor jaded horses were turned out to graze, and take their rest: the weary journey up the mountains had worn them down in flesh and spirit; but this last march across the thirsty plain had nearly finished them.

[9] If the previous date, "July 26th," is correct, the date "July 27th" should read "July 28th," because a day had intervened since Bonneville had met Fontenelle.

The ADVENTURES of CAPTAIN BONNEVILLE

The captain had here the first taste of the boasted strategy of the fur trade. During his brief, but social encampment, in company with Fontenelle, that experienced trapper had managed to win over a number of Delaware Indians whom the captain had brought with him, by offering them four hundred dollars each for the ensuing autumnal hunt. The captain was somewhat astonished when he saw these hunters, on whose services he had calculated securely, suddenly pack up their traps, and go over to the rival camp. That he might in some measure, however, be even with his competitor, he dispatched two scouts to look out for the band of free trappers who were to meet Fontenelle in this neighborhood, and to endeavor to bring them to his camp.

As it would be necessary to remain some time in this neighborhood, that both men and horses might repose, and recruit their strength; and as it was a region full of danger, Captain Bonneville proceeded to fortify his camp with breastworks of logs and pickets.[10]

---

[10] This was the construction of Fort Bonneville during August, 1832. A large granite boulder on a weathered cement base today marks the location of this post. This marker is on the north side of a gravel road three miles west of the junction of U. S. Highways 189 and 187 near Daniel, Wyoming. The site was determined by the late Perry W. Jenkins on the basis of evidence summarized in a letter written July 27, 1954, to the editor when Mr. Jenkins was eighty-seven. This evidence is too complex to be recorded here, but one sentence warrants quotation:

"I found the outline of the foundation which I cut with trenches and found the rotted ends of the stockade. The rotton [sic] wood was that of cottonwood logs." In Chapter VIII, Irving states that Bonneville dug several *caches*, or pits, for the concealment of goods and dismantled wagons. Mr. Jenkins recalled that excavation for an irrigation ditch nearby unearthed one of these *caches* and bits of scrap metal. Another *cache* was dug within the stockade, and is marked today by a depression in the surface. The stockade was several hundred yards south of the Green River, which here flows southeasterly at the base of a high gravel terrace covered with sagebrush. Horse Creek flows about two miles south across a level plain at the base of another terrace. It joins the Green River between four and five miles below the site of Fort Bonneville. In this vicinity were held most of the annual rendezvous after 1832.

The best contemporary description of Fort Bonneville is that by Ferris in *Life in the Rocky Mountains*, 206–207. He described it as being a square stockade built of upright logs a foot in diameter and fifteen feet high. Two block houses stood at diagonally opposite corners. These were constructed of unhewn timbers. Bonneville's competitors called it "Fort Nonsense" and "Bonneville's Folly" because the fort was considered to be poorly located, but DeVoto in *Across the Wide*

The ADVENTURES *of* CAPTAIN BONNEVILLE

These precautions were, at that time, peculiarly necessary, from the bands of Blackfeet Indians which were roving about the neighborhood. These savages are the most dangerous banditti of the mountains, and the inveterate foe of the trappers. They are Ishmaelites of the first order, always with weapon in hand, ready for action. The young braves of the tribe, who are destitute of property, go to war for booty; to gain horses, and acquire the means of setting up a lodge, supporting a family, and entitling themselves to a seat in the public councils. The veteran warriors fight merely for the love of the thing, and the consequence which success gives them among their people.

They are capital horsemen, and are generally well mounted on short, stout horses, similar to the prairie ponies to be met with at St. Louis. When on a war party, however, they go on foot, to enable them to skulk through the country with greater secrecy; to keep in thickets and ravines, and use more adroit subterfuges and stratagems. Their mode of warfare is entirely by ambush, surprise, and sudden assaults in the night time. If they succeed in causing a panic, they dash forward with headlong fury: if the enemy is on the alert, and shows no signs of fear, they become wary and deliberate in their movements.

Some of them are armed in the primitive style, with bows and arrows; the greater part have American fusees, made after the fashion of those of the Hudson's Bay Company. These they procure at the trading post of the American Fur Company, on Marias River,[11] where they traffic their peltries for arms, ammunition, clothing, and trinkets. They are extremely fond of spirituous liquors and tobacco; for which nuisances they are ready to exchange not merely their guns and horses, but even their wives and daughters. As they are a treacherous race, and have cherished a lurking hostility to the whites ever since one of their tribe was killed by Mr.

Missouri, 58–60, reassessed the value of its location. It should also be added that the numerous rendezvous held in this area in subsequent years argue that Bonneville chose wisely even though he occupied the fort only briefly.

[11] Fort Piegan, built by James Kipp in 1831. When this burned, Fort McKenzie was built in 1832.

Lewis,[12] the associate of General Clarke, in his exploring expedition across the Rocky Mountains, the American Fur Company is obliged constantly to keep at that post a garrison of sixty or seventy men.

Under the general name of Blackfeet are comprehended several tribes: such as the Surcies, the Peagans, the Blood Indians, and the Gros Ventres of the Prairies: who roam about the southern branches of the Yellowstone and Missouri Rivers, together with some other tribes further north.

The bands infesting the Wind River Mountains and the country adjacent at the time of which we are treating, were Gros Ventres *of the Prairies*, which are not to be confounded with Gros Ventres *of the Missouri*, who keep about the *lower* part of that river, and are friendly to the white men.

This hostile band keeps about the headwaters of the Missouri, and numbers about nine hundred fighting men. Once in the course of two or three years they abandon their usual abodes, and make a visit to the Arapahoes of the Arkansas. Their route lies either through the Crow country, and the Black Hills, or through the lands of the Nez Percés, Flatheads, Bannacks, and Shoshonies. As they enjoy their favorite state of hostility with all these tribes, their expeditions are prone to be conducted in the most lawless and predatory style; nor do they hesitate to extend their maraudings to any party of white men they meet with; following their trails; hovering about their camps; waylaying and dogging the caravans of the free traders, and murdering the solitary trapper. The consequences are frequent and desperate fights between them and the "mountaineers," in the wild defiles and fastnesses of the Rocky Mountains.

The band in question was, at this time, on their way homeward from one of their customary visits to the Arapahoes; and in the ensuing chapter we shall treat of some bloody encounters between them and the trappers, which had taken place just before the arrival of Captain Bonneville among the mountains.

[12] This incident occurred in 1806 on the Marias River during the return journey of the Lewis and Clark Expedition. See *Original Journals of the Lewis and Clark Expedition* (ed. by Reuben Gold Thwaites), V, 223–25.

6.

Sublette and his band—Robert Campbell—Mr. Wyeth and a band of "down-easters"—Yankee enterprise—Fitzpatrick—His adventure with the Blackfeet—A rendezvous of mountaineers—The battle of Pierre's Hole—An Indian ambuscade—Sublette's return

LEAVING CAPTAIN BONNEVILLE and his band ensconced within their fortified camp in the Green River valley, we shall step back and accompany a party of the Rocky Mountain Fur Company in its progress, with supplies from St. Louis, to the annual rendezvous at Pierre's Hole. This party consisted of sixty men, well mounted, and conducting a line of packhorses. They were commanded by Captain William Sublette, a partner in the company, and one of the most active, intrepid, and renowned leaders in this half military kind of service. He was accompanied by his associate in business, and tried companion in danger, Mr. Robert Campbell, one of the pioneers of the trade beyond the mountains, who had commanded trapping parties there in times of the greatest peril.[1]

As these worthy compeers were on their route to the frontier, they fell in with another expedition, likewise on its way to the mountains. This was a party of regular "down-easters," that is to say, people of New England, who, with the all-penetrating and all-pervading spirit of their race, were now pushing their way into a new field of enterprise with which they were totally unacquainted. The party had been fitted out and was maintained and commanded by Mr. Nathaniel J. Wyeth, of Boston.[2] This gentleman had con-

---

[1] For William Sublette's 1832 expedition, see Sunder, *Bill Sublette*, 101–13.

ceived an idea that a profitable fishery for salmon might be established on the Columbia River, and connected with the fur trade. He had, accordingly, invested capital in goods, calculated, as he supposed, for the Indian trade, and had enlisted a number of eastern men in his employ, who had never been in the Far West, nor knew anything of the wilderness. With these, he was bravely steering his way across the continent, undismayed by danger, difficulty, or distance, in the same way that a New England coaster and his neighbors will coolly launch forth on a voyage to the Black Sea, or a whaling cruise to the Pacific.

With all their national aptitude at expedient and resource, Wyeth and his men felt themselves completely at a loss when they reached the frontier, and found that the wilderness required experience and habitudes of which they were totally deficient. Not one of the party, excepting the leader, had ever seen an Indian or handled a rifle; they were without guide or interpreter, and totally unacquainted with "wood craft" and the modes of making their way among savage hordes, and subsisting themselves during long marches over wild mountains and barren plains.

In this predicament, Captain Sublette found them, in a manner becalmed, or rather run aground, at the little frontier town of Independence, in Missouri, and kindly took them in tow.[3] The two

---

[2] In the former editions of this work we have erroneously given this enterprising individual the title of captain (Irving's note).

Wyeth was born in 1802 and died in 1856. His experiences as a fur trader are recounted in *The Correspondence and Journals of Captain Nathaniel J. Wyeth* (ed. by F. G. Young). Wyeth lent the two journals published in this work to Irving in manuscript form while Irving was writing *Bonneville*, and he drew upon them frequently during the writing of this book. These borrowings are noted below. For Wyeth's first expedition, see also *Oregon; or a Short History of a Long Journey* by John B. Wyeth, a young relative, who went as far as Pierre's Hole in 1832; and *Narrative of a Journey across the Rocky Mountains to the Columbia River* by John K. Townsend, who traveled with Nathaniel Wyeth in 1834. Both books are reprinted in *Early Western Travels* (ed. by R. G. Thwaites), XXI. For the men who were with N. J. Wyeth in 1832, see Philip Henry Overmyer, "Members of the First Wyeth Expedition," *Oregon Historical Quarterly*, Vol. XXXVI (March, 1935), 95–101.

[3] Unfortunately, Wyeth's letters and his first journal are both incomplete and say nothing about this meeting nor of the arrangement whereby he and his in-

parties travelled amicably together; the frontier men of Sublette's party gave their Yankee comrades some lessons in hunting, and some insight into the art and mystery of dealing with the Indians, and they all arrived without accident at the upper branches of the Nebraska or Platte River.

In the course of their march, Mr. Fitzpatrick,[4] the partner of the company who was resident at that time beyond the mountains, came down from the rendezvous at Pierre's Hole to meet them and hurry them forward. He travelled in company with them until they reached the Sweet Water; then taking a couple of horses, one for the saddle, and the other as a pack-horse, he started off express for Pierre's Hole, to make arrangements against their arrival, that he might commence his hunting campaign before the rival company.

Fitzpatrick was a hardy and experienced mountaineer, and knew all the passes and defiles. As he was pursuing his lonely course up the Green River valley, he described several horsemen at a distance, and came to a halt to reconnoitre. He supposed them to be some

---

experienced men were to travel with Sublette. Irving may have drawn upon John Wyeth's *Oregon;* see *Early Western Travels,* XXI, 43–48.

[4] Thomas Fitzpatrick (c. 1799–1854); see Hafen and Ghent, *Broken Hand.* Like Sublette, Fitzpatrick was a former Ashley man, and was now one of the owners, with Milton Sublette, Bridger, Fraeb, and Gervais, of the Rocky Mountain Fur Company, for whom William Sublette and Robert Campbell had agreed to carry supplies to the 1832 rendezvous at Pierre's Hole. Contrary to what Irving says about Fitzpatrick's coming from the mountains to meet Sublette, he had been traveling with him from the beginning. At the Laramie River he started ahead in order to carry news of Sublette's approach with supplies. Both Wyeth's *Correspendence and Journals,* 156, as well as Leonard's *Adventures* confirm this fact. See also Sunder, *Bill Sublette,* 102. Leonard was one of nineteen trappers (Wyeth, *Correspondence and Journals,* 156) whom Sublette met at the Laramie River. They had been originally employed by Gantt and Blackwell but were now separated from them. Leonard is well known today as the author of *Adventures of Zenas Leonard,* most recently edited by John C. Ewers, to which edition all subsequent references will be made. Leonard reports 115 men in the Sublette-Fitzpatrick outfit, which he and his 18 friends now joined (Leonard, *Adventures,* 28–29). Wyeth's *Correspondence and Journals* shows that they met Leonard's group on June 13 and that the combined party left the Laramie River on the fourteenth, thus correcting Leonard's date of July 1 for their departure. Fitzgerald started ahead, consequently on either June 13 or 14.

detachment from the rendezvous, or a party of friendly Indians. They perceived him, and setting up the war-whoop, dashed forward at full speed: he saw at once his mistake and his peril—they were Blackfeet. Springing upon his fleetest horse, and abandoning the other to the enemy, he made for the mountains, and succeeded in escaping up one of the most dangerous defiles. Here he concealed himself until he thought the Indians had gone off, when he returned into the valley. He was again pursued, lost his remaining horse, and only escaped by scrambling up among the cliffs. For several days he remained lurking among rocks and precipices, and almost famished, having but one remaining charge in his rifle, which he kept for self-defence.

In the meantime, Sublette and Campbell, with their fellow-traveller, Wyeth, had pursued their march unmolested, and arrived in the Green River valley, totally unconscious that there was any lurking enemy at hand. They had encamped one night on the banks of a small stream, which came down from the Wind River Mountains, when about midnight, a band of Indians burst upon their camp, with horrible yells and whoops, and a discharge of guns and arrows. Happily no other harm was done than wounding one mule, and causing several horses to break loose from their pickets. The camp was instantly in arms; but the Indians retreated with yells of exultation, carrying off several of the horses under cover of the night.[5]

This was somewhat of a disagreeable foretaste of mountain life to some of Wyeth's band, accustomed only to the regular and peaceful life of New England; nor was it altogether to the taste of Captain Sublette's men, who were chiefly creoles and townsmen from St. Louis. They continued their march the next morning,

[5] It was probably this encounter that Nathaniel Wyeth described.
"This night [July 1 or 2] at about 12 ock. we were attacked by Indians probably the Blackfoot. They approached within 50 yds. and fired about 40 shots into the camp and some arrows they wounded three animals and got 5 from Mr. Sublette One from an Independent hunter and 4 which I left out of camp for better feed mine were all poor and sore backed and useless." *Correspondence and Journals*, 158.

keeping scouts ahead and upon their flanks, and arrived without further molestation at Pierre's Hole.[6]

The first inquiry of Captain Sublette, on reaching the rendezvous, was for Fitzpatrick. He had not arrived, nor had any intelligence been received concerning him. Great uneasiness was now entertained, lest he should have fallen into the hands of the Blackfeet who had made the midnight attack upon the camp. It was a matter of general joy, therefore, when he made his appearance, conducted by two half-breed Iroquois hunters. He had lurked for several days among the mountains, until almost starved; at length he escaped the vigilance of his enemies in the night, and was so fortunate as to meet the two Iroquois hunters, who, being on horseback, conveyed him without further difficulty to the rendezvous. He arrived there so emaciated that he could scarcely be recognized.[7]

The valley called Pierre's Hole is about thirty miles in length and fifteen in width, bounded to the west and south by low and broken ridges, and overlooked to the east by three lofty mountains, called the three Tetons, which domineer as landmarks over a vast extent of country.

A fine stream, fed by rivulets and mountain springs, pours through the valley toward the north, dividing it into nearly equal parts. The meadows on its borders are broad and extensive, covered with willow and cotton-wood trees, so closely interlocked and matted together as to be nearly impassable.

In this valley was congregated the motley populace connected with the fur trade. Here the two rival companies[8] had their encampments, with their retainers of all kinds: traders, trappers, hunters, and half-breeds, assembled from all quarters, awaiting their

[6] Wyeth's journal shows that they arrived at the rendezvous on July 8. Besides "about 100 men of the Rocky Mountain Fur Co," there were Lucien Fontenelle's partner, Andrew Dripps, of the rival American Fur Company, with around ninety men; "many independent Hunters"; and "about 120 Lodges of the Nez Perces and about 80 of the Flatheads." *Correspondence and Journals*, 159. Bonneville's company was not present nor was Fontenelle's, but William H. Vanderburgh was with Dripps. Ferris, *Life in the Rocky Mountains*, 156.

[7] The fullest account of Fitzpatrick's experience is in Leonard's *Adventures*, 35–40.

[8] The Rocky Mountain Fur Company and the American Fur Company.

yearly supplies, and their orders to start off in new directions. Here, also, the savage tribes connected with the trade, the Nez Percés or Chopunnish Indians, and Flatheads, had pitched their lodges beside the streams, and with their squaws, awaited the distribution of goods and finery. There was, moreover, a band of fifteen free trappers, commanded by a gallant leader from Arkansas, named Sinclair,[9] who held their encampment a little apart from the rest. Such was the wild and heterogeneous assemblage, amounting to several hundred men, civilized and savage, distributed in tents and lodges in the several camps.

The arrival of Captain Sublette with supplies put the Rocky Mountain Fur Company in full activity. The wares and merchandise were quickly opened, and as quickly disposed of to trappers and Indians; the usual excitement and revelry took place, after which all hands began to disperse to their several destinations.

On the 17th of July,[10] a small brigade of fourteen trappers, led by Milton Sublette, brother of the captain, set out with the intention of proceeding to the southwest. They were accompanied by Sinclair and his fifteen free trappers; Wyeth, also, and his New England band of beaver hunters and salmon fishers, now dwindled down to eleven, took this opportunity to prosecute their cruise in the wilderness, accompanied with such experienced pilots. On the first day, they proceeded about eight miles to the southeast, and encamped for the night, still in the valley of Pierre's Hole. On the following morning, just as they were raising their camp, they observed a long line of people pouring down a defile of the mountains. They at first supposed them to be Fontenelle and his party, whose arrival had been daily expected. Wyeth, however, reconnoitred them with a spy-glass, and soon perceived they were Indians. They were divided

[9] Alexander Sinclair (also St. Clair). See LeRoy R. Hafen, "The Bean-Sinclair Party of Rocky Mountain Trappers, 1830–32," *Colorado Magazine*, Vol. XXXI (July, 1954), 161–71.

[10] This date agrees with Wyeth's. His statement that "On the 17th we put out and ste[e]red S.E. in direction to a pass through the same mountains by which we entered the valley," *Correspondence and Journals*, 158, indicates that Milton Sublette's and Wyeth's intention was to cross the Teton Range via Teton Pass and descend into Jackson Hole.

into two parties, forming, in the whole, about one hundred and fifty persons, men, women, and children. Some were on horseback, fantastically painted and arrayed, with scarlet blankets fluttering in the wind. The greater part, however, were on foot. They had perceived the trappers before they were themselves discovered, and came down yelling and whooping into the plain. On nearer approach, they were ascertained to be Blackfeet.

One of the trappers of Sublette's brigade, a half-breed named Antoine Godin, now mounted his horse, and rode forth as if to hold a conference. He was the son of an Iroquois hunter, who had been cruelly murdered by the Blackfeet at a small stream below the mountains, which still bears his name. In company with Antoine rode forth a Flathead Indian, whose once powerful tribe had been completely broken down in their wars with the Blackfeet. Both of them, therefore, cherished the most vengeful hostility against these marauders of the mountains. The Blackfeet came to a halt. One of the chiefs advanced singly and unarmed, bearing the pipe of peace. This overture was certainly pacific; but Antoine and the Flathead were predisposed to hostility, and pretended to consider it a treacherous movement.

"Is your piece charged?" said Antoine to his red companion.

"It is."

"Then cock it, and follow me."

They met the Blackfoot chief half way, who extended his hand in friendship. Antoine grasped it.

"Fire!" cried he.

The Flathead levelled his piece, and brought the Blackfoot to the ground. Antoine snatched off his scarlet blanket, which was richly ornamented, and galloped off with it as a trophy to the camp, the bullets of the enemy whistling after him. The Indians immediately threw themselves into the edge of a swamp, among willows and cotton-wood trees, interwoven with vines. Here they began to fortify themselves; the women digging a trench, and throwing up a breastwork of logs and branches, deep hid in the bosom of the wood, while the warriors skirmished at the edge to keep the trappers at bay.

The latter took their station in a ravine in front, whence they kept up a scattering fire. As to Wyeth, and his little band of "down-easters," they were perfectly astounded by this second specimen of life in the wilderness; the men, being especially unused to bush-fighting and the use of the rifle, were at a loss how to proceed. Wyeth, however, acted as a skilful commander. He got all his horses into camp and secured them; then, making a breastwork of his packs of goods, he charged his men to remain in garrison, and not to stir out of their fort. For himself, he mingled with the other leaders, determined to take his share in the conflict.

In the meantime, an express had been sent off to the rendezvous for reinforcements. Captain Sublette, and his associate, Campbell, were at their camp when the express came galloping across the plain, waving his cap, and giving the alarm; "Blackfeet! Blackfeet! a fight in the upper part of the valley!—to arms! to arms!"

The alarm was passed from camp to camp. It was a common cause. Every one turned out with horse and rifle. The Nez Percés and Flatheads joined. As fast as horseman could arm and mount he galloped off; the valley was soon alive with white men and red men scouring at full speed.

Sublette ordered his men to keep to the camp, being recruits from St. Louis, and unused to Indian warfare. He and his friend Campbell prepared for action. Throwing off their coats, rolling up their sleeves, and arming themselves with pistols and rifles, they mounted their horses and dashed forward among the first. As they rode along, they made their wills in soldier-like style; each stating how his effects should be disposed of in case of his death, and appointing the other his executor.

The Blackfeet warriors had supposed the brigade of Milton Sublette all the foes they had to deal with, and were astonished to behold the whole valley suddenly swarming with horsemen, galloping to the field of action. They withdrew into their fort, which was completely hid from sight in the dark and tangled wood. Most of their women and children had retreated to the mountains. The trappers now sallied forth and approached the swamp, firing into the thickets at random; the Blackfeet had a better sight at their adversaries, who were in the open field, and a half-breed was wounded in the shoulder.

When Captain Sublette arrived, he urged to penetrate the swamp and storm the fort, but all hung back in awe of the dismal horrors of the place, and the danger of attacking such desperadoes in their savage den. The very Indian allies, though accustomed to bush-fighting, regarded it as almost impenetrable, and full of frightful danger. Sublette was not to be turned from his purpose, but offered to lead the way into the swamp. Campbell stepped forward to accompany him. Before entering the perilous wood, Sublette took his brothers aside, and told them that in case he fell, Campbell, who knew his will, was to be his executor.[11] This done, he grasped his rifle and pushed into the thickets, followed by Campbell. Sinclair, the partisan from Arkansas, was at the edge of the wood with his brother and a few of his men. Excited by the gallant example of the two friends, he pressed forward to share their dangers.

The swamp was produced by the labors of the beaver, which, by damming up a stream, had inundated a portion of the valley. The place was all overgrown with woods and thickets, so closely matted and entangled that it was impossible to see ten paces ahead, and the three associates in peril had to crawl along, one after another, making their way by putting the branches and vines aside; but doing it with caution, lest they should attract the eye of some lurking marksman. They took the lead by turns, each advancing about twenty yards at a time, and now and then hallooing to their men to follow. Some of the latter gradually entered the swamp, and followed a little distance in their rear.

They had now reached a more open part of the wood, and had glimpses of the rude fortress from between the trees. It was a mere breastwork, as we have said, of logs and branches, with blankets, buffalo robes, and the leathern covers of lodges, extended round the top as a screen. The movements of the leaders, as they groped their way, had been descried by the sharp-sighted enemy. As Sin-

---

[11] A letter by Robert Campbell to his brother, Hugh, written July 18 and 19, 1832, at the site of the battle confirms this fact. See Campbell's *Rocky Mountain Letters*, 8–9.

clair, who was in the advance, was putting some branches aside, he was shot through the body. He fell on the spot. "Take me to my brother,"[12] said he to Campbell. The latter gave him in charge to some of the men, who conveyed him out of the swamp.

Sublette now took the advance. As he was reconnoitring the fort, he perceived an Indian peeping through an aperture. In an instant his rifle was levelled and discharged, and the ball struck the savage in the eye. While he was reloading, he called to Campbell, and pointed out to him the hole; "Watch that place," said he, "and you will soon have a fair chance for a shot." Scarce had he uttered the words, when a ball struck him in the shoulder, and almost wheeled him around. His first thought was to take hold of his arm with his other hand, and move it up and down. He ascertained, to his satisfaction, that the bone was not broken. The next moment he was so faint that he could not stand. Campbell took him in his arms and carried him out of the thicket. The same shot that struck Sublette wounded another man in the head.

A brisk fire was now opened by the mountaineers from the wood, answered occasionally from the fort. Unluckily, the trappers and their allies, in searching for the fort, had got scattered, so that Wyeth, and a number of Nez Percés, approached the fort on the northwest side, while others did the same on the opposite quarter. A cross-fire thus took place, which occasionally did mischief to friends as well as foes. An Indian was shot down, close to Wyeth, by a ball which, he was convinced, had been sped from the rifle of a trapper on the other side of the fort.

The number of whites and their Indian allies had by this time so much increased by arrivals from the rendezvous, that the Blackfeet were completely overmatched. They kept doggedly in their fort, however, making no offer of surrender. An occasional firing into the breastwork was kept up during the day. Now and then, one of the Indian allies, in bravado, would rush up to the fort, fire over the ramparts, tear off a buffalo robe or a scarlet blanket, and return

[12] This was Pruett (or Prewitt) Sinclair. Hafen, "The Bean-Sinclair Party," *op. cit.*, 165, 171.

with it in triumph to his comrades. Most of the savage garrison that fell, however, were killed in the first part of the attack.

At one time it was resolved to set fire to the fort; and the squaws belonging to the allies were employed to collect combustibles. This, however, was abandoned; the Nez Percés being unwilling to destroy the robes and blankets, and other spoils of the enemy, which they felt sure would fall into their hands.

The Indians, when fighting, are prone to taunt and revile each other. During one of the pauses of the battle, the voice of the Blackfeet chief was heard.

"So long," said he, "as we had powder and ball, we fought you in the open field: when those were spent, we retreated here to die with our women and children. You may burn us in our fort; but, stay by our ashes, and you who are so hungry for fighting will soon have enough. There are four hundred lodges of our brethren at hand. They will soon be here—their arms are strong—their hearts are big—they will avenge us!"

This speech was translated two or three times by Nez Percé and creole interpreters. By the time it was rendered into English, the chief was made to say that four hundred lodges of his tribe were attacking the encampment at the other end of the valley. Every one now was for hurrying to the defence of the rendezvous. A party was left to keep watch upon the fort; the rest galloped off to the camp. As night came on, the trappers drew out of the swamp, and remained about the skirts of the wood. By morning, their companions returned from the rendezvous with the report that all was safe. As the day opened, they ventured within the swamp and approached the fort. All was silent. They advanced up to it without opposition. They entered: it had been abandoned in the night, and the Blackfeet had effected their retreat, carrying off their wounded on litters made of branches, leaving bloody traces on the herbage. The bodies of ten Indians were found within the fort; among them the one shot in the eye by Sublette. The Blackfeet afterward reported that they had lost twenty-six warriors in this battle. Thirty-two horses were likewise found killed; among them were some of those recently carried off from Sublette's party, in the night; which showed that these were the very savages that had attacked him. They proved to be an advance party of the main body of Blackfeet, which had been upon the trail of Sublette's party. Five white men and one half-breed were killed, and several wounded. Seven of the Nez Percés were also killed, and six wounded.[13] They had an old chief, who was reputed as invulnerable. In the course of the action he was hit by a spent ball, and threw up blood; but his skin was unbroken. His people were now fully convinced that he was proof against powder and ball.

A striking circumstance is related as having occurred the morning after the battle. As some of the trappers and their Indian allies were approaching the fort through the woods, they beheld an Indian woman, of noble form and features, leaning against a tree. Their surprise at her lingering here alone, to fall into the hands of her enemies, was dispelled, when they saw the corpse of a warrior at her feet. Either she was so lost in grief as not to perceive their approach; or a proud spirit kept her silent and motionless. The Indians set up a yell, on discovering her, and before the trappers could interfere, her mangled body fell upon the corpse which she had refused to abandon. We have heard this anecdote discredited by one of the leaders who had been in the battle: but the fact may have taken place without his seeing it, and been concealed from him. It is an instance of female devotion, even to the death, which we are well disposed to believe and to record.

After the battle, the brigade of Milton Sublette, together with the free trappers, and Wyeth's New England band, remained some days at the rendezvous, to see if the main body of Blackfeet intended to make an attack; nothing of the kind occurring, they once more put themselves in motion, and proceeded on their route toward the southwest.[14]

[13] Estimates of the killed and wounded on both sides vary in every account written by a participant in the battle. Irving's figures and those of Nathaniel Wyeth are the most conservative and, therefore, probably the most accurate. Wyeth thought that about twenty of the Blackfeet (actually Gros Ventres) were killed; he states that three trappers were killed and eight badly wounded, and that about ten Nez Percés and Flatheads lost their lives.

[14] The battle of Pierre's Hole was the most intense conflict between whites and

The ADVENTURES *of* CAPTAIN BONNEVILLE

Captain Sublette having distributed his supplies, had intended to set off on his return to St. Louis, taking with him the peltries collected from the trappers and Indians. His wound, however, obliged him to postpone his departure. Several who were to have

---

Indians in the annals of the Rocky Mountain fur trade, and Irving's account of it is the most complete. A year after its publication in *Bonneville,* Samuel Parker, missionary colleague of Dr. Marcus Whitman, attacked Irving in print without naming him:

"I have seen an account of this battle, written by a graphic hand, in all the fascinating style of romance, representing the Indians as having entrenched themselves in a swamp, so densely wooded as to be almost impenetrable.... With those who have seen the field of battle [James Bridger showed it to Parker in 1835], the glowing description, drawn out in long detail, looses [*sic*] its interest; for although I saw it, yet I did not see the dense woods, nor a swamp of any magnitude any where near." *Journal of an Exploring Tour beyond the Rocky Mountains,* 90 n.

Yet an examination of all accounts reveals that Irving's is sound in essential details. A number of descriptions of the battle were available to him. Before him on his desk were Wyeth's journals, where under date of July 18, Irving read one version *(Correspondence and Journals,* 159–60). He could also have read the detailed version by Robert Campbell written to his brother Hugh in the *Rocky Mountain Letters,* 8–11, which was published in 1836 in the *National Atlas, and Tuesday Morning Mail.* Available also were Wyeth's *Oregon,* 48–51, and a letter from William L. Sublette to William Ashley, September 21, 1832, published in the *Missouri Republican,* October 16, 1832. As Irving indicates later in this chapter, he had also met William Sublette personally when the latter was returning from the mountains after the battle of Pierre's Hole. The meeting had taken place about September 24 or 25 near Lexington, Missouri, as Irving was traveling from St. Louis to Independence, and there is a good possibility that Irving had the story of the battle from Sublette himself. If he made notes of this conversation, they have disappeared. Since the notebook of Irving's trip from St. Louis to Independence is missing (McDermott, ed., *Western Journals of Washington Irving,* 89 n.), it is possible that this notebook may have been separated from the others relating to his tour during Irving's composition of Chapter VI of *Bonneville* and that if Bonneville's manuscript journal, from which Irving worked, were found, the notebook of the trip from St. Louis to Independence might be with it.

Other eyewitness accounts not available to Irving are: John Ball, "Across the Continent Seventy Years Ago," *Oregon Historical Quarterly,* Vol. III (1902), 91–92, and the *Autobiography of John Ball,* 77–79; Ferris, *Life in the Rocky Mountains,* 201–12; George Nidever, *The Life and Adventures of George Nidever* (ed. by William H. Ellison), 26–30; and Leonard, *Adventures,* 42–46. Since Bonneville was not present at the Pierre's Hole rendezvous nor a participant in the battle, any information about the battle in his manuscript journal could only have been secondhand.

The ADVENTURES *of* CAPTAIN BONNEVILLE

accompanied him became impatient of this delay. Among these was a young Bostonian, Mr. Joseph More, one of the followers of Mr. Wyeth, who had seen enough of mountain life and savage warfare, and was eager to return to the abodes of civilization. He and six others, among whom were a Mr. Foy, of Mississippi, Mr. Alfred K. Stephens,[15] of St. Louis, and two grandsons of the celebrated Daniel Boon, set out together, in advance of Sublette's party, thinking they would make their way through the mountains.

It was just five days after the battle of the swamp that these seven companions were making their way through Jackson's Hole, a valley not far from the three Tetons,[16] when, as they were descending a hill, a party of Blackfeet that lay in ambush started up with terrific yells. The horse of the young Bostonian, who was in front, wheeled round with affright, and threw his unskilled rider. The young man scrambled up the side of the hill, but, unaccustomed to such wild scenes, lost his presence of mind, and stood, as if paralyzed, on the edge of a bank, until the Blackfeet came up and slew him on the spot. His comrades had fled on the first alarm; but two of them, Foy and Stephens, seeing his danger, paused when they got half way up the hill, turned back, dismounted, and hastened to his assistance. Foy was instantly killed. Stephens was severely wounded, but escaped, to die five days afterward.[17] The survivors returned to the camp of Captain Sublette, bringing tidings of this new disaster.

[15] "Mr. Foy" was John Foy, one of the party led by Alexander Sinclair, killed in the battle of Pierre's Hole. Alfred K. Stephens had been a member of the Gantt-Blackwell expedition. He was leader of the group of trappers that with Zenas Leonard attached themselves to the Sublette-Fitzgerald forces at Laramie River the previous June 13.

[16] The Teton Range forms the western rim of Jackson Hole, which lies immediately below its towering peaks.

[17] From evidence in Ferris, *Life in the Rocky Mountains*, 157 and 159, and in Wyeth, *Correspondence and Journals*, 204, the place where they were killed was on the Hoback River. A later entry in Wyeth's journal (213) locates it in Little Jackson Hole, through which the Hoback flows. Wyeth's testimony (213) and Ferris' (159) are in conflict as to the exact location, although in agreement as to the general area. Ferris states that his group deposited the remains of the murdered men in a branch of Hoback River on August 14, 1832. On the other hand, Wyeth wrote to Francis Ermatinger on July 18, 1833 *(Correspondence and Journals,* 69), and reported that two days before he had buried More's bones.

The ADVENTURES *of* CAPTAIN BONNEVILLE

That hardy leader, as soon as he could bear the journey, set out on his return to St. Louis, accompanied by Campbell. As they had a number of pack-horses richly laden with peltries to convoy, they chose a different route through the mountains, out of the way, as they hoped, of the lurking bands of Blackfeet. They succeeded in making the frontier in safety. We remember to have seen them with their band, about two or three months afterward, passing through a skirt of woodland in the upper part of Missouri.[18] Their long cavalcade stretched in single file for nearly half a mile. Sublette still wore his arm in a sling. The mountaineers in their rude hunting dresses, armed with rifles and roughly mounted, and leading their pack-horses down a hill of the forest, looked like banditti returning with plunder. On the top of some of the packs were perched several half-breed children, perfect little imps, with wild black eyes glaring from among elf locks. These, I was told, were children of the trappers; pledges of love from their squaw spouses in the wilderness.

[18] Latrobe's *The Rambler* reveals that this meeting took place a few miles from Lexington, Missouri. Since Irving was at Independence by September 26 and Lexington was not far east of there, the meeting with Sublette probably occurred on September 24 or 25. According to an article in *Niles' Register*, Sublette's train carried $80,000 worth of furs packed on mules and stretched out over the prairies for a full mile. *Niles' Register*, Vol. XLIII (October 27, 1832), 131.

7.

Retreat of the Blackfeet—Fontenelle's camp in danger—Captain Bonneville and the Blackfeet—Free trappers—Their character, habits, dress, equipments, horses—Game fellows of the mountains—Their visit to the camp—Good fellowship and good cheer—A carouse—A swagger, a brawl, and a reconciliation

THE BLACKFEET WARRIORS, when they effected their midnight retreat from their wild fastness in Pierre's Hole, fell back into the valley of the Seeds-ke-dee, or Green River, where they joined the main body of their band. The whole force amounted to several hundred fighting men, gloomy and exasperated by their late disaster. They had with them their wives and children, which incapacitated them from any bold and extensive enterprise of a warlike nature; but when, in the course of their wanderings, they came in sight of the encampment of Fontenelle, who had moved some distance up Green River valley in search of the free trappers, they put up tremendous war-cries, and advanced fiercely as if to attack it. Second thoughts caused them to moderate their fury. They recollected the severe lesson just received, and could not but remark the strength of Fontenelle's position; which had been chosen with great judgment.

A formal talk ensued. The Blackfeet said nothing of the late battle, of which Fontenelle had as yet received no accounts; the latter, however, knew the hostile and perfidious nature of these savages, and took care to inform them of the encampment of Captain Bonneville, that they might know there were more white men in the neighborhood.

The ADVENTURES *of* CAPTAIN BONNEVILLE

The conference ended, Fontenelle sent a Delaware Indian of his party to conduct fifteen of the Blackfeet to the camp of Captain Bonneville. There was [*sic*] at that time two Crow Indians in the captain's camp, who had recently arrived there. They looked with dismay at this deputation from their implacable enemies, and gave the captain a terrible character of them, assuring him that the best thing he could possibly do, was to put those Blackfeet deputies to death on the spot. The captain, however, who had heard nothing of the conflict at Pierre's Hole, declined all compliance with this sage counsel. He treated the grim warriors with his usual urbanity. They passed some little time at the camp; saw, no doubt, that everything was conducted with military skill and vigilance; and that such an enemy was not to be easily surprised, nor to be molested with impunity, and then departed, to report all that they had seen to their comrades.

The two scouts which Captain Bonneville had sent out to seek for the band of free trappers, expected by Fontenelle, and to invite them to his camp, had been successful in their search, and on the 12th of August those worthies made their appearance.

To explain the meaning of the appellation, free trapper, it is necessary to state the terms on which the men enlist in the service of the fur companies. Some have regular wages, and are furnished with weapons, horses, traps, and other requisites. These are under command, and bound to do every duty required of them connected with the service; such as hunting, trapping, loading and unloading the horses, mounting guard; and, in short, all the drudgery of the camp. These are the hired trappers.

The free trappers are a more independent class; and in describing them, we shall do little more than transcribe the graphic description of them by Captain Bonneville. "They come and go," says he, "when and where they please; provide their own horses, arms, and other equipments; trap and trade on their own account, and dispose of their skins and peltries to the highest bidder. Sometimes, in a dangerous hunting ground, they attach themselves to the camp of some trader for protection. Here they come under some restrictions; they have to conform to the ordinary rules for trapping, and to submit to such restraints, and to take part in such general duties, as are established for the good order and safety of the camp. In return for this protection, and for their camp keeping, they are bound to dispose of all the beaver they take, to the trader who commands the camp, at a certain rate per skin; or, should they prefer seeking a market elsewhere, they are to make him an allowance, of from thirty to forty dollars for the whole hunt."

There is an inferior order, who, either from prudence or poverty, come to these dangerous hunting grounds without horses or accoutrements, and are furnished by the traders. These, like the hired trappers, are bound to exert themselves to the utmost in taking beaver, which, without skinning, they render in at the trader's lodge, where a stipulated price for each is placed to their credit. These, though generally included in the generic name of free trappers, have the more specific title of skin trappers.

The wandering whites who mingle for any length of time with the savages have invariably a proneness to adopt savage habitudes; but none more so than the free trappers. It is a matter of vanity and ambition with them to discard everything that may bear the stamp of civilized life, and to adopt the manners, habits, dress, gesture, and even walk of the Indian. You cannot pay a free trapper a greater compliment, than to persuade him you have mistaken him for an Indian brave; and, in truth, the counterfeit is complete. His hair, suffered to attain to a great length, is carefully combed out, and either left to fall carelessly over his shoulders, or plaited neatly and tied up in otter skins, or parti-colored ribands. A hunting-shirt of ruffled calico of bright dyes, or of ornamented leather, falls to his knee; below which, curiously fashioned leggins, ornamented with strings, fringes, and a profusion of hawks' bells, reach to a costly pair of moccasons of the finest Indian fabric, richly embroidered with beads. A blanket of scarlet, or some other bright color, hangs from his shoulders, and is girt around his waist with a red sash, in which he bestows his pistols, knife, and the stem of his Indian pipe; preparations either for peace or war. His gun is lavishly decorated with brass tacks and vermilion, and provided with a fringed cover, occasionally of buckskin, ornamented here and there with a feather.

His horse, the noble minister to the pride, pleasure, and profit of the mountaineer, is selected for his speed and spirit, and prancing gait, and holds a place in his estimation second only to himself. He shares largely of his bounty, and of his pride and pomp of trapping. He is caparisoned in the most dashing and fantastic style; the bridles and crupper are weightily embossed with beads and cockades; and head, mane, and tail, are interwoven with abundance of eagles' plumes, which flutter in the wind. To complete this grotesque equipment, the proud animal is bestreaked and bespotted with vermilion, or with white clay, whichever presents the most glaring contrast to his real color.

Such is the account given by Captain Bonneville of these rangers of the wilderness, and their appearance at the camp was strikingly characteristic. They came dashing forward at full speed, firing their fusees, and yelling in Indian style. Their dark sunburned faces, and long flowing hair, their leggins, flaps, moccasons, and richly-dyed blankets, and their painted horses gaudily caparisoned, gave them so much the air and appearance of Indians, that it was difficult to persuade one's self that they were white men, and had been brought up in civilized life.

Captain Bonneville, who was delighted with the game look of these cavaliers of the mountains, welcomed them heartily to his camp, and ordered a free allowance of grog to regale them, which soon put them in the most braggart spirits. They pronounced the captain the finest fellow in the world, and his men all *bons garçons*, jovial lads, and swore they would pass the day with them. They did so; and a day it was, of boast, and swagger, and rodomontade. The prime bullies and braves among the free trappers had each his circle of novices, from among the captain's band; mere greenhorns, men unused to Indian life; *mangeurs de lard*, or pork-eaters; as such new-comers are superciliously called by the veterans of the wilderness. These he would astonish and delight by the hour, with prodigious tales of his doings among the Indians; and of the wonders he had seen, and the wonders he had performed, in his adventurous peregrinations among the mountains.

In the evening, the free trappers drew off, and returned to the camp of Fontenelle, highly delighted with their visit and with their new acquaintances, and promising to return the following day. They kept their word: day after day their visits were repeated; they became "hail fellow well met" with Captain Bonneville's men; treat after treat succeeded, until both parties got most potently convinced, or rather confounded, by liquor. Now came on confusion and uproar. The free trappers were no longer suffered to have all the swagger to themselves. The camp bullies and prime trappers of the party began to ruffle up, and to brag, in turn, of their perils and achievements. Each now tried to out-boast and out-talk the other; a quarrel ensued as a matter of course, and a general fight, according to frontier usage. The two factions drew out their forces for a pitched battle. They fell to work and belabored each other with might and main; kicks and cuffs and dry blows were as well bestowed as they were well merited, until, having fought to their hearts' content, and been drubbed into a familiar acquaintance with each other's prowess and good qualities, they ended the fight by becoming firmer friends than they could have been rendered by a year's peaceable companionship.

While Captain Bonneville amused himself by observing the habits and characteristics of this singular class of men, and indulged them, for the time, in all their vagaries, he profited by the opportunity to collect from them information concerning the different parts of the country about which they had been accustomed to range; the characters of the tribes, and, in short, everything important to his enterprise. He also succeeded in securing the services of several to guide and aid him in his peregrinations among the mountains, and to trap for him during the ensuing season. Having strengthened his party with such valuable recruits, he felt in some measure consoled for the loss of the Delaware Indians, decoyed from him by Mr. Fontenelle.

8.

Plans for the winter—Salmon River—Abundance of salmon west of the mountains—New arrangements—Caches—Cerré's detachment—Movements in Fontenelle's camp—Departure of the Blackfeet—Their fortunes—Wind Mountain streams—Buckeye, the Delaware hunter, and the grizzly bear—Bones of murdered travellers—Visit to Pierre's Hole—Traces of the battle—Nez Percé Indians—Arrival at Salmon River

THE INFORMATION derived from the free trappers determined Captain Bonneville as to his further movements. He learned that in the Green River valley the winters were severe, the snow frequently falling to the depth of several feet; and that there was no good wintering ground in the neighborhood. The upper part of Salmon River was represented as far more eligible, besides being in an excellent beaver country; and thither the captain resolved to bend his course.

The Salmon River is one of the upper branches of the Oregon or Columbia; and takes its rise from various sources, among a group of mountains to the northwest of the Wind River chain.[1] It owes its name to the immense shoals of salmon which ascend it in the months of September and October. The salmon on the west side of the Rocky Mountains are, like the buffalo on the eastern plains, vast migratory supplies for the wants of man, that come and go

---

[1] The Salmon River and its branches drain central Idaho. It joins the Snake River a short distance south of the Oregon-Washington line. The Snake—trappers called it the Lewis River—an important tributary of the Columbia, was often referred to by the latter name.

with the seasons. As the buffalo in countless throngs find their certain way in the transient pasturage on the prairies, along the fresh banks of the rivers, and up every valley and green defile of the mountains, so the salmon, at their allotted seasons, regulated by a sublime and all-seeing Providence, swarm in myriads up the great rivers, and find their way up their main branches, and into the minutest tributary streams; so as to pervade the great arid plains, and to penetrate even among barren mountains. Thus wandering tribes are fed in the desert places of the wilderness, where there is no herbage for the animals of the chase, and where, but for these periodical supplies, it would be impossible for man to subsist.

The rapid currents of the rivers which run into the Pacific render the ascent of them very exhausting to the salmon. When the fish first run up the rivers, they are fat and in fine order. The struggle against impetuous streams and frequent rapids gradually renders them thin and weak, and great numbers are seen floating down the rivers on their backs. As the season advances and the water becomes chilled, they are flung in myriads on the shores, where the wolves and bears assemble to banquet on them. Often they rot in such quantities along the river banks as to taint the atmosphere. They are commonly from two to three feet long.

Captain Bonneville now made his arrangements for the autumn and the winter. The nature of the country through which he was about to travel rendered it impossible to proceed with wagons. He had more goods and supplies of various kinds, also, than were required for present purposes, or than could be conveniently transported on horseback; aided, therefore, by a few confidential men, he made *caches*, or secret pits, during the night, when all the rest of the camp were asleep, and in these deposited the superfluous effects, together with the wagons. All traces of the caches were then carefully obliterated. This is a common expedient with the traders and trappers of the mountains. Having no established posts and magazines, they make these caches or deposits at certain points, whither they repair, occasionally, for supplies. It is an expedient derived from the wandering tribes of Indians.

Many of the horses were still so weak and lame, as to be unfit for a long scramble through the mountains. These were collected into one cavalcade, and given in charge to an experienced trapper, of the name of Matthieu.[2] He was to proceed westward, with a brigade of trappers, to Bear River;[3] a stream to the west of the Green River or Colorado, where there was good pasturage for the horses. In this neighborhood it was expected he would meet the Shoshonie villages or bands,[4] on their yearly migrations, with whom he was to trade for peltries and provisions. After he had traded with these people, finished his trapping, and recruited the strength of the horses, he was to proceed to Salmon River and rejoin Captain Bonneville, who intended to fix his quarters there for the winter.

While these arrangements were in progress in the camp of Captain Bonneville, there was a sudden bustle and stir in the camp of Fontenelle. One of the partners[5] of the American Fur Company had arrived, in all haste, from the rendezvous at Pierre's Hole, in quest of the supplies. The competition between the two rival companies was just now at its height, and prosecuted with unusual zeal. The tramontane concerns of the Rocky Mountain Fur Company were managed by two resident partners, Fitzpatrick and Bridger;[6] those of the American Fur Company, by Vanderburgh[7] and Dripps.

[2] Nothing is apparently known of this trapper beyond what Irving writes here and in Chapter XVI.

[3] Bear River rises in Bear Lake on the Utah-Idaho line. After flowing north, it bends to the west and south and empties into Great Salt Lake.

[4] A *village* of Indians, in trappers' language, does not always imply a fixed community, but often a wandering horde or band. The Shoshonies, like most of the mountain tribes, have no settled residences; but are a nomadic people, dwelling in tents or lodges, and shifting their encampments from place to place, according as fish and game abound (Irving's note).

[5] This was probably Andrew Dripps.

[6] James Bridger (1804–81). Born in Virginia, Bridger as a young man was employed by William Ashley in 1822. His career thereafter was a prominent one in the fur trade and the expanding West. He is credited with the discovery of Great Salt Lake. In 1843 he built Fort Bridger in southern Wyoming on a branch of the Oregon Trail. His life has been written by Alter in *James Bridger*.

[7] William Henry Vanderburgh (c. 1798–1832). He attended West Point and soon thereafter entered the fur trade on the Missouri as an associate of Joshua Pilcher in the Missouri Fur Company. Later he joined the American Fur Company. His death resulted from a conflict with Blackfeet Indians (see Ferris, *Life*

Denver Public Library

"Buffalo Hunting"
From a Painting by George Catlin

Denver Public Library

"Buffalo Hunt, Under the White Wolf Skin"
From a Painting by George Catlin

The latter were ignorant of the mountain regions, but trusted to make up by vigilance and activity for their want of knowledge of the country.

Fitzpatrick, an experienced trader and trapper, knew the evils of competition in the same hunting grounds, and had proposed that the two companies should divide the country, so as to hunt in different directions: this proposition being rejected, he had exerted himself to get first into the field. His exertions, as have already been shown, were effectual. The early arrival of Sublette, with supplies, had enabled the various brigades of the Rocky Mountain Company to start off to their respective hunting grounds. Fitzpatrick himself, with his associate, Bridger, had pushed off with a strong party of trappers, for a prime beaver country to the north-northwest.

This had put Vanderburgh upon his mettle. He had hastened on to meet Fontenelle. Finding him at his camp in Green River valley, he immediately furnished himself with the supplies; put himself at the head of the free trappers and Delawares, and set off with all speed, determined to follow hard upon the heels of Fitzpatrick and Bridger. Of the adventures of these parties among the mountains, and the disastrous effects of their competition, we shall have occasion to treat in a future chapter.

Fontenelle having now delivered his supplies and accomplished his errand, struck his tents and set off on his return to the Yellowstone. Captain Bonneville and his band, therefore, remained alone in the Green River valley; and their situation might have been perilous, had the Blackfeet band still lingered in the vicinity. Those marauders, however, had been dismayed at finding so many resolute and well-appointed parties of white men in the neighborhood. They had, therefore, abandoned this part of the country, passing over the headwaters of the Green River, and bending their course towards the Yellowstone. Misfortune pursued them. Their route lay through the country of their deadly enemies, the Crows. In the Wind River valley, which lies east of the mountains, they were encountered by a powerful war party of that tribe, and completely put to rout.

in the Rocky Mountains, 175–78). Irving narrates this battle and Vanderburgh's death in Chapter XI.

Forty of them were killed, many of their women and children captured, and the scattered fugitives hunted like wild beasts until they were completely chased out of the Crow country.

On the 22d of August Captain Bonneville broke up his camp, and set out on his route for Salmon River. His baggage was arranged in packs, three to a mule, or pack-horse; one being disposed on each side of the animal and one on the top; the three forming a load of from one hundred and eighty to two hundred and twenty pounds. This is the trappers' style of loading pack-horses; his men, however, were inexpert at adjusting the packs, which were prone to get loose and slip off, so that it was necessary to keep a rear-guard to assist in reloading. A few days' experience, however, brought them into proper training.

Their march lay up the valley of the Seeds-ke-dee, overlooked to the right by the lofty peaks of the Wind River Mountains. From bright little lakes and fountain-heads of this remarkable bed of mountains poured forth the tributary streams of the Seeds-ke-dee. Some came rushing down gullies and ravines; others tumbled in crystal cascades from inaccessible clefts and rocks, and others winding their way in rapid and pellucid currents across the valley, to throw themselves into the main river. So transparent were these waters that the trout with which they abounded could be seen gliding about as if in the air; and their pebbly beds were distinctly visible at the depth of many feet. This beautiful and diaphanous quality of the Rocky Mountain streams prevails for a long time after they have mingled their waters and swollen into important rivers.

Issuing from the upper part of the valley, Captain Bonneville continued to the east-northeast, across rough and lofty ridges, and deep rocky defiles, extremely fatiguing both to man and horse.[8] Among his hunters was a Delaware Indian who had remained faithful to him. His name was Buckeye. He had often prided himself on

[8] The direction plus the first sentence of the previous paragraph indicates that Bonneville followed the Green River near to the place where it issues from the Green River Lakes on the west side of the Wind River Range, and then made his way over intervening ridges to a tributary (Fish Creek on modern maps) of the Gros Ventre River, which he then followed to Jackson Hole. Why he chose this route instead of the more direct one by way of the Hoback River is not clear.

his skill and success in coping with the grizzly bear, that terror of the hunters. Though crippled in the left arm, he declared he had no hesitation to close with a wounded bear, and attack him with a sword. If armed with a rifle, he was willing to brave the animal when in full force and fury. He had twice an opportunity of proving his prowess, in the course of this mountain journey, and was each time successful. His mode was to seat himself upon the ground, with his rifle cocked and resting on his lame arm. Thus prepared, he would await the approach of the bear with perfect coolness, nor pull trigger until he was close at hand. In each instance, he laid the monster dead upon the spot.

A march of three or four days, through savage and lonely scenes, brought Captain Bonneville to the fatal defile of Jackson's Hole, where poor More and Foy had been surprised and murdered by the Blackfeet. The feelings of the captain were shocked at beholding the bones of these unfortunate young men bleaching among the rocks; and he caused them to be decently interred.[9]

On the 3d of September he arrived on the summit of a mountain[10] which commanded a full view of the eventful valley of Pierre's Hole; whence he could trace the winding of its stream through green meadows, and forests of willow and cotton-wood, and have a prospect, between distant mountains, of the lava plains of Snake River, dimly spread forth like a sleeping ocean below.

After enjoying this magnificent prospect, he descended into the

---

[9] That Bonneville found the remains of More and Foy in Jackson Hole near the Gros Ventre River is at variance with the evidence of Ferris and Wyeth that their bones were found on the Hoback River; see Chapter VI, note 16. It is impossible to reconcile Irving's statements as to Bonneville's route after he left Fort Bonneville with the evidence from Ferris and Wyeth as to where More and Foy were murdered. Furthermore, Wyeth wrote in his journal, "Mr. Bonneville informs me that when he passed last year [1832] in August their bones were lying about the valley. I am apprehensive that More, a sick man whom I left in charge of Stevens, must be one of them." *Correspondence and Journals*, 204.

But Bonneville could not have seen the bones of More and Foy because Ferris' group had deposited them on August 14 in a branch of the Hoback River, and Bonneville did not leave his fort until August 22. Obviously, he was mistaken as to whose bones he saw. The question is important for the bearing it has upon a determination of Bonneville's route from his fort to Jackson Hole.

[10] Teton Pass, nearly due west of modern Jackson, Wyoming.

valley, and visited the scenes of the late desperate conflict. There were the remains of the rude fortress in the swamp, shattered by rifle shot, and strewed with the mingled bones of savages and horses. There was the late populous and noisy rendezvous, with the traces of trappers' camps and Indian lodges; but their fires were extinguished, the motley assemblage of trappers and hunters, white traders and Indian braves, had all dispersed to different points of the wilderness, and the valley had relapsed into its pristine solitude and silence.

That night the captain encamped upon the battle ground; the next day he resumed his toilsome peregrinations through the mountains. For upwards of two weeks he continued his painful march; both men and horses suffering excessively at times from hunger and thirst. At length, on the 19th of September, he reached the upper waters of Salmon River.

The weather was cold, and there were symptoms of an impending storm. The night set in, but Buckeye, the Delaware Indian, was missing. He had left the party early in the morning, to hunt by himself, according to his custom. Fears were entertained lest he should lose his way and become bewildered in tempestuous weather. These fears increased on the following morning, when a violent snow-storm came on, which soon covered the earth to the depth of several inches. Captain Bonneville immediately encamped, and sent out scouts in every direction. After some search Buckeye was discovered, quietly seated at a considerable distance in the rear, waiting the expected approach of the party, not knowing that they had passed, the snow having covered their trail.

On the ensuing morning they resumed their march at an early hour, but had not proceeded far when the hunters, who were beating up the country in the advance, came galloping back, making signals to encamp, and crying Indians! Indians!

Captain Bonneville immediately struck into a skirt of wood and prepared for action. The savages were now seen trooping over the hills in great numbers. One of them left the main body and came forward singly, making signals of peace. He announced them as a band of Nez Percés[11] or Pierced-nose Indians, friendly to the whites, whereupon an invitation was returned by Captain Bonneville for them to come and encamp with him. They halted for a short time to make their toilette, an operation as important with an Indian warrior as with a fashionable beauty. This done, they arranged themselves in martial style, the chiefs leading the van, the braves following in a long line, painted and decorated, and topped off with fluttering plumes. In this way they advanced, shouting and singing, firing off their fusees, and clashing their shields. The two parties encamped hard by each other. The Nez Percés were on a hunting expedition, but had been almost famished on their march. They had no provisions left but a few dried salmon, yet finding the white men equally in want, they generously offered to share even this meager pittance, and frequently repeated the offer, with an earnestness that left no doubt of their sincerity. Their generosity won the heart of Captain Bonneville, and produced the most cordial good will on the part of his men. For two days that the parties remained in company, the most amicable intercourse prevailed, and they parted the best of friends. Captain Bonneville detached a few men, under Mr. Cerré, an able leader, to accompany the Nez Percés on their hunting expedition, and to trade with them for meat for the winter's supply. After this, he proceeded down the river, about five miles below the forks, when he came to a halt on the 26th of September, to establish his winter quarters.[12]

---

[11] We should observe that this tribe is universally called by its French name, which is pronounced by the trappers, *Nepercy*. There are two main branches of this tribe, the upper Nepercys and the lower Nepercys, as we shall show hereafter (Irving's note).

[12] This, the first winter camp, was located on the Salmon River below the junction of the Lemhi River. He was thus in modern Idaho north of the town of Salmon.

9.

Horses turned loose—Preparations for winter quarters—Hungry times—Nez Percés, their honesty, piety, pacific habits, religious ceremonies—Captain Bonneville's conversations with them—Their love of gambling

IT WAS GRATIFYING to Captain Bonneville, after so long and toilsome a course of travel, to relieve his poor jaded horses of the burden under which they were almost ready to give out, and to behold them rolling upon the grass, and taking a long repose after all their sufferings. Indeed, so exhausted were they, that those employed under the saddle were no longer capable of hunting for the daily subsistence of the camp.

All hands now set to work to prepare a winter cantonment. A temporary fortification was thrown up for the protection of the party; a secure and comfortable pen, into which the horses could be driven at night; and huts were built for the reception of the merchandise.[1]

This done, Captain Bonneville made a distribution of his forces: twenty men were to remain with him in garrison to protect the property; the rest were organized into three brigades,[2] and sent off

---

[1] W. A. Ferris and two trappers visited Bonneville's fort early in November, 1832. He described it as being in a cottonwood grove on the west side of the Salmon River. "This miserable establishment, consisted entirely of several log cabins, low, badly constructed, and admirably situated for besiegers only, who would be sheltered on every side, by timber, brush, etc." Ferris, *Life in the Rocky Mountains*, 184. The site is now on grazing land nearly opposite Carmen, Idaho.

[2] One group was led by Joseph Reddeford Walker, and a second by Michel S. Cerré. Who the third leader was has not been determined.

The ADVENTURES of CAPTAIN BONNEVILLE

in different directions, to subsist themselves by hunting the buffalo, until the snow should become too deep.

Indeed, it would have been impossible to provide for the whole party in this neighborhood. It was at the extreme western limit of the buffalo range, and these animals had recently been completely hunted out of the neighborhood by the Nez Percés, so that, although the hunters of the garrison were continually on the alert, ranging the country round, they brought in scarce game sufficient to keep famine from the door. Now and then there was a scanty meal of fish or wild-fowl, occasionally an antelope; but frequently the cravings of hunger had to be appeased with roots, or the flesh of wolves and muskrats. Rarely could the inmates of the cantonment boast of having made a full meal, and never of having wherewithal for the morrow. In this way they starved along until the 8th of October, when they were joined by a party of five families of Nez Percés, who in some measure reconciled them to the hardships of their situation by exhibiting a lot still more destitute. A more forlorn set they had never encountered: they had not a morsel of meat or fish; nor anything to subsist on, excepting roots, wild rosebuds, the barks of certain plants, and other vegetable production; neither had they any weapon for hunting or defence, excepting an old spear: yet the poor fellows made no murmur nor complaint; but seemed accustomed to their hard fare. If they could not teach the white men their practical stoicism, they at least made them acquainted with the edible properties of roots and wild rosebuds, and furnished them a supply from their own store. The necessities of the camp at length became so urgent that Captain Bonneville determined to dispatch a party to the Horse Prairie, a plain to the north of his cantonment,[3] to procure a supply of provisions. When the men were about to depart, he proposed to the Nez Percés that they, or some of them, should join the hunting-party. To his surprise, they promptly declined. He inquired the reason for their refusal, seeing that they

[3] Not north but east across the Continental Divide and the Bitterroot Range, in the general area of modern Dillon, Montana. The party Bonneville sent out at this time is apparently the group, accompanied by a few Flathead Indians, that W. A. Ferris met late in October on the "Gates" of Beaverhead River in Horse Prairie (see Ferris, *Life in the Rocky Mountains*, 182).

were in nearly as starving a situation as his own people. They replied that it was a sacred day with them, and the Great Spirit would be angry should they devote it to hunting. They offered, however, to accompany the party if it would delay its departure until the following day; but this the pinching demands of hunger would not permit, and the detachment proceeded.

A few days afterward, four of them signified to Captain Bonneville that they were about to hunt. "What!" exclaimed he, "without guns or arrows; and with only one old spear? What do you expect to kill?" They smiled among themselves, but made no answer. Preparatory to the chase, they performed some religious rites, and offered up to the Great Spirit a few short prayers for safety and success; then, having received the blessings of their wives, they leaped upon their horses and departed, leaving the whole party of Christian spectators amazed and rebuked by this lesson of faith and dependence on a supreme and benevolent Being. "Accustomed," adds Captain Bonneville, "as I had heretofore been, to find the wretched Indian revelling in blood, and stained by every vice which can degrade human nature, I could scarcely realize the scene which I had witnessed. Wonder at such unaffected tenderness and piety, where it was least to have been sought, contended in all our bosoms with shame and confusion, at receiving such pure and wholesome instructions from creatures so far below us in the arts and comforts of life." The simple prayers of the poor Indians were not unheard. In the course of four or five days they returned, laden with meat. Captain Bonneville was curious to know how they had attained such success with such scanty means. They gave him to understand that they had chased the buffalo at full speed, until they tired them down, when they easily dispatched them with the spear, and made use of the same weapon to flay the carcasses. To carry through their lessons to their Christian friends, the poor savages were as charitable as they had been pious, and generously shared with them the spoils of their hunting, giving them food enough to last for several days.

A further and more intimate intercourse with this tribe gave Captain Bonneville still greater cause to admire their strong devotional feeling. "Simply to call these people religious," says he, "would convey but a faint idea of the deep hue of piety and devotion which pervades their whole conduct. Their honesty is immaculate, and their purity of purpose, and their observance of the rites of their religion, are most uniform and remarkable. They are, certainly, more like a nation of saints than a horde of savages."

In fact, the antibelligerent policy of this tribe may have sprung from the doctrines of Christian charity, for it would appear that they had imbibed some notions of the Christian faith from Catholic missionaries and traders who had been among them. They even had a rude calendar of the fasts and festivals of the Romish Church, and some traces of its ceremonials. These have become blended with their own wild rites, and present a strange medley; civilized and barbarous. On the Sabbath, men, women, and children array themselves in their best style, and assemble round a pole erected at the head of the camp. Here they go through a wild fantastic ceremonial; strongly resembling the religious dance of the Shaking Quakers; but from its enthusiasm, much more striking and impressive. During the intervals of the ceremony, the principal chiefs, who officiate as priests, instruct them in their duties, and exhort them to virtue and good deeds.

"There is something antique and patriarchal," observes Captain Bonneville, "in this union of the offices of leader and priest; as there is in many of their customs and manners, which are all strongly imbued with religion."

The worthy captain, indeed, appears to have been strongly interested by this gleam of unlooked for light amidst the darkness of the wilderness. He exerted himself, during his sojourn among this simple and well-disposed people, to inculcate, as far as he was able, the gentle and humanizing precepts of the Christian faith, and to make them acquainted with the leading points of its history; and it speaks highly for the purity and benignity of his heart, that he derived unmixed happiness from the task.

"Many a time," says he, "was my little lodge thronged, or rather piled with hearers, for they lay on the ground, one leaning over the other, until there was no further room, all listening with greedy ears to the wonders which the Great Spirit had revealed to the white man. No other subject gave them half the satisfaction, or commanded half the attention; and but few scenes in my life remain so freshly on my memory, or are so pleasurably recalled to my contemplation, as these hours of intercourse with a distant and benighted race in the midst of the desert."

The only excesses indulged in by this temperate and exemplary people, appear to be gambling and horseracing. In these they engage with an eagerness that amounts to infatuation. Knots of gamblers will assemble before one of their lodge fires, early in the evening, and remain absorbed in the chances and changes of the game until long after dawn of the following day. As the night advances, they wax warmer and warmer. Bets increase in amount, one loss only serves to lead to a greater, until in the course of a single night's gambling, the richest chief may become the poorest varlet in the camp.

10.

Blackfeet in the Horse Prairie—Search after the hunters—Difficulties and dangers—A card party in the wilderness—The card party interrupted—"Old Sledge" a losing game—Visitors to the camp—Iroquois hunters—Hanging-eared Indians

ON THE 12TH of October, two young Indians of the Nez Percé tribe arrived at Captain Bonneville's encampment. They were on their way homeward, but had been obliged to swerve from their ordinary route through the mountains by deep snows. Their new route took them through the Horse Prairie. In traversing it, they had been attracted by the distant smoke of a camp fire, and, on stealing near to reconnoitre, had discovered a war party of Blackfeet. They had several horses with them; and, as they generally go on foot on warlike excursions, it was concluded that these horses had been captured in the course of their maraudings.

This intelligence awakened solicitude on the mind of Captain Bonneville for the party of hunters whom he had sent to that neighborhood; and the Nez Percés, when informed of the circumstance, shook their heads, and declared their belief that the horses they had seen had been stolen from that very party.

Anxious for information on the subject, Captain Bonneville dispatched two hunters to beat up the country in that direction. They searched in vain; not a trace of the men could be found; but they got into a region destitute of game, where they were well-nigh famished. At one time, they were three entire days without a mouthful of food; at length they beheld a buffalo grazing at the foot of a mountain. After manœuvring so as to get within shot, they fired, but merely wounded him. He took to flight, and they followed him over hill and dale with the eagerness and perseverance of starving men. A more lucky shot brought him to the ground. Stanfield sprang upon him, plunged his knife into his throat, and allayed his raging hunger by drinking his blood. A fire was instantly kindled beside the carcass, when the two hunters cooked, and ate again and again, until, perfectly gorged, they sank to sleep before their hunting fire. On the following morning they rose early, made another hearty meal, then loading themselves with buffalo meat, set out on their return to the camp, to report the fruitlessness of their mission.

At length, after six weeks' absence, the hunters made their appearance, and were received with joy, proportioned to the anxiety that had been felt on their account. They had hunted with success on the prairie, but, while busy drying buffalo meat, were joined by a few panic-stricken Flatheads, who informed them that a powerful band of Blackfeet was at hand. The hunters immediately abandoned the dangerous hunting ground, and accompanied the Flatheads to their village. Here they found Mr. Cerré, and the detachment of hunters sent with him to accompany the hunting party of the Nez Percés.

After remaining some time at the village, until they supposed the Blackfeet to have left the neighborhood, they set off with some of Mr. Cerré's men for the cantonment at Salmon River, where they arrived without accident. They informed Captain Bonneville, however, that not far from his quarters, they had found a wallet of fresh meat and a cord, which they supposed had been left by some prowling Blackfeet. A few days afterwards, Mr. Cerré, with the remainder of his men, likewise arrived at the cantonment.

Mr. Walker,[1] one of his subleaders, who had gone with a band of twenty hunters to range the country just beyond the Horse Prairie, had, likewise, his share of adventures with the all-pervading Blackfeet. At one of his encampments, the guard stationed to keep watch round the camp grew weary of their duty, and feeling a little too

---

[1] Ferris reported meeting Walker's group after the skirmish related in this paragraph. The camp the Blackfeet attacked was in the "Little Hole," a valley which Ferris' manuscript map shows was northwest of Horse Prairie (see Ferris, *Life in the Rocky Mountains*, 183).

secure, and too much at home on these prairies, retired to a small grove of willows, to amuse themselves with a social game of cards, called "old sledge," which is as popular among these trampers of the prairies as whist or ecarté among the polite circles of the cities. From the midst of their sport, they were suddenly roused by a discharge of firearms, and a shrill war-whoop. Starting on their feet, and snatching up their rifles, they beheld in dismay their horses and mules already in possession of the enemy, who had stolen upon the camp unperceived, while they were spell-bound by the magic of old sledge. The Indians sprang upon the animals barebacked, and endeavored to urge them off under a galling fire that did some execution. The mules, however, confounded by the hurly-burly and disliking their new riders, kicked up their heels and dismounted half of them, in spite of their horsemanship. This threw the rest into confusion; they endeavored to protect their unhorsed comrades from the furious assaults of the whites; but after a scene of "confusion worse confounded," horses and mules were abandoned, and the Indains betook themselves to the bushes. Here they quickly scratched holes in the earth about two feet deep, in which they prostrated themselves, and while thus screened from the shots of the white men, were enabled to make such use of their bows and arrows, and fusees, as to repulse their assailants, and to effect their retreat. This adventure threw a temporary stigma upon the game of "old sledge."

In the course of the autumn, four Iroquois hunters, driven by the snow from their hunting grounds, made their appearance at the cantonment. They were kindly welcomed, and during their sojourn made themselves useful in a variety of ways, being excellent trappers, and first-rate woodsmen. They were of the remnants of a party of Iroquois hunters that came from Canada into these mountain regions many years previously, in the employ of the Hudson's Bay Company. They were led by a brave chieftain, named Pierre, who fell by the hands of the Blackfeet, and gave his name to the fated valley of Pierre's Hole. This branch of the Iroquois tribe has ever since remained among these mountains, at mortal enmity with the Blackfeet, and have lost many of their prime hunters in their feuds with that ferocious race. Some of them fell in with General Ashley, in the course of one of his gallant excursions into the wilderness, and have continued ever since in the employ of the company.

Among the motley visitors to the winter quarters of Captain Bonneville was a party of Pends Oreilles (or Hanging-ears) and their chief. These Indians have a strong resemblance, in character and customs, to the Nez Percés. They amount to about three hundred lodges, are well armed, and possess great numbers of horses. During the spring, summer, and autumn, they hunt the buffalo about the head-waters of the Missouri, Henry's Fork of the Snake River, and the northern branches of Salmon River. Their winter quarters are upon the Racine Amère,[2] where they subsist upon roots and dried buffalo meat. Upon this river the Hudson's Bay Company have established a trading post,[3] where the Pends Oreilles and the Flatheads bring their peltries to exchange for arms, clothing, and trinkets.

This tribe, like the Nez Percés, evince strong and peculiar feelings of natural piety. Their religion is not a mere superstitious fear, like that of most savages; they evince abstract notions of morality; a deep reverence for an overruling spirit, and a respect for the rights of their fellow-men. In one respect, their religion partakes of the pacific doctrines of the Quakers. They hold that the Great Spirit is displeased with all nations who wantonly engage in war; they abstain, therefore, from all aggressive hostilities. But though thus unoffending in their policy, they are called upon continually to wage defensive warfare; especially with the Blackfeet; with whom, in the course of their hunting expeditions, they come in frequent collision, and have desperate battles. Their conduct as warriors is without fear or reproach, and they can never be driven to abandon their hunting grounds.

Like most savages, they are firm believers in dreams, and in the power and efficacy of charms and amulets, or medicines, as they term them. Some of their braves, also, who have had numerous hairbreadth 'scapes, like the old Nez Percé chief in the battle of

[2] The Bitterroot River, which joins Clark Fork near Missoula, Montana.
[3] Irving may refer to Flathead House on Clark Fork in the Bitterroot Range.

Pierre's Hole, are believed to wear a charmed life, and to be bullet proof. Of these gifted beings marvelous anecdotes are related, which are most potently believed by their fellow-savages, and sometimes almost credited by the white hunters.

II.

Rival trapping parties—Manœuvring—A desperate game—Vanderburgh and the Blackfeet—Deserted camp fire—A dark defile—An Indian ambush—A fierce melée—Fatal consequences—Fitzpatrick and Bridger—Trappers' precautions—Meeting with the Blackfeet—More fighting—Anecdote of a young Mexican and an Indian girl

WHILE CAPTAIN BONNEVILLE and his men are sojourning among the Nez Percés, on Salmon River, we will inquire after the fortunes of those doughty rivals of the Rocky Mountain and American Fur Companies, who started off for the trapping grounds to the north-northwest.

Fitzpatrick and Bridger, of the former company, as we have already shown, having received their supplies, had taken the lead, and hoped to have the first sweep of the hunting grounds. Vanderburgh and Dripps, however, the two resident partners of the opposite company, by extraordinary exertions, were enabled soon to put themselves upon their traces, and pressed forward with such speed as to overtake them just as they had reached the heart of the beaver country.[1] In fact, being ignorant of the best trapping grounds, it

---

[1] From the rendezvous at Pierre's Hole, Dripps and Vanderburgh had moved south to the Green River looking for Fontenelle. There they had joined him, got supplies, given him their furs, and then had set off after Bridger and Fitzpatrick while Fontenelle started back to Fort Union on the Upper Missouri. The movements of Bridger and Fitzpatrick, of Dripps and Vanderburgh, and W. A. Ferris (who was sent by the latter to search for the Flathead Indians) are too complicated to be summarized here. The best account, from the point of view of the American Fur Company, is in Ferris' *Life in the Rocky Mountains*, 156–79; but Ferris says nothing about the fact that the Dripps-Vanderburgh group were delib-

was their object to follow on, and profit by the superior knowledge of the other party.

Nothing could equal the chagrin of Fitzpatrick and Bridger at being dogged by their inexperienced rivals; especially after their offer to divide the country with them. They tried in every way to blind and baffle them; to steal a march upon them, or lead them on a wrong scent; but all in vain. Vanderburgh made up by activity and intelligence for his ignorance of the country; was always wary, always on the alert; discovered every movement of his rivals, however secret, and was not to be eluded or misled.

Fitzpatrick and his colleague now lost all patience; since the others persisted in following them, they determined to give them an unprofitable chase, and to sacrifice the hunting season, rather than share the products with their rivals. They accordingly took up their line of march down the course of the Missouri, keeping the main Blackfoot trail, and tramping doggedly forward, without stopping to set a single trap. The others beat the hoof after them for some time, but by degrees began to perceive that they were on a wild-goose chase, and getting into a country perfectly barren to the trapper. They now came to a halt, and bethought themselves how to make up for lost time, and improve the remainder of the season. It was thought best to divide their forces and try different trapping grounds. While Dripps went in one direction, Vanderburgh, with about fifty men, proceeded in another.[2] The latter, in his headlong march, had got into the very heart of the Blackfoot country, yet seems to have been unconscious of his danger. As his scouts were out one day, they came upon the traces of a recent band

erately trailing Bridger and Fitzpatrick. A brief account from the opposite side is by Frances Fuller Victor in *The River of the West*, 130–32, from information furnished by Joseph Meek, who was with Bridger, and from her reading of *Bonneville*. All parties moved northward into Montana and converged in the area of Three Forks.

[2] This division took place near Three Forks on September 16, 1832. Ferris reveals that Dripps followed the Rocky Mountain Fur Company while Vanderburgh went off on his own with a party of trappers that included Ferris. Bridger's group finally eluded Dripps' party, only to stumble upon Vanderburgh on October 6. Both groups soon separated, Bridger going up the Madison and Vanderburgh down.

of savages.³ There were the deserted fires still smoking, surrounded by the carcasses of buffaloes just killed. It was evident a party of Blackfeet had been frightened from their hunting camp, and had retreated, probably to seek reinforcements. The scouts hastened back to the camp, and told Vanderburgh what they had seen. He made light of the alarm, and, taking nine men with him, galloped off to reconnoitre for himself. He found the deserted hunting camp just as they had represented it; there lay the carcasses of buffaloes, partly dismembered; there were the smouldering fires, still sending up their wreaths of smoke; everything bore traces of recent and hasty retreat; and gave reason to believe that the savages were still lurking in the neighborhood. With heedless daring, Vanderburgh put himself upon their trail, to trace them to their place of concealment. It led him over prairies, and through skirts of woodland, until it entered a dark and dangerous ravine. Vanderburgh pushed in, without hesitation, followed by his little band. They soon found themselves in a gloomy dell, between steep banks overhung with trees; where the profound silence was only broken by the tramp of their own horses.

Suddenly the horrid war-whoop burst on their ears, mingled with the sharp report of rifles, and a legion of savages sprang from their concealments, yelling, and shaking their buffalo robes to frighten the horses. Vanderburgh's horse fell, mortally wounded by the first discharge. In his fall, he pinned his rider to the ground; who called in vain upon his men to assist in extricating him.⁴ One was shot down and scalped a few paces distant; most of the others were severely wounded, and sought their safety in flight. The savages approached to dispatch the unfortunate leader, as he lay strug-

[3] Ferris tells in *Life in the Rocky Mountains*, 175–76, how he and several others, reconnoitering after an Indian alarm on October 14, discovered a butchered buffalo cow and reported the discovery to their leader, Vanderburgh. Irving's narrative of what followed is very close to the facts as given by Ferris, although the latter's *Life in the Rocky Mountains* was not published until six years after *Bonneville*.

[4] Ferris wrote: "The horse of our partisan was shot dead under him, but with unexampled firmness, he stepped calmly from the lifeless animal, presented his gun at the advancing foe, and exclaimed 'boys don't run,'" 177. Moments afterward Ferris was himself shot in the shoulder; he fled, bleeding and weak, barely able to cling to his horse.

gling beneath his horse. He had still his rifle in his hand, and his pistols in his belt. The first savage that advanced received the contents of the rifle in his breast, and fell dead upon the spot; but before Vanderburgh could draw a pistol, a blow from a tomahawk laid him prostrate, and he was dispatched by repeated wounds.

Such was the fate of Major Henry Vanderburgh: one of the best and worthiest leaders of the American Fur Company; who, by his manly bearing and dauntless courage, is said to have made himseld universally popular among the bold-hearted rovers of the wilderness.[5]

Those of the little band who escaped fled in consternation to the camp, and spread direful reports of the force and ferocity of the enemy. The party, being without a head, were in complete confusion and dismay, and made a precipitate retreat, without attempting to recover the remains of their butchered leader. They made no halt until they reached the encampment of the Pends Oreilles, or Hanging-ears, where they offered a reward for the recovery of the body, but without success; it never could be found.

In the meantime Fitzpatrick and Bridger, of the Rocky Mountain Company, fared but little better than their rivals. In their eagerness to mislead them, they had betrayed themselves into danger, and got into a region infested with the Blackfeet. They soon found that foes were on the watch for them; but they were experienced in Indian warfare, and not to be surprised at night, nor drawn into an ambush in the daytime. As the evening advanced, the horses were all brought in and picketed, and a guard was stationed round the camp. At the earliest streak of day one of the leaders would mount his horse, and gallop off full speed for about half a mile; then look round for Indian trails, to ascertain whether there had been any

[5] Irving's account, which agrees very closely with Ferris', could only have been based on the report that Bonneville recorded in his journal after he heard it from Ferris himself when the latter visited Bonneville's camp early in November, less than three weeks after Vanderburgh was killed. Ferris had undoubtedly also told of the affair to the two groups of Bonneville's men whom he had met earlier while moving toward Bonneville's Salmon River headquarters. One can well imagine that the ambush and Vanderburgh's death were the subjects of much talk among the trappers and that Bonneville would not have failed to write it down in detail.

lurkers round the camp: returning slowly, he would reconnoitre every ravine and thicket where there might be an ambush. This done, he would gallop off in an opposite direction and repeat the same scrutiny. Finding all things safe, the horses would be turned loose to graze, but always under the eye of a guard.

A caution equally vigilant was observed in the march, on approaching any defile or place where an enemy might lie in wait; and scouts were always kept in the advance, or along the ridges and rising grounds on the flanks.

At length, one day, a large band of Blackfeet appeared in the open field, but in the vicinity of rocks and cliffs. They kept at a wary distance, but made friendly signs. The trappers replied in the same way, but likewise kept aloof. A small party of Indians now advanced, bearing the pipe of peace; they were met by an equal number of white men, and they formed a group, midway between the two bands, where the pipe was circulated from hand to hand, and smoked with all due ceremony. An instance of natural affection took place at this pacific meeting. Among the free trappers in the Rocky Mountain band was a spirited young Mexican, named Loretto; who, in the course of his wanderings, had ransomed a beautiful Blackfoot girl from a band of Crows by whom she had been captured. He made her his wife, after the Indian style, and she had followed his fortunes ever since, with the most devoted affection.

Among the Blackfeet warriors who advanced with the calumet of peace, she recognized a brother. Leaving her infant with Loretto, she rushed forward and threw herself upon her brother's neck; who clasped his long lost sister to his heart, with a warmth of affection but little compatible with the reputed stoicism of the savage.

While this scene was taking place, Bridger left the main body of trappers, and rode slowly towards the group of smokers, with his rifle resting across the pommel of his saddle. The chief of the Blackfeet stepped forward to meet him. From some unfortunate feeling of distrust, Bridger cocked his rifle just as the chief was extending his hand in friendship. The quick ear of the savage caught the click of the lock; in a twinkling, he grasped the barrel, forced the muzzle downward, and the contents were discharged into the earth at his feet. His next movement was to wrest the weapon from the hand of Bridger, and fell him with it to the earth. He might have found this no easy task, had not the unfortunate leader received two arrows in his back during the struggle.[6]

The chief now sprang into the vacant saddle and galloped off to his band. A wild hurry-skurry scene ensued; each party took to the banks, the rocks, and trees, to gain favorable positions, and an irregular firing was kept up on either side, without much effect. The Indian girl had been hurried off by her people, at the outbreak of the affray. She would have returned, through the dangers of the fight, to her husband and her child, but was prevented by her brother. The young Mexican saw her struggles and her agony, and heard her piercing cries. With a generous impulse, he caught up the child in his arms, rushed forward, regardless of Indian shaft or rifle, and placed it in safety upon her bosom. Even the savage heart of the Blackfoot chief was reached by this noble deed. He pronounced Loretto a madman for his temerity, but bade him depart in peace. The young Mexican hesitated: he urged to have his wife restored to him, but her brother interfered, and the countenance of the chief grew dark. The girl, he said, belonged to his tribe—she must remain with her people. Loretto would still have lingered, but his wife implored him to depart, lest his life should be endangered. It was with the greatest reluctance that he returned to his companions.

The approach of night put an end to the skirmishing fire of the adverse parties, and the savages drew off without renewing their hostilities. We cannot but remark that both in this affair and that of Pierre's Hole, the affray commenced by a hostile act on the part of white men at the moment when the Indian warrior was extending the hand of amity. In neither instance, as far as circumstances have been stated to us by different persons, do we see any reason to suspect the savage chiefs of perfidy in their overtures of friendship. They advanced in the confiding way usual among Indians when they bear the pipe of peace, and consider themselves sacred from attack. If we violate the sanctity of this ceremonial, by any

---

[6] Bridger carried one of these in his back until 1835, when Dr. Marcus Whitman, at the Green River rendezvous, operated and removed it.

hostile movement on our part, it is we who incur the charge of faithlessness; and we doubt not that in both these instances, the white men have been considered by the Blackfeet as the aggressors, and have, in consequence, been held up as men not to be trusted.

A word to conclude the romantic incident of Loretto and his Indian bride. A few months subsequent to the event just related, the young Mexican settled his accounts with the Rocky Mountain Company, and obtained his discharge. He then left his comrades and set off to rejoin his wife and child among her people; and we understand that, at the time we are writing these pages, he resides at a trading-house established of late by the American Fur Company, in the Blackfoot country, where he acts as an interpreter, and has his Indian girl with him.[7]

[7] Irving is the main source for this encounter with the Blackfeet and for the story of Loretto. Mrs. Victor adopted it in *River of the West*, 133–35, although as Joe Meek's biographer she had a different account of what led up to the skirmish:

"When it had reached the head-waters of the Missouri, on the return march, a party of trappers, including Meek, discovered a small band of Indians in a bend of the lake, and thinking the opportunity for sport a good one, commenced firing on them. The Indians, who were without guns, took to the lake for refuge, while the trappers entertained themselves with the rare amusement of keeping them in the water, by shooting at them occasionally. But . . . these were only a few stragglers from the main Blackfoot camp, which soon came up . . . putting the trappers to flight. . . . [They] fled to camp, the Indians pursuing, until the latter discovered that they had been led almost into the large camp of the whites. This occasioned a halt. . . . In the pause which ensued, one of the chiefs came out into the open space, bearing the peace pipe, and Bridger also advanced to meet him . . ." 133.

12.

A winter camp in the wilderness—Medley of trappers, hunters, and Indians—Scarcity of game—New arrangements in the camp—Detachments sent to a distance—Carelessness of the Indians when encamped—Sickness among the Indians—Excellent character of the Nez Percés—The captain's effort as a pacificator—A Nez Percé's argument in favor of war—Robberies by the Blackfeet—Long suffering of the Nez Percés—A hunter's elysium among the mountains—More robberies—The captain preaches up a crusade—The effect upon his hearers

FOR THE GREATER PART of the month of November, Captain Bonneville remained in his temporary post on Salmon River. He was now in the full enjoyment of his wishes; leading a hunter's life in the heart of the wilderness, with all its wild populace around him. Besides his own people, motley in character and costume—creole, Kentuckian, Indian, half-breed, hired trapper, and free trapper—he was surrounded by encampments of Nez Percés and Flatheads, with their droves of horses covering the hills and plains. It was, he declares, a wild and bustling scene. The hunting parties of white men and red men, continually sallying forth and returning; the groups at the various encampments, some cooking, some working, some amusing themselves at different games; the neighing of horses, the braying of asses, the resounding strokes of the axe, the sharp report of the rifle, the whoop, the halloo, and the frequent burst of laughter, all in the midst of a region suddenly roused from perfect silence and loneliness by this transient hunters' sojourn, realized, he says, the idea of a "populous solitude."

The ADVENTURES *of* CAPTAIN BONNEVILLE

The kind and genial character of the captain had, evidently, its influence on the opposite races thus fortuitously congregated together. The most perfect harmony prevailed between them. The Indians, he says, were friendly in their dispositions, and honest to the most scrupulous degree, in their intercourse with the white men. It is true they were somewhat importunate in their curiosity, and apt to be continually in the way, examining everything with keen and prying eye, and watching every movement of the white men. All this, however, was borne with great good-humor by the captain, and through his example by his men. Indeed, throughout all his transactions, he shows himself the friend of the poor Indians, and his conduct toward them is above all praise.

The Nez Percés, the Flatheads, and the Hanging-ears, pride themselves upon the number of their horses, of which they possess more in proportion than any other of the mountain tribes within the buffalo range. Many of the Indian warriors and hunters, encamped around Captain Bonneville, possess from thirty to forty horses each. Their horses are stout, well built ponies, of great wind, and capable of enduring the severest hardship and fatigue. The swiftest of them, however, are those obtained from the whites, while sufficiently young to become acclimated and inured to the rough service of the mountains.

By degrees the populousness of this encampment began to produce its inconveniences. The immense droves of horses owned by the Indians consumed the herbage of the surrounding hills; while, to drive them to any distant pasturage, in a neighborhood abounding with lurking and deadly enemies, would be to endanger the loss both of man and beast. Game, too, began to grow scarce. It was soon hunted and frightened out of the vicinity, and though the Indians made a wide circuit through the mountains in the hope of driving the buffalo toward the cantonment, their expedition was unsuccessful. It was plain that so large a party could not subsist themselves there, nor in any one place throughout the winter. Captain Bonneville, therefore, altered his whole arrangements. He detached fifty men[1] towards the south to winter upon Snake River, and to trap

[1] This brigade was under the leadership of Joseph Reddeford Walker. From

The ADVENTURES of CAPTAIN BONNEVILLE

about its waters in the spring, with orders to rejoin him in the month of July, at Horse Creek, in Green River valley, which he had fixed upon as the general rendezvous of his company for the ensuing year.

Of all his late party, he now retained with him merely a small number of free trappers, with whom he intended to sojourn among

bits of information scattered through Ferris' *Life in the Rocky Mountains*, it is possible to ascertain Walker's approximate movements and those of some of his men. On November 7, 1832, a group of the Rocky Mountain Fur Company had arrived at Bonneville's camp. They left some days later to establish winter quarters on what Ferris calls the Little Salmon River (Pahsimeroi River on modern maps), a small tributary of the Salmon. Walker and his men left about the same time to winter near the Snake River south of Bonneville's Salmon River camp. Ferris decided to go with Walker as far as the Snake and then leave him to join Dripps at his winter camp near Henry's Fork. They followed an Indian trail along the Salmon in a south south-westerly direction as far as the Little Salmon (Pahsimeroi), at the lower end of which they overtook the Rocky Mountain Fur Company group, and ascended it. When the latter detachment stopped to establish winter camp, Walker's group continued south to what Ferris calls Days Creek (now Little Lost River), where they met Fitzpatrick and one other unidentified trapper. Fitzpatrick now joined the Walker party, intending to go with Ferris to locate Dripps in order to transact some business. Still moving south, they proceeded along Gordiez River (modern Big Lost River), and on December 10 reached the Snake River opposite the Portneuf River. On December 11 they forded the Snake and camped on the east side of the Portneuf (near modern Pocatello, Idaho). Here they learned from an unnamed trapper that four of the men whom Bonneville had sent under Matthieu to the Bear River with horses the previous July had been killed by Indians in November; the remainder of this detachment was now wintering in Cache Valley (south of modern Logan, Utah).

On December 17, Ferris separated from Walker's detachment, which he left on the Portneuf, and succeeded in rejoining Dripps near Henry's Fork. A week later, December 24, he went back to the Blackfoot River (east of the Portneuf) to rejoin some men he had left there with baggage, and ran into Walker again on that date.

We hear no more from Ferris of any of Bonneville's men until May 17, 1833, when Ferris met a party of them on the Salt River (near the Idaho-Wyoming line south of the Snake). From them he learned that Walker was now trapping along the Bear River, presumably north of Bear Lake. Two days later Dripps and Ferris, plus the detachment from Walker's party, raised camp and started for the 1833 rendezvous, which had been set to occur on Horse Creek near Bonneville's fort. The Dripps company took the long route via Pierre's Hole, Teton Pass, the Gros Ventre River, and Green River. When Ferris left them to go ahead to Horse Creek, which he reached on June 7, he found Walker already there. Walker's early arrival can be explained on the assumption that he may have traveled east over the Salt Range to the Green and then north to Horse Creek, a route apparently unknown to Dripps and Ferris. See Ferris, *Life in the Rocky Mountains*, 187–202.

the Nez Percés and Flatheads, and adopt the Indian mode of moving with the game and grass. Those bands, in effect, shortly afterward broke up their encampments and set off for a less beaten neighborhood. Captain Bonneville remained behind for a few days, that he might secretly prepare *caches*, in which to deposit everything not required for current use. Thus lightened of all superfluous encumbrance, he set off on the 20th of November to rejoin his Indian allies. He found them encamped in a secluded part of the country, at the head of a small stream. Considering themselves out of all danger in this sequestered spot, from their old enemies, the Blackfeet, their encampment manifested the most negligent security. Their lodges were scattered in every direction, and their horses covered every hill for a great distance round, grazing upon the upland bunch grass, which grew in great abundance, and though dry, retained its nutritious properties, instead of losing them, like other grasses, in the autumn.

When the Nez Percés, Flatheads, and Pends Oreilles are encamped in a dangerous neighborhood, says Captain Bonneville, the greatest care is taken of their horses, those prime articles of Indian wealth, and objects of Indian depredation. Each warrior has his horse tied by one foot at night to a stake planted before his lodge. Here they remain until broad daylight; by that time the young men of the camp are already ranging over the surrounding hills. Each family then drives its horses to some eligible spot, where they are left to graze unattended. A young Indian repairs occasionally to the pasture to give them water, and to see that all is well. So accustomed are the horses to this management, that they keep together in the pasture where they have been left. As the sun sinks behind the hills, they may be seen moving from all points toward the camp, where they surrender themselves to be tied up for the night. Even in situations of danger, the Indians rarely set guards over their camp at night, intrusting that office entirely to their vigilant and well-trained dogs.

In an encampment, however, of such fancied security as that in which Captain Bonneville found his Indian friends, much of these precautions with respect to their horses are omitted. They merely drive them, at nightfall, to some sequestered little dell, and leave them there, at perfect liberty, until the morning.

One object of Captain Bonneville in wintering among these Indians was to procure a supply of horses against the spring. They were, however, extremely unwilling to part with any, and it was with great difficulty that he purchased, at the rate of twenty dollars each, a few for the use of some of his free trappers, who were on foot, and dependent on him for their equipment.

In this encampment Captain Bonneville remained from the 21st of November to the 9th of December. During this period the thermometer ranged from thirteen to forty-two degrees. There were occasional falls of snow; but it generally melted away almost immediately, and the tender blades of new grass began to shoot up among the old. On the 7th of December, however, the thermometer fell to seven degrees.

The reader will recollect that, on distributing his forces, when in Green River valley, Captain Bonneville had detached a party, headed by a leader of the name of Matthieu, with all the weak and disabled horses, to sojourn about Bear River, meet the Shoshonie bands, and afterward to rejoin him at his winter camp on Salmon River.

More than sufficient time had elapsed, yet Matthieu failed to make his appearance, and uneasiness began to be felt on his account. Captain Bonneville sent out four men, to range the country through which he would have to pass, and endeavor to get some information concerning him; for his route lay across the great Snake River plain, which spreads itself out like an Arabian desert, and on which a cavalcade could be descried at a great distance. The scouts soon returned, having proceeded no further than the edge of the plain, pretending that their horses were lame; but it was evident they had feared to venture, with so small a force, into these exposed and dangerous regions.

A disease, which Captain Bonneville supposed to be pneumonia, now appeared among the Indians, carrying off numbers of them, after an illness of three or four days. The worthy captain acted as physician, prescribing profuse sweatings and copious bleedings, and uniformly with success, if the patient were subsequently treated with proper care. In extraordinary cases, the poor savages called in the aid of their own doctors or conjurors, who officiated with great noise and mummery, but with little benefit. Those who died during this epidemic were buried in graves, after the manner of the whites, but without any regard to the direction of the head. It is a fact worthy of notice that, while this malady made such ravages among the natives, not a single white man had the slightest symptom of it.

A familiar intercourse of some standing with the Pierced-nose and Flathead Indians had now convinced Captain Bonneville of their amicable and inoffensive character; he began to take a strong interest in them, and conceived the idea of becoming a pacificator, and healing the deadly feud between them and the Blackfeet, in which they were so deplorably the sufferers. He proposed the matter to some of the leaders, and urged that they should meet the Blackfeet chiefs in a grand pacific conference, offering to send two of his men to the enemy's camp with pipe, tobacco, and flag of truce, to negotiate the proposed meeting.

The Nez Percés and Flathead sages, upon this, held a council of war of two days' duration, in which there was abundance of hard smoking and long talking, and both eloquence and tobacco were nearly exhausted. At length they came to a decision to reject the worthy captain's proposition, and upon pretty substantial grounds, as the reader may judge.

"War," said the chiefs, "is a bloody business, and full of evil; but it keeps the eyes of the chiefs always open, and makes the limbs of the young men strong and supple. In war, every one is on the alert. If we see a trail, we know it must be an enemy; if the Blackfeet come to us, we know it is for war, and we are ready. Peace, on the other hand, sounds no alarm; the eyes of the chiefs are closed in sleep, and the young men are sleek and lazy. The horses stray into the mountains; the women and their little babes go about alone. But the heart of a Blackfoot is a lie, and his tongue is a trap. If he says peace, it is to deceive; he comes to us as a brother: he smokes his pipe with us; but when he sees us weak, and off our guard, he will slay and steal. We will have no such peace; let there be war!"

With this reasoning, Captain Bonneville was fain to acquiesce; but, since the sagacious Flatheads and their allies were content to remain in a state of warfare, he wished them, at least, to exercise the boasted vigilance which war was to produce, and to keep their eyes open. He represented to them the impossibility, that two such considerable clans could move about the country without leaving trails by which they might be traced. Besides, among the Blackfeet braves were several Nez Percés, who had been taken prisoners in early youth, adopted by their captors, and trained up and imbued with warlike and predatory notions; these had lost all sympathies with their native tribe, and would be prone to lead the enemy to their secret haunts. He exhorted them, therefore, to keep upon the alert, and never to remit their vigilance, while within the range of so crafty and cruel a foe. All these counsels were lost upon his easy and simple-minded hearers. A careless indifference reigned throughout their encampments, and their horses were permitted to range the hills at night in perfect freedom. Captain Bonneville had his own horses brought in at night, and properly picketed and guarded. The evil he apprehended soon took place. In a single night, a swoop was made through the neighboring pastures by the Blackfeet, and eighty-six of the finest horses carried off. A whip and a rope were left in a conspicuous situation by the robbers, as a taunt to the simpletons they had unhorsed.

Long before sunrise, the news of this calamity spread like wildfire through the different encampments. Captain Bonneville, whose own horses remained safe at their pickets, watched in momentary expectation of an outbreak of warriors, Pierced-nose and Flathead, in furious pursuit of the marauders; but no such thing—they contented themselves with searching diligently over hill and dale, to glean up such horses as had escaped the hands of the marauders, and then resigned themselves to their loss with the most exemplary quiescence.

Some, it is true, who were entirely unhorsed, set out on a begging visit to their cousins, as they called them, the Lower Nez Percés, who inhabit the lower country about the Columbia, and possess horses in abundance. To these they repair when in difficulty, and seldom fail, by dint of begging and bartering, to get themselves once more mounted on horseback.

Game had now become scarce in the neighborhood of the camp, and it was necessary, according to Indian custom, to move off to a less beaten ground. Captain Bonneville proposed the Horse Prairie;[2] but his Indian friends objected that many of the Nez Percés had gone to visit their cousins, and that the whites were few in number, so that their united force was not sufficient to venture upon the buffalo grounds, which were infested by bands of Blackfeet.

They now spoke of a place at no great distance, which they represented as a perfect hunter's elysium. It was on the right branch, or head stream of the river, locked up among cliffs and precipices, where there was no danger from roving bands, and where the Blackfeet dare not enter. Here, they said, the elk abounded, and the mountain sheep were to be seen trooping upon the rocks and hills. A little distance beyond it, also, herds of buffalo were to be met with, out of range of danger. Thither they proposed to move their camp.

The proposition pleased the captain, who was desirous, through the Indians, of becoming acquainted with all the secret places of the land. Accordingly, on the 9th of December, they struck their tents, and moved forward by short stages, as many of the Indians were yet feeble from the late malady.

Following up the right fork of the river, they came to where it entered a deep gorge of the mountains, up which lay the secluded region so much vaunted by the Indians. Captain Bonneville halted, and encamped for three days, before entering the gorge. In the meantime, he detached five of his free trappers to scour the hills, and kill as many elk as possible, before the main body should enter, as they would then be soon frightened away by the various Indian hunting parties.

While thus encamped, they were still liable to the marauds of the Blackfeet, and Captain Bonneville admonished his Indian friends to be upon their guard. The Nez Percés, however, notwithstanding their recent loss, were still careless of their horses; merely driving

[2] East of the Bitterroot Range and almost due east of where Bonneville was camped.

them to some secluded spot, and leaving them there for the night, without setting any guard upon them. The consequence was a second swoop, in which forty-one were carried off. This was borne with equal philosophy with the first, and no effort was made either to recover the horses, or to take vengeance on the thieves.

The Nez Percés, however, grew more cautious with respect to their remaining horses, driving them regularly to the camp every evening and fastening them to pickets. Captain Bonneville, however, told them that this was not enough. It was evident they were dogged by a daring and persevering enemy, who was encouraged by past impunity; they should, therefore, take more than usual precautions, and post a guard at night over their cavalry. They could not, however, be persuaded to depart from their usual custom. The horse once picketed, the care of the owner was over for the night, and he slept profoundly. None waked in the camp but the gamblers, who, absorbed in their play, were more difficult to be roused to external circumstances than even the sleepers.

The Blackfeet are bold enemies, and fond of hazardous exploits. The band that were hovering about the neighborhood, finding that they had such pacific people to deal with, redoubled their daring. The horses being now picketed before the lodges, a number of Blackfeet scouts penetrated in the early part of the night into the very centre of the camp. Here they went about among the lodges, as calmly and deliberately as if at home, quietly cutting loose the horses that stood picketed by the lodges of their sleeping owners. One of these prowlers, more adventurous than the rest, approached a fire, round which a group of Nez Percés were gambling with the most intense eagerness. Here he stood for some time, muffled up in his robe, peering over the shoulders of the players, watching the changes of their countenances and the fluctuations of the game. So completely engrossed were they, that the presence of this muffled eaves-dropper was unnoticed and having executed his bravado, he retired undiscovered.

Having cut loose as many horses as they could conveniently carry off, the Blackfeet scouts rejoined their comrades, and all remained patiently round the camp. By degrees, the horses, finding themselves at liberty, took their route toward their customary grazing ground. As they emerged from the camp, they were silently taken possession of, until, having secured about thirty, the Blackfeet sprang on their backs and scampered off. The clatter of hoofs startled the gamblers from their game. They gave the alarm, which soon roused the sleepers from every lodge. Still all was quiescent; no marshalling of forces, no saddling of steeds and dashing off in pursuit, no talk of retribution for their repeated outrages. The patience of Captain Bonneville was at length exhausted. He had played the part of a pacificator without success; he now altered his tone, and resolved, if possible to rouse their war spirit.

Accordingly, convoking their chiefs, he inveighed against their craven policy, and urged the necessity of vigorous and retributive measures, that would check the confidence and presumption of their enemies, if not inspire them with awe. For this purpose, he advised that a war party should be immediately sent off on the trail of the marauders, to follow them, if necessary, into the very heart of the Blackfoot country, and not to leave them until they had taken signal vengeance. Beside this, he recommended the organization of minor war parties, to make reprisals to the extent of the losses sustained. "Unless you rouse yourselves from your apathy," said he, "and strike some bold and decisive blow, you will cease to be considered men, or objects of manly warfare. The very squaws and children of the Blackfeet will be sent against you, while their warriors reserve themselves for nobler antagonists."

This harangue had evidently a momentary effect upon the pride of the hearers. After a short pause, however, one of the orators arose. It was bad, he said, to go to war for mere revenge. The Great Spirit had given them a heart for peace, not for war. They had lost horses, it was true, but they could easily get others from their cousins, the Lower Nez Percés, without incurring any risk; whereas, in war they should lose men, who were not so readily replaced. As to their late losses, an increased watchfulness would prevent any more misfortunes of the kind. He disapproved, therefore, of all hostile measures; and all the other chiefs concurred in his opinion.

Captain Bonneville again took up the point. "It is true," said he,

Oregon Historical Collections

NATHANIEL WYETH
Founder of Fort Hall

SOUTH PASS
Bonneville Was the First to Take Wagons Here.
Monuments to Narcissa Whitman and Elizabeth Spalding;
Old Wagon Tracks May Still Be Seen

14.

The party enters the mountain gorge—A wild fastness
among hills—Mountain mutton—Peace and plenty—
The amorous trapper—A piebald wedding—A free
trapper's wife—Her gala equipments—Christmas
in the wilderness

ON THE 19TH of December Captain Bonneville and his confederate Indians raised their camp, and entered the narrow gorge made by the north fork of Salmon River.[1] Up this lay the secure and plenteous hunting region so temptingly described by the Indians.

Since leaving Green River the plains had invariably been of loose sand or coarse gravel, and the rocky formation of the mountains of primitive limestone. The rivers, in general, were skirted with willows and bitter cotton-wood trees, and the prairies covered with wormwood. In the hollow breast of the mountains which they were now penetrating, the surrounding heights were clothed with pine; while the declivities of the lower hills afforded abundance of bunch grass for the horses.

As the Indians had represented, they were now in a natural fastness of the mountains, the ingress and egress of which was by a deep gorge, so narrow, rugged, and difficult, as to prevent secret approach or rapid retreat, and to admit of easy defence. The Blackfeet, therefore, refrained from venturing in after the Nez Percés, awaiting a better chance, when they should once more emerge into the open country.

[1] Bonneville had moved between fifteen and twenty miles north along the Salmon River and was now ascending the fork that enters at the point where the main stream turns abruptly west.

Captain Bonneville soon found that the Indians had not exaggerated the advantages of this region. Besides numerous gangs of elk, large flocks of the ahsahta or bighorn, the mountain sheep, were to be seen bounding among the precipices. These simple animals were easily circumvented and destroyed. A few hunters may surround a flock and kill as many as they please. Numbers were daily brought into camp, and the flesh of those which were young and fat, was extolled as superior to the finest mutton.

Here, then, there was a cessation from toil, from hunger, and alarm. Past ills and dangers were forgotten. The hunt, the game, the song, the story, the rough though good-humored joke, made time pass joyously away, and plenty and security reigned throughout the camp.

Idleness and ease, it is said, lead to love, and love to matrimony, in civilized life, and the same process takes place in the wilderness. Filled with good cheer and mountain mutton, one of the free trappers began to repine at the solitude of his lodge, and to experience the force of that great law of nature, "it is not meet for man to live alone."

After a night of grave cogitation, he repaired to Kowsoter, the Pierced-nose chief; and unfolded to him the secret workings of his bosom.

"I want," said he, "a wife. Give me one from among your tribe. Not a young, giddy-pated girl, that will think of nothing but flaunting and finery, but a sober, discreet, hard-working squaw; one that will share my lot without flinching, however hard it may be; that can take care of my lodge, and be a companion and a helpmate to me in the wilderness." Kowsoter promised to look round among the females of his tribe, and procure such a one as he desired. Two days were requisite for the search. At the expiration of these, Kowsoter called at his lodge and informed him that he would bring his bride to him in the course of the afternoon. He kept his word. At the appointed time he approached, leading the bride, a comely copper-colored dame, attired in her Indian finery. Her father, mother, brothers by the half dozen, and cousins by the score, all followed on to grace the ceremony, and greet the new and important relative.

The trapper received his new and numerous family connection with proper solemnity; he placed his bride beside him, and, filling the pipe, the great symbol of peace, with his best tobacco, took two or three whiffs, then handed it to the chief, who transferred it to the father of the bride, from whom it was passed on from hand to hand and mouth to mouth of the whole circle of kinsmen round the fire, all maintaining the most profound and becoming silence.

After several pipes had been filled and emptied in this solemn ceremonial, the chief addressed the bride; detailing, at considerable length, the duties of a wife; which, among Indians, are little less onerous than those of the pack-horse; this done, he turned to her friends, and congratulated them upon the great alliance she had made. They showed a due sense of their good fortune, especially when the nuptial presents came to be distributed among the chiefs and relatives, amounting to about one hundred and eighty dollars. The company soon retired, and now the worthy trapper found, indeed, that he had no green girl to deal with; for the knowing dame at once assumed the style and dignity of a trapper's wife, taking possession of the lodge as her undisputed empire; arranging everything according to her own taste and habitudes; and appearing as much at home, and on as easy terms with the trapper, as if they had been man and wife for years.

We have already given a picture of a free trapper and his horse, as furnished by Captain Bonneville: we shall here subjoin, as a companion picture, his description of a free trapper's wife, that the reader may have a correct idea of the kind of blessing the worthy hunter in question had invoked to solace him in the wilderness.

"The free trapper, while a bachelor, has no greater pet than his horse; but the moment he takes a wife, (a sort of brevet rank in matrimony occasionally bestowed upon some Indian fair one, like the heroes of ancient chivalry, in the open field,) he discovers that he has a still more fanciful and capricious animal on which to lavish his expenses.

"No sooner does an Indian belle experience this promotion, than all her notions at once rise and expand to the dignity of her situation; and the purse of her lover, and his credit into the bargain, are taxed to the utmost to fit her out in becoming style. The wife of a free trapper to be equipped and arrayed like any ordinary and undistinguished squaw? Perish the grovelling thought! In the first place, she must have a horse for her own riding; but no jaded, sorry, earth-spirited hack; such as is sometimes assigned by an Indian husband for the transportation of his squaw and her pappooses: the wife of a free trapper must have the most beautiful animal she can lay her eyes on. And then, as to his decoration: headstall, breast-bands, saddle and crupper, are lavishly embroidered with beads, and hung with thimbles, hawks' bells, and bunches of ribands. From each side of the saddle hangs an *esquimoot*, a sort of pocket, in which she bestows the residue of her trinkets and knick-knacks, which cannot be crowded on the decoration of her horse or herself. Over this she folds, with great care, a drapery of scarlet and bright-colored calicoes, and now considers the caparison of her steed complete.

"As to her own person, she is even still more extravagant. Her hair, esteemed beautiful in proportion to its length, is carefully plaited, and made to fall with seeming negligence over either breast. Her riding hat is stuck full of parti-colored feathers; her robe, fashioned somewhat after that of the whites, is of red, green, and sometimes gray cloth, but always of the finest texture that can be procured. Her leggins and moccasons are of the most beautiful and expensive workmanship, and fitted neatly to the foot and ankle, which with the Indian woman are generally well formed and delicate. Then as to jewelry: in the way of finger-rings, ear-rings, necklaces, and other female glories, nothing within reach of the trapper's means is omitted, that can tend to impress the beholder with an idea of the lady's high estate. To finish the whole, she selects from among her blankets of various dyes, one of some glowing color, and throwing it over her shoulders with a native grace, vaults into the saddle of her gay, prancing steed, and is ready to follow her mountaineer 'to the last gasp with love and loyalty.'"

Such is the general picture of the free trapper's wife, given by Captain Bonneville; how far it applied in its details to the one in question does not altogether appear, though it would seem from the outset of her connubial career, that she was ready to avail herself of all the pomp and circumstance of her new condition. It is worthy of mention, that wherever there are several wives of free trappers in a camp, the keenest rivalry exists between them, to the sore detriment of their husbands' purses. Their whole time is expended, and their ingenuity tasked by endeavors to eclipse each other in dress and decoration. The jealousies and heart-burnings thus occasioned among these, so-styled, children of nature, are equally intense with those of the rival leaders of style and fashion in the luxurious abodes of civilized life.

The genial festival of Christmas, which throughout all Christendom lights up the fireside of home with mirth and jollity, followed hard upon the wedding just described. Though far from kindred and friends, Captain Bonneville and his handful of free trappers were not disposed to suffer the festival to pass unenjoyed; they were in a region of good cheer, and were disposed to be joyous; so it was determined to "light up the yule log," and celebrate a merry Christmas in the heart of the wilderness.

On Christmas day, accordingly, they began their rude fêtes and rejoicings. In the course of the night the free trappers surrounded the lodge of the Pierced-nose chief, and in lieu of Christmas carols, saluted him with *feu de joie*.

Kowsoter received it in a truly Christian spirit, and after a speech, in which he expressed his high gratification at the honor done him, invited the whole company to a feast on the following day. His invitation was gladly accepted. A Christmas dinner in the wigwam of an Indian chief! There was novelty in the idea. Not one failed to be present. The banquet was served up in primitive style: skins of various kinds, nicely dressed for the occasion, were spread upon the ground; upon these were heaped up abundance of venison, elk meat, and mountain mutton; with various bitter roots, which the Indians use as condiments.

After a short prayer, the company all seated themselves cross-legged, in Turkish fashion, to the banquet, which passed off with great hilarity. After which various games of strength and agility, by both white men and Indians, closed the Christmas festivities.

15.

A hunt after hunters—Hungry times—A voracious repast—Wintry weather—Godin's River—Splendid winter scene on the great lava plain of Snake River—Severe travelling and tramping in the snow—Manœuvres of a solitary Indian horseman—Encampment on Snake River—Bannack Indians—The Horse chief—His charmed life

THE CONTINUED ABSENCE of Matthieu and his party had, by this time, caused great uneasiness in the mind of Captain Bonneville; and, finding there was no dependence to be placed upon the perseverance and courage of scouting parties in so perilous a quest, he determined to set out himself on the search, and to keep on until he should ascertain something of the object of his solicitude.

Accordingly, on the 26th December, he left the camp, accompanied by thirteen stark trappers and hunters, all well mounted and armed for dangerous enterprise. On the following morning they passed out at the head of the mountain gorge, and sallied forth into the open plain. As they confidently expected a brush with the Blackfeet, or some other predatory horde, they moved with great circumspection, and kept vigilant watch in their encampments.

In the course of another day they left the main branch of Salmon River, and proceeded south toward a pass called John Day's defile.[1] It was severe and arduous travelling. The plains were swept by keen and bitter blasts of wintry wind; the ground was generally covered with snow, game was scarce, so that hunger generally pre-

[1] They probably went up the Salmon River to the Little Salmon (Pahsimeroi), then to Day's Creek (Little Lost River) via John Day's Defile.

vailed in the camp, while the want of pasturage soon began to manifest itself in the declining vigor of the horses.

The party had scarcely encamped on the afternoon of the 28th, when two of the hunters who had sallied forth in quest of game came galloping back in great alarm. While hunting they had perceived a party of savages, evidently manœuvring to cut them off from the camp; and nothing had saved them from being entrapped but the speed of their horses.

These tidings struck dismay into the camp. Captain Bonneville endeavored to reassure his men by representing the position of their encampment, and its capability of defence. He then ordered the horses to be driven in and picketed, and threw up a rough breastwork of fallen trunks of trees and the vegetable rubbish of the wilderness. Within this barrier was maintained a vigilant watch throughout the night, which passed away without alarm. At early dawn they scrutinized the surrounding plain, to discover whether any enemies had been lurking about during the night: not a footprint, however, was to be discovered in the coarse gravel with which the plain was covered.

Hunger now began to cause more uneasiness than the apprehensions of surrounding enemies. After marching a few miles they encamped at the foot of a mountain, in hopes of finding buffalo. It was not until the next day that they discovered a pair of fine bulls on the edge of the plain, among rocks and ravines. Having now been two days and a half without a mouthful of food, they took especial care that these animals should not escape them. While some of the surest marksmen advanced cautiously with their rifles into the rough ground, four of the best mounted horsemen took their stations in the plain, to run the bulls down should they only be maimed.

The buffalo were wounded, and set off in headlong flight. The half-famished horses were too weak to overtake them on the frozen ground, but succeeded in driving them on the ice, where they slipped and fell, and were easily dispatched. The hunters loaded themselves with beef for present and future supply, and then returned and encamped at the last night's fire. Here they passed the remainder of the day, cooking and eating with a voracity proportioned to previous starvation; forgetting in the hearty revel of the moment the certain dangers with which they were environed.

The cravings of hunger being satisfied, they now began to debate about their further progress. The men were much disheartened by the hardships they had already endured. Indeed, two who had been in the rear guard, taking advantage of their position, had deserted and returned to the lodges of the Nez Percés. The prospect ahead was enough to stagger the stoutest heart. They were in the dead of winter. As far as the eye could reach the wild landscape was wrapped in snow; which was evidently deepening as they advanced. Over this they would have to toil, with the icy wind blowing in their faces: their horses might give out through want of pasturage; and they themselves must expect intervals of horrible famine like that they had already experienced.

With Captain Bonneville, however, perseverance was a matter of pride; and, having undertaken this enterprise, nothing could turn him back until it was accomplished: though he declares that, had he anticipated the difficulties and sufferings which attended it, he should have flinched from the undertaking.

Onward, therefore, the little band urged their way, keeping along the course of a stream called John Day's Creek.[2] The cold was so intense that they had frequently to dismount and travel on foot, lest they should freeze in their saddles. The days, which, at this season, are short enough even in the open prairies, were narrowed to a few hours by the high mountains, which allowed the travellers but a brief enjoyment of the cheering rays of the sun. The snow was, generally, at least twenty inches in depth, and in many places much more: those who dismounted had to beat their way with toilsome steps. Eight miles were considered a good day's journey. The horses were almost famished; for the herbage was covered by the deep snow, so that they had nothing to subsist upon but scanty wisps of the dry bunch grass which peered above the surface, and the small branches and twigs of frozen willows and wormwood.

In this way they urged their slow and painful course to the south down John Day's Creek, until it lost itself in a swamp.[3] Here they

[2] Little Lost River.

The Adventures of Captain Bonneville

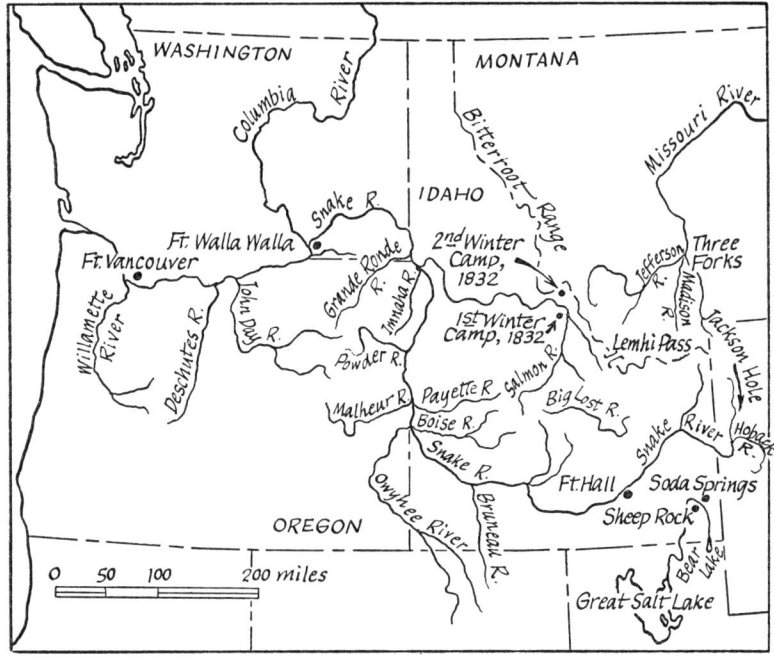

The Pacific Northwest

encamped upon the ice among stiffened willows, where they were obliged to beat down and clear away the snow to procure pasturage for their horses.

Hence, they toiled on to Godin's River;[4] so called after an Iroquois hunter in the service of Sublette, who was murdered there by the Blackfeet.[5] Many of the features of this remote wilderness are

---

[3] Little Lost River Sinks on the northern edge of the Snake River Plain.

[4] Big Lost River, which forms a big elbow south of Little Lost River Sinks before disappearing in the lava. Godin (or Goddin's) River was also known to trappers as Gordiez River.

[5] Godin has been identified as Thyery Godin (or Goddin), whose death occurred in 1829 or 1830. Townsend states that the creek was "so called from a Canadian of that name who was killed in this country by the Blackfeet" *Narrative*, 114. Alexander Ross, on the other hand, said it was named for one of his men who had discovered it; see *Fur Hunters of the Far West* (ed. by Kenneth A. Spaulding), 248.

thus named after scenes of violence and bloodshed that occurred to the early pioneers. It was an act of filial vengeance on the part of Godin's son, Antoine, that, as the reader may recollect, brought on the recent battle at Pierre's Hole.

From Godin's River, Captain Bonneville and his followers came out upon the plain of the Three Butes,[6] so called from three singular and isolated hills that rise from the midst. It is a part of the great desert of Snake River, one of the most remarkable tracts beyond the mountains. Could they have experienced a respite from their sufferings and anxieties, the immense landscape spread out before them was calculated to inspire admiration. Winter has its beauties and glories, as well as summer; and Captain Bonneville had the soul to appreciate them.

Far away, says he, over the vast plains, and up the steep sides of the lofty mountains, the snow lay spread in dazzling whiteness: and whenever the sun emerged in the morning above the giant peaks, or burst forth from among clouds in his mid-day course, mountain and dell, glazed rock and frosted tree, glowed and sparkled with surpassing lustre. The tall pines seemed sprinkled with a silver dust, and the willows, studded with minute icicles reflecting the prismatic rays, brought to mind the fairy trees conjured up by the caliph's story-teller, to adorn his vale of diamonds.

The poor wanderers, however, nearly starved with hunger and cold, were in no mood to enjoy the glories of these brilliant scenes; though they stamped pictures on their memory which have been recalled with delight in more genial situations.

Encamping at the west bute, they found a place swept by the winds, so that it was bare of snow, and there was abundance of bunch grass. Here the horses were turned loose to graze throughout the night. Though for once they had ample pasturage, yet the keen winds were so intense, that in the morning, a mule was found frozen to death. The trappers gathered round and mourned over him as over a cherished friend. They feared their half-famished horses

[6] Bonneville had traversed the same route that Walker had covered earlier in the month. These buttes appear on both of Bonneville's maps. Today they are known as Twin Buttes and Big Southern Butte.

would soon share his fate, for there seemed scarce blood enough left in their veins to withstand the freezing cold. To beat the way further through the snow with these enfeebled animals seemed next to impossible; and despondency began to creep over their hearts, when, fortunately, they discovered a trail made by some hunting party. Into this they immediately entered, and proceeded with less difficulty. Shortly afterward, a fine buffalo bull came bounding across the snow, and was instantly brought down by the hunters. A fire was soon blazing and crackling, and an ample repast soon cooked, and sooner dispatched, after which they made some further progress and then encamped. One of the men reached the camp nearly frozen to death; but good cheer and a blazing fire gradually restored life, and put his blood in circulation.

Having now a beaten path, they proceeded the next morning with more facility; indeed, the snow decreased in depth as they receded from the mountains, and the temperature became more mild. In the course of the day, they discovered a solitary horseman hovering at a distance before them on the plain. They spurred on to overtake him; but he was better mounted on a fresher steed, and kept at a wary distance, reconnoitring them with evident distrust; for the wild dress of the free trappers, their leggins, blankets, and cloth caps garnished with fur and topped off with feathers, even their very elf-locks and weather-bronzed complexions, gave them the look of Indians rather than white men, and made him mistake them for a war party of some hostile tribe.

After much manœuvring, the wild horseman was at length brought to a parley; but even then he conducted himself with the caution of a knowing prowler of the prairies. Dismounting from his horse, and using him as a breastwork, he levelled his gun across his back, and, thus prepared for defence like a wary cruiser upon the high seas, he permitted himself to be approached within speaking distance.

He proved to be an Indian of the Bannack tribe, belonging to a band at no great distance. It was some time before he could be persuaded that he was conversing with a party of white men, and induced to lay aside his reserve and join them. He then gave them the interesting intelligence that there were two companies of white men encamped in the neighborhood.[7] This was cheering news to Captain Bonneville; who hoped to find in one of them the long-sought party of Matthieu. Pushing forward, therefore, with renovated spirits, he reached Snake River by nightfall, and there fixed his encampment.

Early the next morning (13th January, 1833), diligent search was made about the neighborhood for traces of the reported parties of white men. An encampment was soon discovered, about four miles further up the river; in which Captain Bonneville, to his great joy, found two of Matthieu's men, from whom he learned that the rest of his party would be there in the course of a few days. It was a matter of great pride and self-gratulation to Captain Bonneville that he had thus accomplished his dreary and doubtful enterprise; and he determined to pass some time in this encampment, both to await the return of Matthieu, and to give needful repose to men and horses.

It was, in fact, one of the most eligible and delightful wintering grounds in that whole range of country. The Snake River here wound its devious way between low banks through the great plain of the Three Butes; and was bordered by wide and fertile meadows. It was studded with islands, which, like the alluvial bottoms, were covered with groves of cotton-wood, thickets of willow, tracts of good lowland grass, and abundance of green rushes. The adjacent plains were so vast in extent, that no single band of Indians could drive the buffalo out of them; nor was the snow of sufficient depth to give any serious inconvenience. Indeed, during the sojourn of Captain Bonneville in this neighborhood, which was in the heart of winter, he found the weather, with the exception of a few cold and stormy days, generally mild and pleasant; freezing a little at night, but invariably thawing with the morning's sun—resembling the spring weather in the middle parts of the United States.

The lofty range of the Three Tetons, those great landmarks of the Rocky Mountains, rising in the east, and circling away to the north and west of the great plain of Snake River, and the moun-

[7] One of these would have been Walker's.

tains of Salt River and Portneuf toward the south, catch the earliest falls of snow. Their white robes lengthen as the winter advances, and spread themselves far into the plain, driving the buffalo in herds to the banks of the river in quest of food; where they are easily slain in great numbers.

Such were the palpable advantages of this winter encampment; added to which, it was secure from the prowlings and plunderings of any petty band of roving Blackfeet; the difficulties of retreat rendering it unwise for those crafty depredators to venture an attack, unless with an overpowering force.

About ten miles below the encampment lay the Bannack Indians; numbering about one hundred and twenty lodges. They are brave and cunning warriors, and deadly foes of the Blackfeet; whom they easily overcome in battles where their forces are equal. They are not vengeful and enterprising in warfare, however; seldom sending war parties to attack the Blackfeet towns, but contenting themselves with defending their own territories and house. About one-third of their warriors are armed with fusees; the rest with bows and arrows.

As soon as the spring opens, they move down the right bank of Snake River, and encamp at the heads of the Boisée and Payette. Here their horses wax fat on good pasturage, while the tribe revels in plenty upon the flesh of deer, elk, bear, and beaver. They then descend a little further, and are met by the Lower Nez Percés, with whom they trade for horses; giving in exchange beaver, buffalo, and buffalo robes. Hence they strike upon the tributary streams on the left bank of Snake River, and encamp at the rise of the Portneuf and Blackfoot streams, in the buffalo range. Their horses, although of the Nez Percé breed, are inferior to the parent stock, from being ridden at too early an age; being often bought when but two years old, and immediately put to hard work. They have fewer horses, also, than most of these migratory tribes.

At the time that Captain Bonneville came into the neighborhood of these Indians, they were all in mourning for their chief, surnamed The Horse. This chief was said to possess a charmed life, or rather, to be invulnerable to lead; no bullet having ever hit him, though he had been in repeated battles, and often shot at by the surest marksmen. He had shown great magnanimity in his intercourse with the white men. One of the great men of his family had been slain in an attack upon a band of trappers passing through the territories of his tribe. Vengeance had been sworn by the Bannacks; but The Horse interfered, declaring himself the friend of white men, and, having great influence and authority among his people, he compelled them to forego all vindictive plans, and to conduct themselves amicably whenever they came in contact with the traders.

This chief had bravely fallen in resisting an attack made by the Blackfeet upon his tribe, while encamped at the head of Godin's River. His fall in nowise lessened the faith of his people in his charmed life; for they declared that it was not a bullet which laid him low, but a bit of horn which had been shot into him by some Blackfoot marksman; aware, no doubt, of the inefficacy of lead. Since his death, there was no one with sufficient influence over the tribe to restrain the wild and predatory propensities of the young men. The consequence was, they had become troublesome and dangerous neighbors; openly friendly, for the sake of traffic, but disposed to commit secret depredations, and to molest any small party that might fall within their reach.

16.

Misadventures of Matthieu and his party—Return
to the caches at Salmon River—Battle between Nez
Percés and Blackfeet—Heroism of a Nez Percé
woman—Enrolled among the braves

ON THE 3D OF FEBRUARY, Matthieu, with the residue of his band, arrived in camp. He had a disastrous story to relate. After parting with Captain Bonneville in Green River valley, he had proceeded to the westward, keeping to the north of the Eutaw Mountains, a spur of the great Rocky Mountain chain. Here he experienced the most rugged travelling for his horses, and soon discovered that there was but little chance of meeting the Shoshonie bands. He now proceeded along Bear River, a stream much frequented by trappers; intending to shape his course to Salmon River, to rejoin Captain Bonneville.

He was misled, however, either through the ignorance or treachery of an Indian guide, and conducted into a wild valley, where he lay encamped during the autumn and the early part of the winter, nearly buried in snow, and almost starved. Early in the season he detached five men, with nine horses, to proceed to the neighborhood of the Sheep Rock, on Bear River, where game was plenty, and there to procure a supply for the camp. They had not proceeded far on their expedition when their trail was discovered by a party of nine or ten Indians, who immediately commenced a lurking pursuit, dogging them secretly for five or six days. So long as their encampments were well chosen, and a proper watch maintained, the wary savages kept aloof; at length, observing that they were badly encamped, in a situation where they might be approached with secrecy, the enemy crept stealthily along under cover of the river bank, preparing to burst suddenly upon their prey.

They had not advanced within striking distance, however, before they were discovered by one of the trappers. He immediately, but silently, gave the alarm to his companions. They all sprang upon their horses, and prepared to retreat to a safe position. One of the party, however, named Jennings, doubted the correctness of the alarm, and, before he mounted his horse, wanted to ascertain the fact. His companions urged him to mount, but in vain; he was incredulous and obstinate. A volley of firearms by the savages dispelled his doubts; but so overpowered his nerves that he was unable to get into his saddle. His comrades, seeing his peril and confusion, generously leapt from their horses to protect him. A shot from a rifle brought him to the earth; in his agony he called upon the others not to desert him. Two of them, Le Roy and Ross, after fighting desperately, were captured by the savages; the remaining two vaulted into their saddles and saved themselves by headlong flight, being pursued for nearly thirty miles.[1] They got safe back to Matthieu's camp, where their story inspired such dread of lurking Indians, that the hunters could not be prevailed upon to undertake another foray in quest of provisions. They remained, therefore, almost starving in their camp; now and then killing an old or disabled horse for food, while the elk and the mountain sheep roamed unmolested among the surrounding mountains.

The disastrous surprisal of this hunting party is cited by Captain Bonneville to show the importance of vigilant watching and judicious encampments in the Indian country. Most of these kinds of disasters to traders and trappers arise from some careless inattention to the state of their arms and ammunition, the placing of their horses at night, the position of their camping ground, and the posting of their night watches. The Indian is a vigilant and crafty foe; by no means given to hair-brained assaults; he seldom attacks when he finds his

[1] These were the men whom Walker had learned about in mid-December. Both Ferris and Irving identified the location of the attack as Sheep Rock, although Ferris reported the deaths of four, rather than three, men. Ferris, *Life in the Rocky Mountains*, 189.

The ADVENTURES of CAPTAIN BONNEVILLE

foe well prepared and on the alert. Caution is at least as efficacious a protection against him as courage.

The Indians who made this attack were at first supposed to be Blackfeet; until Captain Bonneville found, subsequently, in the camp of the Bannacks a horse, saddle, and bridle, which he recognized as having belonged to one of the hunters. The Bannacks, however, stoutly denied having taken these spoils in fight, and persisted in affirming that the outrage had been perpetrated by a Blackfoot band.

Captain Bonneville remained on Snake River nearly three weeks after the arrival of Matthieu and his party. At length his horses having recovered strength sufficient for a journey, he prepared to return to the Nez Percés, or rather to visit his *caches* on Salmon River; that he might take thence goods and equipments for the opening season. Accordingly, leaving sixteen men at Snake River, he set out on the 19th of February, with sixteen others, on his journey to the caches.[2]

Fording the river, he proceeded to the borders of the deep snow, when he encamped under the lee of immense piles of burnt rock. On the 21st he was again floundering through the snow, on the great Snake River plain, where it lay to the depth of thirty inches. It was sufficiently incrusted to bear a pedestrian, but the poor horses broke through the crust, and plunged and strained at every step. So lacerated were they by the ice, that it was necessary to change the front every hundred yards, and put a different one in the advance, to break the way. The open prairies were swept by a piercing and biting wind from the northwest. At night, they had to task their ingenuity to provide shelter and keep from freezing. In the first place, they dug deep holes in the snow, piling it up in ramparts to windward as a protection against the blast. Beneath these, they spread buffalo skins; upon which they stretched themselves in full dress, with caps, cloaks, and moccasons, and covered themselves with numerous blankets; notwithstanding all which, they were often severely pinched with the cold.

On the 28th of February, they arrived on the banks of Godin's

[2] This meant a return journey of well over two hundred miles.

River. This stream emerges from the mountains opposite an eastern branch of the Malade River, running southeast, forms a deep and swift current about twenty yards wide, passing rapidly through a defile to which it gives its name, and then enters the great plain, where, after meandering about forty miles, it is finally lost in the region of the Burnt Rocks.[3]

On the banks of this river, Captain Bonneville was so fortunate as to come upon a buffalo trail. Following it up, he entered the defile, where he remained encamped for two days to allow the hunters time to kill and dry a supply of buffalo beef. In this sheltered defile, the weather was moderate, and grass was already sprouting more than an inch in height. There was abundance, too, of the salt weed;[4] which grows most plentiful in clayey and gravelly barrens. It resembles pennyroyal, and derives its name from a partial saltness. It is a nourishing food for the horses in the winter, but they reject it the moment the young grass affords sufficient pasturage.

On the 6th of March, having cured sufficient meat, the party resumed their march, and moved on with comparative ease, excepting where they had to make their way through snow-drifts which had been piled up by the wind.

On the 11th, a small cloud of smoke was observed rising in a deep part of the defile. An encampment was instantly formed, and scouts were sent out to reconnoitre. They returned with intelligence that it was a hunting party of Flatheads, returning from the buffalo range laden with meat. Captain Bonneville joined them the next day, and persuaded them to proceed with his party a few miles below, to the caches, whither he proposed also to invite the Nez Percés, whom he hoped to find somewhere in this neighborhood. In fact, on the 13th, he was rejoined by that friendly tribe, who, since he separated from them on Salmon River, had likewise been out to hunt the buffalo, but had continued to be haunted and harassed

---

[3] The Goddin (Big Lost River) disappears in lava formations in the Snake River Plain. The Malade River, so named because trappers who ate beaver caught on it became ill, is now Big Wood River.

[4] *Atriplex confertifolia.*

by their old enemies the Blackfeet, who, as usual, had contrived to carry off many of their horses.

In the course of this hunting expedition, a small band of ten lodges separated from the main body, in search of better pasturage for their horses. About the 1st of March, the scattered parties of Blackfoot banditti united to the number of three hundred fighting men, and determined upon some signal blow. Proceeding to the former camping ground of the Nez Percés, they found the lodges deserted; upon which, they hid themselves among the willows and thickets, watching for some straggler, who might guide them to the present "whereabout" of their intended victims. As fortune would have it, Kosato, the Blackfoot renegade, was the first to pass along, accompanied by his blood-bought bride. He was on his way from the main body of hunters to the little band of ten lodges. The Blackfeet knew and marked him as he passed; he was within bowshot of their ambuscade; yet, much as they thirsted for his blood, they forebore to launch a shaft; sparing him for the moment, that he might lead them to their prey. Secretly following his trail, they discovered the lodges of the unfortunate Nez Percés, and assailed them with shouts and yellings. The Nez Percés numbered only twenty men, and but nine were armed with fusees. They showed themselves, however, as brave and skilful in war as they had been mild and long-suffering in peace. Their first care was to dig holes inside of their lodges; thus ensconced, they fought desperately, laying several of the enemy dead upon the ground; while they, though some of them were wounded, lost not a single warrior.

During the heat of the battle, a woman of the Nez Percés, seeing her warrior badly wounded and unable to fight, seized his bow and arrows, and bravely and successfully defended his person, contributing to the safety of the whole party.

In another part of the field of action, a Nez Percé had crouched behind the trunk of a fallen tree, and kept up a galling fire from his covert. A Blackfoot seeing this, procured a round log, and placing it before him as he lay prostrate, rolled it forward toward the trunk of the tree behind which his enemy lay crouched. It was a moment of breathless interest: whoever first showed himself would be in danger of a shot. The Nez Percé put an end to the suspense. The moment the logs touched, he sprang upon his feet, and discharged the contents of his fusee into the back of his antagonist. By this time, the Blackfeet had got possession of the horses; several of their warriors lay dead on the field, and the Nez Percés, ensconced in their lodges, seemed resolved to defend themselves to the last gasp. It so happened that the chief of the Blackfeet party was a renegade from the Nez Percés; unlike Kosato, however, he had no vindictive rage against his native tribe, but was rather disposed, now he had got the booty, to spare all unnecessary effusion of blood. He held a long parley, therefore, with the besieged, and finally drew off his warriors, taking with him seventy horses. It appeared, afterwards, that the bullets of the Blackfeet had been entirely expended in the course of the battle, so that they were obliged to make use of stones as substitute.

At the outset of the fight, Kosato, the renegade, fought with fury rather than valor: animating the others by word as well as deed. A wound in the head from a rifle ball laid him senseless on the earth. There his body remained when the battle was over, and the victors were leading off the horses. His wife hung over him with frantic lamentations. The conquerors paused and urged her to leave the lifeless renegade, and return with them to her kindred. She refused to listen to their solicitations, and they passed on. As she sat watching the features of Kosato, and giving way to passionate grief, she thought she perceived him to breathe. She was not mistaken. The ball, which had been nearly spent before it struck him, had stunned instead of killing him. By the ministry of his faithful wife, he gradually recovered; reviving to a redoubled love for her, and hatred of his tribe.

As to the female who had so bravely defended her husband, she was elevated by the tribe to a rank far above her sex, and, beside other honorable distinctions, was thenceforward permitted to take a part in the war dances of the braves!

17.

Opening of the caches—Detachments of Cerré and Hodgkiss—Salmon River Mountains—Superstition of an Indian trapper—Godin's River—Preparations for trapping—An alarm—An interruption—A rival band—Phenomena of Snake River Plain—Vast clefts and chasms—Ingulfed streams—Sublime scenery—A grand buffalo hunt

CAPTAIN BONNEVILLE found his caches perfectly secure, and having secretly opened them, he selected such articles as were necessary to equip the free trappers, and to supply the inconsiderable trade with the Indians, after which he closed them again. The free trappers, being newly rigged out and supplied, were in high spirits, and swaggered gayly about the camp. To compensate all hands for past sufferings, and to give a cheerful spur to further operations, Captain Bonneville now gave the men what, in frontier phrase, is termed "a regular blow out." It was a day of uncouth gambols and frolics, and rude feasting. The Indians joined in the sports and games, and all was mirth and good fellowship.

It was now the middle of March, and Captain Bonneville made preparations to open the spring campaign. He had pitched upon Malade River[1] for his main trapping ground for the season. This is a stream which rises among the great bed of mountains north of the lava plain, and after a winding course, falls into Snake River. Previous to his departure, the captain dispatched Mr. Cerré with a few men, to visit the Indian villages and purchase horses; he

[1] Big Wood River, which originates in the Sawtooth Mountains above Sun Valley and flows south to join the Snake in Gooding County.

furnished his clerk, Mr. Hodgkiss, also, with a small stock of goods, to keep up a trade with the Indians during the spring, for such peltries as they might collect, appointing the caches on Salmon River as the point of rendezvous, where they were to rejoin him on the 15th of June following.

This done, he set out for Malade River, with a band of twenty-eight men composed of hired and free trappers, and Indian hunters, together with eight squaws. Their route lay up along the right fork of Salmon River, as it passes through the deep defile of the mountains. They travelled very slowly, not above five miles a day, for many of the horses were so weak that they faltered and staggered as they walked. Pasturage, however, was now growing plentiful. There was abundance of fresh grass, which in some places had attained such height as to wave in the wind. The native flocks of the wilderness, the mountain sheep, as they are called by the trappers, were continually to be seen upon the hills between which they passed, and a good supply of mutton was provided by the hunters, as they were advancing toward a region of scarcity.

In the course of his journey, Captain Bonneville had occasion to remark an instance of the many notions, and almost superstitions, which prevail among the Indians, and among some of the white men, with respect to the sagacity of the beaver. The Indian hunters of his party were in the habit of exploring all the streams along which they passed, in search of "beaver lodges," and occasionally set their traps with some success. One of them, however, though an experienced and skilful trapper, was invariably unsuccessful. Astonished and mortified at such unusual bad luck, he at length conceived the idea that there was some odor about his person of which the beaver got scent, and retreated at his approach. He immediately set about a thorough purification. Making a rude sweating house on the banks of the river, he would shut himself up until in a reeking perspiration, and then suddenly emerging, would plunge into the river. A number of these sweatings and plungings having, as he supposed, rendered his person perfectly "inodorous," he resumed his trapping with renovated hope.

About the beginning of April, they encamped upon Godin's River,[2] where they found the swamp full of "muskrat houses." Here, therefore, Captain Bonneville determined to remain a few days and make his first regular attempt at trapping. That his maiden campaign might open with spirit, he promised the Indians and free trappers an extra price for every muskrat they should take. All now set to work for the next day's sport. The utmost animation and gayety prevailed throughout the camp. Everything looked auspicious for their spring campaign. The abundance of muskrats in the swamp was but an earnest of the nobler game they were to find when they should reach the Malade River, and have a capital beaver country all to themselves, where they might trap at their leisure without molestation.

In the midst of their gayety, a hunter came galloping into the camp, shouting, or rather yelling, "A trail! a trail!—lodge poles! lodge poles!"

These were words full of meaning to a trapper's ear. They intimated that there was some band in the neighborhood, and probably a hunting party, as they had lodge poles for an encampment. The hunter came up and told his story. He had discovered a fresh trail, in which the traces made by the dragging of lodge poles were distinctly visible. The buffalo, too, had just been driven out of the neighborhood, which showed that the hunters had already been on the range.

The gayety of the camp was at an end; all preparations for muskrat trapping were suspended, and all hands sallied forth to examine the trail. Their worst fears were soon confirmed. Infallible signs showed the unknown party in the advance to be white men; doubtless, some rival band of trappers! Here was competition when least expected; and that, too, by a party already in the advance, who were driving the game before them. Captain Bonneville had now a taste

---

[2] They had thus left the Salmon River, probably because of deep snow or rough terrain, and moved in a southeasterly direction to Big Lost River. To get to the Malade they would have to move west across a pass which they were soon to discover was still blocked with snow.

of the sudden transitions to which a trapper's life is subject. The buoyant confidence in an uninterrupted hunt was at an end; every countenance lowered with gloom and disappointment.

Captain Bonneville immediately dispatched two spies to overtake the rival party, and endeavor to learn their plans; in the meantime, he turned his back upon the swamp and its muskrat houses and followed on at "long camps," which in trapper's language is equivalent to long stages. On the 6th of April, he met his spies returning. They had kept on the trail like hounds, until they overtook the party at the south end of Godin's defile. Here they found them comfortably encamped, twenty-two prime trappers, all well appointed, with excellent horses in capital condition, led by Milton Sublette, and an able coadjutor, named Jarvie,[3] and in full march for the Malade hunting ground.

This was stunning news. The Malade River was the only trapping ground within reach; but to have to compete there with veteran trappers, perfectly at home among the mountains, and admirably mounted, while they were so poorly provided with horses and trappers, and had but one man in their party acquainted with the country—it was out of the question![4]

The only hope that now remained was that the snow, which still lay deep among the mountains of Godin's River, and blocked up the usual pass to the Malade country, might detain the other party, until Captain Bonneville's horses should get once more into good condition in their present ample pasturage.

The rival parties now encamped together, not out of companionship, but to keep an eye upon each other. Day after day passed by, without any possibility of getting to the Malade country. Sublette and Jarvie endeavored to force their way across the mountain; but the snows lay so deep as to oblige them to turn back. In the meantime, the captain's horses were daily gaining strength, and their hoofs improving, which had been worn and battered by moun-

---

[3] Jean Baptiste Gervais, one of the partners of Bridger, Fitzpatrick, Fraeb, and Milton Sublette in the Rocky Mountain Fur Company.

[4] This candid admission of inexperience points to the chief reason for Bonneville's failure as a fur trader.

The Adventures of Captain Bonneville

tain service. The captain, also, was increasing his stock of provisions, so that the delay was all in his favor.

To any one who merely contemplates a map of the country, this difficulty of getting from Godin's to Malade River will appear inexplicable, as the intervening mountains terminate in the great Snake River Plain, so that, apparently, it would be perfectly easy to proceed round their bases.

Here, however, occur some of the striking phenomena of this wild and sublime region. The great lower plain which extends to the feet of these mountains is broken up near their bases into crests and ridges, resembling the surges of the ocean breaking on a rocky shore.

In a line with the mountains, the plain is gashed with numerous and dangerous chasms, from four to ten feet wide, and of great depth. Captain Bonneville attempted to sound some of these openings, but without any satisfactory result. A stone dropped into one of them reverberated against the sides for apparently a very great depth, and, by its sound, indicated the same kind of substance with the surface, as long as the strokes could be heard. The horse, instinctively sagacious in avoiding danger, shrinks back in alarm from the least of these chasms; pricking up his ears, snorting and pawing, until permitted to turn away.

We have been told by a person well acquainted with the country that it is sometimes necessary to travel fifty and sixty miles to get round one of these tremendous ravines.[5] Considerable streams, like that of Godin's River, that run with a bold, free current, lose themselves in this plain; some of them end in swamps, others suddenly disappear; finding, no doubt, subterranean outlets.

Opposite to these chasms, Snake River makes two desperate leaps

---

[5] It is possible that Irving's source for this information was one of the Astorians, whose failures he had recounted in *Astoria*. Referring to this same area, Frémont wrote in 1843:

"Between the [Snake] river and the distant Salmon river range, the plain is represented by Mr. [Thomas] Fitzpatrick as so entirely broken up and rent into chasms as to be impracticable for a man even on foot." *Expedition to the Rocky Mountains*, 219.

over precipices, at a short distance from each other; one twenty, the other forty feet in height.

The volcanic plain[6] in question forms an area of about sixty miles in diameter, where nothing meets the eye but a desolate and awful waste; where no grass grows nor water runs, and where nothing is to be seen but lava. Ranges of mountains skirt this plain, and, in Captain Bonneville's opinion, were formerly connected, until rent asunder by some convulsion of nature. Far to the east, the Three Tetons lift their heads sublimely, and dominate this wide sea of lava—one of the most striking features of a wilderness where everything seems on a scale of stern and simple grandeur.

We look forward with impatience for some able geologist to explore this sublime, but almost unknown region.

It was not until the 25th of April that the two parties of trappers broke up their encampments, and undertook to cross over the southwest end of the mountain by a pass explored by their scouts. From various points of the mountain, they commanded boundless prospects of the lava plain, stretching away in cold and gloomy barrenness as far as the eye could reach. On the evening of the 26th, they reached the plain west of the mountain, watered by the Malade, the Boisée, and other streams, which comprised the contemplated trapping ground.

The country about the Boisée (or Woody) River,[7] is extolled by Captain Bonneville as the most enchanting he had seen in the Far West: presenting the mingled grandeur and beauty of mountain and plain; of bright running streams and vast grassy meadows waving to the breeze.

We shall not follow the captain throughout his trapping campaign, which lasted until the beginning of June; nor detail all the manœuvres of the rival trapping parties, and their various schemes to outwit and out-trap each other. Suffice it to say, that after having visited and camped about various streams with varying success, Captain Bonneville set forward early in June for the appointed rendez-

[6] Craters of the Moon National Monument is today in the heart of this area.

[7] The Boise rises just west of the Malade or Big Wood River and, like it, flows out of the Sawtooth Mountains.

vous at the caches.[8] On the way, he treated his party to a grand buffalo hunt. The scouts had reported numerous herds in a plain beyond an intervening height. There was an immediate halt; the fleetest horses were forthwith mounted, and the party advanced to the summit of the hill. Hence they beheld the great plain below absolutely swarming with buffalo. Captain Bonneville now appointed the place where he would encamp; and toward which the hunters were to drive the game. He cautioned the latter to advance slowly, reserving the strength and speed of the horses, until within a moderate distance of the herds. Twenty-two horsemen descended cautiously into the plain, conformably to these directions. "It was a beautiful sight," says the captain, "to see the runners, as they are called, advancing in column, at a slow trot, until within two hundred and fifty yards of the outskirts of the herd, then dashing on at full speed, until lost in the immense multitude of buffaloes scouring the plain in every direction." All was now tumult and wild confusion. In the meantime, Captain Bonneville and the residue of the party moved on to the appointed camping ground; thither the most expert runners succeeded in driving numbers of buffalo, which were killed hard by the camp, and the flesh transported thither without difficulty. In a little while the whole camp looked like one great slaughter house; the carcasses were skilfully cut up, great fires were made, scaffolds erected for drying and jerking beef, and an ample provision was made for future subsistence. On the 15th of June, the precise day appointed for the rendezvous, Captain Bonneville and his party arrived safely at the caches.

Here he was joined by the other detachments of his main party, all in good health and spirits. The *caches* were again opened, supplies of various kinds taken out, and a liberal allowance of *aqua vitae* distributed throughout the camp, to celebrate with proper conviviality this merry meeting.

[8] On the Salmon, where he had agreed to meet M. S. Cerré after the spring hunt.

18.

Meeting with Hodgkiss—Misfortunes of the Nez Percés—Schemes of Kosato, the renegado—His foray into the Horse Prairie—Invasion of Blackfeet—Blue John and his forlorn hope—Their generous enterprise—Their fate—Consternation and despair of the village—Solemn obsequies—Attempt at Indian trade—Hudson's Bay Company's monopoly—Arrangements for autumn—Breaking up of an encampment

HAVING NOW a pretty strong party, well armed and equipped, Captain Bonneville no longer felt the necessity of fortifying himself in the secret places and fastnesses of the mountains; but sallied forth boldly into the Snake River Plain, in search of his clerk, Hodgkiss, who had remained with the Nez Percés. He found him on the 24th of June,[1] and learned from him

[1] An interesting development took place at about this time which does not appear in Irving's pages. On June 22, camped on Camas Creek west of Henry's Fork with Francis Ermatinger of the Hudson's Bay Company, Wyeth made the following entry in his journal: "arrived this mng. an express from Bonneville. . . . this afternoon Mr. Hodge [Hodgkiss, Bonneville's clerk] left to go to Bonneville." *Correspondence and Journals*, 202.

Two days later (June 24), Hodgkiss reached Bonneville's camp and placed in Bonneville's hands a letter dated June 22 from Wyeth which began: "I send you the following proposition for a mutual hunt in the country south of the Columbia river. . . ." *Ibid.*, 58.

The hunt was to take place during the coming fall and spring trapping season, and Wyeth was confident that by pooling resources they could obtain three hundred skins which would be divided equally between them. Bonneville agreed to the proposal, in spite of the fact that he would be obliged to furnish most of the men, animals, and supplies. On July 3, Wyeth joined Bonneville, and on July 4 wrote to his brother Charles in Baltimore, "A meeting with Mr. Bonneville gives me the

another chapter of misfortunes which had recently befallen that ill-fated race.

After the departure of Captain Bonneville in March, Kosato, the renegade Blackfoot, had recovered from the wound received in battle; and with his strength revived all his deadly hostility to his native tribe. He now resumed his efforts to stir up the Nez Percés to reprisals upon their old enemies; reminding them incessantly of all the outrages and robberies they had recently experienced, and assuring them that such would continue to be their lot, until they proved themselves men by some signal retaliation.

The impassioned eloquence of the desperado at length produced an effect; and a band of braves enlisted under his guidance, to penetrate into the Blackfoot country, harass their villages, carry off their horses, and commit all kinds of depredations.

Kosato pushed forward on his foray as far as the Horse Prairie, where he came upon a strong party of Blackfeet. Without waiting to estimate their force, he attacked them with characteristic fury, and was bravely seconded by his followers. The contest, for a time, was hot and bloody: at length, as is customary with these two tribes, they paused, and held a long parley, or rather a war of words.

"What need," said the Blackfoot chief, tauntingly, "have the Nez Percés to leave their homes, and sally forth on war parties,

power to make up jointly with him a party for a hunt for this season [1833–34]. I shall not come home this year." *Ibid.*, 65. He added that they might extend their trapping into California.

Another letter written on the same day to his uncle, Leonard Jarvis, adds that the hunt might extend into California and that Wyeth himself was to lead it. But this letter was never sent because, owing to some sudden and unexplainable circumstance, Wyeth or Bonneville changed his mind. The next day (July 5), as a result, Wyeth wrote to Dr. John McLoughlin at Fort Vancouver that he was "in a direct train for the States" and expected to reach his home in Cambridge, Massachusetts, by October. *Ibid.*, 68.

Whatever the cause of this sudden abandonment of plans, it was not because of any dispute. The two camps remained together and on July 6 both set out for the rendezvous on Green River. They reached Henry's Fork on July 7. Bonneville arrived at Green River on July 13, Wyeth two days later. There seems to have been some business connection still in Wyeth's mind, for on July 18 he wrote to Francis Ermatinger: "I find Bonneville's connections are responsible." *Ibid.*, 69. The two men continued on friendly terms, as subsequent events will show.

when they have danger enough at their own doors? If you want fighting, return to your villages; you will have plenty of it there. The Blackfeet warriors have hitherto made war upon you as children. They are now coming as men. A great force is at hand; they are on their way to your towns, and are determined to rub out the very name of the Nez Percés from the mountains. Return, I say, to your towns, and fight there, if you wish to live any longer as a people."

Kosato took him at his word; for he knew the character of his native tribe. Hastening back with his band to the Nez Percés village, he told all that he had seen and heard, and urged the most prompt and strenuous measures for defence. The Nez Percés, however, heard him with their accustomed phlegm: the threat of the Blackfeet had been often made, and as often had proved a mere bravado; such they pronounced it to be at present, and, of course, took no precautions.

They were soon convinced that it was no empty menace. In a few days, a band of three hundred Blackfeet warriors appeared upon the hills. All now was consternation in the village. The force of the Nez Percés was too small to cope with the enemy in open fight; many of the young men having gone to their relatives on the Columbia to procure horses. The sages met in hurried council. What was to be done to ward off a blow which threatened annihilation? In this moment of imminent peril, a Pierced-nose chief, named Blue John by the whites, offered to approach secretly with a small, but chosen band, through a defile which led to the encampment of the enemy, and, by a sudden onset, to drive off the horses. Should this blow be successful, the spirit and strength of the invaders would be broken, and the Nez Percés, having horses, would be more than a match for them. Should it fail, the village would not be worse off than at present, when destruction appeared inevitable.

Twenty-nine of the choicest warriors instantly volunteered to follow Blue John in this hazardous enterprise. They prepared for it with the solemnity and devotion peculiar to the tribe. Blue John consulted his medicine, or talismanic charm, such as every chief keeps in his lodge as a supernatural protection. The oracle assured him that his enterprise would be completely successful, provided no rain should fall before he had passed through the defile; but should it rain, his band would be utterly cut off.

The day was clear and bright; and Blue John anticipated that the skies would be propitious. He departed in high spirits with his forlorn hope; and never did band of braves make a more gallant display—horsemen and horses being decorated and equipped in the fiercest and most glaring style—glittering with arms and ornaments, and fluttering with feathers.

The weather continued serene until they reached the defile; but just as they were entering it, a black cloud rose over the mountain crest, and there was a sudden shower. The warriors turned to their leader as if to read his opinion of this unlucky omen; but the countenance of Blue John remained unchanged, and they continued to press forward. It was their hope to make their way, undiscovered, to the very vicinity of the Blackfoot camp; but they had not proceeded far in the defile, when they met a scouting party of the enemy. They attacked and drove them among the hills, and were pursuing them with great eagerness, when they heard shouts and yells behind them, and beheld the main body of the Blackfeet advancing.

The second chief wavered a little at the sight, and proposed an instant retreat. "We came to fight!" replied Blue John, sternly. Then giving his war-whoop, he sprang forward to the conflict. His braves followed him. They made a headlong charge upon the enemy; not with the hope of victory, but the determination to sell their lives dearly. A frightful carnage, rather than a regular battle, succeeded. The forlorn band laid heaps of their enemies dead at their feet, but were overwhelmed with numbers, and pressed into a gorge of the mountain, where they continued to fight until they were cut to pieces. One, only, of the thirty survived. He sprang on the horse of a Blackfoot warrior whom he had slain, and escaping at full speed, brought home the baleful tidings to his village.

Who can paint the horror and desolation of the inhabitants? The flower of their warriors laid low, and a ferocious enemy at their doors. The air was rent by the shrieks and lamentations of the women, who, casting off their ornaments, and tearing their hair, wandered about, frantically bewailing the dead, and predicting destruction to the living. The remaining warriors armed themselves for obstinate defence; but showed by their gloomy looks and sullen silence, that they considered defence hopeless. To their surprise, the Blackfeet refrained from pursuing their advantage; perhaps satisfied with the blood already shed, or disheartened by the loss they had themselves sustained. At any rate, they disappeared from the hills, and it was soon ascertained that they had returned to the Horse Prairie.

The unfortunate Nez Percés now began once more to breathe. A few of their warriors, taking pack-horses, repaired to the defile to bring away the bodies of their slaughtered brethren. They found them mere headless trunks; and the wounds with which they were covered showed how bravely they had fought. Their hearts, too, had been torn out and carried off; a proof of their signal valor; for in devouring the heart of a foe renowned for bravery, or who has distinguished himself in battle, the Indian victor thinks he appropriates to himself the courage of the deceased.

Gathering the mangled bodies of the slain, and strapping them across their pack-horses, the warriors returned, in dismal procession, to the village. The tribe came forth to meet them; the women with piercing cries and wailings; the men with downcast countenances, in which gloom and sorrow seemed fixed as if in marble. The mutilated and almost undistinguishable bodies were placed in rows upon the ground, in the midst of the assemblage; and the scene of heart-rending anguish and lamentation that ensued would have confounded those who insist on Indian stoicism.

Such was the disastrous event that had overwhelmed the Nez Percés tribe, during the absence of Captain Bonneville; and he was informed that Kosato, the renegade, who, being stationed in the village, had been prevented from going on the forlorn hope, was again striving to rouse the vindictive feelings of his adopted brethren, and to prompt them to revenge the slaughter of their devoted braves.

During his sojourn on the Snake River Plain, Captain Bonneville

The ADVENTURES *of* CAPTAIN BONNEVILLE

made one of his first essays at the strategy of the fur trade. There was at this time an assemblage of Nez Percés, Flatheads, and Cottonois[2] Indians, encamped together upon the plain; well provided with beaver, which they had collected during the spring. These they were waiting to traffic with a resident trader[3] of the Hudson's Bay Company, who was stationed among them, and with whom they were accustomed to deal. As it happened, the trader was almost entirely destitute of Indian goods; his spring supply not having yet reached him. Captain Bonneville had secret intelligence that the supplies were on their way, and would soon arrive; he hoped, however, by a prompt move, to anticipate their arrival, and secure the market to himself. Throwing himself, therefore, among the Indians, he opened his packs of merchandise, and displayed the most tempting wares; bright cloths, and scarlet blankets, and glittering ornaments, and everything gay and glorious in the eyes of warrior or squaw; all, however, was in vain. The Hudson's Bay trader was a perfect master of his business, thoroughly acquainted with the Indians he had to deal with, and held such control over them, that none dared to act openly in opposition to his wishes: nay more—he came nigh turning the tables upon the captain, and shaking the allegiance of some of his free trappers, by distributing liquors among them. The latter, therefore, was glad to give up a competition, where the war was likely to be carried into his own camp.

In fact, the traders of the Hudson's Bay Company have advantages over all competitors in the trade beyond the Rocky Mountains. That huge monopoly centres within itself not merely its own hereditary and long-established power and influence; but also those of its ancient rival, but now integral part, the famous Northwest Company. It has thus its races of traders, trappers, hunters, and voyageurs, born and brought up in its service, and inheriting from preceding generations a knowledge and aptitude in everything connected with Indian life, and Indian traffic. In the process of years, this company has been enabled to spread its ramifications in every

---

[2] Kutenai; also Kootenay and Kootenai.

[3] Bernard DeVoto thought this was Francis Payette (*Across the Wide Missouri*, 94), but Wyeth's *Correspondence and Journals* shows that it was Francis Ermatinger.

direction; its system of intercourse is founded upon a long and intimate knowledge of the character and necessities of the various tribes; and of all the fastnesses, defiles, and favorable hunting grounds of the country. Their capital, also, and the manner in which their supplies are distributed at various posts, or forwarded by regular caravans, keep their traders well supplied, and enable them to furnish their goods to the Indians at a cheap rate. Their men, too, being chiefly drawn from the Canadas, where they enjoy great influence and control, are engaged at the most trifling wages, and supported at little cost; the provisions which they take with them being little more than Indian corn and grease. They are brought, also, into the most perfect discipline and subordination, especially when their leaders have once got them to their scene of action in the heart of the wilderness.

These circumstances combine to give the leaders of the Hudson's Bay Company a decided advantage over all the American companies that come within their range; so that any close competition with them is almost hopeless.

Shortly after Captain Bonneville's ineffectual attempt to participate in the trade of the associated camp, the supplies of the Hudson's Bay Company arrived; and the resident trader was enabled to monopolize the market.

It was now the beginning of July; in the latter part of which month, Captain Bonneville had appointed a rendezvous at Horse Creek, in Green River valley, with some of the parties which he had detached in the preceding year. He now turned his thoughts in that direction, and prepared for the journey.

The Cottonois were anxious for him to proceed at once to their country; which, they assured him, abounded in beaver. The lands of this tribe lie immediately north of those of the Flatheads, and are open to the inroads of the Blackfeet. It is true, the latter professed to be their allies; but they had been guilty of so many acts of perfidy, that the Cottonois had, latterly, renounced their hollow friendship, and attached themselves to the Flatheads and Nez Percés. These they had accompanied in their migrations, rather than remain alone at home, exposed to the outrages of the Blackfeet.

The Adventures of Captain Bonneville

They were now apprehensive that these marauders would range their country during their absence, and destroy the beaver: this was their reason for urging Captain Bonneville to make it his autumnal hunting ground. The latter, however, was not to be tempted: his engagements required his presence at the rendezvous in Green River valley; and he had already formed his ulterior plans.

An unexpected difficulty now arose. The free trappers suddenly made a stand, and declined to accompany him. It was a long and weary journey; the route lay through Pierre's Hole, and other mountain passes infested by the Blackfeet, and recently the scenes of sanguinary conflicts. They were not disposed to undertake such unnecessary toils and dangers, when they had good and secure trapping grounds nearer at hand, on the headwaters of Salmon River.

As these were free and independent fellows, whose will and whim were apt to be law—who had the whole wilderness before them, "where to choose," and the trader of a rival company at hand, ready to pay for their services—it was necessary to bend to their wishes. Captain Bonneville fitted them out, therefore, for the hunting ground in question; appointing Mr. Hodgkiss to act as their partisan, or leader, and fixing a rendezvous where he should meet them in the course of the ensuing winter. The brigade consisted of twenty-one free trappers, and four or five hired men as camp-keepers. This was not the exact arrangement of a trapping party; which, when accurately organized, is composed of two-thirds trappers, whose duty leads them continually abroad in pursuit of game; and one-third camp-keepers, who cook, pack, and unpack; set up the tents, take care of the horses, and do all other duties usually assigned by the Indians to their women. This part of the service is apt to be fulfilled by French creoles from Canada and the valley of the Mississippi.

In the meantime, the associated Indians, having completed their trade and received their supplies, were all ready to disperse in various directions. As there was a formidable band of Blackfeet just over a mountain to the northeast, by which Hodgkiss and his free trappers would have to pass; and as it was known that those sharp-sighted marauders had their scouts out, watching every movement of the encampments, so as to cut off stragglers or weak detachments,

Captain Bonneville prevailed upon the Nez Percés to accompany Hodgkiss and his party, until they should be beyond the range of the enemy.

The Cottonois, and the Pends Oreilles, determined to move together at the same time, and to pass close under the mountain infested by the Blackfeet; while Captain Bonneville, with his party, was to strike in an opposite direction to the southeast, bending his course for Pierre's Hole, on his way to Green River.

Accordingly, on the 6th of July, all the camps were raised at the same moment; each party taking its separate route. The scene was wild and picturesque: the long line of traders, trappers, and Indians, with their rugged and fantastic dresses and accoutrements; their varied weapons, their innumerable horses, some under the saddle, some burdened with packages, others following in droves; all stretching in lengthening cavalcades across the vast landscape, making for different points of the plains and mountains.

19.

Precautions in dangerous defiles—Trappers' mode of defence on a prairie—A mysterious visitor—Arrival in Green River valley—Adventures of the detachments—The forlorn partisan—His tale of disasters

As THE ROUTE of Captain Bonneville lay through what was considered the most perilous part of this region of dangers, he took all his measures with military skill, and observed the strictest circumspection. When on the march, a small scouting party was thrown in the advance, to reconnoitre the country through which they were to pass. The encampments were selected with great care, and a watch was kept up night and day. The horses were brought in and picketed at night, and at daybreak a party was sent out to scour the neighborhood for half a mile round, beating up every grove and thicket that could give shelter to a lurking foe. When all was reported safe, the horses were cast loose and turned out to graze. Were such precautions generally observed by traders and hunters, we should not so often hear of parties being surprised by the Indians.

Having stated the military arrangements of the captain, we may here mention a mode of defence on the open prairie, which we have heard from a veteran in the Indian trade. When a party of trappers is on a journey with a convoy of goods or peltries, every man has three pack-horses under his care; each horse laden with three packs. Every man is provided with a picket with an iron head, a mallet, and hobbles, or leathern fetters for the horses. The trappers proceed across the prairie in a long line; or sometimes three parallel lines, sufficiently distant from each other to prevent the packs from interfering. At an alarm, when there is no covert at hand, the line wheels so as to bring the front to the rear and form a circle. All then dismount, drive their pickets into the ground in the centre, fasten the horses to them, and hobble their forelegs, so that, in case of alarm, they cannot break away. Then they unload them, and dispose of their packs as breastworks on the periphery of the circle; each man having nine packs behind which to shelter himself. In this promptly-formed fortress, they await the assault of the enemy, and are enabled to set large bands of Indians at defiance.

The first night of his march, Captain Bonneville encamped upon Henry's Fork; an upper branch of Snake River, called after the first American trader that erected a fort beyond the mountains.[1] About an hour after all hands had come to a halt the clatter of hoofs was heard, and a solitary female, of the Nez Percé tribe, came galloping up. She was mounted on a mustang, or half-wild horse, which she managed by a long rope hitched round the under jaw by way of bridle. Dismounting, she walked silently into the midst of the camp, and there seated herself on the ground, still holding her horse by the long halter.

The sudden and lonely apparition of this woman, and her calm, yet resolute demeanor, awakened universal curiosity. The hunters and trappers gathered round, and gazed on her as something mysterious. She remained silent, but maintained her air of calmness and self-possession. Captain Bonneville approached and interrogated her as to the object of her mysterious visit. Her answer was brief but earnest—"I love the whites—I will go with them." She was forthwith invited to a lodge, of which she readily took possession, and from that time forward was considered one of the camp.

In consequence, very probably, of the military precautions of

[1] Henry's Fork, which still bears this name, flows into the Snake in the southwest corner of Madison County. On it, in 1810, Andrew Henry built a fortification not far from modern St. Anthony. An account of the excavation of a cabin here is recorded in M. D. Beal's *A History of Southeastern Idaho*, 397–98. In Chapter XXXI of *Astoria*, Irving had told of the arrival of Wilson Price Hunt and the overland Astorians at Henry's Fort on October 8, 1811. They found deserted log cabins on the bank of Henry's Fork. This fort was distinct from Henry's camp referred to in Chapter I, note 3.

Captain Bonneville, he conducted his party in safety through this hazardous region. No accident of a disastrous kind occurred, excepting the loss of a horse, which, in passing along the giddy edge of the precipice, called the Cornice, a dangerous pass between Jackson's and Pierre's Hole, fell over the brink and was dashed to pieces.

On the 13th of July, (1833,) Captain Bonneville arrived at Green River. As he entered the valley, he beheld it strewed in every direction with the carcasses of buffaloes. It was evident that Indians had recently been there, and in great numbers. Alarmed at this sight, he came to a halt, and as soon as it was dark, sent out spies to his place of rendezvous on Horse Creek, where he had expected to meet with his detached parties of trappers on the following day. Early in the morning, the spies made their appearance in the camp, and with them came three trappers of one of his bands, from the rendezvous, who told him his people were all there expecting him. As to the slaughter among the buffaloes, it had been made by a friendly band of Shoshonies, who had fallen in with one of his trapping parties, and accompanied them to the rendezvous. Having imparted this intelligence, the three worthies from the rendezvous broached a small keg of "alcohol," which they had brought with them, to enliven this merry meeting. The liquor went briskly round; all absent friends were toasted, and the party moved forward to the rendezvous in high spirits.[2]

The meeting of associated bands, who have been separated from each other on these hazardous enterprises, is always interesting; each having its tales of perils and adventures to relate. Such was

[2] In an obscure novel by Sir William George Drummond Stewart appear the most vivid and lifelife scenes of this rendezvous drawn from firsthand observation in 1833. See his *Edward Warren*, I, 251–82. Here is one scene at Fort Bonneville:

"The trading house and camp of Bonneville was at the upper end of those which were scattered nearest to the river bank, and where the timber gave out. We rode through the plain, until we came towards the store, which was surrounded by Indians and whites . . . looking on at the purchases of some Indian squaws; the bucks, as the young Indian fops are called, were parading up and down the camp in all their bravery; the painted robes and shields, the household gods of each lodge, were hung out in their gaudy colours. . . . The horses here were scattered about in every colour and pattern, spotted, pyed, mixed, dun, yellow, red, blue, and violet." *Ibid.*, 270.

the case with the various detachments of Captain Bonneville's company, thus brought together on Horse Creek. Here was the detachment of fifty men which he had sent from Salmon River, in the preceding month of November, to winter on Snake River.[3] They had met with many crosses and losses in the course of their spring hunt, not so much from Indians as from white men. They had come in competition with rival trapping parties, particularly one belonging to the Rocky Mountain Fur Company;[4] and they had long stories to relate of their manœuvres to forestall or distress each other. In fact, in these virulent and sordid competitions, the trappers of each party were more intent upon injuring their rivals, than benefitting themselves; breaking each other's traps, trampling and tearing to pieces the beaver lodges, and doing everything in their power to mar the success of the hunt. We forbear to detail these pitiful contentions.

The most lamentable tale of disasters, however, that Captain Bonneville had to hear, was from a partisan, whom he had detached in the preceding year, with twenty men, to hunt through the outskirts of the Crow country, and on the tributary streams of the Yellowstone; whence he was to proceed and join him in his winter quarters on Salmon River. This partisan appeared at the rendezvous without his party, and a sorrowful tale of disasters had he to relate.[5] In hunting the Crow country, he fell in with a village of that tribe; notorious rogues, jockeys, and horse stealers, and errant scamperers

[3] This was Joseph Walker's detachment. They had reached Horse Creek by June 7 or perhaps earlier.

[4] This was a party led by James Bridger. They had camped at Henry's Fork in December, 1832, and in January, 1833, had moved down to the Portneuf River. Besides Bridger, this group included Joe Meek and Kit Carson. Victor, *River of the West*, 135.

[5] Bonneville told Wyeth of his losses; and Wyeth, writing to Francis Ermatinger on July 18, 1833, from Green River, stated: "He [Bonneville] lost one entire party among the Crows that is the Horses and of course all the Beavers." *Correspondence and Journals*, 69. This party had been led by David Adams, not by Antonio Montero as conjectured by Chittenden, *American Fur Trade*, I, 404, and by Aubrey L. Haines in his edition of Osborne Russell's *Journal of a Trapper*, 167–68 n. See Editor's Introduction, letter to Adams from Bonneville, August 17, 1832. The theft of Adams' horses and equipment by the Crows plus the desertion of his men is related by James Beckwourth in his *Life and Adventures*, 163–66.

of the mountains. These decoyed most of his men to desert, and carry off horses, traps, and accoutrements. When he attempted to retake the deserters, the Crow warriors ruffled up to him and declared the deserters were their good friends, had determined to remain among them, and should not be molested. The poor partisan, therefore, was fain to leave his vagabonds among these birds of their own feather, and, being too weak in numbers to attempt the dangerous pass across the mountains to meet Captain Bonneville on Salmon River, he made, with the few that remained faithful to him, for the neighborhood of Tullock's Fort,[6] on the Yellowstone, under the protection of which he went into winter quarters.

He soon found out that the neighborhood of the fort was nearly as bad as the neighborhood of the Crows. His men were continually stealing away thither, with whatever beaver skins they could secrete or lay their hands on. These they would exchange with the hangers-on of the fort for whisky, and then revel in drunkenness and debauchery.

The unlucky partisan made another move. Associating with his party a few free trappers, whom he met with in this neighborhood, he started off early in the spring to trap on the head waters of Powder River. In the course of the journey, his horses were so much jaded in traversing a steep mountain, that he was induced to turn them loose to graze during the night. The place was lonely; the path was rugged; there was not the sign of an Indian in the neighborhood; not a blade of grass that had been turned by a footstep. But who can calculate on security in the midst of the Indian country, where the foe lurks in silence and secrecy, and seems to come and go on the wings of the wind? The horses had scarce been turned loose, when a couple of Arickara (or Rickaree) warriors entered the camp. They affected a frank and friendly demeanor; but their appearance and movements awakened the suspicions of some of the veteran trappers, well versed in Indian wiles. Convinced that they were spies sent on some sinister errand, they took them in custody, and set to work to drive in the horses. It was too late—

[6] Fort Cass, built in 1832 by Samuel Tulloch at the mouth of the Big Horn River for the American Fur Company.

the horses were already gone. In fact, a war party of Arickaras had been hovering on their trail for several days, watching with the patience and perseverance of Indians, for some moment of negligence and fancied security, to make a successful swoop. The two spies had evidently been sent into the camp to create a diversion, while their confederates carried off the spoil.

The unlucky partisan, thus robbed of his horses, turned furiously on his prisoners, ordered them to be bound hand and foot, and swore to put them to death unless his property were restored. The robbers, who soon found that their spies were in captivity, now made their appearance on horseback, and held a parley. The sight of them, mounted on the very horses they had stolen, set the blood of the mountaineers in a ferment; but it was useless to attack them, as they would have but to turn their steeds and scamper out of the reach of pedestrians. A negotiation was now attempted. The Arickaras offered what they considered fair terms; to barter one horse, or even two horses, for a prisoner. The mountaineers spurned at their offer, and declared that, unless all the horses were relinquished, the prisoners should be burnt to death. To give force to their threat, a pyre of logs and fagots was heaped up and kindled into a blaze.

The parley continued; the Arickaras released one horse and then another, in earnest of their proposition; finding, however, that nothing short of the relinquishment of all their spoils would purchase the lives of the captives, they abandoned them to their fate, moving off with many parting words and lamentable howlings. The prisoners seeing them depart, and knowing the horrible fate that awaited them, made a desperate effort to escape. They partially succeeded, but were severely wounded and retaken; then dragged to the blazing pyre, and burnt to death in the sight of their retreating comrades.

Such are the savage cruelties that white men learn to practise, who mingle in savage life; and such are the acts that lead to terrible recrimination on the part of the Indians. Should we hear of any atrocities committed by the Arickaras upon captive white men, let this signal and recent provocation be borne in mind. Individual cases of the kind dwell in the recollections of whole tribes; and it is a point of honor and conscience to revenge them.

The loss of his horses completed the ruin of the unlucky partisan. It was out of his power to prosecute his hunting, or to maintain his party; the only thought now was how to get back to civilized life. At the first water-course, his men built canoes, and committed themselves to the stream. Some engaged themselves at various trading establishments at which they touched, others got back to the settlements. As to the partisan, he found an opportunity to make his way to the rendezvous at Green River valley; which he reached in time to render to Captain Bonneville this forlorn account of his misadventures.

20.

Gathering in Green River valley—Visitings and feastings of leaders—Rough wassailing among the trappers—Wild blades of the mountains—Indian belles—Potency of bright beads and red blankets—Arrival of supplies—Revelry and extravagance—Mad wolves—The lost Indian

THE GREEN RIVER VALLEY was at this time the scene of one of those general gatherings of traders, trappers, and Indians, that we have already mentioned. The three rival companies, which, for a year past had been endeavoring to out-trade, out-trap and out-wit each other, were here encamped in close proximity, awaiting their annual supplies. About four miles from the rendezvous of Captain Bonneville was that of the American Fur Company, hard by which, was that also of the Rocky Mountain Fur Company.[1]

[1] The names of trappers and traders at this rendezvous constitute a veritable roster of men prominent in the trade. In Bonneville's camp were Walker and Cerré plus their men. The American Fur Company was represented by Dripps and Fontenelle with 160 men, including W. A. Ferris, Robert Newell, and George Holmes, who was destined for an early death. Five miles away was the camp of the Rocky Mountain Fur Company with around 40 men, including Milton Sublette, J. B. Gervais, Fitzpatrick, Louis Vasquez, Bridger, Joe Meek, William Sublette, Robert Campbell, and Charles Larpenteur, who was later to write an important narrative of his fur-trade activities. With them were Dr. Benjamin Harris, Edmund Christy, and Captain William Stewart, sportsman-hunter from Scotland who had come out with the Sublette-Campbell train. Besides these, there were Benjamin O'Fallon, N. J. Wyeth, and Zenas Leonard, who would also write an important account of his fur-trade experiences. Ferris estimated that about 300 whites were present, Wyeth that there were 250. To these must be added 50 to 60 lodges of Snake Indians, trading skins for ammunition, knives, guns, ornaments, etc. This mountain assembly of human beings consumed whisky at a cost of $5.00 a pint. Wyeth's opinion of the lot was that the great majority were "Scoundrels."

After the eager rivalry and almost hostility displayed by these companies in their late campaigns, it might be expected that, when thus brought in juxtaposition, they would hold themselves warily and sternly aloof from each other, and, should they happen to come in contact, brawl and bloodshed would ensue.

No such thing! Never did rival lawyers, after a wrangle at the bar, meet with more social good humor at a circuit dinner. The hunting season over, all past tricks and manœuvres are forgotten, all feuds and bickerings buried in oblivion. From the middle of June to the middle of September, all trapping is suspended; for the beavers are then shedding their furs and their skins are of little value. This, then, is the trapper's holiday, when he is all for fun and frolic, and ready for a saturnalia among the mountains.

At the present season, too, all parties were in good humor. The year had been productive. Competition, by threatening to lessen their profits, had quickened their wits, roused their energies, and made them turn every favorable chance to the best advantage; so that, on assembling at their respective places of rendezvous, each company found itself in possession of a rich stock of peltries.[2]

The leaders of the different companies, therefore, mingled on terms of perfect good fellowship; interchanging visits, and regaling each other in the best style their respective camps afforded. But the rich treat for the worthy captain was to see the "chivalry" of the various encampments, engaged in contests of skill at running, jumping, wrestling, shooting with the rifle, and running horses. And then their rough hunters' feastings and carousals. They drank together, they sang, they laughed, they whooped; they tried to out-brag and out-lie each other in stories of their adventures and achievements. Here the free trappers were in all their glory; they considered themselves the "cocks of the walk," and always carried the highest crests. Now and then familiarity was pushed too far, and would

[2] The Rocky Mountain Fur Company had fifty-five packs of beaver skins to transport to St. Louis; the American Fur Company had fifty-one packs; and Bonneville twenty-two and one-half packs. Wyeth, *Correspondence and Journals*, 69–70.

Packs weighed about one-hundred pounds, each containing approximately eighty skins. These would bring around $3.50 a pound in St. Louis. DeVoto, *Across the Wide Missouri*, 95, 104.

effervesce into a brawl, and a "rough and tumble" fight; but it all ended in cordial reconciliation and maudlin endearment.

The presence of the Shoshonie tribe[3] contributed occasionally to cause temporary jealousies and feuds. The Shoshonie beauties became objects of rivalry among some of the amorous mountaineers. Happy was the trapper who could muster up a red blanket, a string of gay beads, or a paper of precious vermilion, with which to win the smiles of a Shoshonie fair one.

The caravans of supplies arrived at the valley just at this period of gallantry and good fellowship. Now commenced a scene of eager competition and wild prodigality at the different encampments. Bales were hastily ripped open, and their motley contents poured forth. A mania for purchasing spread itself throughout the several bands—munitions for war, for hunting, for gallantry, were seized upon with equal avidity—rifles, hunting knives, traps, scarlet cloth, red blankets, garish beads, and glittering trinkets, were bought at any price, and scores run up without any thought how they were ever to be rubbed off. The free trappers, especially, were extravagant in their purchases. For a free mountaineer to pause at a paltry consideration of dollars and cents, in the attainment of any object that might strike his fancy, would stamp him with the mark of the beast in the estimation of his comrades. For a trader to refuse one of these free and flourishing blades a credit, whatever unpaid scores might stare him in the face, would be a flagrant affront scarcely to be forgiven.

Now succeeded another outbreak of revelry and extravagance. The trappers were newly fitted out and arrayed, and dashed about with their horses caparisoned in Indian style. The Shoshonie beauties also flaunted about in all the colors of the rainbow. Every freak of prodigality was indulged to its fullest extent, and in a little while most of the trappers, having squandered away all their wages, and perhaps run knee-deep in debt, were ready for another hard campaign in the wilderness.[4]

[3] Snake Indians.

[4] At the next year's rendezvous John K. Townsend reported prices that can be assumed comparable to those of 1833. Whisky diluted with water was three dollars

During this season of folly and frolic, there was an alarm of mad wolves in the two lower camps. One or more of these animals entered the camps for three nights successively, and bit several of the people.

Captain Bonneville relates the case of an Indian, who was a universal favorite in the lower camp. He had been bitten by one of these animals. Being out with a party shortly afterwards, he grew silent and gloomy, and lagged behind the rest as if he wished to leave them. They halted and urged him to move faster, but he entreated them not to approach him, and, leaping from his horse, began to roll frantically on the earth, gnashing his teeth and foaming at the mouth. Still he retained his senses, and warned his companions not to come near him, as he should not be able to restrain himself from biting them. They hurried off to obtain relief; but on their return he was nowhere to be found. His horse and his accoutrements remained upon the spot. Three or four days afterwards a solitary Indian, believed to be the same, was observed crossing a valley, and pursued; but he darted away into the fastnesses of the mountains, and was seen no more.

Another instance we have from a different person who was present in the encampment. One of the men of the Rocky Mountain Fur Company had been bitten. He set out shortly afterwards in company with two white men on his return to the settlements. In the course of a few days he showed symptoms of hydrophobia, and became raving toward night. At length, breaking away from his companions, he rushed into a thicket of willows, where they left him to his fate![5]

a pint. Tobacco bought in Philadelphia for ten cents a pound was sold at two dollars for the same amount. In the absence of currency, free trappers paid in beaver pelts, buffalo robes, and other skins; those attached to companies had their purchases deducted from wages. Townsend observed a trapper who ordered *"twenty dollars' worth of rum, and ten dollars worth of sugar,* to treat two of his companions who were about leaving the rendezvous." *Narrative,* 76.

[5] The mad-wolf scare occurs in several narratives besides Irving's. Ferris wrote in his journal (205) that "mad dogs and wolves" attacked during several nights. One rabid wolf was killed. In his camp three persons were bitten and nine in the camp of Dripps and Fontenelle. A young New Yorker named George Holmes was one victim. He later died as a result of an infected bite (see Charles Larpenteur,

The ADVENTURES *of* CAPTAIN BONNEVILLE

Forty Years a Fur Trader on the Upper Missouri [ed. by Milo M. Quaife], 30–31, 33–34). The attack on young Holmes provided material for an incident in Stewart's *Edward Warren*, in which a footnote reads:

"Poor Holmes was seated on the ground, the side of his head and his ear bleeding and torn; a mad wolf was ravaging the camp. . . . Poor Holmes changed from that hour . . . ." (I, 274–76 n.) Larpenteur wrote that Holmes became mad while traveling down the Big Horn with Fontenelle and that he had run away into the wilderness, stark naked, and was never again seen.

21.

Schemes of Captain Bonneville—The Great Salt Lake—Expedition to explore it—Preparations for a journey to the Bighorn

CAPTAIN BONNEVILLE now found himself at the head of a hardy, well-seasoned and well-appointed company of trappers, all benefited by at least one year's experience among the mountains, and capable of protecting themselves from Indian wiles and stratagems, and of providing for their subsistence wherever game was to be found. He had, also, an excellent troop of horses, in prime condition, and fit for hard service. He determined, therefore, to strike out into some of the bolder parts of his scheme. One of these was to carry his expeditions into some of the unknown tracts of the Far West, beyond what is generally termed the buffalo range. This would have something of the merit and charm of discovery, so dear to every brave and adventurous spirit. Another favorite project was to establish a trading post on the lower part of the Columbia River, near the Multnomah valley, and to endeavor to retrieve for his country some of the lost trade of Astoria.

The first of the above mentioned views was, at present, uppermost in his mind—the exploring of unknown regions. Among the grand features of the wilderness about which he was roaming, one had made a vivid impression on his mind, and been clothed by his imagination with vague and ideal charms. This is a great lake of salt water,[1] laving the feet of the mountains, but extending far to

[1] Great Salt Lake. Since Bonneville never visited the lake, the notes in his journal could only have been the results of his talking with trappers who had seen it. By 1833 the existence of this body of water was well known to many mountain men as a result of its discovery in 1825 by James Bridger and its circumnavigation

the west-southwest, into one of those vast and elevated plateaus of land, which range high above the level of the Pacific.

Captain Bonneville gives a striking account of the lake when seen from the land. As you ascend the mountains about its shores, says he, you behold this immense body of water spreading itself before you, and stretching further and further, in one wide and far-reaching expanse, until the eye, wearied with continued and strained attention, rests in the blue dimness of distance, upon lofty ranges of mountains, confidently asserted to rise from the bosom of the waters. Nearer to you, the smooth and unruffled surface is studded with little islands, where the mountain sheep roam in considerable numbers. What extent of lowland may be encompassed by the high peaks beyond, must remain for the present matter of mere conjecture; though from the form of the summits, and the breaks which may be discovered among them, there can be little doubt that they are the sources of streams calculated to water large tracts, which are probably concealed from view by the rotundity of the lake's surface. At some future day, in all probability, the rich harvest of beaver fur, which may be reasonably anticipated in such a spot, will tempt adventurers to reduce all this doubtful region to the palpable certainty of a beaten track.[2] At present, however, destitute of the means of making boats, the trapper stands upon the shore, and gazes upon a promised land which his feet are never to tread.

Such is the somewhat fanciful view which Captain Bonneville

---

in the following year by four of Ashley's men. See letter of Robert Campbell for April 4, 1857, in Lieutenant G. K. Warren's *Memoir* in *Reports of Explorations and Surveys*, 36 Cong., 2 sess., *Sen. Exec. Doc.* [unnumbered] (Washington, 1861), XI, 35–36. This letter also appears in Alter, *James Bridger*, 49–50. See also *Alexandria Gazette*, December 28, 1826; reprinted in Frost, *Notes on General Ashley*, 147–48. Of this exploring party Ferris wrote:

"It was circumnavigated a few years since by four men in a small boat, who were absent on the expedition forty days, and on their return reported that for several days they found no fresh water on its western shore, and nearly perished from the want of that necessary article. They ascertained that it had no visible outlet." *Life in the Rocky Mountains*, 69–70.

[2] These "adventurers" had already thoroughly assessed the fur-bearing potential of the streams flowing into Great Salt Lake (see Dale Morgan, *The Great Salt Lake*, Chapters 5–6).

The ADVENTURES of CAPTAIN BONNEVILLE

gives to this great body of water. He has evidently taken part of his ideas concerning it from the representations of others, who have somewhat exaggerated its features. It is reported to be about one hundred and fifty miles long, and fifty miles broad. The ranges of mountain peaks which Captain Bonneville speaks of, as rising from its bosom, are probably the summits of mountains beyond it, which may be visible at a vast distance, when viewed from an eminence, in the transparent atmosphere of these lofty regions. Several large islands certainly exist in the lake; one of which is said to be mountainous, but not by any means to the extent required to furnish the series of peaks above mentioned.

Captain Sublette, in one of his early expeditions across the mountains, is said to have sent four men in a skin canoe, to explore the lake, who professed to have navigated all round it; but to have suffered excessively from thirst, the water of the lake being extremely salt, and there being no fresh streams running into it.

Captain Bonneville doubts this report, or that the men accomplished the circumnavigation, because, he says, the lake receives several large streams[3] from the mountains which bound it to the east. In the spring, when the streams are swollen by rain and by the melting of the snows, the lake rises several feet above its ordinary level; during the summer, it gradually subsides again, leaving a sparkling zone of the finest salt upon its shores.[4]

The elevation of the vast plateau on which this lake is situated, is estimated by Captain Bonneville at one and three-fourths of a mile above the level of the ocean.[5] The admirable purity and transparency of the atmosphere in this region, allowing objects to be seen, and the report of firearms to be heard, at an astonishing distance; and its extreme dryness, causing the wheels of wagons to fall in pieces, as instanced in former passages of this work, are proofs

[3] The Bear, the Weber, and the Jordon rivers. After leaving these streams the men would have suffered from thirst owing to the absence of streams on the other sides of the lake. Bonneville could not have been aware of the great length of its shore line.

[4] An accurate statement. See Morgan, *Great Salt Lake*, 23–24, for statistics.

[5] According to the Saltair gauge, "zero level," or the point from which fluctuations are measured, is 4,196.85 feet. Morgan, *op. cit.*, 23.

The ADVENTURES *of* CAPTAIN BONNEVILLE

of the great altitude of the Rocky Mountain plains. That a body of salt water should exist at such a height is cited as a singular phenomenon by Captain Bonneville, though the salt lake of Mexico is not much inferior in elevation.[6]

To have this lake properly explored, and all its secrets revealed, was the grand scheme of the captain for the present year; and while it was one in which his imagination evidently took a leading part, he believed it would be attended with great profit, from the numerous beaver streams with which the lake must be fringed.

This momentous undertaking he confided to his lieutenant, Mr. Walker, in whose experience and ability he had great confidence. He instructed him to keep along the shores of the lake, and trap in all the streams on his route; also to keep a journal, and minutely to record the events of his journey, and everything curious or interesting, making maps or charts of his route, and of the surrounding country.

No pains nor expense were spared in fitting out the party, of forty men, which he was to command. They had complete supplies for a year, and were to meet Captain Bonneville in the ensuing summer, in the valley of Bear River, the largest tributary of the Salt Lake, which was to be his point of general rendezvous.[7]

[6] The lake of Tezcuco, which surrounds the city of Mexico, the largest and lowest of the five lakes on the Mexican plateau, and one of the most impregnated with saline particles, is seven thousand four hundred and sixty-eight feet, or nearly one mile and a half above the level of the sea (Irving's note).

[7] The above three paragraphs constitute one of the most perplexing passages in the book because external evidence with one exception indicates that Bonneville's intention was not to send Walker on an exploration of Great Salt Lake but to travel to California. The one conflicting piece of evidence is a statement by Stephen Hall Meek:

"There [at Green River] I hired to Capt. B. L. E. Bonneville to accompany an expedition of 34 men, under Joseph Walker, to explore the Great Salt Lake. We got too far West, and finally started down the Mary's, or Humboldt, river for California, over a country entirely unknown to trappers." *Autobiography of a Mountain Man, 1805–1889* (ed. by Arthur Woodward), 5. But Zenas Leonard, who hired on as Walker's clerk and who would therefore have been in a position to know the purpose of the expedition, declared:

"I was anxious to go to the coast of the Pacific, and for that purpose hired with Mr. Walker as clerk. . . . On the 4th of September we killed our last buffalo on the west side of Salt Lake. We still continued along the margin of the Lake, with

The next care of Captain Bonneville was to arrange for the safe transportation of the peltries which he had collected to the Atlantic States. Mr. Robert Campbell, the partner of Sublette, was at this time in the rendezvous of the Rocky Mountain Fur Company, having brought up their supplies. He was about to set off on his return, with the peltries collected during the year, and intended to proceed through the Crow country, to the head of navigation on the Bighorn River, and to descend in boats down that river, the Missouri, and the Yellowstone, to St. Louis.

Captain Bonneville determined to forward his peltries by the same route, under the especial care of Mr. Cerré. By way of escort, he would accompany Cerré to the point of embarkation, and then make an autumnal hunt in the Crow country.

the intention of leaving it when we got to the extreme west side of it. . . . On the 13th we left the Lake and took a westerly course into the most extensive and barren plains I ever seen." *Adventures*, 65–66.

Another member of the party, George Nidever, had a similar understanding of the purpose of Walker's expedition: "This winter's experience decided me, as also some others of our company, to seek a warmer climate, and having heard many wonderful stories of California, we settled upon coming here. In the spring, there were a large number of trappers gathered at the rendezvous in Green River valley and among them Capt. Walker and Company, bound for California. We joined him, making a party in all of 36. Upon the breaking up of the rendezvous we started southward, intending to trap a short time on the Mary's River." *Life and Adventures*, 31–32. It is important to point out, also, that before leaving for the West Bonneville had obtained Mexican passports, which would have permitted him to enter California; see Editor's Introduction, p. xxv. These passports were later handed over to Walker and his men. One of them, Nathan Daily, in an affidavit stated that he entered Bonneville's service, "under whose passports we entered California in the year 1833" (quoted in Cleland, *This Reckless Breed*, 297–98).

Bonneville's sense of outrage (see Chapter XXXIX) at Walker's alleged duplicity in traveling to California rather than exploring Great Salt Lake can only be wondered at, consequently. To go to California to search for furs had been Wyeth's ambition not many weeks before Walker started. Once Wyeth had abandoned the idea, Bonneville seized upon it by sending one of his most trusted aides, whom he outfitted with provisions for a year's expedition—more than necessary to explore the shores of Great Salt Lake—hoping in this way to reap the harvest that he and his financial backers expected. That Walker failed in returning with a bounty may be justification for Bonneville's disappointment, and indignation in print might serve to throw the burden on Walker's shoulder for Bonneville's financial losses.

The narrative of Walker's expedition is given in Chapters XXXVIII–XLIX.

22.

The Crow country—A Crow paradise—Habits of the Crows—Anecdotes of Rose, the renegade white man—His fights with the Blackfeet—His elevation—His death—Arapooish, the Crow chief—His eagle—Adventure of Robert Campbell—Honor among Crows

BEFORE WE ACCOMPANY Captain Bonneville into the Crow country, we will impart a few facts about this wild region, and the wild people who inhabit it. We are not aware of the precise boundaries, if there are any, of the country claimed by the Crows; it appears to extend from the Black Hills to the Rocky Mountains, including a part of their lofty ranges, and embracing many of the plains and valleys watered by the Wind River, the Yellowstone, the Powder River, the Little Missouri, and the Nebraska. The country varies in soil and climate; there are vast plains of sand and clay, studded with large red sand-hills; other parts are mountainous and picturesque; it possesses warm springs, and coal mines, and abounds with game.

But let us give the account of the country as rendered by Arapooish,[1] a Crow chief, to Mr. Robert Campbell, of the Rocky Mountain Fur Company.

"The Crow country," said he, "is a good country. The Great Spirit has put it exactly in the right place; while you are in it you fare well; whenever you go out of it, whichever way you travel, you fare worse.

---

[1] Arapooish is a central figure in Chapter 18 of Beckwourth's *Life and Adventures*. The means by which Irving obtained his information from Campbell has not come to light, but it was probably through correspondence.

"If you go to the south, you have to wander over great barren plains; the water is warm and bad, and you meet the fever and ague.

"To the north it is cold; the winters are long and bitter, with no grass; you cannot keep horses there, but must travel with dogs. What is a country without horses?

"On the Columbia they are poor and dirty, paddle about in canoes, and eat fish. Their teeth are worn out; they are always taking fish-bones out of their mouths. Fish is poor food.

"To the east, they dwell in villages; they live well; but they drink the muddy water of the Missouri—that is bad. A Crow's dog would not drink such water.

"About the forks of the Missouri is a fine country; good water; good grass; plenty of buffalo. In summer, it is almost as good as the Crow country; but in winter it is cold; the grass is gone; and there is no salt weed for the horses.

"The Crow country is exactly in the right place. It has snowy mountains and sunny plains; all kinds of climates and good things for every season. When the summer heats scorch the prairies, you can draw up under the mountains, where the air is sweet and cool, the grass fresh, and the bright streams come tumbling out of the snow-banks. There you can hunt the elk, the deer, and the antelope, when their skins are fit for dressing; there you will find plenty of white bears and mountain sheep.

"In the autumn, when your horses are fat and strong from the mountain pastures, you can go down into the plains and hunt the buffalo, or trap beaver on the streams. And when winter comes on, you can take shelter in the woody bottoms along the rivers; there you will find buffalo meat for yourselves, and cotton-wood bark for your horses: or you may winter in the Wind River valley, where there is salt weed in abundance.

"The Crow country is exactly in the right place. Everything good is to be found there. There is no country like the Crow country."

Such is the eulogium on his country by Arapooish.

We have had repeated occasions to speak of the restless and

predatory habits of the Crows. They can muster fifteen hundred fighting men; but their incessant wars with the Blackfeet, and their vagabond, predatory habits, are gradually wearing them out.

In a recent work, we related the circumstance of a white man named Rose, an outlaw, and a designing vagabond, who acted as guide and interpreter to Mr. Hunt and his party, on their journey across the mountains to Astoria, who came near betraying them into the hands of the Crows, and who remained among the tribe, marrying one of their women, and adopting their congenial habits.[2] A few anecdotes of the subsequent fortunes of that renegade may not be uninteresting, especially as they are connected with the fortunes of the tribe.

Rose was powerful in frame and fearless in spirit; and soon by his daring deeds took his rank among the first braves of the tribe. He aspired to command, and knew it was only to be attained by desperate exploits. He distinguished himself in repeated actions with Blackfeet. On one occasion, a band of those savages had fortified themselves within a breastwork, and could not be harmed. Rose proposed to storm the work. "Who will take the lead?" was the demand. "I!" cried he; and putting himself at their head, rushed forward. The first Blackfoot that opposed him he shot down with his rifle, and, snatching up the war-club of his victim, killed four others within the fort. The victory was complete, and Rose returned to the Crow village covered with glory, and bearing five Blackfoot scalps, to be erected as a trophy before his lodge. From this time, he was known among the Crows by the name of Che-ku-kaats, or "the man who killed five." He became chief of the village, or rather band, and for a time was the popular idol. His popularity soon awakened envy among the native braves; he was a stranger, an intruder, a white man. A party seceded from his command. Feuds and civil wars succeeded that lasted for two or three years, until Rose, having contrived to set his adopted brethren by the ears, left them, and went down the Missouri in 1823. Here he fell in with one of the earliest trapping expeditions sent by General Ashley across the mountains. It was conducted by Smith, Fitzpatrick, and

[2] See Astoria (Irving's note). The account of Rose is in Chapter XXIV.

The ADVENTURES of CAPTAIN BONNEVILLE

Sublette. Rose enlisted with them as guide and interpreter. When he got them among the Crows, he was exceedingly generous with their goods; making presents to the braves of his adopted tribe, as became a high-minded chief.

This, doubtless, helped to revive his popularity. In that expedition, Smith and Fitzpatrick were robbed of their horses in Green River valley; the place where the robbery took place still bears the name of Horse Creek. We are not informed whether the horses were stolen through the instigation and management of Rose; it is not improbable, for such was the perfidy he had intended to practice on a former occasion toward Mr. Hunt and his party.

The last anecdote we have of Rose is from an Indian trader. When General Atkinson made his military expedition up the Missouri, in 1825,[3] to protect the fur trade, he held a conference with the Crow nation, at which Rose figured as Indian dignitary and Crow interpreter. The military were stationed at some little distance from the scene of the "big talk"; while the general and the chiefs were smoking pipes and making speeches, the officers, supposing all was friendly, left the troops, and drew near the scene of ceremonial. Some of the more knowing Crows, perceiving this, stole quietly to the camp, and, unobserved, contrived to stop the touch-holes of the field-pieces with dirt. Shortly after, a misunderstanding occurred in the conference: some of the Indians, knowing the cannon to be useless, became insolent. A tumult arose. In the confusion, Colonel O'Fallan snapped a pistol in the face of a brave, and knocked him down with the butt end.[4] The Crows were all in a fury. A chance-

---

[3] General Henry Atkinson was one of the commissioners in this peace treaty expedition of 1825. Major Benjamin O'Fallon was the other commissioner. Chittenden in *American Fur Trade*, II, 608–17, reviews the expedition in detail.

[4] Chittenden quotes from a journal kept on this expedition:

". . . the Crows became very hostile in their conduct, and from their attempting to take the presents before they were told to do so, Major O'Fallon struck three or four of the chiefs over the head with his pistol. About this time General Atkinson, who had been absent from the council to get his dinner, on returning to the council saw the commotion and ordered the troops under arms. This probably saved bloodshed." *American Fur Trade*, II, 614.

Rose is not mentioned here, but an eyewitness, Captain Reuben Holmes, reports the incident with the focus on Rose, who was ordered by Major O'Fallon not to

medley fight was on the point of taking place, when Rose, his natural sympathies as a white man suddenly recurring, broke the stock of his fusee over the head of a Crow warrior, and laid so vigorously about him with the barrel, that he soon put the whole throng to flight. Luckily, as no lives had been lost, this sturdy rib roasting calmed the fury of the Crows, and the tumult ended without serious consequences.

What was the ultimate fate of this vagabond hero is not distinctly known.[5] Some report him to have fallen a victim to disease, brought on by his licentious life; others assert that he was murdered in a feud among the Crows. After all, his residence among these savages, and the influence he acquired over them, had, for a time, some beneficial effects. He is said, not merely to have rendered them more formidable to the Blackfeet, but to have opened their eyes to the policy of cultivating the friendship of the white men.[6]

After Rose's death, his policy continued to be cultivated, with indifferent success, by Arapooish, the chief already mentioned, who had been his great friend, and whose character he had contributed to develope. This sagacious chief endeavored, on every occasion, to restrain the predatory propensities of his tribe when directed against the white men. "If we keep friends with them," said he, "we have nothing to fear from the Blackfeet, and can rule the mountains." Arapooish pretended to be a great "medicine man"; a character among the Indians which is a compound of priest, doctor, prophet, and conjurer. He carried about with him a tame eagle, as his "medicine" or familiar. With the white men, he acknowledged that this

---

strike, although "he stood in the act . . . of striking—the gun continued raised above the back of his own head, ready to fall, at any instant on that of the chief." "The Five Scalps," by Captain Reuben Holmes, reprinted in *Glimpses of the Past*, Missouri Historical Society, Vol. V (January–March, 1938), 53–54. The date of the occurrence was August 4, 1825.

[5] "The Crows say, that the Minnatarees . . . killed him; and the Minnatarees say, that the Crows killed him, in consequence of the Council scene. Be this as it may, he is dead." Holmes, "The Five Scalps," *op. cit.*, 54.

[6] The most extensive account of Edward Rose appeared as "The Five Scalps" in 1828 in the *St. Louis Beacon* (see above). See also Chittenden, *American Fur Trade*, II, 684–88.

was all charlatanism; but said it was necessary, to give him weight and influence among his people.

Mr. Robert Campbell, from whom we have most of these facts, in the course of one of his trapping expeditions, was quartered in the village of Arapooish, and a guest in the lodge of the chieftain. He had collected a large quantity of furs, and, fearful of being plundered, deposited but a part in the lodge of the chief; the rest he buried in a cache. One night, Arapooish came into the lodge with a cloudy brow, and seated himself for a time without saying a word. At length, turning to Campbell, "You have more furs with you," said he, "than you have brought into my lodge?"

"I have," replied Campbell.

"Where are they?"

Campbell knew the uselessness of any prevarication with an Indian; and the importance of complete frankness. He described the exact place where he had concealed his peltries.

"'Tis well," replied Arapooish; "you speak straight. It is just as you say. But your cache has been robbed. Go and see how many skins have been taken from it."

Campbell examined the cache, and estimated his loss to be about one hundred and fifty beaver skins.

Arapooish now summoned a meeting of the village. He bitterly reproached his people for robbing a stranger who had confided to their honor; and commanded that whoever had taken the skins, should bring them back: declaring that, as Campbell was his guest and inmate of his lodge, he would not eat nor drink until every skin was restored to him.

The meeting broke up, and every one dispersed. Arapooish now charged Campbell to give neither reward nor thanks to any one who should bring in the beaver skins, but to keep count as they were delivered.

In a little while, the skins began to make their appearance, a few at a time; they were laid down in the lodge, and those who brought them departed without saying a word. The day passed away. Arapooish sat in one corner of his lodge, wrapped up in his robe, scarcely moving a muscle of his countenance. When night arrived, he demanded if all the skins had been brought in. Above a hundred had been given up, and Campbell expressed himself contented. Not so the Crow chieftain. He fasted all that night, nor tasted a drop of water. In the morning, some more skins were brought in, and continued to come, one and two at a time, throughout the day; until but a few were wanting to make the number complete. Campbell was now anxious to put an end to this fasting of the old chief, and again declared that he was perfectly satisfied. Arapooish demanded what number of skins were yet wanting. On being told, he whispered to some of his people, who disappeared. After a time the number were brought in, though it was evident they were not any of the skins that had been stolen, but others gleaned in the village.

"Is all right now?" demanded Arapooish.

"All is right," replied Campbell.

"Good! Now bring me meat and drink!"

When they were alone together, Arapooish had a conversation with his guest.

"When you come another time among the Crows," said he, "don't hide your goods: trust to them and they will not wrong you. Put your goods in the lodge of a chief, and they are sacred; hide them in a cache, and any one who finds will steal them. My people have now given up your goods for my sake; but there are some foolish young men in the village, who may be disposed to be troublesome. Don't linger, therefore, but pack your horses and be off."

Campbell took his advice, and made his way safely out of the Crow country. He has ever since maintained that the Crows are not so black as they are painted. "Trust to their honor," says he, "and you are safe: trust to their honesty, and they will steal the hair off your head."

Having given these few preliminary particulars, we will resume the course of our narrative.

23.

Departure from Green River valley—Popo Agie—
Its course—The rivers into which it runs—Scenery of
the Bluffs—the great Tar Spring—Volcanic tracts
in the Crow country—Burning Mountain of Powder
River—Sulphur springs—Hidden fires—Colter's
Hell—Wind River—Campbell's party—Fitzpatrick
and his trappers—Captain Stewart, an amateur
traveller—Nathaniel Wyeth—Anecdotes of his
expedition to the Far West—Disaster of Campbell's
party—A union of bands—The Bad Pass—The
rapids—Departure of Fitzpatrick—Embarkation of
peltries—Wyeth and his bull boat—Adventures of
Captain Bonneville in the Bighorn Mountains—
Adventures in the plain—Traces of Indians—
Travelling precautions—Dangers of making a smoke—
The rendezvous

ON THE 25TH of July, Captain Bonneville struck his tents, and set out on his route for the Bighorn, at the head of a party of fifty-six men, including those who were to embark with Cerré. Crossing the Green River valley, he proceeded along the south point of the Wind River range of mountains, and soon fell upon the track of Mr. Robert Campbell's party, which had preceded him by a day.[1] This he pursued, until he perceived that it led down the banks of the Sweet Water to the southeast. As this was different from his proposed direction, he left it; and turning

---

[1] Larpenteur's *Forty Years a Fur Trader* and Wyeth's *Correspondence and Journals* also detail the movements of the trappers from the Green River to the Big Horn in this year.

to the northeast, soon came upon the waters of the Popo Agie.[2] This stream takes its rise in the Wind River Mountains. Its name, like most Indian names, is characteristic. *Popo,* in the Crow language, signifies head; and *A gie,* river. It is the head of a long river, extending from the south end of the Wind River Mountains in a northeast direction, until it falls into the Yellowstone. Its course is generally through plains, but is twice crossed by chains of mountains; the first called the Littlehorn; the second, the Bighorn. After it has forced its way through the first chain, it is called the Horn River; after the second chain, it is called the Bighorn River.[3] Its passage through this last chain is rough and violent; making repeated falls, and rushing down long and furious rapids, which threaten destruction to the navigator; though a hardy trapper is said to have shot down them in a canoe. At the foot of these rapids, is the head of navigation; where it was the intention of the parties to construct boats, and embark.

Proceeding down along the Popo Agie, Captain Bonneville came again in full view of the "Bluffs," as they are called, extending from the base of the Wind River Mountains far away to the east, and presenting to the eye a confusion of hills and cliffs of red sandstone, some peaked and angular, some round, some broken into crags and precipices, and piled up in fantastic masses; but all naked and sterile. There appeared to be no soil favorable to vegetation, nothing but coarse gravel; yet, over all this isolated, barren landscape, were diffused such atmospherical tints and hues, as to blend the whole into harmony and beauty.

In this neighborhood, the captain made search for "the great Tar Spring,"[4] one of the wonders of the mountains; the medicinal prop-

[2] Trapper journals reveal various attempts to render the Crow pronunciation phonetically: *Popoasia* (Leonard), *Po po azia* (Russell), *Popoise* (Wyeth), *Pappah-ah-je* (Larpenteur).

[3] The Big Horn today is considered to begin at the junction of Wind River and the Popo Agie near Riverton, Wyoming.

[4] Larpenteur recorded that Dr. Benjamin Harrison, travelling with Campbell ahead of Bonneville, also visited it "on account of the remarkable oil spring. . . ." *Forty Years a Fur Trader,* 32. An interesting account is in Russell, *Journal of a Trapper,* 57–58. C. G. Coutant wrote: ". . . Bonneville made the mistake of sup-

The ADVENTURES of CAPTAIN BONNEVILLE

erties of which, he had heard extravagantly lauded by the trappers. After a toilsome search, he found it at the foot of a sand-bluff, a little east of the Wind River Mountains; where it exuded in a small stream of the color and consistency of tar. The men immediately hastened to collect a quantity of it, to use as an ointment for the galled backs of their horses, and as a balsam for their own pains and aches. From the description given of it, it is evidently the bituminous oil, called petrolium or naphtha, which forms a principal ingredient in the potent medicine called British Oil. It is found in various parts of Europe and Asia, in several of the West India islands, and in some places of the United States. In the state of New York, it is called Seneca Oil, from being found near the Seneca lake.

The Crow country has other natural curiosities, which are held in superstitious awe by the Indians, and considered great marvels by the trappers. Such is the Burning Mountain, on Powder River, abounding with anthracite coal. Here the earth is hot and cracked; in many places emitting smoke and sulphurous vapors, as if covering concealed fires. A volcanic tract of similar character is found on Stinking River,[5] one of the tributaries of the Bighorn, which takes its unhappy name from the odor derived from sulphurous springs and streams. This last mentioned place was first discovered by Colter, a hunter belonging to Lewis and Clarke's exploring party, who came upon it in the course of his lonely wanderings, and gave such an account of its gloomy terrors, its hidden fires, smoking pits, noxious streams, and the all-pervading "smell of brimstone," that it received, and has ever since retained among trappers, the name of "Colter's Hell!"[6]

posing he was on the Popo Agie, whereas he had only reached the south branch of that stream, known ... as the Little Popo Agie." *The History of Wyoming*, 172. An oil well is in this vicinity today.

[5] Now the Shoshone River, a tributary of the Big Horn. A volcanic, thermal area on this river is to be seen today near Cody, Wyoming, the true location of the place designated Colter's Hell, where Irving correctly places it. The fullest account is in Burton Harris' *John Colter*.

[6] John Colter (1770?–1813), employed by Manuel Lisa in 1807, had left Lisa's newly constructed fort at the mouth of the Big Horn that autumn to wander among the Indians and urge them to bring their trade to Lisa's post. In these wanderings he crossed the Shoshone River, climbed the Wind River Range, and

The ADVENTURES *of* CAPTAIN BONNEVILLE

Resuming his descent along the left bank of the Popo Agie, Captain Bonneville soon reached the plains; where he found several large streams entering from the west. Among these was Wind River, which gives its name to the mountains among which it takes its rise. This is one of the most important streams of the Crow country. The river being much swollen, Captain Bonneville halted at its mouth, and sent out scouts to look for a fording place. While thus encamped, he beheld in the course of the afternoon a long line of horsemen descending the slope of the hills on the opposite side of the Popo Agie. His first idea was that they were Indians; he soon discovered, however, that they were white men, and, by the long line of pack-horses, ascertained them to be the convoy of Campbell, which, having descended the Sweet Water,[7] was now on its way to the Horn River.

The two parties came together two or three days afterwards, on the 4th of August, after having passed through the gap of the Littlehorn Mountain. In company with Campbell's convoy was a trapping party of the Rocky Mountain Company, headed by Fitzpatrick; who, after Campbell's embarkation on the Bighorn, was to take charge of all the horses, and proceed on a trapping campaign. There were, moreover, two chance companions in the rival camp. One was Captain Stewart,[8] of the British army, a gentleman of noble connections, who was amusing himself by a wandering tour in the Far

---

descended it into Jackson Hole. Then he probably entered modern Idaho west of the Tetons, and returned by way of the Yellowstone Park area in the following spring (1808). In *Astoria*, Chapter XV, Irving recounted Colter's celebrated race for life from the Blackfeet Indians in the summer of 1808. For a brief account of Colter's career, see Edgeley W. Todd, "John Colter, Mountain Man," *Colorado Quarterly*, Vol. II (1953), 79–91.

[7] This would have taken them far off course. Instead, they crossed South Pass and also the Sweetwater, and then veered northeast.

[8] William George Drummond Stewart (1796–1871). The fullest account of his activities in the West, with the exception of 1843, is in DeVoto's *Across the Wide Missouri*. For the 1843 expedition, see Edgeley W. Todd, "Scotsman in Buckskin," *Colorado Quarterly*, Vol. IV (1956), 309–36; also Matthew C. Field, *Prairie and Mountain Sketches* (ed. by Kate L. Gregg and John F. McDermott).

Stewart was the author of two novels, *Altowan* and *Edward Warren*, both reflecting his experiences among the mountain men and often presenting vivid descriptions of trapper and mountain life.

West; in the course of which, he had lived in hunter's style; accompanying various bands of traders, trappers, and Indians; and manifesting that relish for the wilderness that belongs to men of game spirit.

The other casual inmate of Mr. Campbell's camp was Mr. Nathaniel Wyeth;[9] the self-same leader of the band of New England salmon fishers, with whom we parted company in the valley of Pierre's Hole, after the battle with the Blackfeet. A few days after that affair, he again set out from the rendezvous in company with Milton Sublette and his brigade of trappers. On his march, he visited the battle ground, and penetrated to the deserted fort of the Blackfeet in the midst of the wood. It was a dismal scene. The fort was strewed with the mouldering bodies of the slain; while vultures soared aloft, or sat brooding on the trees around; and Indian dogs howled about the place, as if bewailing the death of their masters.[10] Wyeth travelled for a considerable distance to the southwest, in company with Milton Sublette, when they separated; and the former, with eleven men, the remnant of his band, pushed on for Snake River; kept down the course of that eventful stream; traversed the Blue Mountains, trapping beaver occasionally by the way, and finally, after hardships of all kinds, arrived, on the 29th of October,[11] at Vancouver, on the Columbia, the main factory of the Hudson's Bay Company.

He experienced hospitable treatment at the hands of the agents of that company; but his men, heartily tired of wandering in the wilderness, or tempted by other prospects, refused, for the most part, to continue any longer in his service. Some set off for the Sand-

---

[9] Wyeth's journal for August 1 reads: "Same camp find Mr. Bonneville camped a few miles above us." *Correspondence and Journals,* 207.

[10] Irving paraphrased Wyeth's manuscript journal for July 24, 1832:
"On the 24th we again moved out of the valley in the same direction as at first viz about S.E. and encamped . . . [.] during the march I visited the scene of our conflict for the first time since the battle   the din of arms was now changed into the noise of the vulture and the howling of masterless dogs   the stench was extreme   most of the men in the fort must have perished   I soon retired from this scene of disgusting butchery." *Correspondence and Journals,* 160.

[11] Wyeth's *Correspondence and Journals,* 176, confirms this date.

wich Islands; some entered into other employ. Wyeth found, too, that a great part of the goods he had brought with him were unfitted for the Indian trade; in a word, his expedition, undertaken entirely on his own resources, proved a failure. He lost everything invested in it, but his hopes. These were as strong as ever. He took note of every thing, therefore, that could be of service to him in the further prosecution of his project; collected all the information within his reach, and then set off, accompanied by merely two men, on his return journey across the continent. He had got thus far "by hook and by crook," a mode in which a New England man can make his way all over the world, and through all kinds of difficulties, and was now bound for Boston; in full confidence of being able to form a company for the salmon fishery and fur trade of the Columbia.[12]

The party of Mr. Campbell had met with a disaster in the course of their route from the Sweet Water. Three or four of the men, who were reconnoitering the country in advance of the main body, were visited one night in their camp, by fifteen or twenty Shoshonies. Considering this tribe as perfectly friendly, they received them in the most cordial and confiding manner. In the course of the night, the man on guard near the horses fell sound asleep; upon which a Shoshonie shot him in the head, and nearly killed him. The savages then made off with the horses, leaving the rest of the party to find their way to the main body on foot.[13]

The rival companies of Captain Bonneville and Mr. Campbell, thus fortuitously brought together, now prosecuted their journey in great good fellowship; forming a joint camp of about a hundred men. The captain, however, began to entertain doubts that Fitzpatrick and his trappers, who kept profound silence as to their future movements, intended to hunt the same grounds which he had selected for his autumnal campaign; which lay to the west of the Horn River, on its tributary streams. In the course of his march, therefore,

[12] Irving's summary of Wyeth's actions is digested from the latter's *Correspondence and Journals*, 160–206.

[13] This incident is mentioned by Larpenteur, *Forty Years a Fur Trader*, 32. Wyeth in his *Correspondence and Journals*, 207–208, relates it in more detail. Irving summarized Wyeth's journal for August 1, but he probably owed something to Bonneville's journal as well.

he secretly detached a small party of trappers, to make their way to those hunting grounds, while he continued on with the main body; appointing a rendezvous, at the next full moon, about the 28th of August, at a place called the Medicine Lodge.[14]

On reaching the second chain, called the Bighorn Mountains, where the river forced its impetuous way through a precipitous defile, with cascades and rapids, the travellers were obliged to leave its banks, and traverse the mountains by a rugged and frightful route, emphatically called the "Bad Pass." Descending the opposite side, they again made for the river banks; and about the middle of August, reached the point below the rapids where the river becomes navigable for boats. Here Captain Bonneville detached a second party of trappers, consisting of ten men, to seek and join those whom he had detached while on the route; appointing for them the same rendezvous, (at the Medicine Lodge,) on the 28th of August.

All hands now set to work to construct "bull boats," as they are technically called; a light, fragile kind of bark, characteristic of the expedients and inventions of the wilderness; being formed of buffalo skins, stretched on frames.[15] They are sometimes, also, called skin boats. Wyeth was the first ready; and, with his usual promptness and hardihood, launched his frail bark, singly, on this wild and hazardous voyage, down an almost interminable succession of rivers, winding through countries teeming with savage hordes. Milton Sublette, his former fellow traveller, and his companion in the battle scenes of Pierre's Hole, took passage in his boat. His crew

---

[14] This river is difficult to identify on modern maps. A Medicine Lodge Creek flows west from the Big Horn Mountains, joining Paintrock Creek. But Bonneville had despatched his men up the west side of the Big Horn River, not the east side. They went as far north as Greybull River. Medicine Lodge Creek is possibly designated on modern maps as Fifteenmile Creek, opposite Worland, Wyoming, or Owl Creek north of Thermopolis.

[15] These boats were readily improvised as needed. Raw hides, stretched over a green-willow frame, were dried over a slow fire, and the seams waterproofed with elk tallow. Describing his bull boats, Wyeth said, "ours is made of three skins is 18 feet long and about $5\frac{1}{2}$ wde sharp at both ends round bottom." *Correspondence and Journals*, 209. He found that the bottoms should have been flatter; his boats drew one and a half feet, which was too much, and he grounded often as a result.

consisted of two white men, and two Indians. We shall hear further of Wyeth, and his wild voyage, in the course of our wanderings about the Far West.

The remaining parties soon completed their several armaments. That of Captain Bonneville was composed of three bull boats, in which he embarked all his peltries, giving them in charge of Mr. Cerré, with a party of thirty-six men. Mr. Campbell took command of his own boats, and the little squadrons were soon gliding down the bright current of the Bighorn.

The secret precautions which Captain Bonneville had taken to throw his men first into the trapping ground west of the Bighorn, were, probably, superfluous. It did not appear that Fitzpatrick had intended to hunt in that direction. The moment Mr. Campbell and his men embarked with the peltries, Fitzpatrick took charge of all the horses, amounting to above a hundred, and struck off to the east, to trap upon Littlehorn, Powder, and Tongue rivers.[16] He was accompanied by Captain Stewart, who was desirous of having a range about the Crow country. Of the adventures they met with in that region of vagabonds and horse stealers, we shall have something to relate hereafter.

Captain Bonneville being now left to prosecute his trapping campaign without rivalry, set out, on the 17th of August, for the rendezvous at Medicine Lodge. He had but four men remaining with him, and forty-six horses to take care of; with these he had to make his way over mountain and plain, through a marauding, horse-stealing region, full of peril for a numerous cavalcade so slightly manned. He addressed himself to his difficult journey, however, with his usual alacrity of spirit.

In the afternoon of his first day's journey, on drawing near to the Bighorn Mountain, on the summit of which he intended to encamp for the night, he observed, to his disquiet, a cloud of smoke rising from its base. He came to a halt, and watched it anxiously. It was very irregular; sometimes it would almost die away; and then would mount up in heavy volumes. There was, apparently, a

---

[16] Tributaries of the Yellowstone River having their source on the east and north slopes of the Big Horn Mountains.

The Adventures of Captain Bonneville

large party encamped there; probably, some ruffian horde of Blackfeet. At any rate, it would not do for so small a number of men, with so numerous a cavalcade, to venture within sight of any wandering tribe. Captain Bonneville and his companions, therefore, avoided this dangerous neighborhood; and, proceeding with extreme caution, reached the summit of the mountain, apparently without being discovered. Here they found a deserted Blackfoot fort, in which they ensconced themselves; disposed of every thing as securely as possible, and passed the night without molestation. Early the next morning they descended the south side of the mountain into the great plain extending between it and the Littlehorn range. Here they soon came upon numerous footprints, and the carcasses of buffaloes; by which they knew there must be Indians not far off. Captain Bonneville now began to feel solicitude about the two small parties of trappers which he had detached, lest the Indians should have come upon them before they had united their forces. But he felt still more solicitude about his own party; for it was hardly to be expected he could traverse these naked plains undiscovered, when Indians were abroad; and should he be discovered, his chance would be a desperate one. Everything now depended upon the greatest circumspection. It was dangerous to discharge a gun, or light a fire, or make the least noise, where such quick-eared and quick-sighted enemies were at hand. In the course of the day they saw indubitable signs that the buffalo had been roaming there in great numbers, and had recently been frightened away. That night they encamped with the greatest care; and threw up a strong breastwork for their protection.

For the two succeeding days they pressed forward rapidly, but cautiously, across the great plain; fording the tributary streams of the Horn River; encamping one night among thickets; the next, on an island; meeting, repeatedly, with traces of Indians; and now and then, in passing through a defile, experiencing alarms that induced them to cock their rifles.

On the last day of their march hunger got the better of their caution, and they shot a fine buffalo bull at the risk of being betrayed by the report. They did not halt to make a meal, but carried the meat on with them to the place of rendezvous, the Medicine Lodge, where they arrived safely, in the evening, and celebrated their arrival by a hearty supper.

The next morning they erected a strong pen for the horses, and a fortress of logs for themselves; and continued to observe the greatest caution. Their cooking was all done at mid-day, when the fire makes no glare, and a moderate smoke cannot be perceived at any great distance. In the morning and the evening, when the wind is lulled, the smoke rises perpendicularly in a blue column, or floats in light clouds above the tree-tops, and can be discovered from afar.

In this way the little party remained for several days, cautiously encamped, until, on the 29th of August, the two detachments they had been expecting, arrived together at the rendezvous. They, as usual, had their several tales of adventures to relate to the captain, which we will furnish to the reader in the next chapter.

24.

Adventures of the party of ten—The Balaamite mule—
A dead point—The mysterious elks—A night attack—
A retreat—Travelling under an alarm—A joyful
meeting—Adventures of the other party—A decoy
elk—Retreat to an island—A savage dance of
triumph—Arrival at Wind River

THE ADVENTURES of the detachment of ten are the first in order. These trappers, when they separated from Captain Bonneville at the place where the furs were embarked, proceeded to the foot of the Bighorn Mountain, and having encamped, one of them mounted his mule and went out to set his trap in a neighboring stream. He had not proceeded far when his steed came to a full stop. The trapper kicked and cudgelled, but to every blow and kick the mule snorted and kicked up, but still refused to budge an inch. The rider now cast his eyes warily around in search of some cause for this demur, when, to his dismay, he discovered an Indian fort within gunshot distance, lowering through the twilight. In a twinkling he wheeled about; his mule now seemed as eager to get on as himself, and in a few moments brought him, clattering with his traps, among his comrades. He was jeered at for his alacrity in retreating; his report was treated as a false alarm; his brother trappers contented themselves with reconnoitring the fort at a distance, and pronounced that it was deserted.

As night set in, the usual precaution, enjoined by Captain Bonneville on his men, was observed. The horses were brought in and tied, and a guard stationed over them. This done, the men wrapped themselves in their blankets, stretched themselves before the fire, and being fatigued with a long day's march, and gorged with a hearty supper, were soon in a profound sleep.

The camp fires gradually died away; all was dark and silent; the sentinel stationed to watch the horses had marched as far, and supped as heartily as any of his companions, and while they snored, he began to nod at his post. After a time, a low trampling noise reached his ear. He half opened his closing eyes, and beheld two or three elks moving about the lodges, picking, and smelling, and grazing here and there. The sight of elk within the purlieus of the camp caused some little surprise; but having had his supper, he cared not for elk meat, and, suffering them to graze about unmolested, soon relapsed into a doze.

Suddenly, before daybreak, a discharge of firearms, and a struggle and tramp of horses, made every one start to his feet. The first move was to secure the horses. Some were gone; others were struggling, and kicking, and trembling, for there was a horrible uproar of whoops, and yells, and firearms. Several trappers stole quietly from the camp, and succeeded in driving in the horses which had broken away; the rest were tethered still more strongly. A breastwork was thrown up of saddles, baggage, and camp furniture, and all hands waited anxiously for daylight. The Indians, in the meantime, collected on a neighboring height, kept up the most horrible clamor, in hopes of striking a panic into the camp, or frightening off the horses. When the day dawned, the trappers attacked them briskly and drove them to some distance. A desultory fire was kept up for an hour, when the Indians, seeing nothing was to be gained, gave up the contest and retired. They proved to be a war party of Blackfeet, who, while in search of the Crow tribe, had fallen upon the trail of Captain Bonneville on the Popo Agie, and dogged him to the Bighorn; but had been completely baffled by his vigilance. They had then waylaid the present detachment, and were actually housed in perfect silence within their fort, when the mule of the trapper made such a dead point.

The savages went off uttering the wildest denunciations of hostility, mingled with opprobrious terms in broken English, and gesticulations of the most insulting kind.

In this melée, one white man was wounded, and two horses were killed. On preparing the morning's meal, however, a number of cups, knives, and other articles were missing, which had, doubtless, been carried off by the fictitious elk, during the slumber of the very sagacious sentinel.

As the Indians had gone off in the direction which the trappers had intended to travel, the latter changed their route, and pushed forward rapidly through the "Bad Pass," nor halted until night; when, supposing themselves out of the reach of the enemy, they contented themselves with tying up their horses and posting a guard. They had scarce laid down to sleep, when a dog strayed into the camp with a small pack of moccasons tied upon his back; for dogs are made to carry burdens among the Indians. The sentinel, more knowing than he of the preceding night, awoke his companions and reported the circumstance. It was evident that Indians were at hand. All were instantly at work; a strong pen was soon constructed for the horses, after completing which, they resumed their slumbers with the composure of men long inured to dangers.

In the next night, the prowling of dogs about the camp, and various suspicious noises, showed that Indians were still hovering about them. Hurrying on by long marches, they at length fell upon a trail, which, with the experienced eye of veteran woodmen, they soon discovered to be that of the party of trappers detached by Captain Bonneville when on his march, and which they were sent to join. They likewise ascertained from various signs, that this party had suffered some maltreatment from the Indians. They now pursued the trail with intense anxiety; it carried them to the banks of the stream called the Gray Bull, and down along its course, until they came to where it empties into the Horn River.[1] Here, to their great joy, they discovered the comrades of whom they were in search, all strongly fortified, and in a state of great watchfulness and anxiety.

We now take up the adventures of this first detachment of trap-

[1] The Greybull River flows from the west into the Big Horn at Greybull, Wyoming. They were thus a short distance north of where Bonneville camped on Medicine Lodge Creek.

pers. These men, after parting with the main body under Captain Bonneville, had proceeded slowly for several days up the course of the river, trapping beaver as they went. One morning, as they were about to visit their traps, one of the camp-keepers pointed to a fine elk, grazing at a distance, and requested them to shoot it. Three of the trappers started off for the purpose. In passing a thicket, they were fired upon by some savages in ambush, and at the same time, the pretended elk, throwing off his hide and his horn, started forth an Indian warrior.

One of the three trappers had been brought down by the volley; the others fled to the camp, and all hands, seizing up whatever they could carry off, retreated to a small island in the river, and took refuge among the willows. Here they were soon joined by their comrade who had fallen, but who had merely been wounded in the neck.

In the meantime the Indians took possession of the deserted camp, with all the traps, accoutrements, and horses. While they were busy among the spoils, a solitary trapper, who had been absent at his work, came sauntering to the camp with his traps on his back. He had approached near by, when an Indian came forward and motioned him to keep away; at the same moment, he was perceived by his comrades on the island, and warned of his danger with loud cries. The poor fellow stood for a moment, bewildered and aghast, then dropping his traps, wheeled and made off at full speed, quickened by a sportive volley which the Indians rattled after him.

In high good humor with their easy triumph, the savages now formed a circle round the fire and performed a war dance, with the unlucky trappers for rueful spectators. This done, emboldened by what they considered cowardice on the part of the white men, they neglected their usual mode of bush-fighting, and advanced openly within twenty paces of the willows. A sharp volley from the trappers brought them to a sudden halt, and laid three of them breathless. The chief, who had stationed himself on an eminence to direct all the movements of his people, seeing three of his warriors laid low, ordered the rest to retire. They immediately did so, and the whole

The Adventures of Captain Bonneville

band soon disappeared behind a point of woods, carrying off with them the horses, traps, and the greater part of the baggage.

It was just after this misfortune that the party of ten men discovered this forlorn band of trappers in a fortress, which they had thrown up after their disaster. They were so perfectly dismayed, that they could not be induced even to go in quest of their traps, which they had set in a neighboring stream. The two parties now joined their forces, and made their way, without further misfortune, to the rendezvous.

Captain Bonneville perceived from the reports of these parties, as well as from what he had observed himself in his recent march, that he was in a neighborhood teeming with danger. Two wandering Snake Indians, also, who visited the camp, assured him that there were two large bands of Crows marching rapidly upon him. He broke up his encampment, therefore, on the 1st of September, made his way to the south, across the Littlehorn Mountain, until he reached Wind River, and then turning westward, moved slowly up the banks of that stream, giving time for his men to trap as he proceeded. As it was not in the plan of the present hunting campaigns to go near the caches on Green River, and as the trappers were in want of traps to replace those they had lost, Captain Bonneville undertook to visit the caches, and procure a supply. To accompany him in this hazardous expedition, which would take him through the defiles of the Wind River Mountains, and up the Green River valley, he took but three men; the main party were to continue on trapping up toward the head of Wind River, near which he was to rejoin them, just about the place where that stream issues from the mountains. We shall accompany the captain on his adventurous errand.

25.

Captain Bonneville sets out for Green River valley—Journey up the Popo Agie—Buffaloes—The staring white bears—The smoke—The warm springs—Attempt to traverse the Wind River Mountains—The Great Slope—Mountain dells and chasms—Crystal lakes—Ascent of a snowy peak—Sublime prospect—A panorama—"Les dignes de pitie," or wild men of the mountains

HAVING FORDED WIND RIVER a little above its mouth, Captain Bonneville and his three companions proceeded across a gravelly plain, until they fell upon the Popo Agie,[1] up the left bank of which they held their course, nearly in a southerly direction. Here they came upon numerous droves of buffalo, and halted for the purpose of procuring a supply of beef. As the hunters were stealing cautiously to get within shot of the game, two small white bears suddenly presented themselves in their path, and, rising upon their hind legs, contemplated them for some time with a whimsically solemn gaze. The hunters remained motionless; whereupon the bears, having apparently satisfied their curiosity, lowered themselves upon all fours, and began to withdraw. The hunters now advanced, upon which the bears turned, rose again upon their haunches, and repeated their serio-comic examination. This was repeated several times, until the hunters, piqued at their unmannerly staring, rebuked it with a discharge of their rifles. The bears made an awkward bound or two, as if wounded, and then walked off with great gravity, seeming to commune together, and every now and then turning to take another look at the hunters. It

[1] A short distance south of modern Riverton, Wyoming.

was well for the latter that the bears were but half grown, and had not yet acquired the ferocity of their kind.

The buffalo were somewhat startled at the report of the firearms; but the hunters succeeded in killing a couple of fine cows, and, having secured the best of the meat, continued forward until some time after dark, when, encamping in a large thicket of willows, they made a great fire, roasted buffalo beef enough for half a score, disposed of the whole of it with keen relish and high glee, and then "turned in" for the night and slept soundly, like weary and well fed hunters.

At daylight they were in the saddle again, and skirted along the river, passing through fresh grassy meadows, and a succession of beautiful groves of willows and cotton-wood. Toward evening, Captain Bonneville observed a smoke at a distance rising from among hills, directly in the route he was pursuing. Apprehensive of some hostile band, he concealed the horses in a thicket, and, accompanied by one of his men, crawled cautiously up a height, from which he could overlook the scene of danger. Here, with a spy-glass, he reconnoitred the surrounding country, but not a lodge nor fire, not a man, horse, nor dog, was to be discovered; in short, the smoke which had caused such alarm proved to be the vapor from several warm, or rather hot springs of considerable magnitude, pouring forth streams in every direction over a bottom of white clay. One of the springs was about twenty-five yards in diameter, and so deep that the water was of a bright green color.

They were now advancing diagonally upon the chain of Wind River Mountains, which lay between them and Green River valley. To coast round their southern points would be a wide circuit; whereas, could they force their way through them, they might proceed in a straight line. The mountains were lofty, with snowy peaks and cragged sides; it was hoped, however, that some practicable defile might be found. They attempted, accordingly, to penetrate the mountains by following up one of the branches of the Popo Agie, but soon found themselves in the midst of stupendous crags and precipices that barred all progress. Retracing their steps, and falling back upon the river, they consulted where to make another attempt. They were too close beneath the mountains to scan them generally, but they now recollected having noticed, from the plain, a beautiful slope rising, at an angle of about thirty degrees, and apparently without any break, until it reached the snowy region. Seeking this gentle acclivity, they began to ascend it with alacrity, trusting to find at the top one of those elevated plains which prevail among the Rocky Mountains. The slope was covered with coarse gravel, interspersed with plates of freestone. They attained the summit with some toil, but found, instead of a level, or rather undulating plain, that they were on the brink of a deep and precipitous ravine, from the bottom of which rose a second slope, similar to the one they had just ascended. Down into this profound ravine they made their way by a rugged path, or rather fissure of the rocks, and then labored up the second slope. They gained the summit only to find themselves on another ravine, and now perceived that this vast mountain, which had presented such a sloping and even side to the distant beholder on the plain, was shagged by frightful precipices, and seamed with longitudinal chasms, deep and dangerous.

In one of these wild dells they passed the night, and slept soundly and sweetly after their fatigues. Two days more of arduous climbing and scrambling only served to admit them into the heart of this mountainous and awful solitude; where difficulties increased as they proceeded. Sometimes they scrambled from rock to rock, up the bed of some mountain stream, dashing its bright way down to the plains; sometimes they availed themselves of the paths made by the deer and the mountain sheep, which, however, often took them to the brinks of fearful precipices, or led to rugged defiles, impassable for their horses. At one place, they were obliged to slide their horses down the face of a rock, in which attempt some of the poor animals lost their footing, rolled to the bottom, and came near being dashed to pieces.

In the afternoon of the second day, the travellers attained one of the elevated valleys locked up in this singular bed of mountains. Here were two bright and beautiful little lakes, set like mirrors in the midst of stern and rocky heights, and surrounded by grassy meadows, inexpressibly refreshing to the eye. These probably were among the sources of those mighty streams which take their rise among these mountains, and wander hundreds of miles through the plains.

In the green pastures bordering upon these lakes, the travellers halted to repose, and to give their weary horses time to crop the sweet and tender herbage. They had now ascended to a great height above the level of the plains, yet they beheld huge crags of granite piled one upon another, and beetling like battlements far above them. While two of the men remained in the camp with the horses, Captain Bonneville, accompanied by the other men [man], set out to climb a neighboring height, hoping to gain a commanding prospect, and discern some practicable route through this stupendous labyrinth. After much toil, he reached the summit of a lofty cliff, but it was only to behold gigantic peaks rising all around, and towering far into the snowy regions of the atmosphere. Selecting one which appeared to be the highest, he crossed a narrow intervening valley, and began to scale it. He soon found that he had undertaken a tremendous task; but the pride of man is never more obstinate than when climbing mountains. The ascent was so steep and rugged that he and his companion were frequently obliged to clamber on hands and knees, with their guns slung upon their backs. Frequently, exhausted with fatigue, and dripping with perspiration, they threw themselves upon the snow, and took handfuls of it to allay their parching thirst. At one place, they even stripped off their coats and hung them upon the bushes, and thus lightly clad, proceeded to scramble over these eternal snows. As they ascended still higher, there were cool breezes that refreshed and braced them, and springing with new ardor to their task, they at length attained the summit.

Here a scene burst upon the view of Captain Bonneville, that for a time astonished and overwhelmed him with its immensity. He stood, in fact, upon that dividing ridge which Indians regard as the crest of the world; and on each side of which, the landscape may be said to decline to the two cardinal oceans of the globe. Whichever way he turned his eye, it was confounded by the vastness and variety of objects. Beneath him, the Rocky Mountains seemed to open all their secret recesses: deep, solemn valleys; treasured lakes; dreary passes; rugged defiles, and foaming torrents; while beyond their savage precincts, the eye was lost in an almost immeasurable landscape; stretching on every side into dim and hazy distance, like the expanse of a summer's sea. Whichever way he looked, he beheld vast plains glimmering with reflected sunshine; mighty streams wandering on their shining course toward either ocean, and snowy mountains, chain beyond chain, and peak beyond peak, till they melted like clouds into the horizon. For a time, the Indian fable seemed realized: he had attained that height from which the Blackfoot warrior, after death, first catches a view of the land of souls, and beholds the happy hunting grounds spread out below him, brightening with the abodes of the free and generous spirits. The captain stood for a long while gazing upon this scene, lost in a crowd of vague and indefinite ideas and sensations. A long-drawn inspiration at length relieved him from this enthralment of the mind, and he began to analyze the parts of this vast panorama. A simple enumeration of a few of its features may give some idea of its collective grandeur and magnificence.

The peak on which the captain had taken his stand commanded the whole Wind River chain; which, in fact, may rather be considered one immense mountain, broken into snowy peaks and lateral spurs, and seamed with narrow valleys. Some of these valleys glittered with silver lakes and gushing streams; the fountain heads, as it were, of the mighty tributaries to the Atlantic and Pacific Oceans. Beyond the snowy peaks, to the south, and far, far below the mountain range, the gentle river, called the Sweet Water, was seen pursuing its tranquil way through the rugged regions of the Black Hills. In the east, the head waters of Wind River wandered through a plain, until, mingling in one powerful current, they forced their way through the range of Horn Mountains, and were lost to view. To the north were caught glimpses of the upper streams of the Yellowstone, that great tributary of the Missouri. In another direction were to be seen some of the sources of the Oregon, or Columbia, flowing to the northwest, past those towering landmarks the Three Tetons, and pouring down into the great lava plain; while, almost at the captain's feet, the Green River, or Colorado of the West, set forth on its wandering pilgrimage to the Gulf of California; at first a mere mountain torrent, dashing northward over a crag and precipice, in a succession of cascades, and tumbling into the plain where, expanding into an ample river, it circled away to the south, and after alternately shining out and disappearing in the mazes of the vast landscape, was finally lost in a horizon of mountains. The day was calm and cloudless, and the atmosphere so pure that objects were discernible at an astonishing distance. The whole of this immense area was inclosed by an outer range of shadowy peaks, some of them faintly marked on the horizon, which seemed to wall it in from the rest of the earth.

It is to be regretted that Captain Bonneville had no instruments with him with which to ascertain the altitude of this peak. He gives it as his opinion that it is the loftiest point of the North American continent; but of this we have no satisfactory proof. It is certain that the Rocky Mountains are of an altitude vastly superior to what was formerly supposed. We rather incline to the opinion that the highest peak is further to the northward, and is the same measured by Mr. Thompson, surveyor to the Northwest Company; who, by the joint means of the barometer and trigonometric measurement, ascertained it to be twenty-five thousand feet above the level of the sea; an elevation only inferior to that of the Himalayas.[2]

For a long time, Captain Bonneville remained gazing around him with wonder and enthusiasm; at length the chill and wintry winds, whirling about the snow-clad height, admonished him to descend. He soon regained the spot where he and his companions [companion] had thrown off their coats, which were now gladly resumed,

[2] See the letter of Professor Renwick, in the Appendix to Astoria (Irving's note).

Irving had appealed to Professor James Renwick, Columbia College, New York, for information about the altitude of the Rocky Mountains. Renwick replied on February 23, 1836. The figure of 25,000 feet is far in excess of the elevation of the highest mountain on the North American continent, which is Mt. McKinley, with an altitude of 20,321 feet.

The ADVENTURES of CAPTAIN BONNEVILLE

and, retracing their course down the peak, they safely rejoined their companions on the border of the lake.[3]

Notwithstanding the savage and almost inaccessible nature of these mountains, they have their inhabitants. As one of the party was out hunting, he came upon the solitary track of a man in a lonely valley. Following it up, he reached the brow of a cliff, whence he beheld three savages running across the valley below him. He fired his gun to call their attention, hoping to induce them to turn back. They only fled the faster, and disappeared among the rocks. The hunter returned and reported what he had seen. Captain Bonneville at once concluded that these belonged to a kind of hermit race, scanty in number, that inhabit the highest and most inaccessible fastnesses. They speak the Shoshonie language, and probably are offsets from that tribe, though they have peculiarities of their own, which distinguish them from all other Indians. They are miserably poor; own no horses, and are destitute of every convenience to be derived from an intercourse with the whites. Their weapons are bows and stone-pointed arrows, with which they hunt the deer, the elk, and the mountain sheep. They are to be found scattered about the countries of the Shoshonie, Flathead, Crow, and Blackfeet tribes; but their residences are always in lonely places, and the clefts of the rocks.

Their footsteps are often seen by the trappers in the high and solitary valleys among the mountains, and the smokes of their fires descried among the precipices, but they themselves are rarely met with, and still more rarely brought to a parley, so great is their shyness, and their dread of strangers.

As their poverty offers no temptation to the marauder, and as they are inoffensive in their habits, they are never the objects of

[3] "The peak on which Captain Bonneville . . . climbed is thirty-six miles on a direct line west from Lander [Wyoming], and will be found on a map of the state marked Mt. Bonneville. The Captain earned the distinction of having his name given to one of the grandest peaks of the Wind River range. . . . Later explorations by the United States government resulted in the selection of this peak as the one Bonneville ascended. . . ." Coutant, *The History of Wyoming*, 176. Irving's description conveys an excellent sense of the ruggedness and grandeur of these mountains.

warfare: should one of them, however, fall into the hands of a war party, he is sure to be made a sacrifice, for the sake of that savage trophy, a scalp, and that barbarous ceremony, a scalp dance. These forlorn beings, forming a mere link between human nature and the brute, have been looked down upon with pity and contempt by the creole trappers, who have given them the appellation of "les dignes de pitie," or "the objects of pity." They appear more worthy to be called the wild men of the mountains.

26.

A retrogade move—Channel of a mountain torrent—
Alpine scenery—Cascades—Beaver valleys—Beavers
at work—Their architecture—Their modes of felling
trees—Mode of trapping beaver—Contests of skill—
A beaver "up to trap"—Arrival at the
Green River caches

THE VIEW from the snowy peak of the Wind River Mountains, while it had excited Captain Bonneville's enthusiasm, had satisfied him that it would be useless to force a passage westward, through multiplying barriers of cliffs and precipices. Turning his face eastward, therefore, he endeavored to regain the plains, intending to make the circuit round the southern point of the mountain. To descend, and to extricate himself from the heart of this rock-piled wilderness, was almost as difficult as to penetrate it. Taking his course down the ravine of a tumbling stream, the commencement of some future river, he descended from rock to rock, and shelf to shelf, between stupendous cliffs and beetling crags that sprang up to the sky. Often he had to cross and recross the rushing torrent, as it wound foaming and roaring down its broken channel, or was walled by perpendicular precipices; and imminent was the hazard of breaking the legs of the horses in the clefts and fissures of slippery rocks. The whole scenery of this deep ravine was of Alpine wildness and sublimity. Sometimes the travellers passed beneath cascades which pitched from such lofty heights that the water fell into the stream like heavy rain. In other places, torrents came tumbling from crag to crag, dashing into foam and spray, and making tremendous din and uproar.

On the second day of their descent, the travellers, having got beyond the steepest pitch of the mountains, came to where the deep and rugged ravine began occasionally to expand into small levels or valleys, and the stream to assume for short intervals a more peaceful character. Here, not merely the river itself, but every rivulet flowing into it, was dammed up by communities of industrious beavers, so as to inundate the neighborhood, and make continual swamps.

During a mid-day halt in one of these beaver valleys, Captain Bonneville left his companions, and strolled down the course of the stream to reconnoitre. He had not proceeded far when he came to a beaver pond, and caught a glimpse of one of its painstaking inhabitants busily at work upon the dam. The curiosity of the captain was aroused, to behold the mode of operating of this far-famed architect; he moved forward, therefore, with the utmost caution, parting the branches of the water willows without making any noise, until having attained a position commanding a view of the whole pond, he stretched himself flat on the ground, and watched the solitary workman. In a little while, three others appeared at the head of the dam, bringing sticks and bushes. With these they proceeded directly to the barrier, which Captain Bonneville perceived was in need of repair. Having deposited their loads upon the broken part, they dived into the water, and shortly reappeared at the surface. Each now brought a quantity of mud, with which he would plaster the sticks and bushes just deposited. This kind of masonry was continued for some time, repeated supplies of wood and mud being brought, and treated in the same manner. This done, the industrious beavers indulged in a little recreation, chasing each other about the pond, dodging and whisking about on the surface, or diving to the bottom; and in their frolic, often slapping their tails on the water with a loud clacking sound. While they were thus amusing themselves, another of the fraternity made his appearance, and looked gravely on their sports for some time, without offering to join in them. He then climbed the bank close to where the captain was concealed, and, rearing himself on his hind quarters, in a sitting position, put his forepaws against a young pine tree,[1] and began to cut the bark with his teeth. At times he would tear off a small piece, and holding it between his paws, and retaining his sedentary position, would feed himself with it, after the fashion of a monkey. The object of the beaver, however, was evidently to cut down the tree; and he was proceeding with his work, when he was alarmed by the approach of Captain Bonneville's men, who, feeling anxious at the protracted absence of their leader, were coming in search of him. At the sound of their voices, all the beavers, busy as well as idle, dived at once beneath the surface, and were no more to be seen. Captain Bonneville regretted this interruption. He had heard much of the sagacity of the beaver in cutting down trees, in which, it is said, they manage to make them fall into the water, and in such a position and direction as may be most favorable for conveyance to the desired point. In the present instance, the tree was a tall straight pine, and as it grew perpendicularly, and there was not a breath of air stirring, the beaver could have felled it in any direction he pleased, if really capable of exercising a discretion in the matter. He was evidently engaged in "belting" the tree, and his first incision had been on the side nearest to the water.

Captain Bonneville, however, discredits, on the whole, the alleged sagacity of the beaver in this particular, and thinks the animal has no other aim than to get the tree down, without any of the subtle calculation as to its mode or direction of falling. This attribute, he thinks, has been ascribed to them from the circumstance that most trees growing near water-courses, either lean bodily toward the stream, or stretch their largest limbs in that direction, to benefit by the space, the light, and the air to be found there. The beaver, of course, attacks those trees which are nearest at hand, and on the banks of the stream or pond. He makes incisions round them, or, in technical phrase, belts them with his teeth, and when they fall, they naturally take the direction in which their trunks or branches preponderate.

"I have often," says Captain Bonneville, "seen trees measuring

[1] The food of the beaver is willow, aspen, alder, birch, poplar, and cottonwood but not pine, although the beaver will sometimes cut down a pine for other purposes.

eighteen inches in diameter, at the places where they had been cut through by the beaver, but they lay in all directions, and often very inconveniently for the after purposes of the animal. In fact, so little ingenuity do they at times display in this particular, that at one of our camps on Snake River, a beaver was found with his head wedged into the cut which he had made, the tree having fallen upon him and held him prisoner until he died."

Great choice, according to the captain, is certainly displayed by the beaver in selecting the wood which is to furnish bark for winter provision. The whole beaver household, old and young, set out upon this business, and will often make long journeys before they are suited. Sometimes they cut down trees of the largest size and then cull the branches, the bark of which is most to their taste. These they cut into lengths of about three feet, convey them to the water, and float them to their lodges, where they are stored away for winter. They are studious of cleanliness and comfort in their lodges, and after their repasts, will carry out the sticks from which they have eaten the bark, and throw them into the current beyond the barrier. They are jealous, too, of their territories, and extremely pugnacious, never permitting a strange beaver to enter their premises, and often fighting with such virulence as almost to tear each other to pieces. In the spring, which is the breeding season, the male leaves the female at home, and sets off on a tour of pleasure, rambling often to a great distance, recreating himself in every clear and quiet expanse of water on his way, and climbing the banks occasionally to feast upon the tender sprouts of the young willows. As summer advances, he gives up his bachelor rambles, and bethinking himself of housekeeping duties, returns home to his mate and his new progeny, and marshals them all for the foraging expedition in quest of winter provisions.

After having shown the public spirit of this praiseworthy little animal as a member of a community, and his amiable and exemplary conduct as the father of a family, we grieve to record the perils with which he is environed, and the snares set for him and his painstaking household.

Practice, says Captain Bonneville, has given such a quickness of eye to the experienced trapper in all that relates to his pursuit, that he can detect the slightest sign of beaver, however wild; and although the lodge may be concealed by close thickets and overhanging willows, he can generally, at a single glance, make an accurate guess at the number of its inmates. He now goes to work to set his trap; planting it upon the shore, in some chosen place, two or three inches below the surface of the water, and secures it by a chain to a pole set deep in the mud. A small twig is then stripped of its bark, and one end is dipped in the "medicine," as the trappers term the peculiar bait which they employ. This end of the stick rises about four inches above the surface of the water, the other end is planted between the jaws of the trap. The beaver, possessing an acute sense of smell, is soon attracted by the odor of the bait. As he raises his nose toward it, his foot is caught in the trap. In his fright he throws a somerset into the deep water. The trap, being fastened to the pole, resists all his efforts to drag it to the shore; the chain by which it is fastened defies his teeth; he struggles for a time, and at length sinks to the bottom and is drowned.

Upon rocky bottoms, where it is not possible to plant the pole, it is thrown into the stream. The beaver, when entrapped, often gets fastened by the chain to sunken logs or floating timber; if he gets to shore, he is entangled in the thickets of brook willows. In such cases, however, it costs the trapper diligent search, and sometimes a bout at swimming, before he finds his game.

Occasionally it happens that several members of a beaver family are trapped in succession. The survivors then become extremely shy, and can scarcely be "brought to medicine," to use the trapper's phrase for "taking the bait." In such case, the trapper gives up the use of the bait, and conceals his traps in the usual paths and crossing-places of the household. The beaver now being completely "up to trap," approaches them cautiously, and springs them ingeniously with a stick. At other times, he turns the traps bottom upwards, by the same means, and occasionally even drags them to the barrier and conceals them in the mud. The trapper now gives up the contest of ingenuity, and shouldering his traps, marches off, admitting that he is not yet "up to beaver."

On the day following Captain Bonneville's supervision of the industrious and frolicsome community of beavers, of which he has given so edifying an account, he succeeded in extricating himself from the Wind River Mountains, and regaining the plain to the eastward, made a great bend to the south, so as to go round the bases of the mountains, and arrived without further incident of importance, at the old place of rendezvous in Green River valley, on the 17th of September.

He found the caches, in which he had deposited his superfluous goods and equipments, all safe, and having opened and taken from them the necessary supplies, he closed them again; taking care to obliterate all traces that might betray them to the keen eyes of Indian marauders.

27.

Route toward Wind River—Dangerous neighborhood—Alarms and precautions—A sham encampment—Apparition of an Indian spy—Midnight move—A mountain defile—The Wind River valley—Tracking a party—Deserted camps—Symptoms of Crows—Meeting of comrades—A trapper entrapped—Crow pleasantry—Crow spies—A decampment—Return to Green River valley—Meeting with Fitzpatrick's party—Their adventures among the Crows—Orthodox Crows

ON THE 18TH of September, Captain Bonneville and his three companions set out, bright and early, to rejoin the main party, from which they had parted on Wind River. Their route lay up the Green River valley, with that stream on their right hand, and beyond it, the range of Wind River Mountains. At the head of the valley, they were to pass through a defile[1] which would bring them out beyond the northern end of these mountains, to the head of Wind River; where they expected to meet the main party, according to arrangement.

We have already adverted to the dangerous nature of this neighborhood, infested by roving bands of Crows and Blackfeet; to whom the numerous defiles and passes of the country afford capital places for ambush and surprise. The travellers, therefore, kept a vigilant eye upon everything that might give intimation of lurking danger.

About two hours after mid-day, as they reached the summit of a hill, they discovered buffalo on the plain below, running in every

[1] Union Pass on the Continental Divide, about thirteen miles west of modern Dubois, Wyoming.

The ADVENTURES of CAPTAIN BONNEVILLE

direction. One of the men, too, fancied he heard the report of a gun. It was concluded, therefore, that there was some party of Indians below, hunting the buffalo.

The horses were immediately concealed in a narrow ravine; and the captain, mounting an eminence, but concealing himself from view, reconnoitred the whole neighborhood with a telescope. Not an Indian was to be seen; so, after halting about an hour, he resumed his journey. Convinced, however, that he was in a dangerous neighborhood, he advanced with the utmost caution; winding his way through hollows and ravines, and avoiding, as much as possible, any open tract, or rising ground, that might betray his little party to the watchful eye of an Indian scout.

Arriving, at length, at the edge of the open meadow-land bordering on the river, he again observed the buffalo, as far as he could see, scampering in great alarm. Once more concealing the horses, he and his companions remained for a long time watching the various groups of the animals, as each caught the panic and started off; but they sought in vain to discover the cause.

They were now about to enter the mountain defile, at the head of Green River valley, where they might be waylaid and attacked; they, therefore, arranged the packs on their horses, in the manner most secure and convenient for sudden flight, should such be necessary. This done, they again set forward, keeping the most anxious look-out in every direction.

It was now drawing toward evening; but they could not think of encamping for the night, in a place so full of danger. Captain Bonneville, therefore, determined to halt about sunset, kindle a fire, as if for encampment, cook and eat supper; but, as soon as it was sufficiently dark, to make a rapid move for the summit of the mountain, and seek some secluded spot for their night's lodgings.

Accordingly, as the sun went down, the little party came to a halt, made a large fire, spitted their buffalo meat on wooden sticks, and, when sufficiently roasted, planted the savory viands before them; cutting off huge slices with their hunting knives, and supping with a hunter's appetite. The light of their fire would not fail, as they knew, to attract the attention of any Indian horde in the neighborhood; but they trusted to be off and away, before any prowlers could reach the place. While they were supping thus hastily, however, one of their party suddenly started up and shouted "Indians!" All were instantly on their feet, with their rifles in their hands; but could see no enemy. The man, however, declared that he had seen an Indian advancing, cautiously, along the trail which they had made in coming to the encampment; who, the moment he was perceived, had thrown himself on the ground, and disappeared. He urged Captain Bonneville instantly to decamp. The captain, however, took the matter more coolly. The single fact, that the Indian had endeavored to hide himself, convinced him that he was not one of a party, on the advance to make an attack. He was, probably, some scout, who had followed up their trail, until he came in sight of their fire. He would, in such case, return, and report what he had seen to his companions. These, supposing the white men had encamped for the night, would keep aloof until very late, when all should be asleep. They would, then, according to Indian tactics, make their stealthy approaches, and place themselves in ambush around, preparatory to their attack, at the usual hour of daylight.

Such was Captain Bonneville's conclusion; in consequence of which, he counselled his men to keep perfectly quiet, and act as if free from all alarm, until the proper time arrived for a move. They, accordingly, continued their repast with pretended appetite and jollity; and then trimmed and replenished their fire, as if for a bivouac. As soon, however, as the night had completely set in, they left their fire blazing; walked quietly among the willows, and then leaping into their saddles, made off as noiselessly as possible. In proportion as they left the point of danger behind them, they relaxed in their rigid and anxious taciturnity, and began to joke at the expense of their enemy; whom they pictured to themselves mousing in the neighborhood of their deserted fire, waiting for the proper time of attack, and preparing for a grand disappointment.

About midnight, feeling satisfied that they had gained a secure distance, they posted one of their number to keep watch, in case the enemy should follow on their trail, and then, turning abruptly into a dense and matted thicket of willows, halted for the night at

Yale University Press

FORT VANCOUVER
Hudson's Bay Company Outpost
From a Drawing by Henry James Warre

Green River Site of the Trappers' Rendezvous
Wind River Mountains in Background

the foot of the mountain, instead of making for the summit, as they had originally intended.

A trapper in the wilderness, like a sailor on the ocean, snatches morsels of enjoyment in the midst of trouble, and sleeps soundly when surrounded by danger. The little party now made their arrangements for sleep with perfect calmness; they did not venture to make a fire and cook, it is true, though generally done by hunters whenever they come to a halt, and have provisions. They comforted themselves, however, by smoking a tranquil pipe; and then calling in the watch, and turning loose the horses, stretched themselves on their pallets, agreed that whoever should first awake, should rouse the rest, and in a little while were all as sound asleep as though in the midst of a fortress.

A little before day, they were all on the alert; it was the hour for Indian maraud. A sentinel was immediately detached, to post himself at a little distance on their trail, and give the alarm, should he see or hear an enemy.

With the first blink of dawn, the rest sought the horses; brought them to the camp, and tied them up, until an hour after sunrise; when, the sentinel having reported that all was well, they sprang once more into their saddles, and pursued the most covert and secret paths up the mountain, avoiding the direct route.

At noon, they halted and made a hasty repast; and then bent their course so as to regain the route from which they had diverged. They were now made sensible of the danger from which they had just escaped. There were tracks of Indians, who had evidently been in pursuit of them; but had recently returned, baffled in their search.

Trusting that they had now got a fair start, and could not be overtaken before night, even in case the Indians should renew the chase, they pushed briskly forward, and did not encamp until late; when they cautiously concealed themselves in a secure nook of the mountains.

Without any further alarm, they made their way to the head waters of Wind River, and reached the neighborhood in which they had appointed the rendezvous with their companions. It was within the precincts of the Crow country; the Wind River valley being one of the favorite haunts of that restless tribe. After much searching, Captain Bonneville came upon a trail which had evidently been made by his main party. It was so old, however, that he feared his people might have left the neighborhood; driven off, perhaps by some of those war parties which were on the prowl. He continued his search with great anxiety, and no little fatigue; for his horses were jaded, and almost crippled, by their forced marches and scramblings through rocky defiles.

On the following day, about noon, Captain Bonneville came upon a deserted camp of his people, from which they had, evidently, turned back; but he could find no signs to indicate why they had done so; whether they had met with misfortune, or molestation, or in what direction they had gone. He was now, more than ever, perplexed.

On the following day, he resumed his march with increasing anxiety. The feet of his horses had by this time become so worn and wounded by the rocks, that he had to make moccasons for them of buffalo hide. About noon, he came to another deserted camp of his men; but soon after lost their trail. After great search, he once more found it, turning in a southerly direction along the eastern bases of the Wind River Mountains, which towered to the right. He now pushed forward with all possible speed, in hopes of overtaking the party. At night, he slept at another of their camps, from which they had but recently departed. When the day dawned sufficiently to distinguish objects, he perceived the danger that must be dogging the heels of his main party. All about the camp were traces of Indians who must have been prowling about it at the time his people had passed the night there; and who must still be hovering about them. Convinced, now, that the main party could not be at any great distance, he mounted a scout on the best horse, and sent him forward to overtake them, to warn them of their danger, and to order them to halt, until he should rejoin them.

In the afternoon, to his great joy, he met the scout returning, with six comrades from the main party, leading fresh horses for his accommodation; and on the following day (September 25th), all hands were once more reunited, after a separation of nearly three weeks. Their meeting was hearty and joyous; for they had both experienced dangers and perplexities.

The main party, in pursuing their course up the Wind River valley, had been dogged the whole way by a war party of Crows. In one place, they had been fired upon, but without injury; in another place, one of their horses had been cut loose, and carried off. At length, they were so closely beset, that they were obliged to make a retrograde move, lest they should be surprised and overcome. This was the movement which had caused such perplexity to Captain Bonneville.

The whole party now remained encamped for two or three days, to give repose to both men and horses. Some of the trappers, however, pursued their vocations about the neighboring streams. While one of them was setting his traps, he heard the tramp of horses, and looking up, beheld a party of Crow braves moving along at no great distance, with a considerable cavalcade. The trapper hastened to conceal himself, but was discerned by the quick eye of the savages. With whoops and yells, they dragged him from his hiding-place, flourished over his head their tomahawks and scalping-knives, and for a time, the poor trapper gave himself up for lost. Fortunately, the Crows were in a jocose, rather than a sanguinary mood. They amused themselves heartily, for a while, at the expense of his terrors; and after having played off divers Crow pranks and pleasantries, suffered him to depart unharmed. It is true, they stripped him completely, one taking his horse, another his gun, a third his traps, a fourth his blanket, and so on, through all his accoutrements, and even his clothing, until he was stark naked; but then they generously made him a present of an old tattered buffalo robe, and dismissed him, with many complimentary speeches, and much laughter. When the trapper returned to the camp, in such sorry plight, he was greeted with peals of laughter from his comrades, and seemed more mortified by the style in which he had been dismissed, than rejoiced at escaping with his life. A circumstance which he related to Captain Bonneville, gave some insight into the cause of this extreme jocularity on the part of the Crows. They had evidently had a run of luck, and, like winning gamblers, were in high good humor. Among twenty-six fine horses, and some mules, which composed their cavalcade, the trapper recognized a number which had belonged to Fitzpatrick's brigade, when they parted company on the Bighorn. It was supposed, therefore, that these vagabonds had been on his trail, and robbed him of part of his cavalry.

On the day following this affair, three Crows came into Captain Bonneville's camp, with the most easy, innocent, if not impudent air imaginable; walking about with the imperturbable coolness and unconcern, in which the Indian rivals the fine gentleman. As they had not been of the set which stripped the trapper, though evidently of the same band, they were not molested. Indeed, Captain Bonneville treated them with his usual kindness and hospitality; permitting them to remain all day in the camp, and even to pass the night there. At the same time, however, he caused a strict watch to be maintained on all their movements; and at night, stationed an armed sentinel near them. The Crows remonstrated against the latter being armed. This only made the captain suspect them to be spies, who meditated treachery; he redoubled, therefore, his precautions. At the same time, he assured his guests, that while they were perfectly welcome to the shelter and comfort of his camp, yet, should any of their tribe venture to approach during the night, they would certainly be shot; which would be a very unfortunate circumstance, and much to be deplored. To the latter remark, they fully assented; and shortly afterward commenced a wild song, or chant, which they kept up for a long time, and in which they very probably gave their friends, who might be prowling round the camp, notice that the white men were on the alert. The night passed away without disturbance. In the morning, the three Crow guests were very pressing that Captain Bonneville and his party should accompany them to their camp, which they said was close by. Instead of accepting their invitation, Captain Bonneville took his departure with all possible dispatch, eager to be out of the vicinity of such a piratical horde; nor did he relax the diligence of his march, until, on the second day, he reached the banks of the Sweet Water, beyond the limits of the Crow country, and a heavy fall of snow had obliterated all traces of his course.

The ADVENTURES *of* CAPTAIN BONNEVILLE

He now continued on for some few days, at a slower pace, round the point of the mountain toward Green River, and arrived once more at the caches, on the 14th of October.

Here they found traces of the band of Indians who had hunted them in the defile toward the head waters of Wind River. Having lost all trace of them on their way over the mountains, they had turned and followed back their trail down the Green River valley to the caches. One of these they had discovered and broken open, but it fortunately contained nothing but fragments of old iron, which they had scattered about in all directions, and then departed. In examining their deserted camp, Captain Bonneville discovered that it numbered thirty-nine fires, and had more reason than ever to congratulate himself on having escaped the clutches of such a formidable band of freebooters.

He now turned his course southward, under cover of the mountains, and on the 25th of October reached Liberge's Ford,[2] a tributary of the Colorado, where he came suddenly upon the trail of this same war party, which had crossed the stream so recently that the banks were yet wet with the water that had been splashed upon them. To judge from their tracks, they could not be less than three hundred warriors, and apparently of the Crow nation.

Captain Bonneville was extremely uneasy lest this overpowering force should come upon him in some place where he would not have the means of fortifying himself promptly. He now moved toward Hane's Fork,[3] another tributary of the Colorado, where he encamped, and remained during the 26th of October. Seeing a large cloud of smoke to the south, he supposed it to arise from some encampment of Shoshonies, and sent scouts to procure information, and to purchase a lodge. It was, in fact, a band of Shoshonies, but with them were encamped Fitzpatrick and his party of trappers. That active leader had an eventful story to relate of his fortunes in the country of the Crows. After parting with Captain Bonneville on the banks of the Bighorn, he made for the west, to trap upon Powder

[2] LaBarge Creek, a tributary of Green River, approximately forty-five miles south of Fort Bonneville.
[3] Hams Fork, about thirty miles due south of LaBarge Creek.

and Tongue Rivers. He had between twenty and thirty men with him, and about one hundred horses. So large a cavalcade could not pass through the Crow country without attracting the attention of its freebooting hordes. A large band of Crows was soon on their traces, and came up with them on the 5th of September, just as they had reached Tongue River. The Crow chief came forward with great appearance of friendship, and proposed to Fitzpatrick that they should encamp together. The latter, however, not having any faith in Crows, declined the invitation, and pitched his camp three miles off. He then rode over with two or three men, to visit the Crow chief, by whom he was received with great apparent cordiality. In the meantime, however, a party of young braves, who considered them absolved by his distrust from all scruples of honor, made a circuit privately, and dashed into his encampment. Captain Stewart, who had remained there in the absence of Fitzpatrick, behaved with great spirit; but the Crows were too numerous and active. They had got possession of the camp, and soon made booty of every thing —carrying off all the horses. On their way back they met Fitzpatrick returning to his camp; and finished their exploit by rifling and nearly stripping him.

A negotiation now took place between the plundered white men and the triumphant Crows; what eloquence and management Fitzpatrick made use of, we do not know, but he succeeded in prevailing upon the Crow chieftain to return him his horses and many of his traps; together with his rifles and a few rounds of ammunition for each man. He then set out with all speed to abandon the Crow country, before he should meet with any fresh disasters.

After his departure, the consciences of some of the most orthodox Crows pricked them sorely for having suffered such a cavalcade to escape out of their hands. Anxious to wipe off so foul a stigma on the reputation of the Crow nation, they followed on his trial, nor quit hovering about him on his march until they had stolen a number of his best horses and mules. It was, doubtless, this same band which came upon the lonely trapper on the Popo Agie, and generously gave him an old buffalo robe in exchange for his rifle, his traps, and all his accoutrements. With these anecdotes, we shall, for

The ADVENTURES of CAPTAIN BONNEVILLE

the present, take our leave of the Crow country and its vagabond chivalry.[4]

[4] Fitzpatrick's difficulty with the Crows has often been recounted in fur-trade literature. Irving's version is the earliest. James P. Beckwourth, who was with the Crows as an agent of the American Fur Company, told of it in his typically vainglorious way in his *Life and Adventures*, 181–87. Mrs. Victor's account in *River of the West*, 160–161, is derived from Irving. In more recent literature the incident appears in Chittenden, *American Fur Trade*, I, 301–302, 351–52; in Hafen and Ghent, *Broken Hand*, 110–11, where it is presented as an event in Fitzpatrick's biography; and in DeVoto's *Across the Wide Missouri*, 127–31.

28.

A region of natural curiosities—The plain of white clay—Hot springs—The Beer Spring—Departure to seek the free trappers—Plain of Portneuf—Lava—Chasms and gullies—Bannack Indians—Their hunt of the buffalo—Hunter's feast—Trencher heroes—Bullying of an absent foe—The damp comrade—The Indian spy—Meeting with Hodgkiss—His adventures—Poordevil Indians—Triumph of the Bannacks—Blackfeet policy in war

CROSSING AN ELEVATED RIDGE, Captain Bonneville now came upon Bear River,[1] which, from its source to its entrance into the Great Salt Lake, describes the figure of a horse-shoe. One of the principal head waters of this river, although supposed to abound with beaver, has never been visited by the trapper; rising among rugged mountains, and being barricadoed [sic] by fallen pine trees and tremendous precipices.

Proceeding down this river, the party encamped, on the 6th of November, at the outlet of a lake[2] about thirty miles long, and from two to three miles in width, completely imbedded in low ranges of mountains, and connected with Bear River by an impassable swamp. It is called the Little Lake, to distinguish it from the great one of salt water.

On the 10th of November, Captain Bonneville visited a place in the neighborhood which is quite a region of natural curiosities. An

[1] He moved west from Hams Fork to the Bear. The easiest route is that followed today by U. S. Highway 30N west of Kemerer, Wyoming, but from Irving's statement Bonneville may have followed Hams Fork north of this point and crossed nearer to its source.

[2] Bear Lake, lying in northern Utah and southern Idaho.

area of about half a mile square presents a level surface of white clay or fuller's earth, perfectly spotless, resembling a great slab of Parian marble, or a sheet of dazzling snow. The effect is strikingly beautiful at all times: in summer, when it is surrounded with verdure, or in autumn, when it contrasts its bright immaculate surface with the withered herbage. Seen from a distant eminence, it then shines like a mirror, set in the brown landscape. Around this plain are clustered numerous springs of various sizes and temperatures. One of them, of scalding heat, boils furiously and incessantly, rising to the height of two or three feet. In another place, there is an aperture in the earth, from which rushes a column of steam that forms a perpetual cloud. The ground for some distance around sounds hollow, and startles the solitary trapper, as he hears the tramp of his horse giving the sound of a muffled drum. He pictures to himself a mysterious gulf below, a place of hidden fires, and gazes round him with awe and uneasiness.

The most noted curiosity, however, of this singular region, is the *Beer Spring*,[3] of which trappers give wonderful accounts. They are said to turn aside from their route through the country to drink of its waters, with as much eagerness as the Arab seeks some famous well of the desert. Captain Bonneville describes it as having the taste of beer. His men drank it with avidity, and in copious draughts. It did not appear to him to possess any medicinal properties, or to produce any peculiar effects. The Indians, however, refuse to taste it, and endeavor to persuade the white men from doing so.

We have heard this also called the Soda Spring, and described as containing iron and sulphur. It probably possesses some of the properties of the Ballston water.[4]

The time had now arrived for Captain Bonneville to go in quest

[3] Beer Spring (or Soda Spring) on Bear River is located at modern Soda Springs, Idaho, but is now submerged by a reservoir. Actually there were many springs in the area. Fremont visited it in August, 1843, and left a detailed account of his observations (see *Expedition to the Rocky Mountains*, 173–78). Indians and certain trappers regarded the springs with superstition, believing them inhabited by spirits (see George F. Ruxton, *Life in the Far West* (ed. by LeRoy R. Hafen), 79–80).

[4] The water of Ballston Spa, New York, near Saratoga Springs.

of the party of free trappers, detached in the beginning of July, under the command of Mr. Hodgkiss, to trap upon the head waters of Salmon River. His intention was to unite them with the party with which he was at present travelling, that all might go into quarters together for the winter. Accordingly, on the 11th of November, he took a temporary leave of his band, appointing a rendezvous on Snake River, and, accompanied by three men, set out upon his journey. His route lay across the plain of the Portneuf, a tributary stream of Snake River, called after an unfortunate Canadian trapper murdered by the Indians. The whole country through which he passed bore evidence of volcanic convulsions and conflagrations in the olden time. Great masses of lava lay scattered about in every direction; the crags and cliffs had apparently been under the action of fire; the rocks in some places seemed to have been in a state of fusion; the plain was rent and split with deep chasms and gullies, some of which were partly filled with lava.

They had not proceeded far, however, before they saw a party of horsemen, galloping full tilt toward them. They instantly turned, and made full speed for the covert of a woody stream, to fortify themselves among the trees. The Indians came to a halt, and one of them came forward alone. He reached Captain Bonneville and his men just as they were dismounting and about to post themselves. A few words dispelled all uneasiness. It was a party of twenty-five Bannack Indians, friendly to the whites, and they proposed, through their envoy, that both parties should encamp together, and hunt the buffalo, of which they had discovered several large herds hard by. Captain Bonneville cheerfully assented to their proposition, being curious to see their manner of hunting.

Both parties accordingly encamped together on a convenient spot, and prepared for the hunt. The Indians first posted a boy on a small hill near the camp, to keep a look-out for enemies. The "runners," then, as they are called, mounted on fleet horses, and armed with bows and arrows, moved slowly and cautiously toward the buffalo, keeping as much as possible out of sight, in hollows and ravines. When within a proper distance, a signal was given, and they all opened at once like a pack of hounds, with a full chorus of yells,

The ADVENTURES of CAPTAIN BONNEVILLE

dashing into the midst of the herds, and launching their arrows to the right and left. The plain seemed absolutely to shake under the tramp of the buffalo, as they scoured off. The cows in headlong panic, the bulls furious with rage, uttering deep roars, and occasionally turning with a desperate rush upon their pursuers. Nothing could surpass the spirit, grace, and dexterity, with which the Indians managed their horses; wheeling and coursing among the affrighted herd, and launching their arrows with unerring aim. In the midst of the apparent confusion, they selected their victims with perfect judgment, generally aiming at the fattest of the cows, the flesh of the bull being nearly worthless, at this season of the year. In a few minutes, each of the hunters had cripppled three or four cows. A single shot was sufficient for the purpose, and the animal, once maimed, was left to be completely dispatched at the end of the chase. Frequently, a cow was killed on the spot by a single arrow. In one instance, Captain Bonneville saw an Indian shoot his arrow completely through the body of a cow, so that it struck in the ground beyond. The bulls, however, are not so easily killed as the cows, and always cost the hunter several arrows; sometimes making battle upon the horses, and chasing them furiously, though severely wounded, with the darts still sticking in their flesh.

The grand scamper of the hunt being over, the Indians proceeded to dispatch the animals that had been disabled; then cutting up the carcasses, they returned with loads of meat to the camp, where the choicest pieces were soon roasting before large fires, and a hunters' feast succeeded; at which Captain Bonneville and his men were qualified, by previous fasting, to perform their parts with great vigor.

Some men are said to wax valorous upon a full stomach, and such seemed to be the case with the Bannack braves, who, in proportion as they crammed themselves with buffalo meat, grew stout of heart, until, the supper at an end, they began to chant war songs, setting forth their mighty deeds, and the victories they had gained over the Blackfeet. Warming with the theme, and inflating themselves with their own eulogies, these magnanimous heroes of the trencher would start up, advance a short distance beyond the light of the fire, and apostrophize most vehemently their Blackfeet enemies, as though they had been within hearing. Ruffling, and swelling, and snorting, and slapping their breasts, and brandishing their arms, they would vociferate all their exploits; reminding the Blackfeet how they had drenched their towns in tears and blood; enumerate the blows they had inflicted, the warriors they had slain, the scalps they had brought off in triumph. Then, having said everything that could stir a man's spleen or pique his valor, they would dare their imaginary hearers, now that the Bannacks were few in number, to come and take their revenge—receiving no reply to this valorous bravado, they would conclude by all kinds of sneers and insults, deriding the Blackfeet for dastards and poltroons, that dared not accept their challenge. Such is the kind of swaggering and rhodomontade in which the "red men" are prone to indulge in their vainglorious moments; for, with all their vaunted taciturnity, they are vehemently prone at times to become eloquent about their exploits, and to sound their own trumpet.

Having vented their valor in this fierce effervescence, the Bannack braves gradually calmed down, lowered their crests, smoothed their ruffled feathers, and betook themselves to sleep, without placing a single guard over their camp; so that, had the Blackfeet taken them at their word, but few of these braggart heroes might have survived for any further boasting.

On the following morning, Captain Bonneville purchased a supply of buffalo meat from his braggadocio friends; who, with all their vaporing, were in fact a very forlorn horde, destitute of firearms, and of almost everything that constitutes riches in savage life. The bargain concluded, the Bannacks set off for their village, which was situated, they said, at the mouth of the Portneuf, and Captain Bonneville and his companions shaped their course toward Snake River.

Arrived on the banks of that river, he found it rapid and boisterous, but not too deep to be forded. In traversing it, however, one of the horses was swept suddenly from his footing, and his rider was flung from the saddle into the midst of the stream. Both horse and horseman were extricated without any damage, excepting that the latter was completely drenched, so that it was necessary to kindle a fire to dry him. While they were thus occupied, one of the party looking up, perceived an Indian scout cautiously reconnoitring them from the summit of a neighboring hill. The moment he found himself discovered, he disappeared behind the hill. From his furtive movements, Captain Bonneville suspected him to be a scout from the Blackfeet camp, and that he had gone to report what he had seen to his companions. It would not do to loiter in such a neighborhood, so the kindling of the fire was abandoned, the drenched horseman mounted in dripping condition, and the little band pushed forward directly into the plain, going at a smart pace, until they had gained a considerable distance from the place of supposed danger. Here encamping for the night, in the midst of abundance of sage, or wormwood, which afforded fodder for their horses, they kindled a huge fire for the benefit of their damp comrade, and then proceeded to prepare a sumptuous supper of buffalo humps and ribs, and other choice bits, which they had brought with them. After a hearty repast, relished with an appetite unknown to city epicures, they stretched themselves upon their couches of skins, and under the starry canopy of heaven, enjoyed the sound and sweet sleep of hardy and well-fed mountaineers.

They continued on their journey for several days, without any incident worthy of notice, and on the 19th of November, came upon traces of the party of which they were in search; such as burned patches of prairie, and deserted camping grounds. All these were carefully examined, to discover by their freshness or antiquity the probable time that the trappers had left them; at length, after much wandering and investigating, they came upon the regular trail of the hunting party, which led into the mountains, and following it up briskly, came about two o'clock in the afternoon of the 20th, upon the encampment of Hodgkiss and his band of free trappers, in the bosom of a mountain valley.

It will be recollected that these free trappers, who were masters of themselves and their movements, had refused to accompany Captain Bonneville back to Green River in the preceding month of July, preferring to trap about the upper waters of the Salmon River, where they expected to find plenty of beaver, and a less dangerous neighborhood. Their hunt had not been very successful. They had penetrated the great range of mountains among which some of the upper branches of Salmon River take their rise, but had become so entangled among immense and almost impassable barricades of fallen pines, and so impeded by tremendous precipices, that a great part of their season had been wasted among these mountains. At one time, they had made their way through them, and reached the Boisée River; but meeting with a band of Bannack Indians, from whom they apprehended hostilities, they had again taken shelter among the mountains, where they were found by Captain Bonneville. In the neighborhood of their encampment, the captain had the good fortune to meet with a family of those wanderers of the mountains, emphatically called "les dignes de pitie," or Poordevil Indians. These, however, appear to have forfeited the title, for they had with them a fine lot of skins of beaver, elk, deer, and mountain sheep. These, Captain Bonneville purchased from them at a fair valuation, and sent them off astonished at their own wealth, and no doubt objects of envy to all their pitiful tribe.

Being now reinforced by Hodgkiss and his band of free trappers, Captain Bonneville put himself at the head of the united parties, and set out to rejoin those he had recently left at the Beer Spring, that they might all go into winter quarters on Snake River. On his route, he encountered many heavy falls of snow, which melted almost immediately, so as not to impede his march, and on the 4th of December, he found his other party, encamped at the very place where he had partaken in the buffalo hunt with the Bannacks.

That braggart horde was encamped but about three miles off, and were just then in high glee and festivity, and more swaggering than ever, celebrating a prodigious victory. It appeared that a party of their braves being out on a hunting excursion, discovered a band of Blackfeet moving, as they thought, to surprise their hunting camp. The Bannacks immediately posted themselves on each side of a dark ravine, through which the enemy must pass, and, just as they were entangled in the midst of it, attacked them with great fury. The Blackfeet, struck with sudden panic, threw off their buffalo robes and fled, leaving one of their warriors dead on the spot. The victors eagerly gathered up the spoils; but their greatest prize was the scalp of the Blackfoot brave. This they bore off in triumph to their village, where it had ever since been an object of the greatest exultation and rejoicing. It had been elevated upon a pole in the centre of the village, where the warriors had celebrated the scalp dance round it, with war feasts, war songs, and warlike harangues. It had then been given up to the women and boys; who had paraded it up and down the village with shouts and chants and antic dances; occasionally saluting it with all kinds of taunts, invectives, and revilings.

The Blackfeet, in this affair, do not appear to have acted up to the character which has rendered them objects of such terror. Indeed, their conduct in war, to the inexperienced observer, is full of inconsistencies; at one time they are headlong in courage, and heedless of danger; at another time cautious almost to cowardice. To understand these apparent incongruities, one must know their principles of warfare. A war party, however triumphant, if they lose a warrior in the fight, bring back a cause of mourning to their people, which casts a shade over the glory of their achievement. Hence, the Indian is often less fierce and reckless in general battle, than he is in a private brawl; and the chiefs are checked in their boldest undertakings by the fear of sacrificing their warriors.

This peculiarity is not confined to the Blackfeet. Among the Osages, says Captain Bonneville, when a warrior falls in battle, his comrades, though they may have fought with consummate valor, and won a glorious victory, will leave their arms upon the field of battle, and returning home with dejected countenances, will halt without the encampment, and wait until the relatives of the slain come forth and invite them to mingle again with their people.

29.

Winter camp at the Portneuf—Fine springs—The Bannack Indians—Their honesty—Captain Bonneville prepares for an expedition—Christmas—The American Falls—Wild scenery—Fishing Falls—Snake Indians—Scenery on the Bruneau—View of volcanic country from a mountain—Powder River—Shoshokoes, or Root Diggers—Their character, habits, habitations, dogs—Vanity at its last shift

IN ESTABLISHING his winter camp near the Portneuf, Captain Bonneville had drawn off to some little distance from his Bannack friends, to avoid all annoyance from their intimacy or intrusions. In so doing, however, he had been obliged to take up his quarters on the extreme edge of the flat land, where he was encompassed with ice and snow, and had nothing better for his horses to subsist on than wormwood. The Bannacks, on the contrary, were encamped among fine springs of water, where there was grass in abundance. Some of these springs gush out of the earth in sufficient quantity to turn a mill; and furnish beautiful streams, clear as crystal, and full of trout of a large size, which may be seen darting about the transparent water.

Winter now set in regularly. The snow had fallen frequently, and in large quantities, and covered the ground to a depth of a foot; and the continued coldness of the weather prevented any thaw.

By degrees, a distrust which at first subsisted between the Indians and the trappers, subsided, and gave way to mutual confidence and good will. A few presents convinced the chiefs that the white men were their friends; nor were the white men wanting in proofs of the honesty and good faith of their savage neighbors. Occasionally, the deep snow and the want of fodder obliged them to turn their weakest horses out to roam in quest of sustenance. If they at any time strayed to the camp of the Bannacks, they were immediately brought back. It must be confessed, however, that if the stray horse happened, by any chance, to be in vigorous plight and good condition, though he was equally sure to be returned by the honest Bannacks, yet it was always after the lapse of several days, and in a very gaunt and jaded state; and always with the remark that they had found him a long way off. The uncharitable were apt to surmise that he had, in the interim, been well used up in a buffalo hunt; but those accustomed to Indian morality in the matter of horseflesh, considered it a singular evidence of honesty that he should be brought back at all.

Being convinced, therefore, from these, and other circumstances, that his people were encamped in the neighborhood of a tribe as honest as they were valiant, and satisfied that they would pass their winter unmolested, Captain Bonneville prepared for a reconnoitring expedition of great extent and peril. This was, to penetrate to the Hudson's Bay establishments on the banks of the Columbia, and to make himself acquainted with the country and the Indian tribes; it being one part of his scheme to establish a trading post somewhere on the lower part of the river, so as to participate in the trade lost to the United States by the capture of Astoria.[1] This expedition would, of course, take him through the Snake River country, and across the Blue Mountains,[2] the scenes of so much hardship and disaster to Hunt and Crooks, and their Astorian bands, who first explored it, and he would have to pass through it in the same frightful season, the depth of winter.

The idea of risk and hardship, however, only served to stimulate the adventurous spirit of the captain. He chose three companions for his journey, put up a small stock of necessaries in the most port-

---

[1] See Editor's Introduction, xxxi, for a discussion of Bonneville's observation of British interests in the Northwest.

[2] The Blue Mountains lie in the northeast corner of Oregon. For Hunt and Crooks' difficult trek, see *Astoria*, II, Chapters IV–VII; in one-volume editions, Chapters XXXIV–XXXVII.

able form, and selected five horses and mules for themselves and their baggage. He proposed to rejoin his band in the early part of March, at the winter encampment near the Portneuf. All these arrangements being completed, he mounted his horse on Christmas morning, and set off with his three comrades. They halted a little beyond the Bannack camp, and made their Christmas dinner, which, if not a very merry, was a very hearty one, after which they resumed their journey.

They were obliged to travel slowly, to spare their horses; for the snow had increased in depth to eighteen inches; and though somewhat packed and frozen, was not sufficiently so to yield firm footing. Their route lay to the west, down along the left side of Snake River; and they were several days in reaching the first, or American Falls.[3] The banks of the river, for a considerable distance, both above and below the falls, have a volcanic character: masses of basaltic rock are piled one upon another; the water makes its way through their broken chasms, boiling through narrow channels, or pitching in beautiful cascades over ridges of basaltic columns.

Beyond these falls, they came to a picturesque, but inconsiderable stream, called the Cassié.[4] It runs through a level valley, about four miles wide, where the soil is good; but the prevalent coldness and dryness of the climate is unfavorable to vegetation. Near to this stream there is a small mountain of mica slate, including garnets. Granite, in small blocks, is likewise seen in this neighborhood, and white sandstone.[5] From this river, the travellers had a prospect of the snowy heights of the Salmon River Mountains to the north; the nearest, at least fifty miles distant.

In pursuing his course westward, Captain Bonneville generally kept several miles from Snake River, crossing the heads of its tribu-

[3] The community of American Falls, Idaho, stands at this point today on the south side of the Snake.

[4] The Raft River in Cassia County, Idaho.

[5] These details came from Wyeth's manuscript journal for August 18, 1832:
"in this region I found one mountain of Mica Slate enclosing garnetts. The Basaltic rock appears to be the same formerly [*sic*] and the remains of the Garnetts are in some cases to be seen. also I have found here granite in small blocks   there is also much white sandstone compact." *Correspondence and Journals,* 163–64.

tary streams; though he often found the open country so encumbered by volcanic rocks, as to render travelling extremely difficult. Whenever he approached Snake River, he found it running through a broad chasm, with steep, perpendicular sides of basaltic rock. After several days' travel across a level plain, he came to a part of the river which filled him with astonishment and admiration. As far as the eye could reach, the river was walled in by perpendicular cliffs two hundred and fifty feet high, beetling like dark and gloomy battlements, while blocks and fragments lay in masses at their feet, in the midst of the boiling and whirling current. Just above, the whole stream pitched in one cascade above forty feet in height, with a thundering sound, casting up a volume of spray that hung in the air like a silver mist. These are called by some the Fishing Falls,[6] as the salmon are taken here in immense quantities. They cannot get by these falls.

After encamping at this place all night, Captain Bonneville, at sunrise, descended with his party through a narrow ravine, or rather crevice, in the vast wall of basaltic rock which bordered the river; this being the only mode, for many miles, of getting to the margin of the stream.

The snow lay in a thin crust along the banks of the river, so that their travelling was much more easy than it had been hitherto. There were foot tracks, also, made by the natives, which greatly facilitated their progress. Occasionally, they met the inhabitants of this wild region; a timid race, and but scantily provided with the necessaries of life. Their dress consisted of a mantle about four feet square, formed of strips of rabbit skins sewed together; this they hung over their shoulders, in the ordinary Indian mode of wearing the blanket. Their weapons were bows and arrows; the latter tipped with obsidian, which abounds in the neighborhood. Their huts were shaped like haystacks, and constructed of branches of willow covered with long grass, so as to be warm and comfortable. Occasionally, they were surrounded by small inclosures of wormwood, about three feet high, which gave them a cottage-like appearance. Three or four of these tenements were occasionally grouped together in some wild

[6] Probably Twin Falls.

and striking situation, and had a picturesque effect. Sometimes they were in sufficient number to form a small hamlet. From these people, Captain Bonneville's party frequently purchased salmon, dried in an admirable manner, as were likewise the roes. This seemed to be their prime article of food; but they were extremely anxious to get buffalo meat in exchange.

The high walls and rocks, within which the travellers had been so long inclosed, now occasionally presented openings, through which they were enabled to ascend to the plain, and to cut off considerable bends of the river.

Throughout the whole extent of this vast and singular chasm, the scenery of the river is said to be of the most wild and romantic character. The rocks present every variety of masses and grouping. Numerous small streams come rushing and boiling through narrow clefts and ravines: one of a considerable size issued from the face of a precipice, within twenty-five feet of its summit; and after running in nearly a horizontal line for about one hundred feet, fell, by numerous small cascades, to the rocky bank of the river.

In its career through this vast and singular defile, Snake River is upward of three hundred yards wide, and as clear as spring water. Sometimes it steals along with a tranquil and noiseless course; at other times, for miles and miles, it dashes on in a thousand rapids, wild and beautiful to the eye, and lulling the ear with the soft tumult of plashing waters.

Many of the tributary streams of Snake River, rival it in the wildness and picturesqueness of their scenery. That called the Bruneau[7] is particularly cited. It runs through a tremendous chasm, rather than a valley, extending upwards of a hundred and fifty miles. You come upon it on a sudden, in traversing a level plain. It seems as if you could throw a stone across from cliff to cliff; yet, the valley

[7] The Bruneau joins the Snake west of Glenns Ferry in Owyhee County, Idaho. It is labeled Powder River on Bonneville's map. Owing to Bonneville's omission of the name Bruneau, it may be presumed that Irving supplied this name from another source, failing to recognize its identity with the river Bonneville called the Powder. This same double terminology appears later in the book, and is responsible for most of the confusion resulting from an effort to trace Bonneville's route of travel.

is near two thousand feet deep: so that the river looks like an inconsiderable stream. Basaltic rocks rise perpendicularly, so that it is impossible to get from the plain to the water, or from the river margin to the plain. The current is bright and limpid. Hot springs are found on the borders of this river. One bursts out of the cliffs forty feet above the river, in a stream sufficient to turn a mill, and sends up a cloud of vapor.

We find a characteristic picture of this volcanic region of mountains and streams, furnished by the journal of Mr. Wyeth, which lies before us;[8] who ascended a peak in the neighborhood we are describing. From this summit, the country, he says, appears an indescribable chaos; the tops of the hills exhibit the same strata as far as the eye can reach; and appear to have once formed the level of the country; and the valleys to be formed by the sinking of the earth, rather than the rising of the hills. Through the deep cracks and chasms thus formed, the rivers and brooks make their way, which renders it difficult to follow them. All these basaltic channels are called cut rocks by the trappers. Many of the mountain streams disappear in the plains; either absorbed by their thirsty soil, and by the porous surface of the lava, or swallowed up in gulfs and chasms.

On the 12th of January (1834), Captain Bonneville reached Powder River;[9] much the largest stream that he had seen since leaving the Portneuf. He struck it about three miles above its entrance into Snake River. Here he found himself above the lower narrows and defiles of the latter river, and in an open and level country. The natives now made their appearance in considerable

[8] Irving had Wyeth's manuscript journal, not published until 1899. The passage Irving draws upon at this point is Wyeth's entry for August 30, 1832:

"This day we assended the highest mountain in sight and found the exhibit an indescribable chaos the tops of the hills exhibit the same strata as far as the eye can reach and appear to [have] once form[ed] the level of the country and the vall[ey] to be formed by the sinking of the earth rather than the rising of the hills through the deep cracks and chasms thus formed the rivers and creeks of this country creep which renders them of the most difficult to follow." *Correspondence and Journals*, 166.

[9] Now the Bruneau River, which appears on Bonneville's map as the Powder River.

numbers, and evinced the most insatiable curiosity respecting the white men; sitting in groups for hours together, exposed to the bleakest winds, merely for the pleasure of gazing upon the strangers, and watching every movement. These are of that branch of the great Snake tribe called Shoshokoes, or Root Diggers, from their subsisting, in a great measure, on the roots of the earth; though they likewise take fish in great quantities, and hunt, in a small way. They are, in general, very poor; destitute of most of the comforts of life, and extremely indolent: but a mild, inoffensive race. They differ, in many respects, from the other branch of the Snake tribe, the Shoshonies; who possess horses, are more roving and adventurous, and hunt the buffalo.

On the following day, as Captain Bonneville approached the mouth of Powder River, he discovered at least a hundred families of these Diggers, as they are familiarly called, assembled in one place. The women and children kept at a distance, perched among the rocks and cliffs; their eager curiosity being somewhat dashed with fear. From their elevated posts, they scrutinized the strangers with the most intense earnestness; regarding them with almost as much awe as if they had been beings of a supernatural order.

The men, however, were by no means so shy and reserved; but importuned Captain Bonneville and his companions excessively by their curiosity. Nothing escaped their notice; and any thing they could lay their hands on underwent the most minute examination. To get rid of such inquisitive neighbors, the travellers kept on for a considerable distance, before they encamped for the night.

The country, hereabout, was generally level and sandy; producing very little grass, but a considerable quantity of sage or wormwood. The plains were diversified by isolated hills, all cut off, as it were, about the same height, so as to have tabular summits. In this they resembled the isolated hills of the great prairies, east of the Rocky Mountains; especially those found on the plains of the Arkansas.

The high precipices which had hitherto walled in the channel of Snake River had now disappeared; and the banks were of the ordinary height. It should be observed, that the great valleys or plains, through which the Snake River wound its course, were generally of great breadth, extending on each side from thirty to forty miles; where the view was bounded by unbroken ridges of mountains.

The travellers found but little snow in the neighborhood of Powder River, though the weather continued intensely cold. They learned a lesson, however, from their forlorn friends, the Root Diggers, which they subsequently found of great service in their wintry wanderings. They frequently observed them to be furnished with long ropes, twisted from the bark of the wormwood. This they used as a slow match, carrying it always lighted. Whenever they wished to warm themselves, they would gather together a little dry wormwood, apply the match, and in an instant produce a cheering blaze.

Captain Bonneville gives a cheerless account of a village of these Diggers, which he saw in crossing the plain below Powder River. "They live," says he, "without any further protection from the inclemency of the season, than a sort of break-weather, about three feet high, composed of sage (or wormwood), and erected around them in the shape of a half moon." Whenever he met with them, however, they had always a large suite of half-starved dogs: for these animals, in savage as well as in civilized life, seem to be the concomitants of beggary.

These dogs, it must be allowed, were of more use than the beggary curs of cities. The Indian children used them in hunting the small game of the neighborhood, such as rabbits and prairie dogs; in which mongrel kind of chase they acquitted themselves with some credit.

Sometimes the Diggers aspire to nobler game, and succeed in entrapping the antelope, the fleetest animal of the prairies. The process by which this is effected is somewhat singular. When the snow has disappeared, says Captain Bonneville, and the ground become soft, the women go into the thickest fields of wormwood, and pulling it up in great quantities, construct with it a hedge, about three feet high, inclosing about a hundred acres. A single opening is left for the admission of the game. This done, the women conceal themselves behind the wormwood, and wait patiently for the coming of the antelopes; which sometimes enter this spacious trap in considerable numbers. As soon as they are in, the women give the signal, and the men hasten to play their part. But one of them enters the pen at a time; and, after chasing the terrified animals round the inclosure, is relieved by one of his companions. In this way the hunters take their turns, relieving each other, and keeping up a continued pursuit by relays, without fatigue to themselves. The poor antelopes, in the end, are so wearied down, that the whole party of men enter and dispatch them with clubs; not one escaping that has entered the inclosure. The most curious circumstance in this chase is, that an animal so fleet and agile as the antelope, and straining for its life, should range round and round this fated inclosure, without attempting to overleap the low barrier which surrounds it. Such, however, is said to be the fact; and such their only mode of hunting the antelope.

Notwithstanding the absence of all comfort and convenience in their habitations, and the general squalidness of their appearance, the Shoshokoes do not appear to be destitute of ingenuity. They manufacture good ropes, and even a tolerably fine thread, from a sort of weed found in their neighborhood; and construct bowls and jugs out of a kind of basket-work formed from small strips of wood plaited: these, by the aid of a little wax, they render perfectly water tight. Beside the roots on which they mainly depend for subsistence, they collect great quantities of seed, of various kinds, beaten with one hand out of the tops of the plants into wooden bowls held for that purpose. The seed thus collected is winnowed and parched, and ground between two stones into a kind of meal or flour; which, when mixed with water, forms a very palatable paste or gruel.

Some of these people, more provident and industrious than the rest, lay up a stock of dried salmon, and other fish, for winter: with these, they were ready to traffic with the travellers for any objects of utility in Indian life; giving a large quantity in exchange for an awl, a knife, or a fish-hook. Others were in the most abject state of want and starvation; and would even gather up the fish-bones which the travellers threw away after a repast, warm them over again at the fire, and pick them with the greatest avidity.

The farther Captain Bonneville advanced into the country of these Root Diggers, the more evidence he perceived of their rude and forlorn condition. "They were destitute," says he, "of the necessary covering to protect them from the weather; and seemed to be in the most unsophisticated ignorance of any other propriety or advantage in the use of clothing. One old dame had absolutely nothing on her person but a thread round her neck, from which was pendant a solitary bead."

What stage of human destitution, however, is too destitute for vanity! Though these naked and forlorn-looking beings had neither toilet to arrange, nor beauty to contemplate, their greatest passion was for a mirror. It was a "great medicine," in their eyes. The sight of one was sufficient, at any time, to throw them into a paroxysm of eagerness and delight; and they were ready to give anything they had for the smallest fragment in which they might behold their squalid features. With this simple instance of vanity, in its primitive but vigorous state, we shall close our remarks on the Root Diggers.

30.

Temperature of the climate—Root Diggers on horseback—An Indian guide—Mountain prospects—The Grand Rond—Difficulties on Snake River—A scramble over the Blue Mountains—Sufferings from hunger—Prospect of the Immahah Valley—The exhausted traveller

THE TEMPERATURE of the regions west of the Rocky Mountains is much milder than in the same latitudes on the Atlantic side; the upper plains, however, which lie at a distance from the sea-coast, are subject in winter to considerable vicissitude; being traversed by lofty "sierras," crowned with perpetual snow, which often produce flaws and streaks of intense cold. This was experienced by Captain Bonneville and his companions in their progress westward. At the time when they left the Bannacks, Snake River was frozen hard: as they proceeded, the ice became broken and floating; it gradually disappeared, and the weather became warm and pleasant, as they approached a tributary stream called the Little Wyer;[1] and the soil, which was generally of a watery clay, with occasional intervals of sand, was soft to the tread of the horses. After a time, however, the mountains approached and flanked the river; the snow lay deep in the valleys, and the current was once more icebound.

Here they were visited by a party of Root Diggers, who were apparently rising in the world, for they had "horse to ride and weapon to wear," and were altogether better clad and equipped than any of the tribe that Captain Bonneville had met with. They

[1] From its position opposite the Payette River on Bonneville's map, the Little Wyer is identifiable as the Malheur River of eastern Oregon.

were just from the plain of Boisée River, where they had left a number of their tribe, all as well provided as themselves; having guns, horses, and comfortable clothing. All these they obtained from the Lower Nez Percés, with whom they were in habits [*sic*] of frequent traffic. They appeared to have imbibed from that tribe their noncombative principles, being mild and inoffensive in their manners. Like them, also, they had something of religious feelings; for Captain Bonneville observed that, before eating, they washed their hands, and made a short prayer; which he understood was their invariable custom. From these Indians, he obtained a considerable supply of fish, and an excellent and well-conditioned horse, to replace one which had become too weak for the journey.

The travellers now moved forward with renovated spirits; the snow, it is true, lay deeper and deeper as they advanced, but they trudged on merrily, considering themselves well provided for the journey, which could not be of much longer duration.

They had intended to proceed up the banks of Gun Creek,[2] a stream which flows into Snake River from the west; but were assured by the natives that the route in that direction was impracticable. The latter advised them to keep along Snake River, where they would not be impeded by the snow. Taking one of the Diggers for a guide, they set off along the river, and to their joy soon found the country free from snow, as had been predicted, so that their horses once more had the benefit of tolerable pasturage. Their Digger proved an excellent guide, trduging cheerily in the advance. He made an unsuccessful shot or two at a deer and a beaver; but at night found a rabbit hole, whence he extracted the occupant, upon which, with the addition of a fish given him by the travellers, he made a hearty supper, and retired to rest, filled with good cheer and good humor.

The next day the travellers came to where the hills closed upon the river, leaving here and there intervals of undulating meadow land. The river was sheeted with ice, broken into hills at long intervals. The Digger kept on ahead of the party, crossing and recrossing

---

[2] Gun Creek appears on Bonneville's map. On modern maps it is the Powder River of eastern Oregon.

the river in pursuit of game, until, unluckily, encountering a brother Digger, he stole off with him, without the ceremony of leave-taking.

Being now left to themselves, they proceeded until they came to some Indian huts, the inhabitants of which spoke a language totally different from any they had yet heard. One, however, understood the Nez Percé language, and through him they made inquiries as to their route. These Indians were extremely kind and honest, and furnished them with a small quantity of meat; but none of them could be induced to act as guides.

Immediately in the route of the travellers lay a high mountain, which they ascended with some difficulty. The prospect from the summit was grand but disheartening. Directly before them towered the loftiest peaks of Immahah,[3] rising far higher than the elevated ground on which they stood: on the other hand, they were enabled to scan the course of the river,[4] dashing along through deep chasms, between rocks and precipices, until lost in a distant wilderness of mountains, which closed the savage landscape.

They remained for a long time contemplating, with perplexed and anxious eye, this wild congregation of mountain barriers, and seeking to discover some practicable passage. The approach of evening obliged them to give up the task, and to seek some camping ground for the night. Moving briskly forward, and plunging and tossing through a succession of deep snow-drifts, they at length reached a valley known among trappers as the "Grand Rond,"[5] which they found entirely free from snow.

This is a beautiful and very fertile valley, about twenty miles long and five or six broad; a bright cold stream called the *Fourche de Glace,* or Ice River,[6] runs through it. Its sheltered situation,

---

[3] Now the Wallowa Mountains.

[4] The Snake, which they continued to follow north of Gun (Powder) Creek.

[5] Keeping along the Snake as the text clearly indicates, Bonneville could not have come to the Grande Ronde Valley. This reference is the one confusing element in Bonneville's movements through this area. He would not meet the Grande Ronde River until he had crossed the Imnaha River.

[6] Usually identified as the Grande Ronde River, but open to the objections stated above. *Fourche de Glace* means literally "Ice Fork." Since early references to the Grande Ronde sometimes call it Clay River because of its color at the lower end,

The ADVENTURES of CAPTAIN BONNEVILLE

embosomed in mountains, renders it good pasturaging ground in the winter time; when the elk come down to it in great numbers, driven out of the mountains by the snow. The Indians then resort to it to hunt. They likewise come to it in the summer time to dig the camash root,[7] of which it produces immense quantities. When this plant is in blossom, the whole valley is tinted by its blue flowers, and looks like the ocean when overcast by a cloud.

After passing a night in this valley, the travellers in the morning scaled the neighboring hills, to look out for a more eligible route than that upon which they had unluckily fallen; and, after much reconnoitring, determined to make their way once more to the river, and to travel upon the ice when the banks should prove impassable.

On the second day after this determination, they were again upon Snake River, but, contrary to their expectations, it was nearly free from ice. A narrow riband ran along the shore, and sometimes there was a kind of bridge across the stream, formed of old ice and snow. For a short time, they jogged along the bank, with tolerable facility, but at length came to where the river forced its way into the heart of the mountains, winding between tremendous walls of basaltic rock, that rose perpendicularly from the water['s] edge, frowning in bleak and gloomy grandeur. Here difficulties of all kinds beset their path. The snow was from two to three feet deep, but soft and yielding, so that the horses had no foothold, but kept plunging forward, straining themselves by perpetual efforts. Sometimes the crags and promontories forced them upon the narrow riband of ice that bordered the shore; sometimes they had to scramble over vast masses of rock which had tumbled from the impending precipices; sometimes they had to cross the stream upon the hazardous bridges of ice and snow, sinking to the knee at every step; sometimes they had to scale slippery acclivities, and to pass along narrow cornices, glazed with ice and sleet, a shouldering wall of rock on one side, a yawning precipice on the other, where a single false step

Phillip A. Rollins has suggested that Irving's *glace* is an error for *glaise* (clay); see Stuart, *Discovery of the Oregon Trail*, 76 ff., and Lewis A. McArthur, *Oregon Geographic Names*, 233.

[7] Camass plant (genus *Camassia*), with edible bulbs.

would have been fatal. In a lower and less dangerous pass, two of their horses actually fell into the river; one was saved with much difficulty, but the boldness of the shore prevented their rescuing the other, and he was swept away by the rapid current.

In this way they struggled forward, manfully braving difficulties and dangers, until they came to where the bed of the river was narrowed to a mere chasm, with perpendicular walls of rock that defied all further progress.[8] Turning their faces now to the mountain, they endeavored to cross directly over it; but, after clambering nearly to the summit, found their path closed by insurmountable barriers.

Nothing now remained but to retrace their steps. To descend a cragged mountain, however, was more difficult and dangerous than to ascend it. They had to lower themselves cautiously and slowly, from steep to steep; and, while they managed with difficulty to maintain their own footing, to aid their horses by holding on firmly to the rope halters, as the poor animals stumbled among slippery rocks, or slid down icy declivities. Thus, after a day of intense cold, and severe and incessant toil, amidst the wildest of scenery, they managed, about nightfall, to reach the camping ground, from which they had started in the morning, and for the first time in the course of their rugged and perilous expedition, felt their hearts quailing under their multiplied hardships.

A hearty supper, a tranquillizing pipe, and a sound night's sleep, put them all in better mood, and in the morning they held a consultation as to their future movements. About four miles behind, they had remarked a small ridge of mountains approaching closely to the river. It was determined to scale this ridge, and seek a passage into the valley which must lie beyond. Should they fail in this, but one alternative remained. To kill their horses, dry the flesh for provisions, make boats of the hides, and, in these, commit themselves to the stream—a measure hazardous in the extreme.

A short march brought them to the foot of the mountain, but its steep and cragged sides almost discouraged hope. The only chance of scaling it was by broken masses of rock, piled one upon another,

[8] The Grand Canyon of the Snake.

which formed a succession of crags, reaching nearly to the summit. Up these they wrought their way with indescribable difficulty and peril, in a zigzag course, climbing from rock to rock, and helping their horses up after them; which scrambled among the crags like mountain goats; now and then dislodging some huge stone, which, the moment they had left it, would roll down the mountain, crashing and rebounding with terrific din. It was some time after dark before they reached a kind of platform on the summit of the mountain, where they could venture to encamp. The winds, which swept this naked height, had whirled all the snow into the valley beneath, so that the horses found tolerable winter pasturage on the dry grass which remained exposed. The travellers, though hungry in the extreme, were fain to make a very frugal supper; for they saw their journey was likely to be prolonged much beyond the anticipated term.

In fact, on the following day they discerned that, although already at a great elevation, they were only as yet upon the shoulder of the mountain. It proved to be a great sierra, or ridge, of immense height, running parallel to the course of the river, swelling by degrees to lofty peaks, but the outline gashed by deep and precipitous ravines. This, in fact, was a part of the chain of Blue Mountains, in which the first adventurers to Astoria experienced such hardships.

We will not pretend to accompany the travellers step by step in this tremendous mountain scramble, into which they had unconsciously betrayed themselves. Day after day did their toil continue; peak after peak had they to traverse, struggling with difficulties and hardships known only to the mountain trapper. As their course lay north, they had to ascend the southern faces of the heights, where the sun had melted the snow, so as to render the ascent wet and slippery, and to keep both men and horses continually on the strain; while on the northern sides, the snow lay in such heavy masses, that it was necessary to beat a track down which the horses might be led. Every now and then, also, their way was impeded by tall and numerous pines, some of which had fallen, and lay in every direction.

In the midst of these toils and hardships, their provisions gave out. For three days they were without food, and so reduced that they could scarcely drag themselves along. At length one of the mules, being about to give out from fatigue and famine, they hastened to dispatch him. Husbanding this miserable supply, they dried the flesh, and for three days subsisted upon the nutriment extracted from the bones. As to the meat, it was packed and preserved as long as they could do without it, not knowing how long they might remain bewildered in these desolate regions.

One of the men was now dispatched ahead, to reconnoitre the country, and to discover, if possible, some more practicable route. In the meantime, the rest of the party moved on slowly. After a lapse of three days, the scout rejoined them. He informed them that Snake River ran immediately below the sierra or mountainous ridge, upon which they were travelling; that it was free from precipices, and was at no great distance from them in a direct line; but that it would be impossible for them to reach it without making a weary circuit. Their only course would be to cross the mountain ridge to the left.

Up this mountain, therefore, the weary travellers directed their steps; and the ascent, in their present weak and exhausted state, was one of the severest parts of this most painful journey. For two days were they toiling slowly from cliff to cliff, beating at every step a path through the snow for their faltering horses. At length they reached the summit, where the snow was blown off; but in descending on the opposite side, they were often plunging through deep drifts, piled in the hollows and ravines.

Their provisions were now exhausted, and they and their horses almost ready to give out with fatigue and hunger; when one afternoon, just as the sun was sinking behind a blue line of distant mountain, they came to the brow of a height from which they beheld the smooth valley of the Immahah[9] stretched out in smiling verdure below them.

The sight inspired almost a frenzy of delight. Roused to new ardor, they forgot, for a time, their fatigues, and hurried down the

[9] The valley of the Imnaha River, which flows northward and joins the Snake south of the Oregon-Washington line. Bonneville's map correctly shows its location, although he did not label it.

MOUTH OF HORSE CREEK ON GREEN RIVER
Below Site of Fort Bonneville

Mouth of Horse River
August 17th 1832

Mr David Adams
Sir,
Your known intelligence and integrity warrants me in placing you at the head of our eastern Trapping party consisting of twenty one men and forty Animals with their necessary equipment, and sundry Merchandise as per enclosed Invoice —

Your route will lay as marked out upon Mr Meldrum Map — round the foot of the Wind River Mountains, down Wind River up Stinking and upon the small streams keeping up the Yellow Stone, crossing over to the Galatin and Medicine Rivers, from which you will cross over to Salmon River and descend it to the forks where you will find a letter at the foot of the tree marked thus — instructing you where the Main body will Winter, which it is believed will be there or very near it —

You should consider trapping your business, yet should an advantageous trade offer either for horses or Beaver you would of course improve it — but let nothing induce you to deviate your course for precarious trade. Nightly parks and close staking you are aware are the only true methods of keeping your animals in security —

The signals for our parties this fall are these — a blaze upon the tree opposite the course pursued. One notch over it untill the 15th Septr. two from that day untill 25th October and three from that to the wintering grounds; for distress blaze upon both sides of the notches and first blaze — for loss of horses leave the side blazes plain — for dispute hack thus one of the side blazes — for a Cache or some writing hack both side blazes which would induce us to dig at the foot of the 2nd nearest tree for information

Missouri Historical Society

LETTER FROM CAPTAIN BONNEVILLE TO DAVID ADAMS
Mouth of Horse River, 1832

mountain, dragging their jaded horses after them, and sometimes compelling them to slide a distance of thirty or forty feet at a time. At length they reached the banks of the Immahah. The young grass was just beginning to sprout, and the whole valley wore an aspect of softness, verdure, and repose, heightened by the contrast of the frightful region from which they had just descended. To add to their joy, they observed Indian trails along the margin of the stream, and other signs, which gave them reason to believe that there was an encampment of the Lower Nez Percés in the neighborhood, as it was within the accustomed range of that pacific and hospitable tribe.

The prospect of a supply of food stimulated them to new exertion, and they continued on as fast as the enfeebled state of themselves and their steeds would permit. At length, one of the men, more exhausted than the rest, threw himself upon the grass, and declared he could go no further. It was in vain to attempt to rouse him; his spirit had given out, and his replies only showed the dogged apathy of despair. His companions, therefore, encamped on the spot, kindled a blazing fire, and searched about for roots with which to strengthen and revive him. They all then made a starveling repast; but gathering round the fire, talked over past dangers and troubles, soothed themselves with the persuasion that all were now at an end, and went to sleep with the comforting hope that the morrow would bring them into plentiful quarters.

31.

Progress in the valley—An Indian cavalier—The captain falls into a lethargy—A Nez Percé patriarch—Hospitable treatment—The bald head—Bargaining—Value of an old plaid cloak—The family horse—The cost of an Indian present

A TRANQUIL NIGHT'S REST had sufficiently restored the broken down traveller to enable him to resume his wayfaring, and all hands set forward on the Indian trail. With all their eagerness to arrive within reach of succor, such was their feeble and emaciated condition, that they advanced but slowly. Nor is it a matter of surprise that they should almost have lost heart, as well as strength. It was now (the 16th of February) fifty-three days that they had been travelling in the midst of winter, exposed to all kinds of privations and hardships: and for the last twenty days, they had been entangled in the wild and desolate labyrinths of the snowy mountains; climbing and descending icy precipices, and nearly starved with cold and hunger.

All the morning they continued following the Indian trail, without seeing a human being, and were beginning to be discouraged, when, about noon, they discovered a horseman at a distance. He was coming directly toward them; but on discovering them, suddenly reined up his steed, came to a halt, and, after reconnoitring them for a time with great earnestness, seemed about to make a cautious retreat. They eagerly made signs of peace, and endeavored, with the utmost anxiety, to induce him to approach. He remained for some time in doubt; but at length, having satisfied himself that they were not enemies, came galloping up to them. He was a fine, haughty-looking savage, fancifully decorated, and mounted on a high-mettled steed, with gaudy trappings and equipments. It was evident that he was a warrior of some consequence among his tribe. His whole deportment had something in it of barbaric dignity; he felt, perhaps, his temporary superiority in personal array, and in the spirit of his steed, to the poor, ragged, travel-worn trappers and their half-starved horses. Approaching them with an air of protection, he gave them his hand, and, in the Nez Percé language, invited them to his camp, which was only a few miles distant; where he had plenty to eat, and plenty of horses, and would cheerfully share his good things with them.

His hospitable invitation was joyfully accepted: he lingered but a moment, to give directions by which they might find his camp, and then, wheeling round, and giving the reins to his mettlesome steed, was soon out of sight. The travellers followed, with gladdened hearts, but at a snail's pace; for their poor horses could scarcely drag one leg after the other. Captain Bonneville, however, experienced a sudden and singular change of feeling. Hitherto, the necessity of conducting his party, and of providing against every emergency, had kept his mind upon the stretch, and his whole system braced and excited. In no one instance had he flagged in spirit, or felt disposed to succumb. Now, however, that all danger was over, and the march of a few miles would bring them to repose and abundance, his energies suddenly deserted him; and every faculty, mental and physical, was totally relaxed. He had not proceeded two miles from the point where he had had the interview with the Nez Percé chief, when he threw himself upon the earth, without the power or will to move a muscle, or exert a thought, and sank almost instantly into a profound and dreamless sleep. His companions again came to a halt, and encamped beside him, and there they passed the night.

The next morning, Captain Bonneville awakened from his long and heavy sleep, much refreshed; and they all resumed their creeping progress. They had not long been on the march, when eight or ten of the Nez Percé tribe came galloping to meet them, leading fresh horses to bear them to their camp. Thus gallantly mounted, they felt new life infused into their languid frames, and dashing forward, were soon at the lodges of the Nez Percés. Here they found about twelve families living together, under the patriarchal sway of an ancient and venerable chief. He received them with the hospitality of the golden age, and with something of the same kind of fare; for, while he opened his arms to make them welcome, the only repast he set before them consisted of roots. They could have wished for something more hearty and substantial; but, for want of better, made a voracious meal on these humble viands. The repast being over, the best pipe was lighted and sent round: and this was a most welcome luxury, having lost their smoking apparatus twelve days before, among the mountains.

While they were thus enjoying themselves, their poor horses were led to the best pastures in the neighborhood, where they were turned loose to revel on the fresh sprouting grass; so that they had better fare than their masters.

Captain Bonneville soon felt himself quite at home among these quiet, inoffensive people. His long residence among their cousins, the Upper Nez Percés, had made him conversant with their language, modes of expression, and all their habitudes. He soon found, too, that he was well known among them, by report, at least, from the constant interchange of visits and messages between the two branches of the tribe. They at first addressed him by his name; giving him his title of captain, with a French accent: but they soon gave him a title of their own; which, as usual with Indian titles, had a peculiar signification. In the case of the captain, it had somewhat of a whimsical origin.

As he sat chatting and smoking in the midst of them, he would occasionally take off his cap. Whenever he did so, there was a sensation in the surrounding circle. The Indians would half rise from their recumbent posture, and gaze upon his uncovered head, with their usual exclamation of astonishment. The worthy captain was completely bald; a phenomenon very surprising in their eyes. They were at a loss to know whether he had been scalped in battle, or enjoyed a natural immunity from that belligerent infliction. In a little while, he became known among them by an Indian name, signifying "the bald chief." "A sobriquet," observes the captain, "for which

I can find no parallel in history since the days of 'Charles the Bald.' "

Although the travellers had banqueted on roots, and been regaled with tobacco smoke, yet their stomachs craved more generous fare. In approaching the lodges of the Nez Percés, they had indulged in fond anticipations of venison and dried salmon; and dreams of the kind still haunted their imaginations, and could not be conjured down. The keen appetites of mountain trappers, quickened by a fortnight's fasting, at length got the better of all scruples of pride, and they fairly begged some fish or flesh from the hospitable savages. The latter, however, were slow to break in upon their winter store, which was very limited; but were ready to furnish roots in abundance, which they pronounced excellent food. At length, Captain Bonneville thought of a means of attaining the much-coveted gratification.

He had about him, he says, a trusty plaid; an old and valued travelling companion and comforter; upon which the rains had descended, and the snows and winds beaten, without further effect than somewhat to tarnish its primitive lustre. This coat of many colors had excited the admiration, and inflamed the covetousness of both warriors and squaws, to an extravagant degree. An idea now occurred to Captain Bonneville, to convert this rainbow garment into the savory viands so much desired. There was a momentary struggle in his mind, between old associations and projected indulgence; and his decision in favor of the latter was made, he says, with a greater promptness, perhaps, than true taste and sentiment might have required. In a few moments, his plaid cloak was cut into numerous strips. "Of these," continues he, "with the newly developed talent of a man-milliner, I speedily constructed turbans *à la Turque*, and fanciful head-gears of divers conformations. These, judiciously distributed among such of the womenkind as seemed of most consequence and interest in the eyes of the *patres conscripti*, brought us, in a little while, abundance of dried salmon and deers' hearts; on which we made a sumptous supper. Another, and a more satisfactory smoke, succeeded this repast, and sweet slumbers answering the peaceful invocation of our pipes, wrapped us in that delicious rest, which is only won by toil and travail."

As to Captain Bonneville, he slept in the lodge of the venerable patriarch, who had evidently conceived a most disinterested affection for him; as was shown on the following morning. The travellers, invigorated by a good supper, and "fresh from the bath of repose," were about to resume their journey, when this affectionate old chief took the captain aside, to let him know how much he loved him. As a proof of his regard, he had determined to give him a fine horse, which would go further than words, and put his good will beyond all question. So saying, he made a signal, and forthwith a beautiful young horse, of a brown color, was led, prancing and snorting, to the place. Captain Bonneville was suitably affected by this mark of friendship; but his experience in what is proverbially called "Indian giving," made him aware that a parting pledge was necessary on his own part, to prove that his friendship was reciprocated. He accordingly placed a handsome rifle in the hands of the venerable chief, whose benevolent heart was evidently touched and gratified by this outward and visible sign of amity.

Having now, as he thought, balanced this little account of friendship, the captain was about to shift his saddle to this noble gift-horse, when the affectionate patriarch plucked him by the sleeve, and introduced to him a whimpering, whining, leathern-skinned old squaw, that might have passed for an Egyptian mummy, without drying. "This," said he, "is my wife; she is a good wife—I love her very much.—She loves the horse—she loves him a great deal—she will cry very much at losing him.—I do not know how I shall comfort her—and that makes my heart very sore."

What could the worthy captain do, to console the tender-hearted old squaw, and, peradventure, to save the venerable patriarch from a curtain lecture? He bethought himself of a pair of ear-bobs: it was true, the patriarch's better-half was of an age and appearance that seemed to put personal vanity out of the question, but when is personal vanity extinct? The moment he produced the glittering ear-bobs, the whimpering and whining of the sempiternal beldame was at an end. She eagerly placed the precious baubles in her ears, and, though as ugly as the Witch of Endor, went off with a sideling gait, and coquettish air, as though she had been a perfect Semiramis.

The captain had now saddled his newly acquired steed, and his foot was in the stirrup, when the affectionate patriarch again stepped forward, and presented to him a young Pierced-nose, who had a peculiarly sulky look. "This," said the venerable chief, "is my son: he is very good; a great horseman—he always took care of this very fine horse—he brought him up from a colt, and made him what he is.—He is very fond of this fine horse—he loves him like a brother—his heart will be very heavy when this fine horse leaves the camp."

What could the captain do, to reward the youthful hope of this venerable pair, and comfort him for the loss of his foster-brother, the horse? He bethought him of a hatchet, which might be spared from his slender stores. No sooner did he place the implement into the hands of the young hopeful, than his countenance brightened up, and he went off rejoicing in his hatchet, to the full as much as did his respectable mother in her ear-bobs.

The captain was now in the saddle, and about to start, when the affectionate old patriarch stepped forward, for the third time, and, while he laid one hand gently on the mane of the horse, held up the rifle in the other. "This rifle," said he, "shall be my great medicine. I will hug it to my heart—I will always love it, for the sake of my good friend, the bald-headed chief.—But a rifle, by itself, is dumb—I cannot make it speak. If I had a little powder and ball, I would take it out with me, and would now and then shoot a deer; and when I brought the meat home to my hungry family, I would say—This was killed by the rifle of my friend, the bald-headed chief, to whom I gave that very fine horse."

There was no resisting this appeal; the captain, forthwith, furnished the coveted supply of powder and ball; but at the same time, put spurs to his very fine gift-horse, and the first trial of his speed was to get out of all further manifestation of friendship, on the part of the affectionate old patriarch and his insinuating family.

32.

Nez Percé camp—A chief with a hard name—The Big Hearts of the East—Hospitable treatment—The Indian guides—Mysterious councils—The loquacious chief—Indian tomb—Grand Indian reception—An Indian feast—Town-criers—Honesty of the Nez Percés—The captain's attempt at healing.

FOLLOWING THE COURSE of the Immahah, Captain Bonneville and his three companions soon reached the vicinity of Snake River. Their route now lay over a succession of steep and isolated hills, with profound valleys. On the second day, after taking leave of the affectionate old patriarch, as they were descending into one of those deep and abrupt intervals, they descried a smoke, and shortly afterward came in sight of a small encampment of Nez Percés.

The Indians, when they ascertained that it was a party of white men approaching, greeted them with a salute of firearms, and invited them to encamp. This band was likewise under the sway of a venerable chief named Yo-mus-ro-y-e-cut; a name which we shall be careful not to inflict oftener than is necessary upon the reader. This ancient and hard-named chieftain welcomed Captain Bonneville to his camp with the same hospitality and loving kindness that he had experienced from his predecessor. He told the captain he had often heard of the Americans and their generous deeds, and that his buffalo brethren (the Upper Nez Percés) had always spoken of them as the Big-hearted whites of the East, the very good friends of the Nez Percés.

Captain Bonneville felt somewhat uneasy under the responsibility of this magnanimous but costly appellation; and began to fear he might be involved in a second interchange of pledges of friendship. He hastened, therefore, to let the old chief know his poverty-stricken state, and how little there was to be expected from him.

He informed him that he and his comrades had long resided among the Upper Nez Percés, and loved them so much, that they had thrown their arms around them, and now held them close to their hearts. That he had received such good accounts from the Upper Nez Percés of their cousins, the Lower Nez Percés, that he had become desirous of knowing them as friends and brothers. That he and his companions had accordingly loaded a mule with presents and set off for the country of the Lower Nez Percés; but, unfortunately, had been entrapped for many days among the snowy mountains; and that the mule with all the presents had fallen into Snake River, and been swept away by the rapid current. That instead, therefore, of arriving among their friends, the Nez Percés, with light hearts and full hands, they came naked, hungry, and broken down; and instead of making them presents, must depend upon them even for food. "But," concluded he, "we are going to the white men's fort on the Wallah-Wallah, and will soon return; and then we will meet our Nez Percé friends like the true Big Hearts of the East."

Whether the hint thrown out in the latter part of the speech had any effect, or whether the old chief acted from the hospitable feelings which, according to the captain, are really inherent in the Nez Percé tribe, he certainly showed no disposition to relax his friendship on learning the destitute circumstances of his guests. On the contrary, he urged the captain to remain with them until the following day, when he would accompany him on his journey, and make him acquainted with all his people. In the meantime, he would have a colt killed, and cut up for travelling provisions. This, he carefully explained, was intended not as an article of traffic, but as a gift; for he saw that his guests were hungry and in need of food.

Captain Bonneville gladly assented to this hospitable arrangement. The carcass of the colt was forthcoming in due season, but the captain insisted that one half of it should be set apart for the use of the chieftain's family.

At an early hour of the following morning, the little party resumed their journey, accompanied by the old chief and an Indian guide. Their route was over a rugged and broken country; where the hills were slippery with ice and snow. Their horses, too, were so weak and jaded, that they could scarcely climb the steep ascents, or maintain their foothold on the frozen declivities. Throughout the whole of the journey, the old chief and the guide were unremitting in their good offices, and continually on the alert to select the best roads, and assist them through all difficulties. Indeed, the captain and his comrades had to be dependent on their Indian friends for almost every thing, for they had lost their tobacco and pipes, those great comforts of the trapper, and had but a few charges of powder left, which it was necessary to husband for the purpose of lighting their fires.

In the course of the day the old chief had several private consultations with the guide, and showed evident signs of being occupied with some mysterious matter of mighty import. What it was, Captain Bonneville could not fathom, nor did he make much effort to do so. From some casual sentences that he overheard, he perceived that it was something from which the old man promised himself much satisfaction, and to which he attached a little vainglory, but which he wished to keep a secret; so he suffered him to spin out his petty plans unmolested.

In the evening when they encamped, the old chief and his privy counsellor, the guide, had another mysterious colloquy, after which the guide mounted his horse and departed on some secret mission, while the chief resumed his seat at the fire, and sat humming to himself in a pleasing but mystic reverie.

The next morning, the travellers descended into the valley of the Way-lee-way,[1] a considerable tributary of Snake River. Here they met the guide returning from his secret errand. Another private conference was held between him and the old managing chief, who now seemed more inflated than ever with mystery and self-importance. Numerous fresh trails, and various other signs, persuaded Cap-

---

[1] Grande Ronde River. This river is correctly shown on Bonneville's map without being labelled *Grande Ronde*. The name Way-lee-way appears instead on the lower part of the river.

tain Bonneville that there must be a considerable village of Nez Percés in the neighborhood; but as his worthy companion, the old chief, said nothing on the subject, and as it appeared to be in some way connected with his secret operations, he asked no questions, but patiently awaited the development of his mystery.

As they journeyed on, they came to where two or three Indians were bathing in a small stream. The good old chief immediately came to a halt, and had a long conversation with them, in the course of which he repeated to them the whole history which Captain Bonneville had related to him. In fact, he seems to have been a very sociable, communicative old man; by no means afflicted with that taciturnity generally charged upon the Indians. On the contrary, he was fond of long talks and long smokings, and evidently was proud of his new friend, the bald-headed chief, and took a pleasure in sounding his praises, and setting forth the power and glory of the Big Hearts of the East.

Having disburdened himself of everything he had to relate to his bathing friends, he left them to their aquatic disports, and proceeded onward with the captain and his companions. As they approached the Way-lee-way, however, the communicative old chief met with another and a very different occasion to exert his colloquial powers. On the banks of the river stood an isolated mound covered with grass. He pointed to it with some emotion. "The big heart and the strong arm," said he, "lie buried beneath that sod."

It was, in fact, the grave of one of his friends; a chosen warrior of the tribe; who had been slain on this spot when in pursuit of a war party of Shoshokoes, who had stolen the horses of the village. The enemy bore off his scalp as a trophy; but his friends found his body in this lonely place, and committed it to the earth with ceremonials characteristic of their pious and reverential feelings. They gathered round the grave and mourned; the warriors were silent in their grief; but the women and children bewailed their loss with loud lamentations. "For three days," said the old man, "we performed the solemn dances for the dead, and prayed the Great Spirit that our brother might be happy in the land of brave warriors and hunters. Then we killed at his grave fifteen of our best and strongest horses, to serve him when he should arrive at the happy hunting grounds; and having done all this, we returned sorrowfully to our homes."

While the chief was still talking, an Indian scout came galloping up, and, presenting him with a powder-horn, wheeled round, and was speedily out of sight. The eyes of the old chief now brightened; and all his self-importance returned. His petty mystery was about to explode. Turning to Captain Bonneville, he pointed to a hill hard by, and informed him, that behind it was a village governed by a little chief, whom he had notified of the approach of the bald-headed chief, and a party of the Big Hearts of the East, and that he was prepared to receive them in becoming style. As, among other ceremonials, he intended to salute them with a discharge of firearms, he had sent the horn of gunpowder that they might return the salute in a manner correspondent to his dignity.

They now proceeded on until they doubled the point of the hill, when the whole population of the village broke upon their view, drawn out in the most imposing style, and arrayed in all their finery. The effect of the whole was wild and fantastic, yet singularly striking. In the front rank were the chiefs and principal warriors, glaringly painted and decorated; behind them were arranged the rest of the people, men, women, and children.

Captain Bonneville and his party advanced slowly, exchanging salutes of firearms. When arrived within a respectful distance, they dismounted. The chiefs then came forward successively, according to their respective characters and consequence, to offer the hand of good fellowship; each filing off when he had shaken hands, to make way for his successor. Those in the next rank followed in the same order, and so on, until all had given the pledge of friendship. During all this time, the chief, according to custom, took his stand beside the guests. If any of his people advanced whom he judged unworthy of the friendship or confidence of the white men, he motioned them off by a wave of the hand, and they would submissively walk away. When Captain Bonneville turned upon him an inquiring look, he would observe, "he was a bad man," or something quite as concise, and there was an end of the matter.

Mats, poles, and other materials were now brought, and a comfortable lodge was soon erected for the strangers, where they were kept constantly supplied with wood and water, and other necessaries; and all their effects were placed in safe keeping. Their horses, too, were unsaddled, and turned loose to graze, and a guard set to keep watch upon them.

All this being adjusted, they were conducted to the main building or council house of the village, where an ample repast, or rather banquet, was spread, which seemed to realize all the gastronomical dreams that had tantalized them during their long starvation; for here they beheld not merely fish and roots in abundance, but the flesh of deer and elk, and the choicest pieces of buffalo meat. It is needless to say how vigorously they acquitted themselves on this occasion, and how unnecessary it was for their hosts to practice the usual cramming principle of Indian hospitality.

When the repast was over, a long talk ensued. The chief showed the same curiosity evinced by his tribe generally, to obtain information concerning the United States, of which they knew little but what they derived through their cousins, the Upper Nez Percés; as their traffic is almost exclusively with the British traders of the Hudson's Bay Company. Captain Bonneville did his best to set forth the merits of his nation, and the importance of their friendship to the red men, in which he was ably seconded by his worthy friend, the old chief with the hard name, who did all that he could to glorify the Big Hearts of the East.

The chief, and all present, listened with profound attention, and evidently with great interest; nor were the important facts thus set forth, confined to the audience in the lodge; for sentence after sentence was loudly repeated by a crier for the benefit of the whole village.

This custom of promulgating everything by criers, is not confined to the Nez Percés, but prevails among many other tribes. It has its advantage where there are no gazettes to publish the news of the day, or to report the proceedings of important meetings. And in fact, reports of this kind, viva voce, made in the hearing of all parties, and liable to be contradicted or corrected on the spot, are more likely to convey accurate information to the public mind than those circulated through the press. The office of crier is generally filled by some old man, who is good for little else. A village has generally several of these walking newspapers, as they are termed by the whites, who go about proclaiming the news of the day, giving notice of public councils, expeditions, dances, feasts, and other ceremonials, and advertising anything lost. While Captain Bonneville remained among the Nez Percés, if a glove, handkerchief, or anything of similar value, was lost or mislaid, it was carried by the finder to the lodge of the chief, and proclamation was made by one of their criers, for the owner to come and claim his property.

How difficult it is to get at the true character of these wandering tribes of the wilderness! In a recent work, we have had to speak of this tribe of Indians from the experience of other traders who had casually been among them, and who represented them as selfish, inhospitable, exorbitant in their dealings, and much addicted to thieving:[2] Captain Bonneville, on the contrary, who resided much among them, and had repeated opportunities of ascertaining their real character, invariably speaks of them as kind and hospitable, scrupulously honest, and remarkable, above all other Indians that he had met with, for a strong feeling of religion. In fact, so enthusiastic is he in their praise, that he pronounces them, all ignorant and barbarous as they are by their condition, one of the purest-hearted people on the face of the earth.

Some cures which Captain Bonneville had effected in simple cases, among the Upper Nez Percés, had reached the ears of their cousins here, and gained for him the reputation of a great medicine man. He had not been long in the village, therefore, before his lodge began to be the resort of the sick and the infirm. The captain felt the value of the reputation thus accidentally and cheaply acquired, and endeavored to sustain it. As he had arrived at that age when every man is, experimentally, something of a physician, he was enabled to turn to advantage the little knowledge in the healing art which he had casually picked up; and was sufficiently successful in two or three cases, to convince the simple Indians that report had

[2] Vide Astoria, chap. lii (Irving's note).

not exaggerated his medical talents. The only patient that effectually baffled his skill, or rather discouraged any attempt at relief, was an antiquated squaw with a churchyard cough, and one leg in the grave; it being shrunk and rendered useless by a rheumatic affection. This was a case beyond his mark; however, he comforted the old woman with a promise that he would endeavor to procure something to relieve her, at the fort on the Wallah-Wallah, and would bring it on his return; with which assurance her husband was so well satisfied, that he presented the captain with a colt, to be killed as provisions for the journey: a medical fee which was thankfully accepted.

While among these Indians, Captain Bonneville unexpectedly found an owner for the horse which he had purchased from a Root Digger at the Big Wyer.[3] The Indian satisfactorily proved that the horse had been stolen from him some time previous, by some unknown thief. "However," said the considerate savage, "you got him in fair trade—you are more in want of horses than I am: keep him; he is yours—he is a good horse; use him well."

Thus, in the continued experience of acts of kindness and generosity, which his destitute condition did not allow him to reciprocate, Captain Bonneville passed some short time among these good people, more and more impressed with the general excellence of their character.

[3] Bonneville's map shows the Big Wyre flowing from the southwest into the Snake opposite the Boise River. On modern maps it is the Owyhee River in eastern Oregon.

33.

Scenery of the Way-lee-way—A substitute for tobacco—Sublime scenery of Snake River—The garrulous old chief and his cousin—A Nez Percé meeting—A stolen skin—The scapegoat dog—Mysterious conferences—The little chief—His hospitality—The captain's account of the United States—His healing skill

IN RESUMING HIS JOURNEY, Captain Bonneville was conducted by the same Nez Percé guide, whose knowledge of the country was important in choosing the routes and resting places. He also continued to be accompanied by the worthy old chief with the hard name, who seemed bent upon doing the honors of the country, and introducing him to every branch of his tribe. The Way-lee-way, down the banks of which Captain Bonneville and his companions were now travelling,[1] is a considerable stream winding through a succession of bold and beautiful scenes. Sometimes the landscape towered into bold and mountainous heights that partook of sublimity; at other times, it stretched along the water side in fresh smiling meadows, and graceful undulating valleys.

Frequently in their route they encountered small parties of the Nez Percés, with whom they invariably stopped to shake hands; and who, generally, evinced great curiosity concerning them and their adventures; a curiosity which never failed to be thoroughly satisfied by the replies of the worthy Yo-mus-ro-y-e-cut, who kindly took upon himself to be spokesman of the party.

The incessant smoking of pipes incident to the long talks of this

[1] They were traveling east toward the Snake.

excellent, but somewhat garrulous old chief, at length exhausted all his stock of tobacco, so that he had no longer a whiff with which to regale his white companions. In this emergency, he cut up the stem of his pipe into fine shavings, which he mixed with certain herbs, and thus manufactured a temporary succedaneum to enable him to accompany his long colloquies and harangues with the customary fragrant cloud.

If the scenery of the Way-lee-way had charmed the travellers with its mingled amenity and grandeur, that which broke upon them on once more reaching Snake River, filled them with admiration and astonishment. At times, the river was overhung by dark and stupendous rocks, rising like gigantic walls and battlements; these would be rent by wide and yawning chasms, that seemed to speak of past convulsions of nature. Sometimes the river was of a glassy smoothness and placidity; at other times it roared along in impetuous rapids and foaming cascades. Here, the rocks were piled in the most fantastic crags and precipices; and in another place, they were succeeded by delightful valleys carpeted with green-sward. The whole of this wild and varied scenery was dominated by immense mountains rearing their distant peaks into the clouds. "The grandeur and originality of the views, presented on every side," says Captain Bonneville, "beggar both the pencil and the pen. Nothing we had ever gazed upon in any other region could for a moment compare in wild majesty and impressive sternness, with the series of scenes which here at every turn astonished our senses, and filled us with awe and delight."

Indeed, from all that we can gather from the journal before us, and the accounts of other travellers, who passed through these regions in the memorable enterprise of Astoria, we are inclined to think that Snake River must be one of the most remarkable for varied and striking scenery of all the rivers of this continent. From its head waters in the Rocky Mountains, to its junction with the Columbia, its windings are upward of six hundred miles[2] through every variety of landscape. Rising in a volcanic region,[3] amid ex-

[2] Actually 1,038 miles.
[3] Yellowstone National Park.

tinguished craters, and mountains awful with the traces of ancient fires, it makes its way through great plains of lava and sandy deserts, penetrates vast sierras or mountainous chains, broken into romantic and often frightful precipices, and crowned with eternal snows; and at other times, careers through green and smiling meadows, and wide landscapes of Italian grace and beauty. Wildness and sublimity, however, appear to be its prevailing characteristics.

Captain Bonneville and his companions had pursued their journey a considerable distance down the course of Snake River, when the old chief halted on the bank, and dismounting, recommended that they should turn their horses loose to graze, while he summoned a cousin of his from a group of lodges on the opposite side of the stream. His summons was quickly answered. An Indian, of an active, elastic form, leaped into a light canoe of cotton-wood, and vigorously plying the paddle, soon shot across the river. Bounding on shore, he advanced with a buoyant air and frank demeanor, and gave his right hand to each of the party in turn. The old chief, whose hard name we forbear to repeat, now presented Captain Bonneville, in form, to his cousin, whose name, we regret to say, was no less hard, being nothing less than Hay-she-in-cow-cow. The latter evinced the usual curiosity to know all about the strangers, whence they came, whither they were going, the object of their journey, and the adventures they had experienced. All these, of course, were ample and eloquently set forth by the communicative old chief. To all his grandiloquent account of the bald-headed chief and his countrymen, the Big Hearts of the East, his cousin listened with great attention, and replied in the customary style of Indian welcome. He then desired the party to await his return, and, springing into his canoe, darted across the river. In a little while he returned, bringing a most welcome supply of tobacco, and a small stock of provisions for the road, declaring his intention of accompanying the party. Having no horse, he mounted behind one of the men, observing that he should procure a steed for himself on the following day.

They all now jogged on very sociably and cheerily together. Not many miles beyond, they met others of the tribe, among whom was one, whom Captain Bonneville and his comrades had known during their residence among the Upper Nez Percés, and who welcomed them with open arms. In this neighborhood was the home of their guide, who took leave of them with a profusion of good wishes for their safety and happiness. That night they put up in the hut of a Nez Percé, where they were visited by several warriors from the other side of the river, friends of the old chief and his cousin, who came to have a talk and a smoke with the white men. The heart of the good old chief was overflowing with good will at thus being surrounded by his new and old friends, and he talked with more spirit and vivacity than ever. The evening passed away in perfect harmony and good-humor, and it was not until a late hour that the visitors took their leave and recrossed the river.

After this constant picture of worth and virtue on the part of the Nez Percé tribe, we grieve to have to record a circumstance calculated to throw a temporary shade upon the name. In the course of the social and harmonious evening just mentioned, one of the captain's men, who happened to be something of a virtuoso in his way, and fond of collecting curiosities, produced a small skin, a great rarity in the eyes of men conversant in peltries. It attracted much attention among the visitors from beyond the river, who passed it from one to the other, examined it with looks of lively admiration, and pronounced it a great medicine.

In the morning, when the captain and his party were about to set off, the precious skin was missing. Search was made for it in the hut, but it was nowhere to be found; and it was strongly suspected that it had been purloined by some of the connoisseurs from the other side of the river.

The old chief and his cousin were indignant at the supposed delinquency of their friends across the water, and called out for them to come over and answer for their shameful conduct. The others answered to the call with all the promptitude of perfect innocence, and spurned at the idea of their being capable of such outrage upon any of the Big-hearted nation. All were at a loss on whom to fix the crime of abstracting the invaluable skin, when by chance the eyes of the worthies from beyond the water fell upon an unhappy cur, belonging to the owner of the hut. He was a gallows-looking dog, but not more so than most Indian dogs, who, take them in the mass, are little better than a generation of vipers. Be that as it may, he was instantly accused of having devoured the skin in question. A dog accused is generally a dog condemned; and a dog condemned is generally a dog executed. So was it in the present instance. The unfortunate cur was arraigned; his thievish looks substantiated his guilt, and he was condemned by his judges from across the river to be hanged. In vain the Indians of the hut, with whom he was a great favorite, interceded in his behalf. In vain Captain Bonneville and his comrades petitioned that his life might be spared. His judges were inexorable. He was doubly guilty: first, in having robbed their good friends, the Big Hearts of the East; secondly, in having brought a doubt on the honor of the Nez Percé tribe. He was, accordingly, swung aloft, and pelted with stones to make his death more certain. The sentence of the judges being thoroughly executed, a post mortem examination of the body of the dog was held, to establish his delinquency beyond all doubt, and to leave the Nez Percés without a shadow of suspicion. Great interest, of course, was manifested by all present, during this operation. The body of the dog was opened, the intestines rigorously scrutinized, but, to the horror of all concerned, not a particle of the skin was to be found—the dog had been unjustly executed!

A great clamor now ensued, but the most clamorous was the party from across the river, whose jealousy of their good name now prompted them to the most vociferous vindications of their innocence. It was with the utmost difficulty that the captain and his comrades could calm their lively sensibilities, by accounting for the disappearance of the skin in a dozen different ways, until all idea of its having been stolen was entirely out of the question.

The meeting now broke up. The warriors returned across the river, the captain and his comrades proceeded on their journey; but the spirits of the communicative old chief, Yo-mus-ro-y-e-cut, were for a time completely dampened, and he evinced great mortification at what had just occurred. He rode on in silence, except, that now and then he would give way to a burst of indignation, and exclaim, with a shake of the head and a toss of the hand toward the opposite shore—"bad men, very bad men across the river"; to each of which brief exclamations, his worthy cousin, Hay-she-in-cow-cow, would respond by a guttural sound of acquiescence, equivalent to an amen.

After some time, the countenance of the old chief again cleared up, and he fell into repeated conferences, in an under tone, with his cousin, which ended in the departure of the latter, who, applying the lash to his horse, dashed forward and was soon out of sight. In fact, they were drawing near to the village of another chief, likewise distinguished by an appellation of some longitude, O-push-y-e-cut; but commonly known as the great chief. The cousin had been sent ahead to give notice of their approach; a herald appeared as before, bearing a powder-horn, to enable them to respond to the intended salute. A scene ensued, on their approach to the village, similar to that which had occurred at the village of the little chief. The whole population appeared in the field, drawn up in lines, arrayed with the customary regard to rank and dignity. Then came on the firing of salutes, and the shaking of hands, in which last ceremonial every individual, man, woman, and child, participated; for the Indians have an idea that it is as indispensable an overture of friendship among the whites as smoking of the pipe is among the red men. The travellers were next ushered to the banquet, where all the choicest viands that the village could furnish, were served up in rich profusion. They were afterwards entertained by feats of agility and horseraces; indeed, their visit to the village seemed the signal for complete festivity. In the meantime, a skin lodge had been spread for their accommodation, their horses and baggage were taken care of, and wood and water supplied in abundance. At night, therefore, they retired to their quarters, to enjoy, as they supposed, the repose of which they stood in need. No such thing, however, was in store for them. A crowd of visitors awaited their appearance, all eager for a smoke and a talk. The pipe was immediately lighted, and constantly replenished and kept alive until the night was far advanced. As usual, the utmost eagerness was evinced by the guests to learn everything within the scope of their comprehension respecting the Americans, for whom they professed the most fraternal regard. The captain, in his replies, made use of familiar illustrations, calculated to strike their minds, and impress them with such an idea of the might of his nation, as would induce them to treat with kindness and respect all stragglers that might fall in their path. To their inquiries as to the numbers of the people of the United States, he assured them that they were as countless as the blades of grass in the prairies, and that, great as Snake River was, if they were all encamped upon its banks, they would drink it dry in a single day. To these and similar statistics, they listened with profound attention, and apparently, implicit belief. It was, indeed, a striking scene: the captain, with his hunter's dress and bald head in the midst, holding forth, and his wild auditors seated around like so many statues, the fire lighting up their painted faces and muscular figures, all fixed and motionless, excepting when the pipe was passed, a question propounded, or a startling fact in statistics received with a movement of surprise and a half-suppressed ejaculation of wonder and delight.

The fame of the captain as a healer of diseases, had accompanied him to this village, and the great chief, O-push-y-e-cut, now entreated him to exert his skill on his daughter, who had been for three days racked with pains, for which the Pierced-nose doctors could devise no alleviation. The captain found her extended on a pallet of mats in excruciating pain. Her father manifested the strongest paternal affection for her, and assured the captain that if he would but cure her, he would place the Americans near his heart. The worthy captain needed no such inducement. His kind heart was already touched by the sufferings of the poor girl, and his sympathies quickened by her appearance; for she was but about sixteen years of age, and uncommonly beautiful in form and feature. The only difficulty with the captain was, that he knew nothing of her malady, and that his medical science was of a most haphazard kind. After considering and cogitating for some time, as a man is apt to do when in a maze of vague ideas, he made a desperate dash at a remedy. By his directions, the girl was placed in a sort of rude vapor bath, much used by the Nez Percés, where she was kept until near fainting. He then gave her a dose of gunpowder dissolved in cold water, and ordered her to be wrapped in buffalo robes and put to sleep under a load of furs and blankets. The remedy succeeded: the next morning she was free from pain, though extremely languid; whereupon, the captain prescribed for her a bowl of colt's head broth, and that she should be kept for a time on simple diet.

The great chief was unbounded in his expressions of gratitude for the recovery of his daughter. He would fain have detained the captain a long time as his guest, but the time for departure had arrived. When the captain's horse was brought for him to mount, the chief declared that the steed was not worthy of him, and sent for one of his best horses, which he presented in its stead; declaring that it made his heart glad to see his friend so well mounted. He then appointed a young Nez Percé to accompany his guest to the next village, and "to carry his talk" concerning them; and the two parties separated with mutual expressions of good will.

The vapor bath of which we have made mention is in frequent use among the Nez Percé tribe, chiefly for cleanliness. Their sweating houses, as they call them, are small and close lodges, and the vapor is produced by water poured slowly upon red-hot stones.

On passing the limits of O-push-y-e-cut's domains, the travellers left the elevated table-lands, and all the wild and romantic scenery which has just been described. They now traversed a gently undulating country, of such fertility that it excited the rapturous admiration of two of the captain's followers, a Kentuckian and a native of Ohio. They declared that it surpassed any land that they had ever seen, and often exclaimed what a delight it would be just to run a plough through such a rich and teeming soil, and see it open its bountiful promise before the share.

Another halt and sojourn of a night was made at the village of a chief named He-mim-el-pilp, where similar ceremonies were observed and hospitality experienced, as at the preceding villages. They now pursued a west-southwest course through a beautiful and fertile region, better wooded than most of the tracts through which they had passed. In their progress, they met with several bands of Nez Percés, by whom they were invariably treated with the utmost kindness. Within seven days after leaving the domain of He-mim-el-pilp, they struck the Columbia River at Fort Wallah-Wallah, where they arrived on the 4th of March, 1834.

34.

Fort Wallah-Wallah—Its commander—Indians in its neighborhood—Exertions of Mr. Pambrune for their improvement—Religion—Code of laws—Range of the Lower Nez Percés—Camash, and other roots—Nez Percé horses—Preparations for departure—Refusal of supplies—Departure—A laggard and glutton

FORT WALLAH-WALLAH is a trading post of the Hudson's Bay Company, situated just above the mouth of the river by the same name, and on the left bank of the Columbia.[1] It is built of drift-wood, and calculated merely for defence against any attack of the natives. At the time of Captain Bonneville's arrival, the whole garrison mustered but six or eight men; and the post was under the superintendence of Mr. Pambrune,[2] an agent of the Hudson's Bay Company.

The great post and fort of the company, forming the emporium of its trade on the Pacific, is Fort Vancouver; situated on the right bank of the Columbia, about sixty miles from the sea, and just above the mouth of the Wallamut.[3] To this point, the company removed

---

[1] The fort was located on the east side of the Columbia River and on the north side of the Walla Walla River. Nathaniel Wyeth had spent five days there in the previous October (1833), and described the fort as being "of no strength merely sufficient to frighten Indians mounting 2 small cannon having bastions at the opposite corners of a square enclosure there were 6 whites there. . . . At the post we saw a bull and cow & calf, hen & cock, punkins, potatoes, corn, all of which looked strange and unnatural and like a dream." *Correspondence and Journals*, 173.

[2] Pierre C. Pambrun (1792–1841). He assumed control of Fort Walla Walla in 1832.

[3] The Willamette River, which flows from the south into the Columbia at Portland, Oregon.

its establishment from Astoria, in 1821, after its coalition with the Northwest Company.

Captain Bonneville and his comrades experienced a polite reception from Mr. Pambrune, the superintendent: for, however hostile the members of the British Company may be to the enterprises of American traders, they have always manifested great courtesy and hospitality to the traders themselves.

Fort Wallah-Wallah is surrounded by the tribe of the same name, as well as by the Skynses[4] and the Nez Percés; who bring to it the furs and peltries collected in their hunting expeditions. The Wallah-Wallahs are a degenerate, worn-out tribe. The Nez Percés are the most numerous and tractable of the three tribes just mentioned. Mr. Pambrune informed Captain Bonneville that he had been at some pains to introduce the Christian religion, in the Roman Catholic form, among them, where it had evidently taken root; but had become altered and modified, to suit their peculiar habits of thought, and motives of action; retaining, however, the principal points of faith, and its entire precepts of morality. The same gentleman had given them a code of laws, to which they conformed with scrupulous fidelity. Polygamy, which once prevailed among them to a great extent, was now rarely indulged. All the crimes denounced by the Christian faith met with severe punishment among them. Even theft, so venial a crime among the Indians, had recently been punished with hanging, by sentence of a chief.

There certainly appears to be a peculiar susceptibility of moral and religious improvement among this tribe, and they would seem to be one of the very, very few that have benefited in morals and manners by an intercourse with white men. The parties which visited them about twenty years previously, in the expedition fitted out by Mr. Astor, complained of their selfishness, their extortion, and their thievish propensities. The very reverse of those qualities prevailed among them during the prolonged sojourns of Captain Bonneville.

The Lower Nez Percés range upon the Way-lee-way, Immahah,

[4] Skin Indians, whom Lewis and Clark called the Eneeshur Indians. John R. Swanton, *The Indian Tribes of North America*, 442–43.

Yenghies,[5] and other of the streams west of the mountains. They hunt the beaver, elk, deer, white bear, and mountain sheep. Besides the flesh of these animals, they use a number of roots for food; some of which would be well worth transplanting and cultivating in the Atlantic States. Among these is the camash,[6] a sweet root, about the form and size of an onion, and said to be really delicious. The cowish,[7] also, or biscuit root, about the size of a walnut, which they reduce to a very palatable flour; together with the jackap, aisish, quako, and others; which they cook by steaming them in the ground.

In August and September, these Indians keep along the rivers, where they catch and dry great quantities of salmon; which, while they last, are their principal food. In the winter, they congregate in villages formed of comfortable huts, or lodges, covered with mats. They are generally clad in deer skins, or woollens, and extremely well armed. Above all, they are celebrated for owning great numbers of horses; which they mark, and then suffer to range in droves in their most fertile plains. These horses are principally of the pony breed; but remarkably stout and long-winded. They are brought in great numbers to the establishments of the Hudson's Bay Company, and sold for a mere trifle.

Such is the account given by Captain Bonneville of the Nez Percés; who, if not viewed by him with too partial an eye, are certainly among the gentlest, and least barbarous people of these remote wildernesses. They invariably signified to him their earnest wish that an American post might be established among them; and repeatedly declared that they would trade with Americans, in preference to any other people.

Captain Bonneville had intended to remain some time in this

---

[5] The Yenghies River has withstood persistent efforts to identify it. No river of this name appears on the maps in either *Astoria* or *Bonneville*. It might be a tributary of the Imnaha or of the Grande Ronde rivers, or possibly modern Clearwater River, which flows into the Snake at Lewiston, Idaho. On the *Astoria* map the Clearwater appears as Kees Kees Kee River and on the western-most map in *Bonneville* as the Kooskoos River.

[6] Camass *(Camassia quamash)*.

[7] Possibly *Lomatium cous*. I have been unable to identify the other plants named in this passage.

The ADVENTURES of CAPTAIN BONNEVILLE

neighborhood, to form an acquaintance with the natives, and to collect information, and establish connections that might be advantageous in the way of trade. The delays, however, which he had experienced on his journey, obliged him to shorten his sojourn, and to set off as soon as possible, so as to reach the rendezvous at the Portneuf at the appointed time. He had seen enough to convince him that an American trade might be carried on with advantage in this quarter; and he determined soon to return with a stronger party, more completely fitted for the purpose.

As he stood in need of some supplies for his journey, he applied to purchase them of Mr. Pambrune; but soon found the difference between being treated as a guest, or as a rival trader. The worthy superintendent, who had extended to him all the genial rites of hospitality, now suddenly assumed a withered-up aspect and demeanor, and observed that, however he might feel disposed to serve him, personally, he felt bound by his duty to the Hudson's Bay Company, to do nothing which should facilitate or encourage the visits of other traders among the Indians in that part of the country. He endeavored to dissuade Captain Bonneville from returning through the Blue Mountains; assuring him it would be extremely difficult and dangerous, if not impracticable, at this season of the year; and advised him to accompany Mr. Payette,[8] a leader of the Hudson's Bay Company, who was about to depart with a number of men, by a more circuitous, but safe route, to carry supplies to the company's agent, resident among the Upper Nez Percés. Captain Bonneville, however, piqued at his having refused to furnish him with supplies, and doubting the sincerity of his advice, determined to return by the more direct route through the mountains; though varying his course, in some respects, from that by which he had come, in consequence of information gathered among the neighboring Indians.

Accordingly, on the 6th of March, he and his three companions, accompanied by their Nez Percé guides, set out on their return. In the early part of their course, they touched again at several of the Nez Percé villages, where they had experienced such kind treat-

[8] Francis Payette.

ment on their way down. They were always welcomed with cordiality; and everything was done to cheer them on their journey.

On leaving the Way-lee-way village, they were joined by a Nez Percé, whose society was welcomed on account of the general gratitude and good will they felt for his tribe. He soon proved a heavy clog upon the little party, being doltish and taciturn, lazy in the extreme, and a huge feeder. His only proof of intellect was in shrewdly avoiding all labor, and availing himself of the toil of others. When on the march, he always lagged behind the rest, leaving to them the task of breaking a way through all difficulties and impediments, and leisurely and lazily jogging along the track, which they had beaten through the snow. At the evening encampment, when others were busy gathering fuel, providing for the horses, and cooking the evening repast, this worthy Sancho of the wilderness would take his seat quietly and cosily by the fire, puffing away at his pipe, and eyeing in silence, but with wistful intensity of gaze, the savory morsels roasting for supper.

When meal-time arrived, however, then came his season of activity. He no longer hung back, and waited for others to take the lead, but distinguished himself by a brilliancy of onset, and a sustained vigor and duration of attack, that completely shamed the efforts of his competitors—albeit, experienced trenchermen of no mean prowess. Never had they witnessed such power of mastication, and such marvellous capacity of stomach, as in this native and uncultivated gastronome. Having, by repeated and prolonged assaults, at length completely gorged himself, he would wrap himself up, and lie with the torpor of an anaconda; slowly digesting his way on to the next repast.

The gormandizing powers of this worthy were, at first, matters of surprise and merriment to the travellers; but they soon became too serious for a joke, threatening devastation to the fleshpots; and he was regarded askance, at his meals, as a regular kill-crop, destined to waste the substance of the party. Nothing but a sense of the obligations they were under to his nation induced them to bear with such a guest; but he proceeded, speedily, to relieve them from the weight of these obligations, by eating a receipt in full.

35.

The uninvited guest—Free and easy manners—
Salutary jokes—A prodigal son—Exit of the glutton—
A sudden change in fortune—Danger of a visit to poor
relations—Plucking of a prosperous man—A vagabond
toilet—A substitute for the very fine horse—Hard
travelling—The uninvited guest and the patriarchal
colt—A beggar on horseback—A catastrophe—
Exit of the merry vagabond

As CAPTAIN BONNEVILLE and his men were encamped one evening among the hills near Snake River, seated before their fire, enjoying a hearty supper, they were suddenly surprised by the visit of an uninvited guest. He was a ragged, half-naked Indian hunter, armed with bow and arrows, and had the carcass of a fine buck thrown across his shoulder. Advancing with an alert step, and free and easy air, he threw the buck on the ground, and, without waiting for an invitation, seated himself at their mess, helped himself without ceremony, and chatted to the right and left in the liveliest and most unembarrassed manner. No adroit and veteran dinner hunter of a metropolis could have acquitted himself more knowingly. The travellers were at first completely taken by surprise, and could not but admire the facility with which this ragged cosmopolite made himself at home among them. While they stared he went on, making the most of the good cheer upon which he had so fortunately alighted; and was soon elbow deep in "pot luck," and greased from the tip of his nose to the back of his ears.

As the company recovered from their surprise, they began to feel annoyed at this intrusion. Their uninvited guest, unlike the generality of his tribe, was somewhat dirty as well as ragged and they had no relish for such a messmate. Heaping up, therefore, an abundant portion of the "provant" upon a piece of bark, which served for a dish, they invited him to confine himself thereto, instead of foraging in the general mess.

He complied with the most accommodating spirit imaginable; and went on eating and chatting, and laughing and smearing himself, until his whole countenance shone with grease and good-humor. In the course of his repast, his attention was caught by the figure of the gastronome, who, as usual, was gorging himself in dogged silence. A droll cut of the eye showed either that he knew him of old, or perceived at once his characteristics. He immediately made him the butt of his pleasantries; and cracked off two or three good hits, that caused the sluggish dolt to prick up his ears, and delighted all the company. From this time, the uninvited guest was taken into favor; his jokes began to be relished; his careless, free and easy air, to be considered singularly amusing; and in the end, he was pronounced by the travellers one of the merriest companions and most entertaining vagabonds they had met with in the wilderness.

Supper being over, the redoubtable Shee-wee-she-ouaiter, for such was the simple name by which he announced himself, declared his intention of keeping company with the party for a day or two, if they had no objection; and by way of backing his self-invitation, presented the carcass of the buck as an earnest of his hunting abilities. By this time, he had so completely effaced the unfavorable impression made by his first appearance, that he was made welcome to the camp, and the Nez Percé guide undertook to give him lodging for the night. The next morning, at break of day, he borrowed a gun, and was off among the hills, nor was anything more seen of him until a few minutes after the party had encamped for the evening, when he again made his appearance, in his usual frank, careless manner, and threw down the carcass of another noble deer, which he had borne on his back for a considerable distance.

This evening he was the life of the party, and his open communicative disposition, free from all disguise, soon put them in possession

The ADVENTURES of CAPTAIN BONNEVILLE

of his history. He had been a kind of prodigal son in his native village; living a loose, heedless life, and disregarding the precepts and imperative commands of the chiefs. He had, in consequence, been expelled from the village, but, in nowise disheartened at this banishment, had betaken himself to the society of the border Indians, and had led a careless, haphazard, vagabond life, perfectly consonant to his humors; heedless of the future, so long as he had wherewithal for the present; and fearing no lack of food, so long as he had the implements of the chase, and a fair hunting ground.

Finding him very expert as a hunter, and being pleased with his eccentricities, and his strange and merry humor, Captain Bonneville fitted him out handsomely as the Nimrod of the party, who all soon became quite attached to him. One of the earliest and most signal services he performed, was to exorcise the insatiate kill-crop that hitherto oppressed the party. In fact, the doltish Nez Percé, who had seemed so perfectly insensible to rough treatment of every kind, by which the travellers had endeavored to elbow him out of their society, could not withstand the good-humored bantering, and occasionally sharp wit of She-wee-she. He evidently quailed under his jokes, and sat blinking like an owl in daylight, when pestered by the flouts and peckings of mischievous birds. At length his place was found vacant at meal-time; no one knew when he went off, or whither he had gone, but he was seen no more, and the vast surplus that remained when the repast was over, showed what a mighty gormandizer had departed.

Relieved from this incubus, the little party now went on cheerily. She-wee-she kept them in fun as well as food. His hunting was always successful; he was ever ready to render any assistance in the camp or on the march; while his jokes, his antics, and the very cut of his countenance, so full of whim and comicality, kept every one in good-humor.

In this way they journeyed on until they arrived on the banks of the Immahah, and encamped near to the Nez Percé lodges. Here She-wee-she took a sudden notion to visit his people, and show off the state of worldly prosperity to which he had so suddenly attained. He accordingly departed in the morning, arrayed in hunter's style, and well appointed with everything benefitting his vocation. The buoyancy of his gait, the elasticity of his step, and the hilarity of his countenance, showed that he anticipated, with chuckling satisfaction, the surprise he was about to give those who had ejected him from their society in rags. But what a change was there in his whole appearance when he rejoined the party in the evening! He came skulking into camp like a beaten cur, with his tail between his legs. All his finery was gone; he was naked as when he was born, with the exception of a scanty flap that answered the purpose of a fig leaf. His fellow-travellers at first did not know him, but supposed it to be some vagrant Root Digger sneaking into the camp; but when they recognized in this forlorn object their prime wag, She-wee-she, whom they had seen depart in the morning in such high glee and high feather, they could not contain their merriment, but hailed him with loud and repeated peals of laughter.

She-wee-she was not of a spirit to be easily cast down; he soon joined in the merriment as heartily as any one, and seemed to consider his reverse of fortune an excellent joke. Captain Bonneville, however, thought proper to check his good-humor, and demanded, with some degree of sternness, the cause of his altered condition. He replied in the most natural and self-complacent style imaginable, "that he had been among his cousins, who were very poor; they had been delighted to see him; still more delighted with his good fortune; they had taken him to their arms; admired his equipments; one had begged for this; another for that"—in fine, what with the poor devil's inherent heedlessness, and the real generosity of his disposition, his needy cousins had succeeded in stripping him of all his clothes and accoutrements, excepting the fig leaf with which he had returned to camp.

Seeing his total want of care and forethought, Captain Bonneville determined to let him suffer a little, in hopes it might prove a salutary lesson; and, at any rate, to make him no more presents while in the neighborhood of his needy cousins. He was left, therefore, to shift for himself in his naked condition; which, however, did not seem to give him any concern, or to abate one jot of his good-humor. In the course of his lounging about the camp, however, he got possession of a deer skin; whereupon, cutting a slit in the middle, he thrust his head through it, so that the two ends hung down before and behind, something like a South American poncho, or the tabard of a herald. These ends he tied together, under the armpits; and thus arrayed, presented himself once more before the captain, with an air of perfect self-satisfaction, as though he thought it impossible for any fault to be found with his toilet.

A little further journeying brought the travellers to the petty village of Nez Percés, governed by the worthy and affectionate old patriarch who had made Captain Bonneville the costly present of the very fine horse. The old man welcomed them once more to his village with his usual cordiality, and his respectable squaw and hopeful son, cherishing grateful recollections of the hatchet and ear-bobs, joined in a chorus of friendly gratulation.

As the much-vaunted steed, once the joy and pride of this interesting family, was now nearly knocked up by travelling, and totally inadequate to the mountain scramble that lay ahead, Captain Bonneville restored him to the venerable patriarch, with renewed acknowledgments for the invaluable gift. Somewhat to his surprise, he was immediately supplied with a fine two years' old colt in his stead, a substitution which, he afterward learnt, according to Indian custom in such cases, he might have claimed as a matter of right. We do not find that any after claims were made on account of this colt. This donation may be regarded, therefore, as a signal punctilio of Indian honor; but it will be found that the animal soon proved an unlucky acquisition to the party.

While at this village, the Nez Percé guide had held consultations with some of the inhabitants as to the mountain tract the party were about to traverse. He now began to wear an anxious aspect, and to indulge in gloomy forebodings. The snow, he had been told, lay to a great depth in the passes of the mountains, and difficulties would increase as he proceeded. He begged Captain Bonneville, therefore, to travel very slowly, so as to keep the horses in strength and spirit for the hard times they would have to encounter. The captain surrendered the regulation of the march entirely to his discretion, and pushed on in the advance, amusing himself with hunting, so as generally to kill a deer or two in the course of the day, and arriving, before the rest of the party, at the spot designated by the guide for the evening's encampment.

In the meantime, the others plodded on at the heels of the guide, accompanied by that merry vagabond, She-wee-she. The primitive garb worn by this droll left all his nether man exposed to the biting blasts of the mountains. Still his wit was never frozen, nor his sunshiny temper beclouded; and his innumerable antics and practical jokes, while they quickened the circulation of his own blood, kept his companions in high good-humor.

So passed the first day after the departure from the patriarch's. The second day commenced in the same manner; the captain in the advance, the rest of the party following on slowly. She-wee-she, for the greater part of the time, trudged on foot over the snow, keeping himself warm by hard exercise, and all kinds of crazy capers. In the height of his foolery, the patriarchal colt, which, unbroken to the saddle, was suffered to follow on at large, happened to come within his reach. In a moment, he was on his back, snapping his fingers, and yelping with delight. The colt, unused to such a burden, and half wild by nature, fell to prancing and rearing and snorting and plunging and kicking; and, at length, set off full speed over the most dangerous ground. As the route led generally along the steep and craggy sides of the hills, both horse and horseman were constantly in danger, and more than once had a hairbreadth escape from deadly peril. Nothing, however, could daunt this madcap savage. He stuck to the colt like a plaister [*sic*], up ridges, down gullies; whooping and yelling with the wildest glee. Never did beggar on horseback display more headlong horsemanship. His companions followed him with their eyes, sometimes laughing, sometimes holding in their breath at his vagaries, until they saw the colt make a sudden plunge or start, and pitch his unlucky rider headlong over a precipice. There was a general cry of horror, and all hastened to the spot. They found the poor fellow lying among the rocks below, sadly bruised and mangled. It was almost a miracle that he had escaped with life. Even in this condition, his merry spirit was not entirely quelled, and he summoned up a feeble laugh at the alarm and anxiety of those who came to his relief. He was extricated from his rocky bed, and a messenger dispatched to inform Captain Bonneville of the accident. The latter returned with all speed, and encamped the party at the first convenient spot. Here the wounded man was stretched upon buffalo skins, and the captain, who officiated on all occasions as doctor and surgeon to the party, proceeded to examine his wounds. The principal one was a long and deep gash in the thigh, which reached to the bone. Calling for a needle and thread, the captain now prepared to sew up the wound, admonishing the patient to submit to the operation with becoming fortitude. His gayety was at an end; he could no longer summon up even a forced smile; and, at the first puncture of the needle, flinched so piteously, that the captain was obliged to pause, and to order him a powerful dose of alcohol. This somewhat rallied up his spirit and warmed his heart; all the time of the operation, however, he kept his eyes riveted on the wound, with his teeth set, and a whimsical wincing of the countenance, that occasionally gave his nose something of its usual comic curl.

When the wound was fairly closed, the captain washed it with rum, and administered a second dose of the same to the patient, who was tucked in for the night, and advised to compose himself to sleep. He was restless and uneasy, however; repeatedly expressing his fears that his leg would be so much swollen the next day, as to prevent his proceeding with the party; nor could he be quieted, until the captain gave a decided opinion favorable to his wishes.

Early the next morning, a gleam of his merry humor returned, on finding that his wounded limb retained its natural proportions. On attempting to use it, however, he found himself unable to stand. He made several efforts to coax himself into a belief that he might still continue forward; but at length, shook his head despondingly, and said, that "as he had but one leg," it was all in vain to attempt a passage of the mountain.

Every one grieved to part with so boon a companion, and under such disastrous circumstances. He was once more clothed and equipped, each one making him some parting present. He was then helped on a horse, which Captain Bonneville presented to him; and after many parting expressions of good will on both sides, set off on his return to his old haunts; doubtless, to be once more plucked by his affectionate but needy cousins.

36.

The difficult mountain—A smoke and consultation—
The captain's speech—An icy turnpike—Danger of a
false step—Arrival on Snake River—Return to
Portneuf—Meeting of comrades

CONTINUING THEIR JOURNEY up the course of the Immahah, the travellers found, as they approached the head waters,[1] the snow increased in quantity, so as to lie two feet deep. They were again obliged, therefore, to beat down a path for their horses, sometimes travelling on the icy surface of the stream. At length they reached the place where they intended to scale the mountains; and, having broken a pathway to the foot, were agreeably surprised to find that the wind had drifted the snow from off the side, so that they attained the summit with but little difficulty. Here they encamped, with the intention of beating a track through the mountains. A short experiment, however, obliged them to give up the attempt, the snow lying in vast drifts, often higher than the horses' heads.

Captain Bonneville now took the two Indian guides, and set out to reconnoitre the neighborhood. Observing a high peak which overtopped the rest, he climbed it, and discovered from the summit a pass about nine miles long, but so heavily piled with snow, that it seemed impracticable. He now lit a pipe, and, sitting down with the two guides, proceeded to hold a consultation after the Indian mode. For a long while they all smoked vigorously and in silence, pondering over the subject matter before them. At length a discussion commenced, and the opinion in which the two guides con-

[1] The Imnaha River rises in the Wallowa Mountains, which Bonneville now had to cross.

curred was, that the horses could not possibly cross the snows. They advised, therefore, that the party should proceed on foot, and they should take the horses back to the village, where they would be well taken care of until Captain Bonneville should send for them. They urged this advice with great earnestness; declaring that their chief would be extremely angry, and treat them severely, should any of the horses of his good friends, the white men, be lost, in crossing under their guidance; and that, therefore, it was good they should not attempt it.

Captain Bonneville sat smoking his pipe, and listening to them with Indian silence and gravity. When they had finished, he replied to them in their own style of language.

"My friends," said he, "I have seen the pass, and have listened to your words; you have little hearts. When troubles and dangers lie in your way, you turn your backs. That is not the way with my nation. When great obstacles present, and threaten to keep them back, their hearts swell, and they push forward. They love to conquer difficulties. But enough for the present. Night is coming on; let us return to our camp."

He moved on, and they followed in silence. On reaching the camp, he found the men extremely discouraged. One of their number had been surveying the neighborhood, and seriously assured them that the snow was at least a hundred feet deep. The captain cheered them up, and diffused fresh spirit in them by his example. Still he was much perplexed how to proceed. About dark there was a slight drizzling rain. An expedient now suggested itself. This was to make two light sleds, place the packs on them, and drag them to the other side of the mountain, thus forming a road in the wet snow, which, should it afterward freeze, would be sufficiently hard to bear the horses. This plan was promptly put into execution; the sleds were constructed, the heavy baggage was drawn backward and forward until the road was beaten, when they desisted from their fatiguing labor. The night turned out clear and cold, and by morning, their road was incrusted with ice sufficiently strong for their purpose. They now set out on their icy turnpike, and got on well enough, excepting that now and then a horse would sidle out of the track, and immediately sink up to the neck. Then came on toil and difficulty, and they would be obliged to haul up the floundering animal with ropes. One, more unlucky than the rest, after repeated falls, had to be abandoned in the snow. Notwithstanding these repeated delays, they succeeded, before the sun had acquired sufficient power to thaw the snow, in getting all the rest of their horses safely to the other side of the mountain.

Their difficulties and dangers, however, were not yet at an end. They had now to descend, and the whole surface of the snow was glazed with ice. It was necessary, therefore, to wait until the warmth of the sun should melt the glassy crust of sleet, and give them a foothold in the yielding snow. They had a frightful warning of the danger of any movement while the sleet remained. A wild young mare, in her restlessness, strayed to the edge of a declivity. One slip was fatal to her; she lost her balance, careered with headlong velocity down the slippery side of the mountain for more than two thousand feet, and was dashed to pieces at the bottom. When the travellers afterward sought the carcass to cut it up for food, they found it torn and mangled in the most horrible manner.

It was quite late in the evening before the party descended to the ultimate skirts of the snow. Here they planted large logs below them to prevent their sliding down, and encamped for the night. The next day they succeeded in bringing down their baggage to the encampment; then packing all up regularly, and loading their horses, they once more set out briskly and cheerfully, and in the course of the following day succeeded in getting to a grassy region.

Here their Nez Percé guides declared that all the difficulties of the mountains were at an end, and their course was plain and simple, and needed no further guidance; they asked leave, therefore, to return home. This was readily granted, with many thanks and presents for their faithful services. They took a long farewell smoke with their white friends, after which they mounted their horses and set off, exchanging many farewells and kind wishes.

On the following day, Captain Bonneville completed his journey down the mountain, and encamped on the borders of Snake River, where he found the grass in great abundance and eight inches in height. In this neighborhood, he saw on the rocky banks of the river several prismoids of basaltes,[2] rising to the height of fifty or sixty feet.

Nothing particularly worthy of note occurred during several days as the party proceeded up along Snake River and across its tributary streams. After crossing Gun Creek, they met with various signs that white people were in the neighborhood, and Captain Bonneville made earnest exertions to discover whether they were any of his own people, that he might join them. He soon ascertained that they had been starved out of this tract of country, and had betaken themselves to the buffalo region, whither he now shaped his course. In proceeding along Snake River, he found small hordes of Shoshonies lingering upon the minor streams, and living upon trout and other fish, which they catch in great numbers at this season in fish-traps. The greater part of the tribe, however, had penetrated the mountains to hunt the elk, deer, and ahsahta or bighorn.

On the 12th of May, Captain Bonneville reached the Portneuf River, in the vicinity of which he had left the winter encampment of his company on the preceding Christmas day. He had then expected to be back by the beginning of March, but circumstances had detained him upward of two months beyond the time, and the winter encampment must long ere this have been broken up. Halting on the banks of the Portneuf, he dispatched scouts a few miles above, to visit the old camping ground and search for signals of the party, or of their whereabouts, should they actually have abandoned the spot. They returned without being able to ascertain anything.

Being now destitute of provisions, the travellers found it necessary to make a short hunting excursion after buffalo. They made caches, therefore, on an island in the river, in which they deposited all their baggage, and then set out on their expedition. They were so fortunate as to kill a couple of fine bulls, and cutting up the carcasses, determined to husband this stock of provisions with the most miserly care, lest they should again be obliged to venture into the open and dangerous hunting grounds. Returning to their island

[2] The great lava flows of the Pacific Northwest characteristically exhibit vertical five- or six-sided columns resulting from cooling and shrinking of the molten basalt.

on the 18th of May, they found that the wolves had been at the caches, scratched up the contents, and scattered them in every direction. They now constructed a more secure one, in which they deposited their heaviest articles, and then descended Snake River again, and encamped just above the American Falls. Here they proceeded to fortify themselves, intending to remain here, and give their horses an opportunity to recruit their strength with good pasturage, until it should be time to set out for the annual rendezvous in Bear River valley.

On the first of June they descried four men on the other side of the river, opposite to the camp, and, having attracted their attention by a discharge of rifles, ascertained to their joy that they were some of their own people. From these men Captain Bonneville learned that the whole party which he had left in the preceding month of December were encamped on Blackfoot River, a tributary of Snake River, not very far above the Portneuf. Thither he proceeded with all possible dispatch, and in a little while had the pleasure of finding himself once more surrounded by his people, who greeted his return among them in the heartiest manner; for his long-protracted absence had convinced them that he and his three companions had been cut off by some hostile tribe.

The party had suffered much during his absence. They had been pinched by famine and almost starved, and had been forced to repair to the caches at Salmon River. Here they fell in with the Blackfeet bands, and considered themselves fortunate in being able to retreat from the dangerous neighborhood without sustaining any loss.

Being thus reunited, a general treat from Captain Bonneville to his men was a matter of course. Two days, therefore, were given up to such feasting and merriment as their means and situation afforded. What was wanting in good cheer was made up in good will; the free trappers in particular, distinguished themselves on the occasion, and the saturnalia was enjoyed with a hearty holiday spirit, that smacked of the game flavor of the wilderness.

37.

Departure for the rendezvous—A war party of
Blackfeet—A mock bustle—Sham fires at night—
Warlike precautions—Dangers of a night attack—
A panic among horses—Cautious march—The Beer
Springs—A mock carousal—Skirmishing with
buffaloes—A buffalo bait—Arrival at the rendezvous—
Meeting of various bands

AFTER THE TWO DAYS of festive indulgence, Captain Bonneville broke up the encampment, and set out with his motley crew of hired and free trappers, half-breeds, Indians, and squaws, for the main rendezvous in Bear River valley. Directing his course up the Blackfoot River, he soon reached the hills among which it takes its rise. Here, while on the march, he descried from the brow of a hill, a war party of about sixty Blackfeet, on the plain immediately below him. His situation was perilous; for the greater part of his people were dispersed in various directions. Still, to betray hesitation or fear would be to discover his actual weakness, and to invite attack. He assumed, instantly, therefore, a belligerent tone; ordered the squaws to lead the horses to a small grove of ashen trees, and unload and tie them; and caused a great bustle to be made by his scanty handful; the leaders riding hither and thither, and vociferating with all their might, as if a numerous force was getting under way for an attack.

To keep up the deception as to his force, he ordered, at night, a number of extra fires to be made in his camp, and kept up a vigilant watch. His men were all directed to keep themselves prepared for instant action. In such cases the experienced trapper sleeps in his clothes, with his rifle beside him, the shot-belt and powder-flask on the stock; so that, in case of alarm, he can lay his hand upon the whole of his equipment at once, and start up, completely armed.

Captain Bonneville was also especially careful to secure the horses, and set a vigilant guard upon them; for there lies the great object and principal danger of a night attack. The grand move of the lurking savage is to cause a panic among the horses. In such cases one horse frightens another, until all are alarmed, and struggle to break loose. In camps where there are great numbers of Indians, with their horses, a night alarm of the kind is tremendous. The running of the horses that have broken loose; the snorting, stamping, and rearing of those which remain fast; the howling of dogs; the yelling of Indians; the scampering of white men, and red men, with their guns; the overturning of lodges, and trampling of fires by the horses; the flashes of the fires, lighting up forms of men and steeds dashing through the gloom, altogether make up one of the wildest scenes of confusion imaginable. In this way, sometimes, all the horses of a camp amounting to several hundred will be frightened off in a single night.

The night passed off without any disturbance; but there was no likelihood that a war party of Blackfeet, once on the track of a camp where there was a chance for spoils, would fail to hover round it. The captain, therefore, continued to maintain the most vigilant precautions; throwing out scouts in the advance, and on every rising ground.

In the course of the day he arrived at the plain of white clay, already mentioned, surrounded by the mineral springs, called Beer Springs, by the trappers.[1] Here the men all halted to have a regale.

[1] In a manuscript journal of Mr. Nathaniel G. Wyeth, we find the following mention of this watering-place:

"There is here a soda spring; or, I may say, fifty of them. These springs throw out lime, which deposits and forms little hillocks of a yellowish-colored stone. There is, also, here, a warm spring, which throws out water, with a jet; which is like bilge-water in taste. There are, also, here, peat beds, which sometimes take fire, and leave behind a deep, light ashes; in which animals sink deep. * * * I ascended a mountain, and from it could see that Bear River took a short turn round Sheep Rock. There were, in the plain, many hundred mounds of yellowish stone, with a crater on the top, formed of the deposits of the impregnated water" (Irving's note).

In a few moments every spring had its jovial knot of hard drinkers, with tin cup in hand, indulging in a mock carouse; quaffing, pledging, toasting, bandying jokes, singing drinking songs, and uttering peals of laughter, until it seemed as if their imaginations had given potency to the beverage, and cheated them into a fit of intoxication. Indeed, in the excitement of the moment, they were loud and extravagant in their commendations of "the mountain tap"; elevating it above every beverage produced from hops or malt. It was a singular and fantastic scene; suited to a region where everything is strange and peculiar:—These groups of trappers, and hunters, and Indians, with their wild costumes, and wilder countenances; their boisterous gayety, and reckless air; quaffing, and making merry round these sparkling fountains; while beside them lay their weapons, ready to be snatched up for instant service. Painters are fond of representing banditti at their rude and picturesque carousals; but here were groups, still more rude and picturesque; and it needed but a sudden onset of Blackfeet, and a quick transition from a fantastic revel to a furious melée, to have rendered this picture of a trapper's life complete.

The beer frolic, however, passed off without any untoward circumstance; and, unlike most drinking bouts, left neither headache nor heartache behind. Captain Bonneville now directed his course up along Bear River; amusing himself, occasionally, with hunting the buffalo, with which the country was covered. Sometimes, when he saw a huge bull taking his repose in a prairie, he would steal along a ravine, until close upon him; then rouse him from his meditations with a pebble, and take a shot at him as he started up. Such is the quickness with which this animal springs upon his legs, that it is not easy to discover the muscular process by which it is effected. The horse rises first upon his fore legs; and the domestic cow, upon her hinder limbs; but the buffalo bounds at once from a couchant to an erect position, with a celerity that baffles the eye. Though from his bulk, and rolling gait, he does not appear to run with

---

This passage is in Wyeth's *Correspondence and Journals*, 226. Irving corrected Wyeth's spelling, punctuation, and capitalization, and took a few liberties with wording.

much swiftness; yet, it takes a stanch horse to overtake him, when at full speed on level ground; and a buffalo cow is still fleeter in her motion.

Among the Indians and half-breeds of the party, were several admirable horsemen and bold hunters; who amused themselves with a grotesque kind of buffalo bait. Whenever they found a huge bull in the plains, they prepared for their teasing and barbarous sport. Surrounding him on horseback, they would discharge their arrows at him in quick succession, goading him to make an attack; which, with a dexterous movement of the horse, they would easily avoid. In this way, they hovered round him, feathering him with arrows, as he reared and plunged about, until he was bristled all over like a porcupine. When they perceived in him signs of exhaustion, and he could no longer be provoked to make battle, they would dismount from their horses, approach him in the rear, and seizing him by the tail, jerk him from side to side, and drag him backward; until the frantic animal, gathering fresh strength from fury, would break from them, and rush, with flashing eyes and a hoarse bellowing, upon any enemy in sight; but in a little while, his transient excitement at an end, would pitch headlong on the ground, and expire. The arrows were then plucked forth, the tongue cut out and preserved as a dainty, and the carcass left a banquet for the wolves.

Pursuing his course up Bear River, Captain Bonneville arrived, on the 13th of June, at the Little Snake Lake;[2] where he encamped for four or five days, that he might examine its shores and outlets. The latter, he found extremely muddy, and so surrounded by swamps and quagmires, that he was obliged to construct canoes of rushes, with which to explore them. The mouths of all the streams which fall into this lake from the west, are marshy and inconsiderable; but on the east side, there is a beautiful beach, broken, occasionally, by high and isolated bluffs, which advance upon the lake, and heighten the character of the scenery. The water is very shallow, but abounds with trout, and other small fish.

Having finished his survey of the lake, Captain Bonneville proceeded on his journey, until on the banks of the Bear River, some

[2] Bear Lake.

distance higher up, he came upon the party which he had detached a year before, to circumambulate the Great Salt Lake, and ascertain its extent, and the nature of its shores. They had been encamped here about twenty days; and were greatly rejoiced at meeting once more with their comrades, from whom they had so long been separated. The first inquiry of Captain Bonneville was about the result of their journey, and the information they had procured as to the Great Salt Lake; the object of his intense curiosity and ambition. The substance of their report will be found in the following chapter.

38.

Plan of the Salt Lake expedition—Great sandy deserts—Sufferings from thirst—Ogden's River—Trails and smoke of lurking savages—Thefts at night—A trapper's revenge—Alarms of a guilty conscience—A murderous victory—Californian mountains—Plains along the Pacific—Arrival at Monterey—Account of the place and neighborhood—Lower California—Its extent—The Peninsula—Soil—Climate—Production—Its settlements by the Jesuits—Their sway over the Indians—Their expulsion—Ruins of a missionary establishment—Sublime scenery—Upper California—Missions—Their power and policy—Resources of the country—Designs of foreign nations

IT WAS ON THE 24TH of July, in the preceding year (1833), that the brigade of forty men set out from Green River valley, to explore the Great Salt Lake.[1] They were to make the complete circuit of it, trapping on all the streams which should fall in their way, and to keep journals and make charts, cal-

[1] See Chapter XXI, note 7. Besides Irving, other firsthand sources for this expedition are Leonard, *Adventures;* Meek, *Autobiography;* Nidever, *Life and Adventures; Niles Register,* Vol. LII (March 25, 1837), 50, publishing information furnished by Stephen H. Meek to the *Sentinel* of Jonesborough, Tennessee; Victor, *River of the West,* Chapter VIII, an unreliable account based upon Joseph Meek's recollections; and *Bonneville.*

Another source is "Recollections of Wm. Craig," by Thomas J. Beall in the *Morning Tribune,* Lewiston, Idaho, March 3, 1918, 8. According to this source members of the Walker expedition included Joseph Meek, Joseph Gale, William S. Williams, Mark Head, Robert Mitchell, Alexis Godey, Antoine Janise, and William Craig. There were some forty men in all. For a thorough examination of the Walker expedition by a modern historian, see Cleland, *This Reckless Breed,* 276–310.

culated to impart a knowledge of the lake and the surrounding country. All the resources of Captain Bonneville had been tasked to fit out this favorite expedition. The country lying to the southwest of the mountains, and ranging down to California, was as yet almost unknown;[2] being out of the buffalo range, it was untraversed by the trapper, who preferred those parts of the wilderness where the roaming herds of that species of animal gave him comparatively an abundant and luxurious life. Still it was said the deer, the elk, and the bighorn were to be found there, so that, with a little diligence and economy, there was no danger of lacking food. As a precaution, however, the party halted on Bear River and hunted for a few days, until they had laid in a supply of dried buffalo meat and venison; they then passed by the head waters of the Cassié River,[3] and soon found themselves launched on an immense sandy desert. Southwardly, on their left, they beheld the Great Salt Lake, spread out like a sea, but they found no stream running into it. A desert extended around them, and stretched to the southwest, as far as the eye could reach, rivalling the deserts of Asia and Africa in sterility. There was neither tree, nor herbage, nor spring, nor pool, nor running stream, nothing but parched wastes of sand, where horse and rider were in danger of perishing.

Their sufferings, at length, became so great that they abandoned their intended course, and made towards a range of snowy mountains, brightening in the north, where they hoped to find water. After a time, they came upon a small stream leading directly towards these mountains. Having quenched their burning thirst, and refreshed themselves and their weary horses for a time, they kept along this stream, which gradually increased in size, being fed by numerous brooks. After approaching the mountains, it took a sweep toward the southwest, and the travellers still kept along it, trapping

[2] Jedediah Strong Smith had explored much of this area in 1826 and 1827. See Morgan's *Jedediah Smith*.

[3] Raft River, which rises in northwest Utah. Irving's account omits the fact that Walker's party had previously followed the west side of Great Salt Lake for nine or ten days before they turned directly away from the Lake. See Leonard, *Adventures*, 65–66.

beaver as they went, on the flesh of which they subsisted for the present, husbanding their dried meat for future necessities.

The stream on which they had thus fallen is called by some, Mary River, but is more generally known as Ogden's River,[4] from Mr. Peter Ogden, an enterprising and intrepid leader of the Hudson's Bay Company, who first explored it. The wild and half-desert region through which the travellers were passing, is wandered over by hordes of Shoshokoes, or Root Diggers, the forlorn branch of the Snake tribe. They are a shy people, prone to keep aloof from the stranger. The travellers frequently met with their trails, and saw the smoke of their fires rising in various parts of the vast landscape, so that they knew there were great numbers in the neighborhood, but scarcely ever were any of them to be met with.

After a time, they began to have vexatious proofs that, if the Shoshokoes were quiet by day, they were busy at night. The camp was dogged by these eavesdroppers; scarce a morning, but various articles were missing, yet nothing could be seen of the marauders. What particularly exasperated the hunters, was to have their traps stolen from the streams. One morning, a trapper of a violent and savage character, discovering that his traps had been carried off in the night, took a horrid oath to kill the first Indian he should meet, innocent or guilty. As he was returning with his comrades to camp, he beheld two unfortunate Diggers, seated on the river bank, fishing. Advancing upon them, he levelled his rifle, shot one upon the spot, and flung his bleeding body into the stream. The other Indian fled, and was suffered to escape. Such is the indifference with which acts of violence are regarded in the wilderness, and such the immunity an armed ruffian enjoys beyond the barriers of the laws, that the only punishment this desperado met with, was a rebuke from the leader of the party.[5]

[4] Humboldt River, rising in the northeast corner of Nevada, runs in a southwesterly direction until it disappears in the Humboldt Sink, 290 miles from its source. Peter Skene Ogden discovered it in 1828. Walker's men called it Barren River because, said Leonard, "the country, natives and everything belonging to it, justly deserves the name. You may travel for many days on the banks of this river, without finding a stick large enough to make a walking cane." Leonard, *Adventures*, 68.

The trappers now left the scene of this infamous tragedy, and kept on westward, down the course of the river, which wound along with a range of mountains on the right hand, and a sandy, but somewhat fertile plain, on the left. As they proceeded, they beheld columns of smoke rising, as before, in various directions, which their guilty consciences now converted into alarm signals, to arouse the country and collect the scattered bands for vengeance.

After a time, the natives began to make their appearance, and sometimes in considerable numbers, but always pacific; the trappers, however, suspected them of deep-laid plans to draw them into ambuscades; to crowd into and get possession of their camp, and various other crafty and daring conspiracies, which, it is probable, never entered into the heads of the poor savages. In fact, they are a simple, timid, inoffensive race, unpractised in warfare, and scarce provided with any weapons, excepting for the chase. Their lives are passed in the great sand plains and along the adjacent rivers; they subsist sometimes on fish, at other times on roots and the seeds of a plant, called the cat's-tail. They are of the same kind of people that Captain Bonneville found upon Snake River, and whom he found so mild and inoffensive.

The trappers, however, had persuaded themselves that they were making their way through a hostile country, and that implacable foes hung round their camp or beset their path, watching for an opportunity to surprise them. At length, one day they came to the banks of a stream emptying into Ogden's River, which they were obliged to ford. Here a great number of Shoshokoes were posted on the opposite bank. Persuaded they were there with hostile intent, they advanced upon them, levelled their rifles, and killed twenty-

[5] Leonard also tells of the Indians stealing traps, and states that some of the men "were for taking vengeance before we left the country—but this was not the disposition of Captain Walker. These discontents being out hunting one day, fell in with a few Indians, two or three of whom they killed, and then returned to camp, not daring to let the Captain know it. The next day while hunting they repeated the same violation—but this time not quite so successful, for the Captain found it out, and immediately took measures for its effectual suppression." Leonard, *Adventures*, 68. Bonneville is reported by Irving to have been horrified at the atrocities committed during the course of the expedition, but Leonard's statement shows that Walker, at least, was opposed to needless bloodshed.

five of them upon the spot. The rest fled to a short distance, then halted and turned about, howling and whining like wolves, and uttering the most piteous wailings. The trappers chased them in every direction; the poor wretches made no defence, but fled with terror; neither does it appear from the accounts of the boasted victors, that a weapon had been wielded or a weapon launched by the Indians throughout the affair. We feel perfectly convinced that the poor savages had no hostile intention, but had merely gathered together through motives of curiosity, as others of their tribe had done when Captain Bonneville and his companions passed along Snake River.[6]

The trappers continued down Ogden's River, until they ascertained that it lost itself in a great swampy lake,[7] to which there was no apparent discharge. They then struck directly westward, across the great chain of California mountains[8] intervening between these interior plains and the shores of the Pacific.

For three and twenty days[9] they were entangled among these

---

[6] Leonard reports this occurrence (*Adventures*, 69–72) in much greater detail and presumably with more accuracy than the later account Bonneville wrote in his journal. The Indians had been given repeated warnings; they had seen the destructiveness of the trappers' rifles; but they persisted in menacing Walker's party. Finally, all his efforts having no effect, Walker ordered an attack. Thirty-nine Indians were killed. "The severity with which we dealt with these Indians," Leonard later wrote, "may be revolting to the heart of the philanthropist; but the circumstances of the case altogether atones [*sic*] for the cruelty." *Adventures*, 72.

Nidever's account of this affair is less detailed than Leonard's, but it also conveys the impression that the trappers had little choice but to fire upon the Indians (see his *Life and Adventures*, 32–33).

[7] Humboldt Sink and Carson Sink, near Lovelock, Nevada. Walker's men named them Battle Lakes. According to Leonard's account, Walker had reached this area about September 4, 1833, and left it on October 10.

[8] The Sierra Nevada. Having reached these mountains, Walker's party became the first organized body of Americans to have blazed the route across the Great Basin of Utah and Nevada that would be followed in the next decade and years to come by countless gold seekers and emigrants to California. But from here on, Walker's route through the mountains is highly conjectural. Leonard's narrative states that on the evening of the same day they left the Humboldt and Carson Sinks they "encamped on the margin of a large lake formed by a river which heads in this mountain." *Adventures*, 73. It is generally assumed that this was Walker Lake in Mineral County, Nevada. From here they cannot be followed with certainty.

[9] This agrees with Leonard's estimate of nearly a month. Irving's meager account of Walker's crossing the Sierra Nevada should be supplemented by Leonard's

mountains, the peaks and ridges of which are in many places covered with perpetual snow. Their passes and defiles present the wildest scenery, partaking of the sublime rather than the beautiful, and abounding with frightful precipices. The sufferings of the travellers among these savage mountains were extreme: for a part of the time they were nearly starved; at length, they made their way through them, and came down upon the plains of New California, a fertile region extending along the coast, with magnificent forests, verdant savannas, and prairies that looked like stately parks. Here they found deer and other game in abundance, and indemnified themselves for past famine. They now turned toward the south, and passing numerous small bands of natives, posted upon various streams, arrived at the Spanish village and post of Monterey.[10]

This is a small place, containing about two hundred houses, situated in latitude 37° north. It has a capacious bay, with indifferent anchorage. The surrounding country is extremely fertile, especially in the valleys; the soil is richer, the further you penetrate into the interior, and the climate is described as a perpetual spring. Indeed, all California, extending along the Pacific Ocean from latitude 19° 30' to 42° north, is represented as one of the most fertile and beautiful regions in North America.

detailed narrative in *Adventures*, 74–83. Owing to the absence of place names, the route of Walker's party is wholly conjectural; for a reasonable description, see Francis P. Farquhar, *Exploration of the Sierra Nevada*, 6–7, which forms the basis of Cleland's account in *This Reckless Breed*, 289–92. It is usually acknowledged that in crossing the range, Walker discovered Yosemite Valley. Once out of the mountains, they crossed the San Joaquin Valley to arrive at the Pacific Coast.

[10] Leonard describes the crossing of the San Joaquin Valley in *Adventures*, 84–96. A reference by Leonard to the great meteor shower of November 12, 1833, accurately establishes the date of their reaching the San Francisco Bay area, which they saw the next morning. They subsequently hailed an American merchant ship, the *Lagoda*, forty miles south of the settlement of San Francisco, and were feasted by Captain Bradshaw and crew aboard ship. On November 25 they arrived at the mission of San Juan Bautista, northeast of Monterey, where the main party halted while Walker went ahead to Monterey to obtain permission for them to remain in the area during the winter. This permission being granted, they camped nearby until most of their horses were stolen. They then moved east about forty miles to a new location, where they remained until setting out on their long return journey on February 14, 1834. Six men chose to remain in California. Leonard, *Adventures*, 97–119.

Lower California, in length about seven hundred miles, forms a great peninsula, which crosses the tropics and terminates in the torrid zone. It is separated from the mainland by the Gulf of California, sometimes called the Vermilion Sea; into this gulf empties the Colorado of the West, the Seeds-ke-dee, or Green River, as it is also sometimes called. The peninsula is traversed by stern and barren mountains, and has many sandy plains, where the only sign of vegetation is the cylindrical cactus growing among the clefts of the rocks. Wherever there is water, however, and vegetable mould, the ardent nature of the climate quickens everything into astonishing fertility. There are valleys luxuriant with the rich and beautiful productions of the tropics. There the sugar-cane and indigo plant attain a perfection unequalled in any other part of North America. There flourish the olive, the fig, the date, the orange, the citron, the pomegranate, and other fruits belonging to the voluptuous climates of the south; with grapes in abundance, that yield a generous wine. In the interior are salt plains; silver mines and scanty veins of gold are said, likewise, to exist; and pearls of a beautiful water are to be fished upon the coast.

The peninsula of California was settled in 1698,[11] by the Jesuits, who, certainly, as far as the natives were concerned, have generally proved the most beneficent of colonists. In the present instance, they gained and maintained a footing in the country without the aid of military force, but solely by religious influence. They formed a treaty, and entered into the most amicable relations with the natives, then numbering from twenty-five to thirty thousand souls, and gained a hold upon their affections, and a control over their minds, that effected a complete change in their condition. They built eleven missionary establishments in the various valleys of the peninsula, which formed rallying places for the surrounding savages, where they gathered together as sheep into the fold, and surrendered themselves and their consciences into the hands of these spiritual pastors. Nothing, we are told, could exceed the implicit and affectionate devotion of the Indian converts to the Jesuit fathers, and the Catholic faith was disseminated widely through the wilderness.

[11] The first permanent settlement was Loreto, founded in 1697.

The growing power and influence of the Jesuits in the New World at length excited the jealousy of the Spanish government, and they were banished from the colonies. The governor, who arrived at California to expel them, and to take charge of the country, expected to find a rich and powerful fraternity, with immense treasures hoarded in their missions, and an army of Indians ready to defend them. On the contrary, he beheld a few venerable silver-haired priests coming humbly forward to meet him, followed by a throng of weeping, but submissive natives. The heart of the governor, it is said, was so touched by this unexpected sight, that he shed tears; but he had to execute his orders. The Jesuits were accompanied to the place of their embarkation by their simple and affectionate parishioners, who took leave of them with tears and sobs. Many of the latter abandoned their heriditary abodes, and wandered off to join their southern brethren, so that but a remnant remained in the peninsula. The Franciscans immediately succeeded the Jesuits, and subsequently the Dominicans; but the latter managed their affairs ill. But two of the missionary establishments are at present occupied by priests; the rest are all in ruins, excepting one, which remains a monument of the former power and prosperity of the order. This is a noble edifice, once the seat of the chief of the resident Jesuits. It is situated in a beautiful valley, about half way between the Gulf of California and the broad ocean, the peninsula being here about sixty miles wide. The edifice is of hewn stone, one story high, two hundred and ten feet in front, and about fifty-five feet deep. The walls are six feet thick, and sixteen feet high, with a vaulted roof of stone, about two feet and a half in thickness. It is now abandoned and desolate; the beautiful valley is without an inhabitant—not a human being resides within thirty miles of the place!

In approaching this deserted mission-house from the south, the traveller passes over the mountain of San Juan, supposed to be the highest peak in the Californias. From this lofty eminence, a vast and magnificent prospect unfolds itself; the great Gulf of California, with the dark blue sea beyond, studded with islands; and in another direction, the immense lava plain of San Gabriel. The splendor of the climate gives an Italian effect to the immense prospect. The sky is of a deep blue color, and the sunsets are often magnificent beyond description. Such is a slight and imperfect sketch of this remarkable peninsula.

Upper California extends from latitude 31° 10′ to 42° on the Pacific, and inland, to the great chain of snow-capped mountains which divide it from the sand plains of the interior. There are about twenty-one missions in this province, most of which were established about fifty years since, and are generally under the care of the Franciscans. These exert a protecting sway over about thirty-five thousand Indian converts, who reside on the lands around the mission houses. Each of these houses has fifteen miles square of land allotted to it, subdivided into small lots, proportioned to the number of Indian converts attached to the mission. Some are enclosed with high walls; but in general they are open hamlets, composed of rows of huts, built of sunburnt bricks; in some instances whitewashed and roofed with tiles. Many of them are far in the interior, beyond the reach of all military protection, and dependent entirely on the good will of the natives, which never fails them. They have made considerable progress in teaching the Indians the useful arts. There are native tanners, shoemakers, weavers, blacksmiths, stonecutters, and other artificers attached to each establishment. Others are taught husbandry, and the rearing of cattle and horses; while the females card and spin wool, weave, and perform the other duties allotted to their sex in civilized life. No social intercourse is allowed between the unmarried of the opposite sexes after working hours; and at night they are locked up in separate apartments, and the keys delivered to the priests.

The produce of the lands, and all the profits arising from sales, are entirely at the disposal of the priests; whatever is not required for the support of the missions, goes to augment a fund which is under their control. Hides and tallow constitute the principal riches of the missions, and, indeed, the main commerce of the country. Grain might be produced to an unlimited extent at the establishments, were there a sufficient market for it. Olives and grapes are also reared at the missions.

Horses and horned cattle abound throughout all this region;

the former may be purchased at from three to five dollars, but they are of an inferior breed. Mules, which are here of a large size and of valuable qualities, cost from seven to ten dollars.

There are several excellent ports along this coast. San Diego, San Barbara, Monterey, the bay of San Francisco, and the northern port of Bondago;[12] all afford anchorage for ships of the largest class. The port of San Francisco is too well known to require much notice in this place. The entrance from the sea is sixty-seven fathoms deep, and within, whole navies might ride with perfect safety. Two large rivers, which take their rise in mountains two or three hundred miles to the east, and run through a country unsurpassed for soil and climate, empty themselves into the harbor. The country around affords admirable timber for ship-building. In a word, this favored port combines advantages which not only fit it for a grand naval dépôt, but almost render it capable of being made the dominant military post of these seas.

Such is a feeble outline of the Californian coast and country, the value of which is more and more attracting the attention of naval powers. The Russians have always a ship of war upon this station, and have already encroached upon the Californian boundaries, by taking possession of the port of Bondago, and fortifying it with several guns. Recent surveys have likewise been made, both by the Russians and the English; and we have little doubt, that, at no very distant day, this neglected, and, until recently, almost unknown region, will be found to possess sources of wealth sufficient to sustain a powerful and prosperous empire. Its inhabitants, themselves, are but little aware of its real riches; they have not enterprise sufficient to acquaint themselves with a vast interior that lies almost a terra incognita; nor have they the skill and industry to cultivate properly the fertile tracts along the coast; nor to prosecute that foreign commerce which brings all the resources of a country into profitable action.

[12] Bodega Bay.

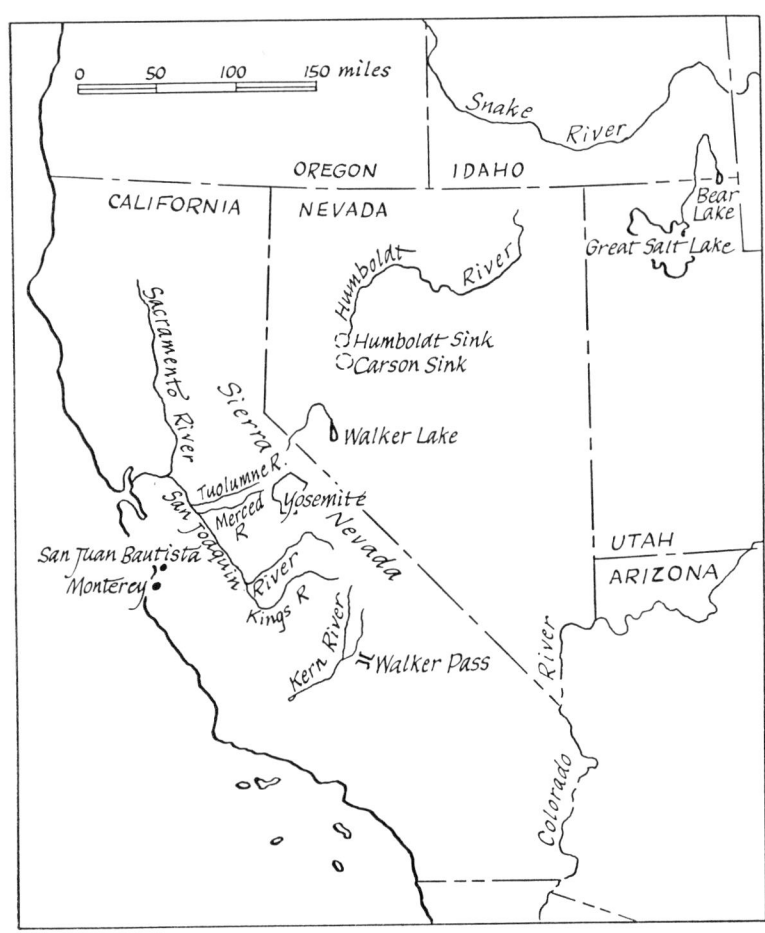

The Walker Expedition Country

39.

Gay life at Monterey—Mexican horsemen—A bold dragoon—Use of the lasso—Vaqueros—Noosing a bear—Fight between a bull and a bear—Departure from Monterey—Indian horse stealers—Outrages committed by the travellers—Indignation of Captain Bonneville

THE WANDERING BAND of trappers was well received at Monterey, the inhabitants were desirous of retaining them among them, and offered extravagant wages to such as were acquainted with any mechanic art. When they went into the country, too, they were kindly treated by the priests at the missions;[1] who are always hospitable to strangers, whatever may be their rank or religion. They had no lack of provisions; being permitted to kill as many as they pleased of the vast herds of cattle that graze the country, on condition, merely, of rendering the hides to the owners. They attended bull-fights and horseraces; forgot all the purposes of their expedition; squandered away, freely, the property that did not belong to them; and, in a word, revelled in a perfect fool's paradise.[2]

What especially delighted them was the equestrian skill of the Californians. The vast number and the cheapness of the horses in this country makes every one a cavalier. The Mexicans and half-breeds of California spend the greater part of their time in the saddle. They are fearless riders; and their daring feats upon unbroken colts and wild horses, astonished our trappers; though accustomed to the bold riders of the prairies.

[1] San Juan Bautista and San Carlos Borroméo de Carmelo.
[2] Leonard's extended account shows this interpretation to be distorted.

292

A Mexican horseman has much resemblance, in many points, to the equestrians of Old Spain; and especially to the vain-glorious caballero of Andalusia. A Mexican dragoon, for instance, is represented as arrayed in a round blue jacket, with red cuffs and collar; blue velvet breeches, unbuttoned at the knees to show his white stockings; bottinas of deer skin; a round-crowned Andalusian hat, and his hair cued. On the pommel of his saddle, he carries balanced a long musket, with fox skin round the lock. He is cased in a cuirass of double-fold deer skin, and carries a bull's hide shield; he is forked in a Moorish saddle, high before and behind; his feet are thrust into wooden box stirrups, of Moorish fashion, and a tremendous pair of iron spurs, fastened by chains, jingle at his heels. Thus equipped, and suitably mounted, he considers himself the glory of California, and the terror of the universe.

The Californian horsemen seldom ride out without the laso [*sic*]; that is to say, a long coil of cord, with a slip noose; with which they are expert, almost to a miracle. The laso, now almost entirely confined to Spanish America, is said to be of great antiquity; and to have come, originally, from the East. It was used, we are told, by a pastoral people of Persian descent; of whom eight thousand accompanied the army of Xerxes. By the Spanish Americans, it is used for a variety of purposes; and among others, for hauling wood. Without dismounting, they cast the noose around a log, and thus drag it to their houses. The vaqueros, or Indian cattle drivers, have also learned the use of the laso from the Spaniards; and employ it to catch the half-wild cattle by throwing it round their horns.

The laso is also of great use in furnishing the public with a favorite, though barbarous sport; the combat between a bear and a wild bull. For this purpose, three or four horsemen sally forth to some wood, frequented by bears, and, depositing the carcass of a bullock, hide themselves in the vicinity. The bears are soon attracted by the bait. As soon as one, fit for their purpose, makes his appearance, they run out, and with the laso, dexterously noose him by either leg. After dragging him at full speed until he is fatigued, they secure him more effectually; and tying him on the carcass of the bullock, draw him in triumph to the scene of action. By this time, he is

The ADVENTURES *of* CAPTAIN BONNEVILLE

exasperated to such frenzy, that they are sometimes obliged to throw cold water on him, to moderate his fury; and dangerous would it be, for horse and rider, were he, while in this paroxysm, to break his bonds.

A wild bull, of the fiercest kind, which has been caught and exasperated in the same manner, is now produced; and both animals are turned loose in the arena of a small amphitheatre. The mortal fight begins instantly; and always, at first, to the disadvantage of Bruin; fatigued, as he is, by his previous rough riding. Roused, at length, by the repeated goring of the bull, he seizes his muzzle with his sharp claws, and clinging to this most sensitive part, causes him to bellow with rage and agony. In his heat and fury, the bull lolls out his tongue; this is instantly clutched by the bear; with a desperate effort he overturns his huge antagonist; and then dispatches him without difficulty.

Beside this diversion, the travellers were likewise regaled with bull-fights, in the genuine style of Old Spain; the Californians being considered the best bull-fighters in the Mexican dominions.

After a considerable sojourn at Monterey, spent in these very edifying, but not very profitable amusements, the leader of this vagabond party set out with his comrades, on his return journey. Instead of retracing their steps through the mountains, they passed round their southern extremity, and, crossing a range of low hills, found themselves in the sandy plains south of Ogden's River; in traversing which, they again suffered, grievously, for want of water.[3]

---

[3] Walker's party moved south through the San Joaquin Valley to the Kern River. Then, with two Indians as guides, they traveled east over the mountains by way of the pass now bearing Walker's name, and descended into the Mojave Desert. At this point they turned north and, during May, followed along the base of the Sierra Nevada. Their march was often difficult owing to lack of water, pasturage, and game. An effort to reach the Humboldt by a shorter route nearly resulted in disaster, and the men were forced to turn west again toward the mountains. This error cost them "sixty-four horses, ten cows, and fifteen dogs." Leonard, *Adventures*, 128. Finally, around June 1, they picked up their old trail of the previous autumn, and within a few days were on the Humboldt. They followed this to its source, it seems, and rather than face the barren wastes west of Great Salt Lake, they then struck north to the Snake River on June 21. They advanced

The ADVENTURES of CAPTAIN BONNEVILLE

In the course of their journey, they encountered a party of Mexicans in pursuit of a gang of natives, who had been stealing horses. The savages of this part of California are represented as extremely poor, and armed only with stone-pointed arrows; it being the wise policy of the Spaniards not to furnish them with firearms. As they find it difficult, with their blunt shafts, to kill the wild game of the mountains, they occasionally supply themselves with food, by entrapping the Spanish horses. Driving them stealthily into fastnesses and ravines, they slaughter them without difficulty, and dry their flesh for provisions. Some they carry off to trade with distant tribes; and in this way, the Spanish horses pass from hand to hand among the Indians, until they even find their way across the Rocky Mountains.

The Mexicans are continually on the alert, to intercept these marauders; but the Indians are apt to outwit them, and force them to make long and wild expeditions in pursuit of their stolen horses.

Two of the Mexican party just mentioned joined the band of trappers, and proved themselves worthy companions. In the course of their journey through the country frequented by the poor Root Diggers, there seems to have been an emulation between them, which could inflict the greatest outrages upon the natives. The trappers still considered them in the light of dangerous foes; and the Mexicans, very probably, charged them with the sin of horse-stealing; we have no other mode of accounting for the infamous barbarities of which, according to their own story, they were guilty; hunting the poor Indians like wild beasts, and killing them without mercy. The Mexicans excelled at this savage sport; chasing their unfortunate victims at full speed; noosing them round the neck with their lasos, and then dragging them to death![4]

along the Snake and rejoined Bonneville about mid-July on Bear River. Leonard, *Adventures*, 131–33.

[4] The three previous paragraphs are a garbled version of two widely separated events. The first occurred while the Walker party was still camped east of San Juan Bautista before the start of their return journey. Some Indians having stolen three hundred horses from the mission, a party of "Spaniards" set out in pursuit, several of Walker's men joining them by invitation. Only a few old and helpless Indians were overtaken, and these the "Spaniards" viciously murdered in spite of

Such are the scanty details of this most disgraceful expedition;[5] at least, such are all that Captain Bonneville had the patience to collect; for he was so deeply grieved by the failure of his plans, and so indignant at the atrocities related to him, that he turned, with disgust and horror, from the narrators. Had he exerted a little of the Lynch law of the wilderness, and hanged those dexterous horsemen[6] in their own lasos, it would but have been a well-merited and salutary act of retributive justice. The failure of this expedition was a blow to his pride, and a still greater blow to his purse. The Great Salt Lake still remained unexplored; at the same time, the means which had been furnished so liberally to fit out this favorite expedition, had all been squandered at Monterey; and the peltries, also, which had been collected on the way.[7] He would have but scanty returns, therefore, to make this year, to his associates in the United States; and there was great danger of their becoming disheartened, and abandoning the enterprise.[8]

the efforts of Walker's men to prevent the slaughter. Leonard, *Adventures*, 115–16. The second event occurred on the Humboldt River when Walker, after trying without success to pacify the Indians there, was forced to fight them in what he regarded as self-defense. Fourteen Indians were killed and many wounded. Three of the Walker party were wounded. Leonard, *Adventures*, 130–31.

[5] The evidence does not justify the term "disgraceful." Irving, in fact, prejudiced by Bonneville's view of the expedition, completely ignores the epic undertaking and historic accomplishment that elevated Walker to top rank among explorers of the Far West.

[6] The Mexicans, two of whom had joined the Walker party while still in the San Joaquin Valley, bringing with them twenty-five good horses. Leonard, *Adventures*, 120.

[7] The word "squandered" misrepresents the case. The majority of Walker's men were never in Monterey, and Leonard furnishes no reason for thinking that Bonneville's supplies were expended in this fashion; ". . . a portion of the peltries," he states, "we had collected whilst crossing the mountains . . . we exchanged with Captain Baggshaw [Bradshaw] for merchandise, such as groceries and ammunition to do us whilst on our return. . . ." *Adventures*, 107.

Later, Walker made further purchases in Monterey to increase their provisions. *Ibid.*, 114–15.

[8] The account of the Walker expedition is the least accurate portion of the book. The responsibility for this inaccuracy must rest upon Bonneville, whose views of the expedition were transmitted to Irving. Irving, furthermore, who worked as a careful historian when corroborative source materials were available to him, was thus handicapped by the absence of parallel versions, such as Leonard's—not published until 1839—, which would have enabled him to correct Bonneville's journal.

40.

Travellers' tales—Indian lurkers—Prognostics of Buckeye—Signs and portents—The medicine wolf—An alarm—An ambush—The captured provant—Triumph of Buckeye—Arrival of supplies—Grand carouse—Arrangements for the year—Mr. Wyeth and his new levied band

THE HORROR AND INDIGNATION felt by Captain Bonneville at the excesses of the Californian adventurers were not participated by his men; on the contrary, the events of that expedition were favorite themes in the camp. The heroes of Monterey bore the palm in all the gossipings among the hunters. Their glowing descriptions of Spanish bear-baits and bull-fights especially, were listened to with intense delight; and had another expedition to California been proposed, the difficulty would have been to restrain a general eagerness to volunteer.

The captain had not long been at the rendezvous when he perceived, by various signs, that Indians were lurking in the neighborhood. It was evident that the Blackfoot band, which he had seen when on his march, had dogged his party, and were intent on mischief. He endeavored to keep his camp on the alert; but it is as difficult to maintain discipline among trappers at a rendezvous as among sailors when in port.

Buckeye, the Delaware Indian, was scandalized at this heedlessness of the hunters when an enemy was at hand, and was continually preaching up caution. He was a little prone to play the prophet, and to deal in signs and portents, which occasionally excited the merriment of his white comrades. He was a great dreamer, and believed in charms and talismans, or medicines, and could foretell the approach of strangers by the howling or barking of the small prairie wolf. This animal, being driven by the larger wolves from the carcasses left on the hunting grounds by the hunters, follows the trail of the fresh meat carried to the camp. Here the smell of the roast and broiled [meat], mingling with every breeze, keeps them hovering about the neighborhood; scenting every blast, turning up their noses like hungry hounds, and testifying their pinching hunger by long whining howls, and impatient barkings. These are interpreted by the superstitious Indians into warnings that strangers are at hand; and one accidental coincidence, like the chance fulfilment of an almanac prediction, is sufficient to cover a thousand failures. This little, whining, feast-smelling animal is, therefore, called among Indians the "medicine wolf"; and such was one of Buckeye's infallible oracles.

One morning early, the soothsaying Delaware appeared with a gloomy countenance. His mind was full of dismal presentiments, whether from mysterious dreams, or the intimations of the medicine wolf, does not appear. "Danger," he said, "was lurking in their path, and there would be some fighting before sunset." He was bantered for his prophecy, which was attributed to his having supped too heartily, and been visited by bad dreams. In the course of the morning, a party of hunters set out in pursuit of buffalo, taking with them a mule to bring home the meat they should procure. They had been some few hours absent, when they came clattering at full speed into camp, giving the war cry of Blackfeet! Blackfeet! Every one seized his weapon, and ran to learn the cause of the alarm. It appeared that the hunters, as they were returning leisurely, leading their mule, well laden with prime pieces of buffalo meat, passed close by a small stream overhung with trees, about two miles from the camp. Suddenly, a party of Blackfeet, who lay in ambush along the thickets, sprang up with a fearful yell, and discharged a volley at the hunters. The latter immediately threw themselves flat on their horses, put them to their speed, and never paused to look behind, until they found themselves in camp. Fortunately, they had escaped without a wound; but the mule, with all the "provant,"[1]

[1] Food.

Site of Fort Bonneville

Denver Public Library

OLD FORT WALLA WALLA

had fallen into the hands of the enemy. This was a loss, as well as an insult, not to be borne. Every man sprang to horse, and with rifle in hand, galloped off to punish the Blackfeet, and rescue the buffalo beef. They came too late; the marauders were off, and all that they found of their mule was the dents of his hoofs, as he had been conveyed off at a round trot, bearing his savory cargo to the hills, to furnish the scampering savages with a banquet of roast meat at the expense of the white men.

The party returned to camp, balked of their revenge, but still more grievously balked of their supper. Buckeye, the Delaware, sat smoking by his fire, perfectly composed. As the hunters related the particulars of the attack, he listened in silence, with unruffled countenance, then pointing to the west, "The sun has not yet set," said he; "Buckeye did not dream like a fool!"

All present now recollected the prediction of the Indian at daybreak, and were struck with what appeared to be its fulfilment. They called to mind, also, a long catalogue of foregone presentiments and predictions made at various times by the Delaware, and, in their superstitious credulity, began to consider him a veritable seer; without thinking how natural it was to predict danger, and how likely to have the prediction verified in the present instance, when various signs gave evidence of a lurking foe.

The various bands of Captain Bonneville's company had now been assembled for some time at the rendezvous;[2] they had had their fill of feasting, and frolicking, and all the species of wild and often uncouth merry-making, which invariably take place on these occasions. Their horses, as well as themselves, had recovered from past famine and fatigue, and were again fit for active service; and an impatience began to manifest itself among the men once more to take the field, and set off on some wandering expedition.

At this juncture, Mr. Cerré arrived at the rendezvous at the head of a supply party, bringing goods and equipments from the

[2] This was Bonneville's rendezvous with his men on Bear River, not the general rendezvous, which, in 1834, was held on Hams Fork, miles east of where Bonneville was camped. One can only speculate as to why he was not also at Hams Fork—probably to avoid competition. Bonneville's rendezvous is described by Leonard, *Adventures*, 133–35.

States. This active leader, it will be recollected, had embarked the year previously in skin-boats on the Bighorn, freighted with the year's collection of peltries. He had met with misfortune in the course of his voyage: one of his frail barks being upset, and part of the furs lost or damaged.

The arrival of the supplies gave the regular finish to the annual revel. A grand outbreak of wild debauch ensued among the mountaineers; drinking, dancing, swaggering, gambling, quarrelling, and fighting. Alcohol, which, from its portable qualities, containing the greatest quantity of fiery spirit in the smallest compass, is the only liquor carried across the mountains, is the inflammatory beverage at these carousals, and is dealt out to the trappers at four dollars a pint. When inflamed by this fiery beverage, they cut all kinds of mad pranks and gambols, and sometimes burn all their clothes in their drunken bravadoes. A camp, recovering from one of these riotous revels, presents a serio-comic spectacle; black eyes, broken heads, lack-lustre visages. Many of the trappers have squandered in one drunken frolic the hard-earned wages of a year; some have run in debt, and must toil on to pay for past pleasure. All are sated with this deep draught of pleasure, and eager to commence another trapping campaign; for hardship and hard work, spiced with the stimulants of wild adventure, and topped off with an annual frantic carousal, is the lot of the restless trapper.

The captain now made his arrangements for the current year. Cerré and Walker,[3] with a number of men who had been to Cali-

---

[3] Following Wyeth's journal, Irving read the following entry for July 4, 1834:

"At the camp we found Mr. Cerry [Cerré] and Mr. Walker who were returning to St. Louis with the furs collected by Mr. Bonneville's company about 10 pack and men going down to whom there is due 10,000$." *Correspondence and Journals*, 225.

The truth is that Walker went into the Crow country and remained there at the head of a band of fifty-five trappers during the ensuing season and was then to meet Bonneville at the mouth of the Popo Agie (see Leonard, *Adventures*, 135–60 *passim*).

Walker's presence in the Crow country has led some writers to assume *Montero* to be a new name for Walker or that the name was fictitious. Failure to solve this problem led W. F. Wagner in his edition of Leonard's *Adventures* (249–250 n.) to conclude that it was a case of "confusion worse confounded." Douglas Watson in

fornia, were to proceed to St. Louis with the packages of furs collected during the past year. Another party, headed by a leader named Montero, was to proceed to the Crow country, trap upon its various streams, and among the Black Hills, and thence to proceed to the Arkansas, where he was to go into winter quarters.

The captain marked out for himself a widely different course. He intended to make another expedition, with twenty-three men to the lower part of the Columbia River, and to proceed to the valley of the Multnomah;[4] after wintering in those parts, and establishing a trade with those tribes, among whom he had sojourned on his first visit, he would return in the spring, cross the Rocky Mountains, and join Montero and his party in the month of July, at the rendezvous of the Arkansas;[5] where he expected to receive his annual supplies from the States.

If the reader will cast his eye upon a map, he may form an idea of the contempt for distance which a man acquires in this vast wilderness, by noticing the extent of country comprised in these projected wanderings. Just as the different parties were about to set out on the 3d of July, on their opposite routes, Captain Bonneville received intelligence that Wyeth, the indefatigable leader of the salmon-fishing enterprise, who had parted with him about a year previously on the banks of the Bighorn, to descend that wild river in a bull boat, was near at hand, with a new levied band of hunters and trappers, and was on his way once more to the banks of the Columbia.

As we take much interest in the novel enterprise of this "eastern man," and are pleased with his pushing and persevering spirit;

West Wind (75–76) erroneously assumed Montero to be "mythical" and hypothesized that Bonneville, angered by Walker's failure on the California expedition, simply obliterated Walker's name by substituting *Montero*. But the fact is that one Antonio Montero was in Bonneville's employ and that both he and Walker led trapping parties that season into various parts of the Crow country. The case for Montero is considered in Chapter XLIX, note 1.

[4] The name Lewis and Clark gave to the Willamette.

[5] As pointed out above, Bonneville was to rendezvous with his men at the mouth of the Popo Agie on the Big Horn River in June, 1835 (see Leonard, *Adventures*, 135).

and as his movements are characteristic of life in the wilderness, we will, with the reader's permission, while Captain Bonneville is breaking up his camp and saddling his horses, step back a year in time, and a few hundred miles in distance, to the bank of the Bighorn, and launch ourselves with Wyeth in his bull boat; and though his adventurous voyage will take us many hundreds of miles further down wild and wandering rivers; yet such is the magic power of the pen, that we promise to bring the reader safe back to Bear River valley, by the time the last horse is saddled.

41.

A voyage in a bull boat

IT WAS ABOUT the middle of August (1830)[1] that Mr. Nathaniel J. Wyeth, as the reader may recollect, launched his bull boat at the foot of the rapids of the Bighorn, and departed in advance of the parties of Campbell and Captain Bonneville.[2] His boat was made of three buffalo skins, stretched on a light frame, stitched together, and the seams payed with elk tallow and ashes. It was eighteen feet long, and about five feet six inches wide, sharp at each end, with a round bottom, and drew about a foot and a half of water; a depth too great for these upper rivers, which abound with shallows and sand-bars.[3] The crew consisted of two half-breeds, who claimed to be white men, though a mixture of the French creole and the Shawnee and Potawattomie. They claimed, moreover, to be thorough mountaineers, and first-rate hunters—the common boast of these vagabonds of the wilderness.

---

[1] 1833 is the correct date and appears in the first edition. The author's revised edition introduced 1830 by mistake.

[2] Irving here picks up the record in Wyeth's journal for August 12, 1833 (*Correspondence and Journals*, 209), and follows it to September 27. Many details are traceable, as the following footnotes show, to this source; but others seem to have originated elsewhere, perhaps in correspondence with Wyeth. Irving's use of Wyeth's manuscript provides an unexcelled opportunity for observing his use of sources.

[3] Irving rewrote Wyeth's journal for August 16:
"Made a start in our boat found travelling quite pleasant but requires much caution on account of some snaggs and bars. We frequently took one half of the river which dividing again gave too little water for our boat which draws 1 ½ feet it is quite too much the [boat] ought to have been flatter. . . . ours is made of three skins is 18 feet long and about 5 ½ feet wide sharp at both ends round bottom." Wyeth, *Correspondence and Journals*, 209.

Besides these, there was a Nez Percé lad of eighteen years of age, a kind of servant of all work, whose great aim, like all Indian servants, was to do as little work as possible; there was, moreover, a half-breed boy, of thirteen, named Baptiste, son of a Hudson's Bay trader by a Flathead beauty; who was travelling with Wyeth to see the world and complete his education. Add to these, Mr. Milton Sublette, who went as passenger, and we have the crew of the little bull boat complete.

It certainly was a slight armament with which to run the gauntlet through countries swarming with hostile hordes, and a slight bark to navigate these endless rivers, tossing and pitching down rapids, running on snags and bumping on sand-bars; such, however, are the cockle-shells with which these hardy rovers of the wilderness will attempt the wildest streams; and it is surprising what rough shocks and thumps these boats will endure, and what vicissitudes they will live through.[4] Their duration, however, is but limited; they require frequently to be hauled out of the water and dried, to prevent the hides from becoming water-soaked; and they eventually rot and go to pieces.

The course of the river was a little to the north of east; it ran about five miles an hour, over a gravelly bottom. The banks were generally alluvial, and thickly grown with cotton-wood trees, intermingled occasionally with ash and plum trees. Now and then limestone cliffs and promontories advanced upon the river, making picturesque headlands. Beyond the woody borders rose ranges of naked hills.

Milton Sublette was the Pelorus of this adventurous bark; being somewhat experienced in this wild kind of navigation. It required all his attention and skill, however, to pilot her clear of sand-bars and snags of sunken trees. There was often, too, a perplexity of choice, where the river branched into various channels, among clusters of islands; and occasionally the voyagers found themselves aground and had to turn back.

[4] On August 16, Wyeth wrote:
"We grounded about 6 times this forenoon it is surprising how hard a thump these bull Boats will stand." *Correspondence and Journals*, 209.

The ADVENTURES of CAPTAIN BONNEVILLE

It was necessary, also, to keep a wary eye upon the land, for they were passing through the heart of the Crow country, and were continually in reach of any ambush that might be lurking on shore. The most formidable foes that they saw, however, were three grizzly bears, quietly promenading along the bank, who seemed to gaze at them with surprise as they glided by.[5] Herds of buffalo, also, were moving about, or lying on the ground, like cattle in a pasture; excepting such inhabitants as these, a perfect solitude reigned over the land. There was no sign of human habitation; for the Crows, as we have already shown, are a wandering people, a race of hunters and warriors, who live in tents and on horseback, and are continually on the move.

At night they landed, hauled up their boat to dry, pitched their tent, and made a rousing fire. Then, as it was the first evening of their voyage, they indulged in a regale, relishing their buffalo beef with inspiring alcohol; after which, they slept soundly, without dreaming of Crows or Blackfeet. Early in the morning, they again launched their boat and committed themselves to the stream.[6]

In this way, they voyaged for two days without any material occurrence, excepting a severe thunder storm, which compelled them to put to shore, and wait until it was passed. On the third morning, they descried some persons at a distance on the river bank. As they were now, by calculation, at no great distance from Fort Cass, a trading post of the American Fur Company, they supposed these might be some of its people. A nearer approach showed them to be Indians. Descrying a woman apart from the rest, they landed and accosted her. She informed them that the main force of the Crow nation, consisting of five bands, under their several chiefs, were but about two or three miles below, on their way up along the river. This was unpleasant tidings, but to retreat was impossible,

---

[5] Wyeth's journal, August 16:
"Have seen on the banks of the river [the Big Horn] this forenoon 3 grisly bears and some Bulls in the river and on the bank   they stare and wonder much." *Correspondence and Journals*, 209-10.

[6] Wyeth's entry for August 16 continues:
"All feel badly today from a severe bout of drinking last night." *Correspondence and Journals*, 210.

The ADVENTURES of CAPTAIN BONNEVILLE

and the river afforded no hiding place. They continued forward, therefore, trusting that, as Fort Cass was so near at hand, the Crows might refrain from any depredations.

Floating down about two miles further, they came in sight of the first band, scattered along the river bank, all well mounted; some armed with guns, others with bows and arrows, and a few with lances. They made a wildly picturesque appearance, managing their horses with their accustomed dexterity and grace. Nothing can be more spirited than a band of Crow cavaliers. They are a fine race of men, averaging six feet in height, lithe and active, with hawks' eyes and Roman noses. The latter feature is common to the Indians on the east side of the Rocky Mountains; those on the western side have generally straight or flat noses.

Wyeth would fain have slipped by this cavalcade unnoticed; but the river, at this place, was not more than ninety yards across; he was perceived, therefore, and hailed by the vagabond warriors, and, we presume, in no very choice language; for, among their other accomplishments, the Crows are famed for possessing a Billingsgate vocabulary[7] of unrivalled opulence, and for being by no means sparing of it whenever an occasion offers. Indeed, though Indians are generally very lofty, rhetorical, and figurative in their language at all great talks, and high ceremonials, yet, if trappers and traders may be believed, they are the most unsavory vagabonds in their ordinary colloquies; they make no hesitation to call a spade a spade; and when they once undertake to call hard names, the famous pot and kettle, of vituperating memory, are not to be compared with them for scurrility of epithet.

To escape the infliction of any compliments of the kind, or the launching, peradventure, of more dangerous missiles, Wyeth landed with the best grace in his power, and approached the chief of the band. It was Arapooish, the quondam friend of Rose the outlaw, and one whom we have already mentioned as being anxious to promote a friendly intercourse between his tribe and the white men. He was a tall, stout man, of good presence, and received the voyagers very graciously. His people, too, thronged around them, and were of-

[7] Foul language associated with the Billingsgate fish market in England.

ficiously attentive after the Crow fashion. One took a great fancy to Baptiste, the Flathead boy, and a still greater fancy to a ring on his finger, which he transposed to his own with surprising dexterity, and then disappeared with a quick step among the crowd.

Another was no less pleased with the Nez Percé lad, and nothing would do but he must exchange knives with him; drawing a new knife out of the Nez Percé's scabbard, and putting an old one in its place. Another stepped up and replaced this old knife with one still older, and a third helped himself to knife, scabbard, and all. It was with much difficulty that Wyeth and his companions extricated themselves from the clutches of these officious Crows before they were entirely plucked.

Falling down the river a little further, they came in sight of the second band, and sheered to the opposite side, with the intention of passing them. The Crows were not to be evaded. Some pointed their guns at the boat, and threatened to fire; others stripped, plunged into the stream, and came swimming across. Making a virtue of necessity, Wyeth threw a cord to the first that came within reach, as if he wished to be drawn to the shore.

In this way he was overhauled by every band, and by the time he and his people came out of the busy hands of the last, they were eased of most of their superfluities. Nothing, in all probability, but the proximity of the American trading post, kept these land pirates from making a good prize of the bull boat and all its contents.[8]

These bands were in full march, equipped for war, and evidently full of mischief. They were, in fact, the very bands that overran the land in the autumn of 1833; partly robbed Fitzpatrick of his horses and effects; hunted and harassed Captain Bonneville and

---

[8] Irving's long account of Wyeth's troubles with the Crows is built up from the following journal entry for August 17, perhaps supplemented by another source.

"at 9 ock. saw several persons ahead on the bank of the river which we at first supposed to be whites from the fort but soon found to be Crow Indians they informed us that the whole nation was behind we were anxious to avoid them but could not as the river afforded us no hiding place they showed us that they meant us to land very soon by stepping and swimming into the river seeing this we chose to land without further trouble in this way we were obliged to make the shore 6 times." *Correspondence and Journals*, 210.

The ADVENTURES *of* CAPTAIN BONNEVILLE

his people; broke up their trapping campaigns, and, in a word, drove them all out of the Crow country. It has been suspected that they were set on to these pranks by some of the American Fur Company, anxious to defeat the plans of their rivals of the Rocky Mountain Company; for at this time, their competition was at its height, and the trade of the Crow country was a great object of rivalry. What makes this the more probable, is, that the Crows in their depredation seemed by no means blood-thirsty, but intent chiefly on robbing the parties of their traps and horses, thereby disabling them from prosecuting their hunting.

We should observe that this year, the Rocky Mountain Company were pushing their way up the rivers, and establishing rival posts near those of the American Company; and that, at the very time of which we are speaking, Captain Sublette was ascending the Yellowstone with a keel boat, laden with supplies; so that there was every prospect of this eager rivalship being carried to extremities.[9]

The last band of Crow warriors had scarcely disappeared in the clouds of dust they had raised, when our voyagers arrived at the mouth of the river, and glided into the current of the Yellowstone. Turning down this stream, they made for Fort Cass, which is situated on the right bank, about three miles below the Bighorn. On the opposite side, they beheld a party of thirty-one savages, which they soon ascertained to be Blackfeet. The width of the river enabled them to keep at a sufficient distance, and they soon landed at Fort Cass.[10] This was a mere fortification against Indians; being a stockade of about one hundred and thirty feet square, with two bastions

---

[9] Robert Campbell, in partnership with William Sublette, was in charge during the fall of 1833 of building a trading post, named Fort William after William Sublette, about three miles below the junction of the Yellowstone and Missouri rivers. See his letters to his brother Hugh Campbell for July 30 and November 16, 1833, in *The Rocky Mountain Letters*, 12–16.

An interesting account of Fort William by one who helped build it and who remained there until it was sold to the American Fur Company in 1834 appears in Larpenteur's *Forty Years a Fur Trader*, 42–55.

[10] On August 17, 1833.

at the extreme corners. M'Tulloch,[11] an agent of the American Company, was stationed there with twenty men; two boats of fifteen tons burden were lying here; but at certain seasons of the year a steamboat can come up to the fort.

They had scarcely arrived, when the Blackfeet warriors made their appearance on the opposite bank, displaying two American flags in token of amity. They plunged into the river, swam across, and were kindly received at the fort. They were some of the very men who had been engaged, the year previously, in the battle at Pierre's Hole, and a fierce-looking set of fellows they were; tall and hawk-nosed, and very much resembling the Crows. They professed to be on an amicable errand, to make peace with the Crows, and set off in all haste, before night, to overtake them. Wyeth predicted that they would lose their scalps; for he had heard the Crows denounce vengeance on them, for having murdered two of their warriors who had ventured among them on the faith of a treaty of peace. It is probable, however, that this pacific errand was all a pretence, and that the real object of the Blackfeet braves was to hang about the skirts of the Crow bands, steal their horses, and take the scalps of stragglers.[12]

At Fort Cass, Mr. Wyeth disposed of some packages of beaver, and a quantity of buffalo robes.[13] On the following morning (August 18th), he once more launched his bull boat, and proceeded down

[11] Samuel Tulloch. Wyeth's journal, August 17, mentions:

"... boats of about 15 tons burthen 2 of which are now laying here and one of them preparing to descend in two days." *Correspondence and Journals*, 210.

Details concerning the fort came from a later entry:

"Fort Cass is scituated on the E. bank of the Yellow stone [*sic*] river is about 130 feet square made of sapling cotton wood pickets with two bastions at the extreme corners and was erected in the fall of 1832." *Ibid.*, 211.

[12] Wyeth's journal, August 17:

"Just as we arrived we saw 31 Indians with two American flags come to the other side of the river they were Gros ventres du Baum the same we fought with last summer at the Trois Tetons [the battle of Pierre's Hole.] they came to make peace with the Crows they were treated civily at the Fort and before night followed the river up to the Crow village where I expect their scalps will be taken...." *Correspondence and Journals*, 210.

[13] "... we traded about 10 packs of Beaver and 150 to 200 pack [of] robes." Wyeth, *Correspondence and Journals*, 210.

the Yellowstone, which inclined in an east-northeast direction. The river had alluvial bottoms, fringed with great quantities of the sweet cotton-wood, and interrupted occasionally by "bluffs" of sandstone. The current occasionally brings down fragments of granite and porphyry.

In the course of the day, they saw something moving on the bank among the trees, which they mistook for game of some kind; and, being in want of provisions, pulled toward shore. They discovered, just in time, a party of Blackfeet, lurking in the thickets, and sheered, with all speed, to the opposite side of the river.

After a time, they came in sight of a gang of elk. Wyeth was immediately for pursuing them, rifle in hand, but saw evident signs of dissatisfaction in his half-breed hunters; who considered him as trenching upon their province, and meddling with things quite above his capacity; for these veterans of the wilderness are exceedingly pragmatical on points of venery and woodcraft, and tenacious of their superiority; looking down with infinite contempt upon all raw beginners. The two worthies, therefore, sallied forth themselves, but after a time, returned empty-handed. They laid the blame, however, entirely on their guns; two miserable old pieces with flint locks, which, with all their picking and hammering, were continually apt to miss fire. These great boasters of the wilderness, however, are very often exceeding bad shots, and fortunate it is for them when they have old flint guns to bear the blame.[14]

The next day they passed where a great herd of buffalo was bellowing on a prairie. Again the Castor and Pollux of the wilderness sallied forth, and again their flint guns were at fault, and missed fire, and nothing went off but the buffalo. Wyeth now found there was danger of losing his dinner if he depended upon his hunters; he took rifle in hand, therefore, and went forth himself. In the course

[14] Wyeth's journal, August 18:
"We saw some large bands of elk but our hunters were more conceited than good which I have generally found to be the case with the hunters in this country they are not willing that a new hand should even try, and are far from good shots themselves and commonly have miserable flint guns which snap continually and afford an excuse for not killing." *Correspondence and Journals,* 211.

of an hour, he returned laden with buffalo meat, to the great mortification of the two regular hunters, who were annoyed at being eclipsed by a greenhorn.[15]

All hands now set to work to prepare the mid-day repast. A fire was made under an immense cotton-wood tree, that overshadowed a beautiful piece of meadow land; rich morsels of buffalo hump were soon roasting before it; in a hearty and prolonged repast, the two unsuccessful hunters gradually recovered from their mortification; threatened to discard their old flint guns as soon as they should reach the settlements, and boasted more than ever of the wonderful shots they had made, when they had guns that never missed fire.

Having hauled up their boat to dry in the sun, previous to making their repast, the voyagers now set it once more afloat, and proceeded on their way. They had constructed a sail out of their old tent, which they hoisted whenever the wind was favorable, and thus skimmed along down the stream. Their voyage was pleasant, notwithstanding the perils by sea and land, with which they were environed. Whenever they could, they encamped on islands for the greater security. If on the mainland, and in a dangerous neighborhood, they would shift their camp after dark, leaving their fire burning, dropping down the river some distance, and making no fire at their second encampment. Sometimes they would float all night with the current; one keeping watch and steering while the rest slept: in such case, they would haul their boat on shore, at noon of the following day, to dry; for notwithstanding every precaution, she was gradually getting water-soaked and rotten.

There was something pleasingly solemn and mysterious in thus floating down these wild rivers at night. The purity of the atmosphere in these elevated regions gave additional splendor to the stars, and heightened the magnificence of the firmament. The occasional rush and laving of the waters; the vague sounds from the surrounding wilderness; the dreary howl, or rather whine of wolves

---

[15] ". . . stopped on hearing the bellowing of Buffaloe on shore to get meat. Our hunters as usual having failed went myself and killed a cow." Wyeth, *Correspondence and Journals*, 211.

from the plains; the low grunting and bellowing of the buffalo, and the shrill neighing of the elk, struck the ear with an effect unknown in the daytime.

The two knowing hunters had scarcely recovered from one mortification when they were fated to experience another. As the boat was gliding swiftly round a low promontory, thinly covered with trees, one of them gave the alarm of Indians. The boat was instantly shoved from shore, and every one caught up his rifle. "Where are they?" cried Wyeth.

"There—there! riding on horseback!" cried one of the hunters.

"Yes; with white scarfs on!" cried the other.

Wyeth looked in the direction they pointed, but descried nothing but two bald eagles, perched on a low dry branch, beyond the thickets, and seeming, from the rapid motion of the boat, to be moving swiftly in an opposite direction. The detection of this blunder in the two veterans, who prided themselves on the sureness and quickness of their sight, produced a hearty laugh at their expense, and put an end to their vauntings.[16]

The Yellowstone, above the confluence of the Bighorn, is a clear stream; its waters were now gradually growing turbid, and assuming the yellow clay color of the Missouri. The current was about four miles an hour, with occasional rapids; some of them dangerous, but the voyagers passed them all without accident. The banks of the river were in many places precipitous with strata of bituminous coal.[17]

[16] Wyeth's journal, August 20:

"we had a good joke on the old hands as they call themselves in distinction to those who have been a short time in the country two bald headed Eagles being perched on a tree on a point and ranged to the other side of the river our motion made them appear moving the old one cried out Les Savvages [sauvages] others of them said on horseback with white scarfs I looked long but not supposing they meant the eagles I saw nothing but the eagles they soon found out their mistake and we had a good laugh at them and a pleasant one as all the Indians we meet here we expect to fight." *Correspondence and Journals*, 212.

[17] On August 20, Wyeth wrote:

"This day and yesterday whenever the river makes perpendicular banks we saw veins of poor bituminous coal in 5 to 7 veins horizontal from 3 ft. to 6 inches thick and 10 to 15 feet above each other rock sandstone." *Correspondence and Journals*, 212.

They now entered a region abounding with buffalo—that ever-journeying animal, which moves in countless droves from point to point of the vast wilderness; traversing plains, pouring through the intricate defiles of mountains, swimming rivers, ever on the move; guided on its boundless migrations by some traditionary knowledge, like the finny tribes of the ocean, which, at certain seasons, find their mysterious paths across the deep, and revisit the remotest shores.

These great migratory herds of buffalo have their hereditary paths and highways, worn deep through the country, and making for the surest passes of the mountains, and the most practicable fords of the rivers. When once a great column is in full career, it goes straight forward, regardless of all obstacles; those in front being impelled by the moving mass behind. At such times, they will break through a camp, trampling down everything in their course.

It was the lot of the voyagers, one night, to encamp at one of these buffalo landing places, and exactly on the trail. They had not been long asleep, when they were awakened by a great bellowing, and tramping, and the rush, and splash, and snorting of animals in the river. They had just time to ascertain that a buffalo army was entering the river on the opposite side, and making toward the landing place. With all haste they moved their boat and shifted their camp, by which time the head of the column had reached the shore, and came pressing up the bank.

It was a singular spectacle, by the uncertain moonlight, to behold this countless throng making their way across the river, blowing, and bellowing, and splashing. Sometimes they pass in such dense and continuous column as to form a temporary dam across the river; the waters of which rise and rush over their backs, or between their squadrons. The roaring and rushing sound of one of these vast herds crossing a river, may sometimes, in a still night, be heard for miles.

The voyagers now had game in profusion. They could kill as many buffalos as they pleased, and, occasionally, were wanton in their havoc; especially among scattered herds, that came swimming near the boat. On one occasion, an old buffalo bull approached so near, that the half-breeds must fain try to noose him as they would

The ADVENTURES *of* CAPTAIN BONNEVILLE

a wild horse. The noose was successfully thrown around his head, and secured him by the horns, and they now promised themselves ample sport. The buffalo made a prodigious turmoil in the water, bellowing, and blowing, and floundering; and they all floated down the stream together. At length he found foothold on a sand-bar, and taking to his heels, whirled the boat after him, like a whale when harpooned; so that the hunters were obliged to cast off their rope, with which strange head-gear the venerable bull made off to the prairies.

On the 24th of August, the bull boat emerged, with its adventurous crew, into the broad bosom of the mighty Missouri. Here, about six miles above the mouth of the Yellowstone, the voyagers landed at Fort Union, the distributing post of the American Fur Company in the western country. It was a stockaded fortress, about two hundred and twenty feet square, pleasantly situated on a high bank. Here they were hospitably entertained by Mr. M'Kenzie,[18] the superintendent, and remained with him three days, enjoying the unusual luxuries of bread, butter, milk, and cheese, for the fort was well supplied with domestic cattle, though it had no garden. The atmosphere of these elevated regions is said to be too dry for the culture of vegetables; yet the voyagers, in coming down the Yellowstone, had met with plums, grapes, cherries, and currants, and had observed ash and elm trees. Where these grow, the climate cannot be incompatible with gardening.

At Fort Union, Wyeth met with a melancholy memento of one of his men. This was a powder-flask, which a clerk had purchased from a Blackfoot warrior. It bore the initials of poor More, the unfortunate youth murdered the year previously, at Jackson's Hole,[19] by the Blackfeet, and whose bones had been subsequently

---

[18] Kenneth McKenzie (1801–61), builder of Fort Union and a noted figure in the fur trade. See Chittenden, *American Fur Trade*, I, 384–87.

For Wyeth's visit to Fort Union from August 24 to August 27 see *Correspondence and Journals*, 212–13.

[19] An error for Jackson's Little Hole, located on the Hoback River and south of Jackson Hole. U. S. Highway 189 passes through it today near Bondurant, Wyoming. Wyeth wrote in his journal on August 27:

"A Mr. Patten shewed me a powder flask which he traded from the Blkft.

found by Captain Bonneville. This flask had either been passed from hand to hand of the tribe, or perhaps, had been brought to the fort by the very savage who slew him.

As the bull boat was now nearly worn out, and altogether unfit for the broader and more turbulent stream of the Missouri, it was given up, and a canoe of cotton-wood,[20] about twenty feet long, fabricated by the Blackfeet, was purchased to supply its place. In this Wyeth hoisted his sail, and bidding adieu to the hospitable superintendent of Fort Union, turned his prow to the east, and set off down the Missouri.

He had not proceeded many hours, before, in the evening, he came to a large keel boat at anchor. It proved to be the boat, of Captain William Sublette,[21] freighted with munitions for carrying on a powerful opposition to the American Fur Company. The voyagers went on board, where they were treated with the hearty hospitality of the wilderness, and passed a social evening, talking over past scenes and adventures, and especially the memorable fight at Pierre's Hole.

Here Milton Sublette determined to give up further voyaging in the canoe, and remain with his brother; accordingly, in the morning, the fellow-voyagers took kind leave of each other, and Wyeth continued on his course. There was now no one on board of his boat

---

I immediately knew it to be one of mine and on examination found No. 4 H.G.O.M. graven with a point on it. It was Mores flask who was killed in Little Jackson Hole last year on his return home after rendezvous." *Correspondence and Journals*, 213.

[20] Commonly called a pirogue and so designated by Wyeth:

"I was here supplied with a peroque traded from the Blackfeet." *Correspondence and Journals*, 213.

[21] Sublette's destination was the fort in process of construction by Robert Campbell. See Chapter XLI, note 8. Wyeth met Sublette on the evening of August 27:

". . . found Mr. Wm. L. Sublette at anchor with a large Bull boat this gentleman we had expected to have found on our arrival at the Missouri he is come to trade furs in opposition to the Am. F. Co. he treated us with much politeness his brother [Milton Sublette, who had been traveling with Wyeth] preferred to remain and come to the states with him we are therefore left without any one who has descended the Missouri but I can go downstream." *Correspondence and Journals*, 213.

that had ever voyaged on the Missouri; it was, however, all plain sailing down the stream, without any chance of missing the way.

All day the voyagers pulled gently along, and landed in the evening and supped; then re-embarking, they suffered the canoe to float down with the current; taking turns to watch and sleep. The night was calm and serene; the elk kept up a continual whinnying or squealing, being the commencement of the season when they are in heat. In the midst of the night, the canoe struck on a sand-bar, and all hands were aroused by the rush and roar of the wild waters, which broke around her. They were all obliged to jump overboard, and work hard to get her off, which was accomplished with much difficulty.[22]

In the course of the following day they saw three grizzly bears at different times along the bank. The last one was on a point of land, and was evidently making for the river, to swim across. The two half-breed hunters were now eager to repeat the maneuvre of the noose; promising to entrap Bruin, and have rare sport in strangling and drowning him. Their only fear was, that he might take fright and return to land before they could get between him and the shore. Holding back, therefore, until he was fairly committed in the centre of the stream, they then pulled forward with might and main, so as to cut off his retreat, and take him in the rear. One of the worthies stationed himself in the bow, with the cord and slip-noose, the other, with the Nez Percé, managed the paddles. There was nothing further from the thoughts of honest Bruin, however, than to beat a retreat. Just as the canoe was drawing near, he turned suddenly round and made for it, with a horrible snarl, and a tremendous show of teeth. The affrighted hunter called to his comrades to paddle off. Scarce had they turned the boat, when the bear laid his enormous claws on the gunwale, and attempted to

[22] Irving failed to read Wyeth's journal for August 29 carefully enough:
"pulled 8½ hours and drifted 11 hours through the night which exposed me to much rain and wind from two thunder showers. I had much difficulty to keep the boat from bars and snaggs ran several times on to Bars all hands being asleep had to jump over board to get [her] off   In the night elk keep up a continual sque[a]ling   it being now the commencement of their running [rutting] season." *Correspondence and Journals*, 213.

get on board. The canoe was nearly overturned, and a deluge of water came pouring over the gunwale. All was clamor, terror, and confusion. Every one bawled out—the bear roared and snarled—one caught up a gun; but water had rendered it useless. Others handled their paddles more effectually, and beating old Bruin about the head and claws, obliged him to relinquish his hold. They now plied their paddles with might and main, the bear made the best of his way to shore, and so ended the second exploit of the noose; the hunters determining to have no more naval contests with grizzly bears.[23]

The voyagers were now out of the range of Crows and Blackfeet; but they were approaching the country of the Rees, or Arickaras; a tribe no less dangerous: and who were, generally, hostile to small parties.

In passing through their country, Wyeth laid by all day, and drifted quietly down the river at night. In this way, he passed on, until he supposed himself safely through the region of danger; when he resumed his voyage in the open day. On the 3d of September he had landed, at mid-day, to dine; and while some were making a fire, one of the hunters mounted a high bank to look out for game. He had scarce glanced his eye round, when he perceived horses grazing on the opposite side of the river. Crouching down he slunk back to the camp, and reported what he had seen. On further reconnoitring, the voyagers counted twenty-one lodges; and, from the number of horses, computed that there must be nearly a hundred Indians encamped there. They now drew their boat, with all speed and caution, into a thicket of water willows, and remained closely concealed all day. As soon as the night closed in they reembarked. The moon would rise early; so that they had but about two hours of darkness to get past the camp. The night, however, was cloudy, with a blustering wind. Silently, and with muffled oars,

[23] Irving got only the first sentence in this paragraph from Wyeth's entry for August 30:
"Saw three white [*i.e.*, grizzly] Bears this day. . . ." *Correspondence and Journals*, 213. The remainder of the paragraph came from an unidentified source or from a portion of the journal that may not have survived. It is possible that Wyeth in correspondence with Irving may have elaborated certain events for him.

they glided down the river, keeping close under the shore opposite to the camp; watching its various lodges and fires, and the dark forms passing to and fro between them. Suddenly, on turning a point of land, they found themselves close upon a camp on their own side of the river. It appeared that not more than one half of the band had crossed. They were within a few yards of the shore; they saw distinctly the savages—some standing, some lying round the fire. Horses were grazing around. Some lodges were set up, others had been sent across the river. The red glare of the fires upon these wild groups and harsh faces, contrasted with the surrounding darkness, had a startling effect, as the voyagers suddenly came upon the scene. The dogs of the camp perceived them, and barked; but the Indians, fortunately, took no heed of their clamor. Wyeth instantly sheered his boat out into the stream; when, unluckily, it struck upon a sand-bar, and stuck fast. It was a perilous and trying situation; for he was fixed between the two camps, and within rifle range of both. All hands jumped out into the water, and tried to get the boat off; but as no one dared to give the word, they could not pull together, and their labor was in vain. In this way they labored for a long time; until Wyeth thought of giving a signal for a general heave, by lifting his hat. The expedient succeeded. They launched their canoe again into deep water, and getting in, had the delight of seeing the camp fires of the savages soon fading in the distance."[24]

[24] Wyeth's journal, September 3, describes this series of events in detail:

"after Breakfast pulled 6 hours when I thought best to go on shore to cook I sent a man out to hunt in the meantime as soon as he assended the high bank he perceived horses on the other side we after[wards] counted 21 lodges and from the number of horses I have no doubt there might have been from 75 to 100. I immediately had the boat put into a little thicket and fortifyed as well as I could then went to fishing and spent the afternoon caught but two large catfish as soon as it was dark we proceeded forward with a high wind and a cloudy sky and no Moon all went well until we were just opposite the village when we perceived lodges and fires on our side also On seeing this I ste[e]red the boat to the middle of the river but unluckily took ground on a sand bar here we worked hard for some time to get off and had the Indians seen or heard us her[e] we were in distance for shot from both sides and could have made little resistance but they did not and after some time we got off and glad we were. We proceed[ed] in all 4 hours pulled, then stopped for the night these were probably the Aricarey and would have scalped us. I feared much for my Nez Perce for we could not speak

They continued under way the greater part of the night, until far beyond all danger from this band, when they pulled to shore, and encamped.

The following day was windy, and they came near upsetting their boat in carrying sail. Towards evening, the wind subsided, and a beautiful calm night succeeded. They floated along with the current throughout the night, taking turns to watch and steer. The deep stillness of the night was occasionally interrupted by the neighing of the elk, the hoarse lowing of the buffalo, the hooting of large owls, and the screeching of the small ones, now and then the splash of a beaver, or the gong-like sound of the swan.[25]

Part of their voyage was extremely tempestuous; with high winds, tremendous thunder, and soaking rain; and they were repeatedly in extreme danger from drift-wood and sunken trees. On one occasion, having continued to float at night, after the moon was down, they ran under a great snag, or sunken tree, with dry branches above the water. These caught the mast, while the boat swung round, broadside to the stream, and began to fill with water. Nothing saved her from total wreck, but cutting away the mast. She then drove down the stream, but left one of the unlucky half-breeds clinging to the snag, like a monkey to a pole. It was necessary to run in shore, toil up, laboriously, along the eddies and to attain some distance above the snag, when they launched forth again into the stream, and floated down with it to his rescue.[26]

to any Indian on the river and all would without explanation have made some fuss and perhaps have killed him." *Correspondence and Journals*, 214–15.

[25] Wyeth's journal, September 4:

". . . floated through the night 11 hours It was a beautiful still night the stillness interrupted only by the neighing of the Elk the continual low of the Buffaloe which we came to soon after starting the hooting of large owls and the screeching of small ones and occasionally the nearer noise of a beaver gnawing a tree or splashing into the water and even the gong like sound of the swan it was really poetical. . . ." *Correspondence and Journals*, 215.

[26] This incident occurred on September 20:

". . . having lost so much time we concluded to run until the moon went down altho we were before informed that it was not safe a few hours we got along well enough but at last went over a snagg with limbs above which taking our mast and the boat swinging broadside she was taking in water at a jolly rate and in a little she would have gone with the suck under the rock I immediately

The ADVENTURES *of* CAPTAIN BONNEVILLE

We forbear to detail all the circumstances and adventures, of upward of a month's voyage, down the windings and doublings of this vast river; in the course of which, they stopped, occasionally, at a post of one of the rival fur companies, or at a government agency for an Indian tribe.[27] Neither shall we dwell upon the changes of climate and productions, as the voyagers swept down from north to south, across several degrees of latitude; arriving at the regions of oaks and sycamores; of mulberry and basswood trees; of paroquets and wild turkeys. This is one of the characteristics of the middle and lower part of the Missouri; but still more so of the Mississippi, whose rapid current traverses a succession of latitudes, so as in a few days to float the voyager almost from the frozen regions to the tropics.

The voyage of Wyeth shows the regular and unobstructed flow of the rivers, on the east side of the Rocky Mountains, in contrast to those of the western side; where rocks and rapids continually menace and obstruct the voyager. We find him in a frail bark of

---

had the mast cut away just in time to save her escaped from this I determined to try more we ran a little and were driven head foremost on a large tree lying across the river. We stopped about midway and lay swinging like a pendulum with much danger and difficulty we extricated her not being yet discourage we ran on but soon were driven into a large drift we narrowly escaped being carried under and half full of water and our oar broke we made the shore as soon as possible resolved to run no more nights." Wyeth, *Correspondence and Journals*, 217–18. There is nothing in Wyeth's journal about a half-breed left clinging to a snag.

[27] On September 2, Wyeth stopped at Fort Clark, built by the American Fur Company in 1831 for trade with the Mandan Indians and headed by James Kipp. On September 8 and 9 he stopped at Fort Pierre, another American Fur Company post which was just being completed, where he was hospitably received by William Laidlow, who treated him to "the good things afforded by the earth and the cellars of the Co." On September 11 he came to the Ponca Post, where a Mr. Bean was agent—"a miserable concern," Wyeth observed. On September 16 he arrived at the Ponca village, where he delivered a message to an agent of one of the Sublettes. On September 21 he stopped at the weed-strewn ruins of an abandoned post at Council Bluffs; the next day at an American Fur Company post below Council Bluffs where Joshua Pilcher was the agent; on September 26 at another post of the American Fur Company at Blacksnake Hills, built by Joseph Robidoux on the site now occupied by St. Joseph, Missouri; and finally on the twenty-seventh at Fort Leavenworth.

skins, launching himself in a stream at the foot of the Rocky Mountains, and floating down from river to river, as they empty themselves into each other; and so he might have kept on upwards of two thousand miles, until his little bark should drift into the ocean. At present, we shall stop with him at Cantonment Leavenworth,[28] the frontier post of the United States; where he arrived on the 27th of September.

Here, his first care was to have his Nez Percé Indian, and his half-breed boy, Baptiste, vaccinated. As they approached the fort, they were hailed by the sentinel. The sight of a soldier in full array, with what appeared to be a long glittering knife on the end of the musket, struck Baptiste with such affright, that he took to his heels, bawling for mercy at the top of his voice. The Nez Percé would have followed him, had not Wyeth assured him of his safety. When they underwent the operation of the lancet, the doctor's wife and another lady were present; both beautiful women. They were the first white women that they had seen, and they could not keep their eyes off of them. On returning to the boat, they recounted to their companions all that they had observed at the fort; but were especially eloquent about the white squaws, who, they said, were white as snow, and more beautiful than any human being they had ever beheld.[29]

We shall not accompany the captain any further in his voyage;

[28] Fort Leavenworth, built in 1827 by Colonel Henry Leavenworth on the west side of the Missouri above the mouth of the Kansas River.

[29] Wyeth's journal, September 27, reads in part:

"My boy Baptiste and the Indian wer[e] vacinated by Doct. Fellows. It was amusing to observe the actions of Baptiste and the Indian when I went from the boat towards the Barracks   the Boy followed me until I was hailed by the sentry at view of one so strangely attired and with a knife on the end of his gun he broke like a quarter Nag crying Pegoni and the Indian was only prevented from taking the run also by being assured that he would not be harmed. I took the two to Doct Fellows quarters to be vaccinated   the Docts wife and another lady happened to be present   they were really beautiful women but the eyes of the two were riveted on the White Squaws   Baptiste who speaks a little English told the other Boys when he returned to the boat that he had seen a white squaw white as snow and so pretty." *Correspondence and Journals*, 218–19.

Wyeth's journal ends with only three more brief entries before he began a new journal with his return to Missouri the following spring.

but will simply state, that he made his way to Boston, where he succeeded in organizing an association under the name of "The Columbia River Fishing and Trading Company," for his original objects of a salmon fishery and a trade in furs. A brig, the May Dacres, had been dispatched for the Columbia with supplies; and he was now on his way to the same point, at the head of sixty men, whom he had enlisted at St. Louis; some of whom were experienced hunters, and all more habituated to the life of the wilderness than his first band of "down-easters."[30]

We will now return to Captain Bonneville and his party, whom we left, making up their packs and saddling their horses, in Bear River valley.

[30] Wyeth left his camp four miles from Independence on April 28, 1834. The number of men is variously stated in contemporary accounts, but among them were two missionaries, Daniel and Jason Lee, plus three or four companions; Milton Sublette, who, as Wyeth's journal reveals, traveled only as far as the Little Vermillion where, on May 8, he turned back owing to an old leg injury; Captain Joseph Thing of Boston, aide to Wyeth; Thomas Nuttall, botanist from Harvard; John Kirk Townsend, a young ornithologist from Philadelphia, whose *Narrative of a Journey across the Rocky Mountains* provides another account of the trip; Isaac P. Rose, whose experiences are recounted in *Four Years in the Rockies; or, the Adventures of Isaac P. Rose*, by James B. Marsh; and Osborne Russell, whose *Journal of a Trapper* not only records the details of the journey but is, in addition, one of the important autobiographical narratives of a trapper.

42.

Departure of Captain Bonneville for the Columbia—
Advance of Wyeth—Efforts to keep the lead—
Hudson's Bay party—A junketing—A delectable
beverage—Honey and alcohol—High carousing—
The Canadian *bon vivant*— A cache—A rapid move—
Wyeth and his plans—His travelling companions—
Buffalo hunting—More conviviality—An interruption

IT WAS THE 3D of July, [1834] that Captain Bonneville set out on his second visit to the banks of the Columbia, at the head of twenty-three men. He travelled leisurely, to keep his horses fresh, until on the 10th of July, a scout brought word that Wyeth, with his band, was but fifty miles in the rear, and pushing forward with all speed. This caused some bustle in the camp; for it was important to get first to the buffalo ground, to secure provisions for the journey. As the horses were too heavily laden to travel fast, a cache was digged, as promptly as possible, to receive all superfluous baggage. Just as it was finished, a spring burst out of the earth at the bottom. Another cache was therefore digged, about two miles further on; when, as they were about to bury the effects, a line of horsemen, with pack-horses, were seen streaking over the plain, and encamped close by.

It proved to be a small band in the service of the Hudson's Bay Company, under the command of a veteran Canadian; one of those petty leaders, who, with a small party of men, and a small supply of goods, are employed to follow up a band of Indians from one hunting ground to another, and buy up their peltries.

Having received numerous civilities from the Hudson's Bay Company, the captain sent an invitation to the officers of the party to an evening regale; and set to work to make jovial preparations. As the night air in these elevated regions is apt to be cold, a blazing fire was soon made, that would have done credit to a Christmas dinner, instead of a midsummer banquet. The parties met in high good fellowship. There was abundance of such hunters' fare as the neighborhood furnished; and it was all discussed with mountain appetites. They talked over all the events of their late campaigns; but the Canadian veteran had been unlucky in some of his transactions; and his brow began to grow cloudy. Captain Bonneville remarked his rising spleen, and regretted that he had no juice of the grape to keep it down.

A man's wit, however, is quick and inventive in the wilderness; a thought suggested itself to the captain, how he might brew a delectable beverage. Among his stores was a keg of honey but half exhausted. This he filled up with alcohol, and stirred the fiery and mellifluous ingredients together. The glorious results may readily be imagined; a happy compound, of strength and sweetness, enough to soothe the most ruffled temper, and unsettle the most solid understanding.

The beverage worked to a charm; the can circulated merrily; the first deep draught washed out every care from the mind of the veteran; the second, elevated his spirit to the clouds. He was, in fact, a boon companion; as all veteran Canadian traders are apt to be. He now became glorious; talked over all his exploits, his huntings, his fightings with Indian braves, his loves with Indian beauties; sang snatches of old French ditties, and Canadian boat songs; drank deeper and deeper, sang louder and louder; until, having reached a climax of drunken gayety, he gradually declined, and at length fell fast asleep upon the ground. After a long nap, he again raised his head, imbibed another potation of the "sweet and strong," flashed up with another slight blaze of French gayety, and again fell asleep.

The morning found him still upon the field of action, but in sad and sorrowful condition; suffering the penalties of past pleasures, and calling to mind the captain's dulcet compound, with many a retch and spasm. It seemed as if the honey and alcohol, which had passed so glibly and smoothly over his tongue, were at war within his stomach; and that he had a swarm of bees within his head. In short, so helpless and woebegone was his plight, that his party proceeded on their march without him; the captain promised to bring him on in safety, in the after part of the day.

As soon as this party had moved off, Captain Bonneville's men proceeded to construct and fill their cache; and just as it was completed, the party of Wyeth was descried at a distance. In a moment, all was activity to take the road. The horses were prepared and mounted; and being lightened of a great part of their burdens, were able to move with celerity. As to the worthy convive of the preceding evening, he was carefully gathered up from the hunter's couch on which he lay, repentant and supine, and, being packed upon one of the horses, was hurried forward with the convoy, groaning and ejaculating at every jolt.

In the course of the day, Wyeth, being lightly mounted, rode ahead of his party, and overtook Captain Bonneville.[1] Their meeting was friendly and courteous; and they discussed, sociably, their respective fortunes since they separated on the banks of the Bighorn. Wyeth announced his intention of establishing a small trading post[2] at the mouth of the Portneuf, and leaving a few men there, with a quantity of goods, to trade with the neighboring Indians. He was

[1] Both Wyeth and Townsend give July 10 as the date, although by Irving's reckoning it was the next day. Osborne Russell also gives July 11. Bonneville was camped on Blackfoot River, east of the Portneuf. Ten days earlier Wyeth, fully awakened to the intense competition among the rival companies, wrote in a letter from Hams Fork:

"Bonneville & Co. I have not seen, but he is not far from me on my proposed route. I fear that he has done nothing of consequence. I shall endeavor to take home his Beaver what there is of it if I get an adequate price. I think his concern is finished. *Correspondence and Journals*, 139.

Lucien Fontenelle also reached the same conclusion. A letter to Pierre Chouteau, dated September 17, 1834, reads in part:

"You must have heard before this of the returns that were made by Mr. Sublette and the company of Bonneville and Company. The latter I think by next year will be at an end with the mountains. They have sent down from twelve to fourteen packs of beaver and admitting that it should sell at a high price it is not enough to pay their retiring hands." Quoted in Chittenden, *American Fur Trade*, I, 305.

[2] Fort Hall, built in 1834 and sold to the Hudson's Bay Company in 1836. It was later of great service to emigrants moving into the Pacific Northwest and California.

compelled, in fact, to this measure, in consequence of the refusal of the Rocky Mountain Fur Company to take a supply of goods, which he had brought out for them according to contract; and which he had no other mode of disposing of.[3] He further informed Captain Bonneville that the competition between the Rocky Mountain and American Fur Companies, which had led to such nefarious stratagems and deadly feuds, was at an end; they having divided the country between them; allotting boundaries within which each was to trade and hunt, so as not to interfere with the other.

In company with Wyeth were travelling two men of science; Mr. Nuttall, the botanist; the same who ascended the Missouri, at the time of the expedition to Astoria;[4] and Mr. Townshend, an ornithologist; from these gentlemen we may look forward to important information concerning these interesting regions. There

---

[3] Wyeth's letters during the winter of 1833–34 while he was in the East make frequent mention of his business plans for the coming trip to the mountains in 1834. Success hinged on the agreement which he had made with Fitzpatrick and Milton Sublette on the Big Horn River on August 14, 1833, by which Wyeth would supply the Rocky Mountain Fur Company with goods (*Correspondence and Journals*, 83; and copy of original contract, Sublette Papers, Missouri Historical Society). The strategy was for him to beat William Sublette to the 1834 rendezvous. But with Sublette ahead of him, Wyeth on May 12 and again on June 9 dispatched letters to Fitzpatrick informing him of his approach. Nonetheless, Fitzpatrick bought his supplies from William Sublette, and when Wyeth arrived at the Hams Fork rendezvous he learned that his contract had been repudiated. Thus, in his journal for July 19, he wrote with understandable irony: ". . . much to my astonishment the goods which I had contracted to bring to the Rocky Mountain Fur Co. were refused by those honorable gentlemen." *Correspondence and Journals*, 225.

As a shrewd businessman, Wyeth had foreseen this eventuality as early as the preceding November and was not wholly unprepared for it. In a letter to businessmen whom he had hoped to interest in his plans, he had then explained:

"If they [the RMF Co.] should not [fulfill this contract], then I will proceed to a safe country on the Columbia [Snake] River where some furs may be traded and there leave them with a few men leaving some men and a trusty person to keep them and trade as many more as he can." *Ibid.*, 77.

It is not surprising, therefore, that Wyeth knew immediately at Hams Fork what his next move was to be—the construction of Fort Hall. In this way he carried out his threat to the partners in the Rocky Mountain Fur Company. "Gentlemen," he warned them at the rendezvous, "I will roll a stone into your garden that you will never be able to get out." Victor, *River of the West*, 164.

[4] *Astoria*, Chapter XV.

were three religious missionaries, also, bound to the shores of the Columbia, to spread the light of the Gospel in that far wilderness.

After riding for some time together, in friendly conversation, Wyeth returned to his party, and Captain Bonneville continued to press forward, and to gain ground. At night, he sent off the sadly sober, and moralizing chief of the Hudson's Bay Company, under a proper escort, to rejoin his people; his route branching off in a different direction. The latter took a cordial leave of his host, hoping, on some future occasion, to repay his hospitality in kind.

In the morning, the captain was early on the march; throwing scouts out far ahead, to scour hill and dale, in search of buffalo. He had confidently expected to find game, in abundance, on the head waters of the Portneuf; but on reaching that region, not a track was to be seen.

At length, one of the scouts, who had made a wide sweep away to the head waters of the Blackfoot River, discovered great herds quietly grazing in the adjacent meadows. He set out on his return, to report his discoveries; but night overtaking him, he was kindly and hospitably entertained at the camp of Wyeth. As soon as day dawned, he hastened to his own camp with the welcome intelligence; and about ten o'clock of the same morning, Captain Bonneville's party were in the midst of the game.

The packs were scarcely off the backs of the mules, when the runners, mounted on the fleetest horses, were full tilt after the buffalo. Others of the men were busied erecting scaffolds, and other contrivances, for jerking or drying meat; others were lighting great fires for the same purpose; soon the hunters began to make their appearance, bringing in the choicest morsels of buffalo meat; these were placed upon the scaffolds, and the whole camp presented a scene of singular hurry and activity. At daylight the next morning, the runners again took the field, with similar success; and, after an interval of repose made their third and last chase, about twelve o'clock; for by this time, Wyeth's party was in sight. The game being now driven into a valley, at some distance, Wyeth was obliged to fix his camp there; but he came in the evening to pay Captain Bonneville a visit. He was accompanied by Captain Stewart,[5] the amateur traveller; who had not yet sated his appetite for the adventurous life of the wilderness. With him, also, was a Mr. M'Kay,[6] a half-breed; son of the unfortunate adventurer of the same name, who came out in the first maritime expedition to Astoria, and was blown up in the Tonquin.[7] His son had grown up in the employ of the British fur companies; and was a prime hunter, and a daring partisan. He held, moreover, a farm, in the valley of the Wallamut.

The three visitors, when they reached Captain Bonneville's camp, were surprised to find no one in it but himself and three men; his party being dispersed in all directions, to make the most of their present chance for hunting. They remonstrated with him on the imprudence of remaining with so trifling a guard, in a region so full of danger. Captain Bonneville vindicated the policy of his conduct. He never hesitated to send out all his hunters, when any important object was to be attained; and experience had taught him that he was most secure, when his forces were thus distributed over the surrounding country. He then was sure that no enemy could approach, from any direction, without being discovered by his hunters; who have a quick eye for detecting the slightest signs of the proximity of Indians; and who would instantly convey intelligence to the camp.

The captain now set to work with his men, to prepare a suitable entertainment for his guests. It was a time of plenty in the camp; of prime hunters' dainties; of buffalo humps, and buffalo tongues; and roasted ribs, and broiled marrowbones: all these were cooked in hunters' style; served up with a profusion known only on a plentiful hunting ground, and discussed with an appetite that would astonish the puny gourmands of the cities. But above all, and to give a bacchanalian grace to this truly masculine repast, the captain produced his mellifluous keg of home-brewed nectar, which had been so potent over the senses of the veteran of Hudson's Bay. Po-

---

[5] Captain William Stewart, who had been traveling with Wyeth since leaving Hams Fork on his way to Fort Vancouver.

[6] Thomas McKay, stepson of Dr. John McLoughlin of Fort Vancouver. His father was Alexander McKay.

[7] *Astoria*, Chapter XI.

tations, pottle deep, again went round: never did beverage excite greater glee, or meet with more rapturous commendation. The parties were fast advancing to that happy state, which would have insured ample cause for the next day's repentance; and the bees were already beginning to buzz about their ears, when a messenger came spurring to the camp with intelligence that Wyeth's people had got entangled in one of those deep and frightful ravines, piled with immense fragments of volcanic rock, which gash the whole country about the head waters of the Blackfoot River. The revel was instantly at an end; the keg of sweet and potent home-brewed was deserted; and the guests departed with all speed, to aid in extricating their companions from the volcanic ravine.[8]

[8] John Townsend's version of this convivial gathering, as reported to him by Wyeth, follows:

"Mr. Wyeth and Captain Stewart visited the lodge of the 'bald chief'. . . . He and Captain Stewart were received very kindly by the veteran, and every delicacy that the lodge afforded was brought forth to do them honor. Among the rest, was some metheglen or diluted alcohol sweetened with honey, which the good host had concocted; this dainty beverage was set before them, and the thirsty guests were not slow in taking advantage of the invitation so obligingly given. Draught after draught of the precious liquor disappeared down the throats of the visitors, until the anxious, but still complaisant captain, began to grow uneasy.

" 'I beg you will help yourselves, gentlemen,' said the host, with a smile which he intended to express the utmost urbanity, but which, in spite of himself, had a certain ghastliness about it.

" 'Thank you, sir, we will do so freely,' replied the two worthies, and away went the metheglen as before.

"Cup after cup was drained, until the hollow sound of the keg indicated that its contents were nearly exhausted, when the company rose, and thanking the kind host for his noble entertainment, were bowed out of the tent with all the polite formality which the accomplished captain knows so well how to assume" *Narrative*, 84.

43.

A rapid march—A cloud of dust—Wild horsemen—
"High jinks"—Horseracing and rifle shooting—
The game of hand—The fishing season—Mode of
fishing—Table-lands—Salmon fishers—The captain's
visit to an Indian lodge—The Indian girl—The
pocket mirror—Supper—Troubles of an evil conscience

"Up and away!" is the first thought at daylight of the Indian trader, when a rival is at hand and distance is to be gained. Early in the morning, Captain Bonneville ordered the half-dried meat to be packed upon the horses, and leaving Wyeth and his party to hunt the scattered buffalo, pushed off rapidly to the east, to regain the plain of the Portneuf. His march was rugged and dangerous; through volcanic hills, broken into cliffs and precipices; and seamed with tremendous chasms, where the rocks rose like walls.

On the second day, however, he encamped once more in the plain, and as it was still early, some of the men strolled out to the neighboring hills. In casting their eyes round the country, they perceived a great cloud of dust rising in the south, and evidently approaching. Hastening back to the camp, they gave the alarm. Preparations were instantly made to receive an enemy; while some of the men, throwing themselves upon the "running horses" kept for hunting, galloped off to reconnoitre. In a little while, they made signals from a distance that all was friendly. By this time, the cloud of dust had swept on as if hurried along by a blast, and a band of wild horsemen came dashing at full leap into the camp, yelling and whooping like so many maniacs. Their dresses, their accoutrements, their mode of riding, and their uncouth clamor, made them seem

Denver Public Library

"Catching the Wild Horse"
From a Painting by George Catlin

Fort Hall Marker
Bannock Indian Reservation

a party of savages arrayed for war: but they proved to be principally half-breeds, and white men grown savage in the wilderness, who were employed as trappers and hunters in the service of the Hudson's Bay Company.[1]

Here was again "high jinks" in the camp. Captain Bonneville's men hailed these wild scamperers as congenial spirits, or rather, as the very game birds of their class. They entertained them with the hospitality of mountaineers, feasting them at every fire. At first, there were mutual details of adventures and exploits, and broad joking mingled with peals of laughter. Then came on boasting of the comparative merits of horses and rifles, which soon engrossed every tongue. This naturally led to racing, and shooting at a mark; one trial of speed and skill succeeded another, shouts and acclamations rose from the victorious parties, fierce altercations succeeded, and a general melée was about to take place, when suddenly the attention of the quarrellers was arrested by a strange kind of Indian chant or chorus, that seemed to operate upon them as a charm. Their fury was at an end; a tacit reconciliation succeeded, and the ideas of the whole mongrel crowd—whites, half-breeds, and squaws—were turned in a new direction. They all formed into groups, and taking their places at the several fires, prepared for one of the most exciting amusements of the Nez Percés, and the other tribes of the Far West.

The choral chant, in fact, which had thus acted as a charm, was a kind of wild accompaniment to the favorite Indian game of "Hand." This is played by two parties drawn out in opposite platoons before a blazing fire. It is in some respects like the old game of passing the ring or the button, and detecting the hand which holds it. In the present game, the object hidden, or the *cache* as it is called by the trappers, is a small splint of wood, or other diminutive article, that may be concealed in the closed hand. This is passed backward and forward among the party "in hand," while the party "out of hand" guess where it is concealed. To heighten the excitement and confuse the guessers, a number of dry poles are laid

[1] Perhaps a detachment of Thomas McKay's brigade, whom Townsend reported meeting in the vicinity on July 16. Townsend, *Narrative*, 92–93.

before each platoon, upon which the members of the party "in hand" beat furiously with short staves, keeping time to the choral chant already mentioned, which waxes fast and furious as the game proceeds. As large bets are staked upon the game, the excitement is prodigious. Each party in turn bursts out in full chorus, beating, and yelling, and working themselves up into such a heat, that the perspiration rolls down their naked shoulders, even in the cold of a winter night. The bets are doubled and trebled as the game advances, the mental excitement increases almost to madness, and all the worldly effects of the gamblers are often hazarded upon the position of a straw.[2]

These gambling games were kept up throughout the night; every fire glared upon a group that looked like a crew of maniacs at their frantic orgies; and the scene would have been kept up throughout the succeeding day, had not Captain Bonneville interposed his authority, and, at the usual hour, issued his marching orders.

Proceeding down the course of Snake River, the hunters regularly returned to camp in the evening laden with wild geese, which were yet scarcely able to fly, and were easily caught in great numbers. It was now the season of the annual fish-feast, with which the Indians in these parts celebrate the first appearance of the salmon in this river. These fish are taken in great numbers at the numerous falls of about four feet pitch. The Indians flank the shallow water just below, and spear them as they attempt to pass. In wide parts of the river, also, they place a sort of chevaux-de-frize, or fence, of poles interwoven with withes, and forming an angle in the middle of the current, where a small opening is left for the salmon to pass. Around this opening the Indians station themselves on small rafts, and ply their spears with great success.

The table lands so common in this region have a sandy soil, inconsiderable in depth, and covered with sage, or more properly speaking, wormwood. Below this, is a level stratum of rock, riven

---

[2] An accurate description of the "hand game," which is still played by Indians. Descriptions of the game appear frequently in early literature of the West, and trappers often joined the Indians in playing it. Irving undoubtedly read Wyeth's description (see *Correspondence and Journals*, 192).

occasionally by frightful chasms. The whole plain rises as it approaches the river, and terminates with high and broken cliffs, difficult to pass, and in many places so precipitous, that it is impossible, for days together, to get down to the water's edge, to give drink to the horses. This obliges the traveller occasionally to abandon the vicinity of the river, and make a wide sweep into the interior.

It was now far in the month of July, and the party suffered extremely from sultry weather and dusty travelling. The flies and gnats, too, were extremely troublesome to the horses; especially when keeping along the edge of the river where it runs between low sand-banks. Whenever the travellers encamped in the afternoon, the horses retired to the gravelly shores and remained there, without attempting to feed until the cool of the evening. As to the travellers, they plunged into the clear and cool current, to wash away the dust of the road, and refresh themselves after the heat of the day. The nights were always cool and pleasant.

At one place where they encamped for some time, the river was nearly five hundred yards wide, and studded with grassy islands, adorned with groves of willow and cotton-wood. Here the Indians were assembled in great numbers, and had barricaded the channels between the islands, to enable them to spear the salmon with greater facility. They were a timid race, and seemed unaccustomed to the sight of white men. Entering one of the huts, Captain Bonneville found the inhabitants just proceeding to cook a fine salmon. It is put into a pot filled with cold water, and hung over the fire. The moment the water begins to boil, the fish is considered cooked.

Taking his seat unceremoniously, and lighting his pipe, the captain awaited the cooking of the fish, intending to invite himself to the repast. The owner of the hut seemed to take his intrusion in good part. While conversing with him, the captain felt something move behind him, and turning round and removing a few skins and old buffalo robes, discovered a young girl, about fourteen years of age, crouched beneath, who directed her large black eyes full in his face, and continued to gaze in mute surprise and terror. The captain endeavored to dispel her fears, and drawing a bright riband from his pocket, attempted repeatedly to tie it round her neck. She jerked back at each attempt, uttering a sound very much like a snarl; nor could all the blandishments of the captain, albeit a pleasant, good-looking, and somewhat gallant man, succeed in conquering the shyness of the savage little beauty. His attentions were now turned to the parents, whom he presented with an awl and a little tobacco, and having thus secured their good will, continued to smoke his pipe and watch the salmon. While thus seated near the threshold, an urchin of the family approached the door, but catching a sight of the strange guest, ran off screaming with terror, and ensconced himself behind the long straw at the back of the hut.

Desirous to dispel entirely this timidity, and to open a trade with the simple inhabitants of the hut, who, he did not doubt, had furs somewhere concealed; the captain now drew forth that grand lure in the eyes of the savage, a pocket mirror. The sight of it was irresistible. After examining it for a long time with wonder and admiration, they produced a muskrat skin, and offered it in exchange. The captain shook his head; but purchased the skin for a couple of buttons—superfluous trinkets! as the worthy lord of the hovel had neither coat nor breeches on which to place them.

The mirror still continued the great object of desire, particularly in the eyes of the old housewife, who produced a pot of parched flour and a string of biscuit roots. These procured her some trifle in return; but could not command the purchase of the mirror. The salmon being now completely cooked, they all joined heartily in supper. A bounteous portion was deposited before the captain by the old woman, upon some fresh grass, which served instead of a platter; and never had he tasted a salmon boiled so completely to his fancy.

Supper being over, the captain lighted his pipe and passed it to his host, who, inhaling the smoke, puffed it through his nostrils so assiduously, that in a little while his head manifested signs of confusion and dizziness. Being satisfied, by this time, of the kindly and companionable qualities of the captain, he became easy and communicative; and at length hinted something about exchanging beaver skins for horses. The captain at once offered to dispose of his steed, which stood fastened at the door. The bargain was soon concluded, whereupon the Indian, removing a pile of bushes under which his valuables were concealed, drew forth the number of skins agreed upon as the price.

Shortly afterwards, some of the captain's people coming up, he ordered another horse to be saddled, and mounting it took his departure from the hut, after distributing a few trifling presents among its simple inhabitants. During all the time of his visit, the little Indian girl had kept her large black eyes fixed upon him, almost without winking, watching every movement with awe and wonder; and as he rode off, remained gazing after him, motionless as a statue. Her father, however, delighted with his new acquaintance, mounted his newly purchased horse, and followed in the train of the captain, to whom he continued to be a faithful and useful adherent during his sojourn in the neighborhood.

The cowardly effects of an evil conscience were evidenced in the conduct of one of the captain's men, who had been in the Californian expedition. During all their intercourse with the harmless people of this place, he had manifested uneasiness and anxiety. While his companions mingled freely and joyously with the natives, he went about with a restless, suspicious look; scrutinizing every painted form and face, and starting often at the sudden approach of some meek and inoffensive savage, who regarded him with reverence as a superior being. Yet this was ordinarily a bold fellow, who never flinched from danger, nor turned pale at the prospect of a battle. At length he requested permission of Captain Bonneville to keep out of the way of these people entirely. Their striking resemblance, he said, to the people of Ogden's River, made him continually fear that some among them might have seen him in that expedition; and might seek an opportunity of revenge. Ever after this, while they remained in this neighborhood, he would skulk out of the way and keep aloof, when any of the native inhabitants approached. "Such," observes Captain Bonneville, "is the effect of self-reproach, even upon the roving trapper in the wilderness, who has little else to fear than the stings of his own guilty conscience."

44.

Outfit of a trapper—Risks to which he is subjected—Partnership of trappers—Enmity of Indians—Distant smoke—A country on fire—Gun Creek—Grand Rond—Fine pastures—Perplexities in a smoky country—Conflagration of forests

IT HAD BEEN the intention of Captain Bonneville, in descending along Snake River, to scatter his trappers upon the smaller streams. In this way, a range of country is trapped by small detachments from a main body. The outfit of a trapper is generally a rifle, a pound of powder, and four pounds of lead, with a bullet mould, seven traps, an axe, a hatchet, a knife and awl, a camp kettle, two blankets, and, where supplies are plenty, seven pounds of flour. He has, generally, two or three horses, to carry himself, and his baggage and peltries. Two trappers commonly go together, for the purposes of mutual assistance and support; a larger party could not easily escape the eyes of the Indians. It is a service of peril, and even more so at present than formerly, for the Indians, since they have got into the habit of trafficking peltries with the traders, have learned the value of the beaver, and look upon the trappers as poachers, who are filching the riches from their streams, and interfering with their market. They make no hesitation, therefore, to murder the solitary trapper, and thus destroy a competitor, while they possess themselves of his spoils. It is with regret we add, too, that this hostility has in many cases been instigated by traders, desirous of injuring their rivals, but who have themselves often reaped the fruits of the mischief they have sown.

When two trappers undertake any considerable stream, their mode of proceeding is to hide their horses in some lonely glen, where

The Adventures of Captain Bonneville

they can graze unobserved. They then build a small hut, dig out a canoe from a cotton-wood tree, and in this, poke along shore silently, in the evening, and set their traps. These they revisit in the same silent way at daybreak. When they take any beaver, they bring it home, skin it, stretch the skin on sticks to dry, and feast upon the flesh. The body, hung up before the fire, turns by its own weight, and is roasted in a superior style; the tail is the trapper's titbit; it is cut off, put on the end of a stick, and toasted, and is considered even a greater dainty than the tongue or the marrow-bone of a buffalo.

With all their silence and caution, however, the poor trappers cannot always escape their hawk-eyed enemies. Their trail has been discovered, perhaps, and followed up for many a mile; or their smoke has been seen curling up out of the secret glen, or has been scented by the savages, whose sense of smell is almost as acute as that of sight. Sometimes they are pounced upon when in the act of setting their traps; at other times, they are roused from their sleep by the horrid war-whoop; or, perhaps, have a bullet or an arrow whistling about their ears, in the midst of one of their beaver banquets. In this way they are picked off, from time to time, and nothing is known of them, until, perchance, their bones are found bleaching in some lonely ravine, or on the banks of some nameless stream, which from that time is called after them. Many of the small streams beyond the mountains thus perpetuate the names of unfortunate trappers that have been murdered on their banks.

A knowledge of these dangers deterred Captain Bonneville, in the present instance, from detaching small parties of trappers as he had intended; for his scouts brought him word that formidable bands of the Bannack Indians were lying on the Boisée and Payette Rivers,[1] at no great distance, so that they would be apt to detect and cut off any stragglers. It behooved him, also, to keep his party together, to guard against any predatory attack upon the main body; he continued on his way, therefore, without dividing his forces. And

---

[1] Both are tributaries of the Snake flowing into it from the east a few miles from each other in western Idaho. Bonneville was retracing his route of the previous winter.

fortunate it was that he did so; for in a little while, he encountered one of the phenomena of the western wilds, that would effectually have prevented his scattered people from finding each other again. In a word, it was the season of setting fire to the prairies. As he advanced, he began to perceive great clouds of smoke at a distance, rising by degrees, and spreading over the whole face of the country. The atmosphere became dry and surcharged with murky vapor, parching to the skin, and irritating to the eyes. When travelling among the hills, they could scarcely discern objects at the distance of a few paces; indeed, the least exertion of the vision was painful. There was evidently some vast conflagration in the direction toward which they were proceeding; it was as yet at a great distance, and during the day, they could only see the smoke rising in larger and denser volumes, and rolling forth in an immense canopy. At night, the skies were all glowing with the reflection of unseen fires, hanging in an immense body of lurid light, high above the horizon.

Having reached Gun Creek,[2] an important stream coming from the left, Captain Bonneville turned up its course, to traverse the mountain and avoid the great bend of Snake River. Being now out of the range of the Bannacks, he sent out his people in all directions to hunt the antelope for present supplies; keeping the dried meats for places where game might be scarce.

During four days that the party were ascending Gun Creek, the smoke continued to increase so rapidly, that it was impossible to distinguish the face of the country and ascertain landmarks. Fortunately, the travellers fell upon an Indian trail, which led them to the head waters of the Fourche de Glace or Ice River, sometimes called the Grand Rond. Here they found all the plains and valleys wrapped in one vast conflagration; which swept over the long grass in billows of flame, shot up every bush and tree, rose in great columns from the groves, and set up clouds of smoke that darkened the atmosphere. To avoid this sea of fire, the travellers had to pursue their course close along the foot of the mountains; but the irritation from the smoke continued to be tormenting.

The country about the head waters of the Grand Rond, spreads

[2] Powder River in eastern Oregon.

The ADVENTURES of CAPTAIN BONNEVILLE

out into broad and level prairies, extremely fertile, and watered by mountain springs and rivulets. These prairies are resorted to by small bands of the Skynses, to pasture their horses, as well as to banquet upon the salmon which abound in the neighboring waters. They take these fish in great quantities and without the least difficulty; simply taking them out of the water with their hands, as they flounder and struggle in the numerous long shoals of the principal streams. At the time the travellers passed over these prairies, some of the narrow deep streams by which they were intersected were completely choked with salmon, which they took in great numbers. The wolves and bears frequent these streams at this season, to avail themselves of these great fisheries.

The travellers continued, for many days, to experience great difficulties and discomforts from this wide conflagration, which seemed to embrace the whole wilderness. The sun was for a great part of the time obscured by the smoke, and the loftiest mountains were hidden from view. Blundering along in this region of mist and uncertainty, they were frequently obliged to make long circuits, to avoid obstacles which they could not perceive until close upon them. The Indian trails were their safest guides, for though they sometimes appeared to lead them out of their direct course, they always conducted them to the passes.

On the 26th of August, they reached the head of the Way-leeway River.[3] Here, in a valley of the mountains through which this head water makes its way, they found a band of the Skynses, who were extremely sociable, and appeared to be well disposed, and as they spoke the Nez Percé language, an intercourse was easily kept up with them.

In the pastures on the bank of this stream, Captain Bonneville encamped for a time, for the purpose of recruiting the strength of his horses.[4] Scouts were now sent out to explore the surrounding

[3] Grande Ronde River. From the context, Bonneville seems to have failed to recognize the identity of the two.
[4] Here Wyeth overtook Bonneville on August 31, 1834. In his journal he wrote: ". . . nooned at the Grand Ronde where I found some Kiuse [Cayuse] Indians, Capt. Bonneville and two of Mckays men and learned that Cpt. Stewart and Mr. [Jason] Lee passed two days before." *Correspondence and Journals*, 231.

The ADVENTURES *of* CAPTAIN BONNEVILLE

country, and search for a convenient pass through the mountains toward the Wallamut or Multnomah. After an absence of twenty days, they returned weary and discouraged. They had been harassed and perplexed in rugged mountain defiles, where their progress was continually impeded by rocks and precipices. Often they had been obliged to travel along the edges of frightful ravines, where a false

---

Townsend, meeting Bonneville for the first time, left an interesting statement of his impression:

"Here we found Captain Bonneville's company, which has been lying here several days, waiting the arrival of its trapping parties. We made a noon camp near it, and were visited by Captain Bonneville. This was the first time I had seen this gentleman. His manners were affable and pleasing, and he seemed possessed of a large share of bold, adventurous, and to a certain extent, romantic spirit, without which no man can expect to thrive as a mountain leader. He stated that he preferred the 'free and easy' life of a mountain hunter and trapper, to the comfortable and luxurious indolence of a dweller in civilized lands, and would not exchange his homely, but wholesome mountain fare, and his buffalo lodge, for the most piquant dishes of the French *artiste*, and the finest palace in the land. This came well from him, and I was pleased with it, although I could not altogether agree with him in sentiment, for I confess I had become somewhat weary of rough travelling and rough fare, and looked forward with no little pleasure to a long rest under a Christian roof, and a general participation in Christian living." *Narrative*, 147.

Wyeth moved on that same afternoon. The next morning he received a letter from Bonneville and a second one in the afternoon in response to his reply. He then answered Bonneville's second letter. There are thus two letters by Wyeth to Bonneville, both dated September 1, 1834, from the Grande Ronde valley (see *Correspondence and Journals*, 141–42). With only Wyeth's side of the correspondence preserved, it is difficult to determine the exact business matters discussed. Apparently they proposed to trade with the Cayuse Indians in the Grande Ronde valley, Wyeth to secure goods necessary for trading from his brig, *May Dacre*, which he was to meet on the Columbia River. Wyeth also offered to convey Bonneville's furs to the eastern seaboard on the *May Dacre* when it returned the next summer for thirty-seven and one-half cents per pound, including insurance. They were both hopeful of cutting in on the Hudson's Bay Company, and Wyeth concluded his second letter by saying, "Your Beaver traded from the Skiuses [Cayuses] is so much seized from the common enemy in trade, so far so good." But these plans all fell through when Wyeth reached the mouth of the Columbia and discovered that the *May Dacre*, having been struck by lightning on the passage out and thus delayed, had missed the salmon season upon which his plans were partly built, thereby making his own business extremely uncertain. Bonneville, likewise, was soon to be rebuffed a second time at Fort Walla Walla. Both men realized that the ground was slipping from under them as fast as possible.

step would have been fatal. In one of these passes, a horse fell from the brink of a precipice, and would have been dashed to pieces, had he not lodged among the branches of a tree, from which he was extricated with great difficulty. These, however, were not the worst of their difficulties and perils. The great conflagration of the country, which had harassed the main party in its march, was still more awful, the further this exploring party proceeded. The flames, which swept rapidly over the light vegetation of the prairies, assumed a fiercer character, and took a stronger hold amidst the wooded glens and ravines of the mountains. Some of the deep gorges and defiles sent up sheets of flame, and clouds of lurid smoke, and sparks and cinders, that in the night made them resemble the craters of volcanoes. The groves and forests, too, which crowned the cliffs, shot up their towering columns of fire, and added to the furnace glow of the mountains. With these stupendous sights were combined the rushing blasts caused by the rarefied air, which roared and howled through the narrow glens, and whirled forth the smoke and flames in impetuous wreaths. Ever and anon, too, was heard the crash of falling trees, sometimes tumbling from crags and precipices, with tremendous sounds.

In the daytime, the mountains were wrapped in smoke so dense and blinding, that the explorers, if by chance they separated, could only find each other by shouting. Often, too, they had to grope their way through the yet burning forests, in constant peril from the limbs and trunks of trees, which frequently fell across their path. At length they gave up the attempt to find a pass as hopeless, under actual circumstances, and made their way back to the camp to report their failure.

45.

The Skynses—Their traffic—Hunting—Food—
Horses—A horserace—Devotional feeling of the
Skynses, Nez Percés, and Flatheads—Prayers—
Exhortations—A preacher on horseback—Effect of
religion on the manners of the tribes—A new light

DURING THE ABSENCE of this detachment, a sociable intercourse had been kept up between the main party and the Skynses, who had removed into the neighborhood of the camp. These people dwell about the waters of the Way-lee-way and the adjacent country, and trade regularly with the Hudson's Bay Company; generally giving horses in exchange for the articles of which they stand in need. They bring beaver skins, also, to the trading posts; not procured by trapping, but by a course of internal traffic with the shy and ignorant Shoshokoes and Too-el-icans,[1] who keep in distant and unfrequented parts of the country, and will not venture near the trading houses. The Skynses hunt the deer and elk, occasionally; and depend, for a part of the year, on fishing. Their main subsistence, however, is upon roots, especially the camash. This bulbous root is said to be of a delicious flavor, and highly nutritious. The women dig it up in great quantities, steam it, and deposit it in caches for winter provisions. It grows spontaneously, and absolutely covers the plains.

This tribe was comfortably clad and equipped. They had a few rifles among them, and were extremely desirous of bartering for

[1] The Shoshokoes were not a tribe but rather poor groups of the Shoshoni, according to Frederick W. Hodge, *Handbook of American Indians*, I, 554.

Concerning the Tooelicans, he cites Irving and remarks: "possibly a Shoshoni band, otherwise unidentified." *Ibid.*, II, 784.

The Adventures of Captain Bonneville

those of Captain Bonneville's men; offering a couple of good running horses for a light rifle. Their first-rate horses, however, were not to be procured from them on any terms. They almost invariably use ponies; but of a breed infinitely superior to any in the United States. They are fond of trying their speed and bottom, and of betting upon them.

As Captain Bonneville was desirous of judging of the comparative merit of their horses, he purchased one of their racers, and had a trial of speed between that, an American, and a Shoshonie, which were supposed to be well matched. The race course was for the distance of one mile and a half out and back. For the first half mile, the American took the lead, by a few hands; but, losing his wind, soon fell far behind; leaving the Shoshonie and Skynse to contend together. For a mile and a half, they went head and head; but at the turn, the Skynse took the lead, and won the race with great ease; scarce drawing a quick breath when all was over.

The Skynses, like the Nez Percés and the Flatheads, have a strong devotional feeling, which has been successfully cultivated by some of the resident personages of the Hudson's Bay Company. Sunday is invariably kept sacred among these tribes. They will not raise their camp on that day, unless in extreme cases of danger or hunger: neither will they hunt, nor fish, nor trade, nor perform any kind of labor on that day. A part of it is passed in prayer and religious ceremonies. Some chief, who is, generally, at the same time what is called a "medicine man," assembles the community. After invoking blessings from the Deity, he addresses the assemblage; exhorting them to good conduct; to be diligent in providing for their families; to obstain from lying and stealing; to avoid quarrelling or cheating in their play, and to be just and hospitable to all strangers who may be among them. Prayers and exhortations are also made, early in the morning, on week days. Sometimes, all this is done by the chief, from horseback; moving slowly about the camp, with his hat on, and uttering his exhortations with a loud voice. On all occasions, the bystanders listen with profound attention; and at the end of every sentence, respond one word in unison; apparently equivalent to an amen. While these prayers and exhortations are going on, every employment in the camp is suspended. If an Indian is riding by the place, he dismounts, holds his horse, and attends with reverence until all is done. When the chief has finished his prayer or exhortation, he says, "I have done"; upon which there is a general exclamation in unison.

With these religious services, probably derived from the white men, the tribes above-mentioned mingle some of their old Indian ceremonials; such as dancing to the cadence of a song or ballad; which is generally done in a large lodge, provided for the purpose. Besides Sundays, they likewise observe the cardinal holidays of the Roman Catholic Church.

Whoever has introduced these simple forms of religion among these poor savages, has evidently understood their characters and capacities, and effected a great melioration of their manners. Of this, we speak not merely from the testimony of Captain Bonneville, but, likewise, from that of Mr. Wyeth, who passed some months in a travelling camp of the Flatheads. "During the time I have been with them," says he, "I have never known an instance of theft among them: the least thing, even to a bead or pin, is brought to you, if found; and often, things that have been thrown way. Neither have I known any quarrelling, nor lying. This absence of all quarrelling the more surprised me, when I came to see the various occasions that would have given rise to it among the whites: the crowding together of from twelve to eighteen hundred horses, which have to be driven into camp at night, to be picketed; to be packed in the morning; the gathering of fuel in places where it is extremely scanty. All this, however, is done without confusion or disturbance.

"They have a mild, playful, laughing disposition; and this is portrayed in their countenances. They are polite, and unobtrusive. When one speaks, the rest pay strict attention: when he is done, another assents by 'yes,' or dissents by 'no'; and then states his reasons, which are listened to with equal attention. Even the children are more peaceable than other children. I never heard an angry word among them, nor any quarrelling; although there were, at least, five hundred of them together, and continually at play. With all this quietness of spirit, they are brave when put to the test; and are an overmatch for an equal number of Blackfeet."[2]

The foregoing observations, though gathered from Mr. Wyeth as relative to the Flatheads, apply, in the main, to the Skynses, also. Captain Bonneville, during his sojourn with the latter, took constant occasion, in conversing with their principal men, to encourage them in the cultivation of moral and religious habits; drawing a comparison between their peaceable and comfortable course of life, and that of other tribes, and attributing it to their superior sense of morality and religion. He frequently attended their religious services, with his people; always enjoining on the latter the most reverential deportment; and he observed that the poor Indians were always pleased to have the white men present.

The disposition of these tribes is evidently favorable to a considerable degree of civilization. A few farmers settled among them, might lead them, Captain Bonneville thinks, to till the earth and cultivate grain; the country of the Skynses, and Nez Percés, is admirably adapted for the raising of cattle. A Christian missionary or two, and some trifling assistance from government, to protect them from the predatory and warlike tribes, might lay the foundation of a Christian people in the midst of the great western wilderness, who would "wear the Americans near their hearts."

We must not omit to observe, however, in qualification of the sanctity of this Sabbath in the wilderness, that these tribes, who are all ardently addicted to gambling and horseracing, make Sunday a peculiar day for recreations of the kind, not deeming them in any wise out of season. After prayers and pious ceremonies are over, there is scarce an hour in the day, says Captain Bonneville, that you do not see several horses racing at full speed; and in every corner of the camp are groups of gamblers, ready to stake everything upon the all-absorbing game of hand. The Indians, says Wyeth, appear to enjoy their amusements with more zest than the whites. They are great gamblers; and in proportion to their means, play bolder, and bet higher than white men.

The cultivation of the religious feeling, above noted, among the

[2] The previous four paragraphs are adapted from Wyeth's journal for April 30, 1833 (see *Correspondence and Journals*, 191–93).

savages, has been, at times, a convenient policy, with some of the more knowing traders; who have derived great credit and influence among them, by being considered "medicine men"; that is, men gifted with mysterious knowledge. This feeling is, also, at times, played upon by religious charlatans; who are to be found in savage, as well as civilized life. One of these was noted by Wyeth, during his sojourn among the Flatheads. A new great man, says he, is rising in the camp, who aims at power and sway. He covers his designs under the ample cloak of religion; inculcating some new doctrines and ceremonials among those who are more simple than himself. He has already made proselytes of one-fifth of the camp; beginning by working on the women, the children, and the weak-minded. His followers are all dancing on the plain, to their own vocal music. The more knowing ones of the tribe look on and laugh; thinking it all too foolish to do harm; but they will soon find that women, children, and fools, form a large majority of every community, and they will have, eventually, to follow the new light, or be considered among the profane. As soon as a preacher, or pseudo prophet of the kind, gets followers enough, he either takes command of the tribe, or branches off and sets up for an independent chief and "medicine man."

46.

Scarcity in the camp—Refusal of supplies by the Hudson's Bay Company—Conduct of the Indians—A hungry retreat—John Day's River—The Blue Mountains—Salmon fishing on Snake River—Messengers from the Crow country—Bear River valley—Immense migration of buffalo—Danger of buffalo hunting—A wounded Indian—Eutaw Indians—A "surround" of antelopes

PROVISIONS WERE NOW GROWING scanty in the camp, and Captain Bonneville found it necessary to seek a new neighborhood. Taking leave, therefore, of his friends, the Skynses, he set off to the westward, and, crossing a low range of mountains, encamped on the head waters of the Ottolais.[1] Being now within thirty miles of Fort Wallah-Wallah, the trading post of the Hudson's Bay Company, he sent a small detachment of men thither, to purchase corn for the subsistence of his party. The men were well received at the fort; but all supplies for their camp were peremptorily refused. Tempting offers were made them, however, if they would leave their present employ, and enter into the service of the company; but they were not to be seduced.[2]

When Captain Bonneville saw his messengers return empty-handed, he ordered an instant move, for there was imminent danger of famine. He pushed forward down the course of the Ottolais, which runs diagonal to the Columbia, and falls into it about fifty

[1] The Umatilla River, south of Fort Walla Walla. It is correctly shown on Bonneville's map, where it is labelled Ottalais River.

[2] This passage and those following reveal what Bonneville was up against in trying to compete with the Hudson's Bay Company in its own territory.

miles below the Wallah-Wallah. His route lay through a beautiful undulating country, covered with horses belonging to the Skynses, who sent them there for pasturage.

On reaching the Columbia, Captain Bonneville hoped to open a trade with the natives, for fish and other provisions, but to his surprise, they kept aloof, and even hid themselves on his approach. He soon discovered that they were under the influence of the Hudson's Bay Company, who had forbidden them to trade, or hold any communion with him. He proceeded along the Columbia, but it was everywhere the same; not an article of provisions was to be obtained from the natives, and he was, at length, obliged to kill a couple of his horses to sustain his famishing people. He now came to a halt, and consulted what was to be done. The broad and beautiful Columbia lay before them, smooth and unruffled as a mirror; a little more journeying would take them to its lower region; to the noble valley of the Wallamut, their projected winter quarters.[3] To advance under present circumstances would be to court starvation. The resources of the country were locked against them, by the influence of a jealous and powerful monopoly. If they reached the Wallamut, they could scarcely hope to obtain sufficient supplies for the winter; if they lingered any longer in the country, the snows would gather upon the mountains and cut off their retreat. By hastening their return, they would be able to reach the Blue Mountains just in time to find the elk, the deer, and the bighorn; and after they had supplied themselves with provisions, they might push through the mountains, before they were entirely blocked up by snow. Influenced by these considerations, Captain Bonneville reluctantly turned his back a second time on the Columbia, and set off for the Blue Mountains. He took his course up John Day's River,[4] so called from one of the hunters in the original Astorian enterprise. As

[3] This had been Bonneville's objective since he left Bear River. He would also be near Wyeth, who early in October took up a large tract of farm land on the Willamette River.

[4] A tributary of the Columbia in Oregon. The John Day River was named for a Virginian who was one of the overland Astorians under Wilson Price Hunt; see *Astoria*, I, 146–47; II, 111–12. The John Day River appears on Bonneville's map.

famine was at his heels, he travelled fast, and reached the mountains[5] by the 1st of October. He entered by the opening made by John Day's River; it was a rugged and difficult defile, but he and his men had become accustomed to hard scrambles of the kind. Fortunately, the September rains had extinguished the fires which recently spread over these regions; and the mountains, no longer wrapped in smoke, now revealed all their grandeur and sublimity to the eye.

They were disappointed in their expectation of finding abundant game in the mountains; large bands of the natives had passed through, returning from their fishing expeditions, and had driven all the game before them. It was only now and then that the hunters could bring in sufficient to keep the party from starvation.

To add to their distress, they mistook their route, and wandered for ten days among high and bald hills of clay. At length, after much perplexity, they made their way to the banks of Snake River, following the course of which, they were sure to reach their place of destination.

It was the 20th of October when they found themselves once more upon this noted stream. The Shoshokoes, whom they had met with in such scanty numbers on their journey down the river, now absolutely thronged its banks to profit by the abundance of salmon, and lay up a stock for winter provisions. Scaffolds were everywhere erected, and immense quantities of fish drying upon them. At this season of the year, however, the salmon are extremely poor, and the travellers needed their keen sauce of hunger to give them a relish.

In some places the shores were completely covered with a stratum of dead salmon, exhausted in ascending the river, or destroyed at the falls; the fetid odor of which tainted the air.

It was not until the travellers reached the head waters of the Portneuf,[6] that they really found themselves in a region of abundance. Here the buffalo were in immense herds; and here they remained for three days, slaying, and cooking, and feasting, and

[5] The western verge of the Blue Mountains.
[6] They were west of Blackfoot River and north of Bear River.

indemnifying themselves by an enormous carnival, for a long and hungry Lent. Their horses, too, found good pasturage, and enjoyed a little rest after a severe spell of hard travelling.

During this period, two horsemen arrived at the camp, who proved to be messengers sent express for supplies from Montero's party; which had been sent to beat up the Crow country and the Black Hills, and to winter on the Arkansas.[7] They reported that all was well with the party, but that they had not been able to accomplish the whole of their mission, and were still in the Crow country, where they should remain until joined by Captain Bonneville in the spring. The captain retained the messengers with him until the 17th of November, when, having reached the caches on Bear River, and procured thence the required supplies, he sent them back to their party; appointing a rendezvous toward the last of June following, on the forks of Wind River valley, in the Crow country.

He now remained several days encamped near the caches, and having discovered a small band of Shoshonies in his neighborhood, purchased from them lodges, furs, and other articles of winter comfort, and arranged with them to encamp together during the winter.

The place designed by the captain for the wintering ground was on the upper part of Bear River, some distance off. He delayed approaching it as long as possible, in order to avoid driving off the buffalo, which would be needed for winter provisions. He accordingly moved forward but slowly, merely as the want of game and grass obliged him to shift his position. The weather had already become extremely cold, and the snow lay to a considerable depth. To enable the horses to carry as much dried meat as possible, he caused a cache to be made, in which all the baggage that could be spared was deposited. This done, the party continued to move slowly toward their winter quarters.

They were not doomed, however, to suffer from scarcity during the present winter. The people upon Snake River having chased off the buffalo before the snow had become deep, immense herds now came trooping over the mountains; forming dark masses on their sides, from which their deep-mouthed bellowing sounded like

[7] See Chapter XL, note 3.

the low peals and mutterings from a gathering thunder-cloud. In effect, the cloud broke, and down came the torrent thundering into the valley. It is utterly impossible, according to Captain Bonneville, to convey an idea of the effect produced by the sight of such countless throngs of animals of such bulk and spirit, all rushing forward as if swept on by a whirlwind.

The long privation which the travellers had suffered gave uncommon ardor to their present hunting. One of the Indians attached to the party, finding himself on horseback in the midst of the buffalo, without either rifle, or bow and arrows, dashed after a fine cow that was passing close by him, and plunged his knife into her side with such lucky aim as to bring her to the ground. It was a daring deed; but hunger had made him almost desperate.

The buffalo are sometimes tenacious of life, and must be wounded in particular parts. A ball striking the shagged frontlet of a bull produces no other effect than a toss of the head, and greater exasperation; on the contrary, a ball striking the forehead of a cow is fatal. Several instances occurred during this great hunting bout, of bulls fighting furiously after having received mortal wounds. Wyeth, also, was witness to an instance of the kind while encamped with Indians. During a grand hunt of the buffalo, one of the Indians pressed a bull so closely that the animal turned suddenly upon him. His horse stopped short, or started back, and threw him. Before he could rise, the bull rushed furiously upon him, and gored him in the chest, so that his breath came out at the aperture. He was conveyed back to the camp, and his wound was dressed. Giving himself up for slain, he called round him his friends, and made his will by word of mouth. It was something like a death chant, and at the end of every sentence those around responded in concord. He appeared no ways intimidated by the approach of death. "I think," adds Wyeth, "the Indians die better than the white men; perhaps, from having less fear about the future."[8]

[8] Wyeth's journal, June 10, 1833, reads:
"To day an Indian was running bulls he turned the horse stopped and threw him the bull gored him into his chest so that his breath was made through the apparture by the help of the women he reached camp. When Mr. Ermatinger

The buffalo may be approached very near, if the hunter keeps to the leeward; but they are quick of scent, and will take the alarm and move off from a party of hunters, to the windward, even when two miles distant.

The vast herds which had poured down into the Bear River valley, were now snow-bound, and remained in the neighborhood of the camp throughout the winter. This furnished the trappers and their Indian friends a perpetual carnival; so that, to slay and eat seemed to be the main occupations of the day. It is astonishing what loads of meat it requires to cope with the appetite of a hunting camp.

The ravens and wolves soon came in for their share of the good cheer. These constant attendants of the hunter gathered in vast numbers as the winter advanced. They might be completely out of sight, but at the report of a gun, flights of ravens would immediately be seen hovering in the air, no one knew whence they came; while the sharp visages of the wolves would peep down from the brow of every hill, waiting for the hunter's departure to pounce upon the carcass.

Beside[s] the buffalo, there were other neighbors snow-bound in the valley, whose presence did not promise to be so advantageous. This was a band of Eutaw Indians, who were encamped higher up on the river. They are a poor tribe, that, in a scale of the various tribes inhabiting these regions, would rank between the Shoshonies and the Shoshokoes or Root Diggers; though more bold and warlike than the latter. They have but few rifles among them, and are generally armed with bows and arrows.

As this band and the Shoshonies were at deadly feud, on account of old grievances, and as neither party stood in awe of the other, it was feared some bloody scenes might ensue. Captain Bonneville, therefore, undertook the office of pacificator, and sent to the Eutaw

---

dressed his wound he very composedly made his will by word of mouth the Indians responding in concert at the end of each sentence. He appeared not in the least intimidated by the approach of death. I think the Indians die better than the whites perhaps they have less superstition in regard to the future and argue that as the deity makes them happy here he will also hereafter if there is existence for them." *Correspondence and Journals,* 200.

chiefs, inviting them to a friendly smoke, in order to bring about a reconciliation. His invitation was proudly declined; whereupon he went to them in person, and succeeded in effecting a suspension of hostilities until the chiefs of the two tribes could meet in council. The braves of the two rival camps sullenly acquiesced in the arrangement. They would take their seats upon the hill tops, and watch their quondam enemies hunting the buffalo in the plain below, and evidently repine that their hands were tied up from a skirmish. The worthy captain, however, succeeded in carrying through his benevolent mediation. The chiefs met; the amicable pipe was smoked, the hatchet buried, and peace formally proclaimed. After this, both camps united and mingled in social intercourse. Private quarrels, however, would occasionally occur in hunting, about the division of the game, and blows would sometimes be exchanged over the carcass of a buffalo; but the chiefs wisely took no notice of these individual brawls.

One day, the scouts, who had been ranging the hills, brought news of several large herds of antelopes in a small valley at no great distance. This produced a sensation among the Indians, for both tribes were in ragged condition, and sadly in want of those shirts made of the skin of the antelope. It was determined to have "a surround," as the mode of hunting that animal is called. Everything now assumed an air of mystic solemnity and importance. The chiefs prepared their medicines or charms, each according to his own method, or fancied inspiration, generally with the compound of certain simples; others consulted the entrails of animals which they had sacrificed, and thence drew favorable auguries. After much grave smoking and deliberating, it was at length proclaimed, that all who were able to lift a club, man, woman, or child, should muster for "the surround." When all had congregated, they moved in rude procession to the nearest point of the valley in question, and there halted. Another course of smoking and deliberating, of which the Indians are so fond, took place among the chiefs. Directions were then issued for the horsemen to make a circuit of about seven miles, so as to encompass the herd. When this was done, the whole mounted force dashed off, simultaneously, at full speed, shouting and yelling at the top of their voices. In a short space of time, the antelopes, started from their hiding places, came bounding from all points into the valley. The riders now gradually contracting their circle, brought them nearer and nearer to the spot, where the senior chief, surrounded by the elders, male and female, was seated in supervision of the chase. The antelopes, nearly exhausted with fatigue and fright, and bewildered by perpetual whooping, made no effort to break through the ring of the hunters, but ran round in small circles, until man, woman, and child beat them down with bludgeons. Such is the nature of that species of antelope hunting, technically called "a surround."

47.

A festive winter—Conversion of the Shoshonies—
Visit of two free trappers—Gayety in the camp—
A touch of the tender passion—The reclaimed squaw—
An Indian fine lady—An elopement—A pursuit—
Market value of a bad wife

GAME CONTINUED to abound throughout the winter, and the camp was overstocked with provisions. Beef and venison, humps and haunches, buffalo tongues and marrow-bones, were constantly cooking at every fire; and the whole atmosphere was redolent with the savory fumes of roast meat. It was, indeed, a continual "feast of fat things," and though there might be a lack of "wine upon the lees,"[1] yet, we have shown that a substitute was occasionally to be found in honey and alcohol.

Both the Shoshonies and the Eutaws conducted themselves with great propriety. It is true, they now and then filched a few trifles from their good friends, the Big Hearts, when their backs were turned; but then, they always treated them, to their faces, with the utmost deference and respect; and good-humoredly vied with the trappers in all kinds of feats of activity and mirthful sports. The two tribes maintained toward each other, also, a friendliness of aspect, which gave Captain Bonneville reason to hope that all past animosity was effectually buried.

The two rival bands, however, had not long been mingled in this social manner, before their ancient jealousy began to break out, in a new form. The senior chief of the Shoshonies was a think-

[1] "And in this mountain shall the Lord of hosts make unto all people a feast of fat things; a feast of wines on the lees, of fat things full of marrow, of wines on the lees well refined" (Isaiah 25:6).

ing man, and a man of observation. He had been among the Nez Percés, listened to their new code of morality and religion received from the white men, and attended their devotional exercises. He had observed the effect of all this, in elevating the tribe in the estimation of the white men; and determined, by the same means, to gain for his own tribe a superiority over their ignorant rivals, the Eutaws. He accordingly assembled his people, and promulgated among them the mongrel doctrines and form of worship of the Nez Percés; recommending the same to their adoption. The Shoshonies were struck with the novelty, at least, of the measure, and entered into it with spirit. They began to observe Sundays and holidays, and to have their devotional dances, and chants, and other ceremonials, about which the ignorant Eutaws knew nothing; while they exerted their usual competition in shooting and horseracing, and the renowned game of hand.

Matters were going on thus pleasantly and prosperously, in this motley community of white and red men, when, one morning, two stark free trappers, arrayed in the height of savage finery, and mounted on steeds as fine and as fiery as themselves, and all jingling with hawks' bells, came galloping, with whoop and halloo, into the camp.

They were fresh from the winter encampment of the American Fur Company, in the Green River valley; and had come to pay their old comrades of Captain Bonneville's company a visit. An idea may be formed, from the scenes we have already given of conviviality in the wilderness, of the manner in which these game birds were received by those of their feather in the camp; what feasting, what revelling, what boasting, what bragging, what ranting and roaring, and racing and gambling, and squabbling and fighting, ensued among these boon companions. Captain Bonneville, it is true, maintained always a certain degree of law and order in his camp, and checked each fierce excess: but the trappers, in their seasons of idleness and relaxation require a degree of license and indulgence, to repay them for the long privations, and almost incredible hardships of their periods of active service.

In the midst of all this feasting and frolicking, a freak of the tender passion intervened, and wrought a complete change in the scene. Among the Indian beauties in the camp of the Eutaws and Shoshonies, the free trappers discovered two, who had whilom figured as their squaws. These connections frequently take place for a season, and sometimes continue for years, if not perpetually; but are apt to be broken when the free trapper starts off, suddenly, on some distant and rough expedition.

In the present instance, these wild blades were anxious to regain their belles; nor were the latter loath once more to come under their protection. The free trapper combines, in the eye of an Indian girl, all that is dashing and heroic in a warrior of her own race, whose gait, and garb, and bravery he emulates, with all that is gallant and glorious in the white man. And then the indulgence with which he treats her, the finery in which he decks her out, the state in which she moves, the sway she enjoys over both his purse and person, instead of being the drudge and slave of an Indian husband; obliged to carry his pack, and build his lodge, and make his fire, and bear his cross humors and dry blows.—No; there is no comparison, in the eyes of an aspiring belle of the wilderness, between a free trapper and an Indian brave.

With respect to one of the parties, the matter was easily arranged. The beauty in question was a pert little Eutaw wench, that had been taken prisoner, in some war excursion, by a Shoshonie. She was readily ransomed for a few articles of trifling value; and forthwith figured about the camp in fine array, "with rings on her fingers, and bells on her toes," and a tossed-up coquetish air, that made her the envy, admiration, and abhorrence, of all the leathern-dressed, hard-working squaws of her acquaintance.

As to the other beauty, it was quite a different matter. She had become the wife of a Shoshonie brave. It is true, he had another wife, of older date than the one in question; who, therefore, took command in his household, and treated his new spouse as a slave; but the latter was the wife of his last fancy, his latest caprice; and was precious in his eyes. All attempt to bargain with him, therefore, was useless; the very proposition was repulsed with anger and disdain. The spirit of the trapper was roused, his pride was piqued as well as his passion. He endeavored to prevail upon his quondam mistress to elope with him. His horses were fleet, the winter nights were long and dark, before daylight they would be beyond the reach of pursuit; and once at the encampment in Green River valley, they might set the whole band of Shoshonies at defiance.

The Indian girl listened and longed. Her heart yearned after the ease and splendor of condition of a trapper's bride, and throbbed to be free from the capricious control of the premier squaw; but she dreaded the failure of the plan, and the fury of a Shoshonie husband. They parted; the Indian girl in tears, and the madcap trapper more mad than ever, with his thwarted passion.

Their interviews had, probably, been detected, and the jealousy of the Shoshonie brave aroused: a clamor of angry voices was heard in his lodge, with the sound of blows, and of female weeping and lamenting. At night, as the trapper lay tossing on his pallet, a soft voice whispered at the door of his lodge. His mistress stood trembling before him. She was ready to follow whithersoever he should lead.

In an instant, he was up and out. He had two prime horses, sure, and swift of foot, and of great wind. With stealthy quiet, they were brought up and saddled; and, in a few moments, he and his prize were careering over the snow, with which the whole country was covered. In the eagerness of escape, they had made no provision for their journey; days must elapse before they could reach their haven of safety, and mountains and prairies be traversed, wrapped in all the desolation of winter. For the present, however, they thought of nothing but flight; urging their horses forward over the dreary wastes, and fancying, in the howling of every blast, they heard the yell of the pursuer.

At early dawn, the Shoshonie became aware of his loss. Mounting his swiftest horse, he set off in hot pursuit. He soon found the trail of the fugitives, and spurred on in hopes of overtaking them. The winds, however, which swept the valley, had drifted the light snow into the prints made by the horses' hoofs. In a little while, he lost all trace of them, and was completely thrown out of the chase. He knew, however, the situation of the camp toward which they were bound, and a direct course through the mountains, by which he might arrive there sooner than the fugitives. Through the most rugged defiles, therefore, he urged his course by day and night, scarce pausing until he reached the camp. It was some time before the fugitives made their appearance. Six days had they been traversing the wintry wilds. They came, haggard with hunger and fatigue, and their horses faltering under them. The first object that met their eyes, on entering the camp was the Shoshonie brave. He rushed, knife in hand, to plunge it in the heart that had proved false to him. The trapper threw himself before the cowering form of his mistress, and, exhausted as he was, prepared for a deadly struggle. The Shoshonie paused. His habitual awe of the white man checked his arm; the trapper's friends crowded to the spot, and arrested him. A parley ensued. A kind of *crim. con.*[2] adjudication took place; such as frequently occurs in civilized life. A couple of horses were declared to be a fair compensation for the loss of a woman who had previously lost her heart; with this, the Shoshonie brave was fain to pacify his passion. He returned to Captain Bonneville's camp, somewhat crest-fallen, it is true; but parried the officious condolements of his friends, by observing that two good horses were very good pay for one bad wife.

[2] Criminal conversation.

48.

Breaking up of winter quarters—Move to Green River—A trapper and his rifle—An arrival in camp—A free trapper and his squaw in distress—Story of a Blackfoot belle

THE WINTER was now breaking up, the snows were melted from the hills, and from the lower parts of the mountains, and the time for decamping had arrived. Captain Bonneville dispatched a party to the caches, who brought away all the effects concealed there, and on the 1st of April (1835), the camp was broken up, and every one on the move. The white men and their allies, the Eutaws and Shoshonies, parted with many regrets and sincere expressions of good will, for their intercourse throughout the winter had been of the most friendly kind.

Captain Bonneville and his party passed by Ham's Fork,[1] and reached the Colorado, or Green River, without accident, on the banks of which they remained during the residue of the spring. During this time, they were conscious that a band of hostile Indians were hovering about their vicinity, watching for an opportunity to slay or steal; but the vigilant precautions of Captain Bonneville baffled all their maneuvres. In such dangerous times, the experienced mountaineer is never without his rifle, even in camp. On going from lodge to lodge to visit his comrades, he takes it with him. On seating himself in a lodge, he lays it beside him, ready to be snatched up; when

---

[1] They had traveled east over the Salt Range to Hams Fork. Upon leaving it they continued in an easterly direction in line with South Pass, which they would have to cross to keep the appointment with Walker's and Montero's trappers at the mouth of the Popo Agie.

he goes out, he takes it up as regularly as a citizen would his walking staff. His rifle is his constant friend and protector.

On the 10th of June, the party were a little to the east of the Wind River Mountains, where they halted for a time in excellent pasturage, to give their horses a chance to recruit their strength for a long journey; for it was Captain Bonneville's intention to shape his course to the settlements; having already been detained by the complication of his duties, and by various losses and impediments, far beyond the time specified in his leave of absence.

While the party was thus reposing in the neighborhood of the Wind River Mountains, a solitary free trapper rode one day into the camp, and accosted Captain Bonneville. He belonged, he said, to a party of thirty hunters, who had just passed through the neighborhood, but whom he had abandoned in consequence of their ill treatment of a brother trapper; whom they had cast off from their party, and left with his bag and baggage, and an Indian wife into the bargain, in the midst of a desolate prairie. The horseman gave a piteous account of the situation of this helpless pair, and solicited the loan of horses to bring them and their effects to the camp.

The captain was not a man to refuse assistance to any one in distress, especially when there was a woman in the case; horses were immediately dispatched, with an escort, to aid the unfortunate couple. The next day, they made their appearance with all their effects: the man, a stalwart mountaineer, with a peculiarly game look; the woman, a young Blackfoot beauty, arrayed in the trappings and trinketry of a free trapper's bride.

Finding the woman to be quick-witted and communicative, Captain Bonneville entered into conversation with her, and obtained from her many particulars concerning the habits and customs of her tribe; especially their wars and huntings. They pride themselves upon being the "best legs of the mountains," and hunt the buffalo on foot. This is done in spring time, when the frosts have thawed and the ground is soft. The heavy buffalo then sink over their hoofs at every step, and are easily overtaken by the Blackfeet; whose fleet steps press lightly on the surface. It is said, however, that the buffalo on the Pacific side of the Rocky Mountains are fleeter and more active than on the Atlantic side; those upon the plains of the Columbia can scarcely be overtaken by a horse that would outstrip the same animal in the neighborhood of the Platte, the usual hunting ground of the Blackfeet. In the course of further conversation, Captain Bonneville drew from the Indian woman her whole story; which gave a picture of savage life, and of the drudgery and hardships to which an Indian wife is subject.

"I was the wife," said she, "of a Blackfoot warrior, and I served him faithfully. Who was so well served as he? Whose lodge was so well provided, or kept so clean? I brought wood in the morning, and placed water always at hand. I watched for his coming; and he found his meat cooked and ready. If he rose to go forth, there was nothing to delay him. I searched the thought that was in his heart, to save him the trouble of speaking. When I went abroad on errands for him, the chiefs and warriors smiled upon me, and the young braves spoke soft things, in secret; but my feet were in the straight path, and my eyes could see nothing but him.

"When he went out to hunt, or to war, who aided to equip him, but I? When he returned, I met him at the door; I took his gun; and he entered without further thought. While he sat and smoked, I unloaded his horses; tied them to the stakes; brought in their loads, and was quickly at his feet. If his moccasons were wet, I took them off and put on others which were dry and warm. I dressed all the skins he had taken in the chase. He could never say to me, why is it not done? He hunted the deer, the antelope, and the buffalo, and he watched for the enemy. Everything else was done by me. When our people moved their camp, he mounted his horse and rode away; free as though he had fallen from the skies. He had nothing to do with the labor of the camp; it was I that packed the horses, and led them on the journey. When we halted in the evening, and he sat with the other braves and smoked, it was I that pitched his lodge; and when he came to eat and sleep, his supper and his bed were ready.

"I served him faithfully; and what was my reward? A cloud was always on his brow, and sharp lightning on his tongue. I was his dog; and not his wife.

"Who was it that scarred and bruised me? It was he. My brother saw how I was treated. His heart was big for me. He begged me to leave my tyrant and fly. Where could I go? If retaken, who would protect me? My brother was not a chief; he could not save me from blows and wounds, perhaps death. At length I was persuaded. I followed my brother from the village. He pointed a way to the Nez Percés, and bade me go and live in peace among them. We parted. On the third day I saw the lodges of the Nez Percés before me. I paused for a moment, and had no heart to go on; but my horse neighed, and I took it as a good sign, and suffered him to gallop forward. In a little while I was in the midst of the lodges. As I sat silent on my horse, the people gathered round me, and inquired whence I came. I told my story. A chief now wrapped his blanket close around him, and bade me dismount. I obeyed. He took my horse to lead him away. My heart grew small within me. I felt, on parting with my horse, as if my last friend was gone. I had no words, and my eyes were dry. As he led off my horse, a young brave stepped forward. 'Are you a chief of the people?' cried he. 'Do we listen to you in council, and follow you in battle? Behold! a stranger flies to our camp from the dogs of Blackfeet, and asks protection. Let shame cover your face! The stranger is a woman, and alone. If she were a warrior, or had a warrior by her side, your heart would not be big enough to take her horse. But he is yours. By the right of war you may claim him; but look!'—his bow was drawn, and the arrow ready!—'you never shall cross his back!' The arrow pierced the heart of the horse, and he fell dead.

"An old woman said she would be my mother. She led me to her lodge: my heart was thawed by her kindness, and my eyes burst forth with tears; like the frozen fountains in springtime. She never changed; but as the days passed away, was still a mother to me. The people were loud in praise of the young brave, and the chief was ashamed. I lived in peace.

"A party of trappers came to the village, and one of them took me for his wife. This is he. I am very happy; he treats me with kindness, and I have taught him the language of my people. As we were travelling this way, some of the Blackfeet warriors beset us, and carried off the horses of the party. We followed, and my husband held a parley with them. The guns were laid down, and the pipe was lighted; but some of the white men attempted to seize the horses by force, and then a battle began. The snow was deep; the white men sank into it at every step; but the red men, with their snow-shoes, passed over the surface like birds, and drove off many of the horses in sight of their owners. With those that remained we resumed our journey. At length words took place between the leader of the party and my husband. He took away our horses, which had escaped in the battle, and turned us from his camp. My husband had one good friend among the trappers. That is he (pointing to the man who had asked assistance for them). He is a good man. His heart is big. When he came in from hunting, and found that we had been driven away, he gave up all his wages, and followed us, that he might speak good words for us to the white captain."

49.

Rendezvous at Wind River—Campaign of Montero and his brigade in the Crow country—Wars between the Crows and Blackfeet—Death of Arapooish—Blackfeet lurkers—Sagacity of the horse—Dependence of the hunter on his horse—Return to the settlements

ON THE 22D of June, Captain Bonneville raised his camp, and moved to the forks of Wind River; the appointed place of rendezvous. In a few days, he was joined there by the brigade of Montero, which had been sent, in the preceding year, to beat up the Crow country, and afterward proceed to the Arkansas.[1] Montero had followed the early part of his instructions;

---

[1] Leonard states that Walker and his men also met Bonneville here:
"About the 19th of June we suspended our trapping and returned to Wind River, where we found Captain Bonneville and his men waiting for us according to appointment, at the mouth of Popoasia Creek." *Adventures*, 160.
Leonard is very explicit as to where they had been since leaving Bonneville the previous June on Bear River:
". . . the tributaries of the Missouri—Tongue, Powder, Yellowstone, Little and Big Porcupine, Musselshell, Priors, Smith's, Gallatin's, Otter, Rosebud, Clark's, and Stinking rivers." *Ibid.*, 160.
Montero's was a second group of trappers, and since his actual existence has been questioned (see Chapter XL, note 3), it is necessary to present the evidence on the other side. (1) The first notice concerning Montero that has come to my attention is a letter from Lucien Fontenelle to William Laidlaw, agent of the American Fur Company at Fort Pierre. It was written on July 20, 1833, at the Green River rendezvous and directs Laidlaw to pay Antonio Montero a balance due him of $260.25. The reverse side of the letter contains Montero's autograph, dated the same day, endorsing the note over to M. S. Cerré. Chouteau-Maffit Collection, Missouri Historical Society. (2) In the Missouri Historical Society collections is an autograph letter to Antonio Montaro [*sic*] by Zenas Leonard for Bonneville and Company, dated January 11, 1835, at Wind River, where Walker had his winter camp. It is a reply to a letter from Montero, January 6, from his

after trapping upon some of the upper streams, he proceeded to Powder River. Here he fell in with the Crow villages or bands, who treated him with unusual kindness, and prevailed upon him to take up his winter quarters among them.

The Crows, at that time, were struggling almost for existence with their old enemies, the Blackfeet; who, in the past year, had picked off the flower of their warriors in various engagements, and among the rest, Arapooish, the friend of the white men. That sagacious and magnanimous chief had beheld, with grief, the ravages

camp on Powder River. Leonard's letter is too long to be quoted here, but Montero had asked for a mule and one or two additional men; the Indians would not arrive until March; Walker was out of meat and had but five horses for hunting, etc. (3) James A. Hamilton, writing from Fort Union, July 18, 1835, to Pratte, Chouteau and Company concerning several boatloads of furs he was sending down the Missouri, stated that "B. Bourdalone No 21 on the List, who works his passage down, came in here half dead, from a Division of Captain Bonnevilles party under Montero, who has been for the last year with 50 Men trapping & trading in the Crow country he tells a wofull tale the leading features whereof Mr Tulloch had previously heard from other quarters." Quoted by Annie Heloise Abel, ed., *Chardon's Journal at Fort Clark, 1834–1839*, 300 n. (4) We learn of Antonio Montero on Powder River in the following year. Joe Meek told Mrs. Victor that "About Christmas [1836 according to Mrs. Victor, but open to question] all the company [Bridger's] went into winter-quarters on Powder River, in the neighborhood of a company of Bonneville's men, left under the command of Antoine Montero, who had established a trading-post and fort at this place [Portuguese Houses; see Chittenden, *American Fur Trade*, II, 966], hoping, no doubt, that here they should be comparatively safe from the injurious competition of the older companies. . . . Montero, who was Bonneville's experienced trader, could not hold his own against so numerous and expert a band of marauders as Bridger's men, assisted by the Crows, proved themselves to be; for by the spring Montero had very little remaining of the property belonging to the fort, nor anything to show for it." *River of the West*, 223–24. (5) Observe Russell refers to Antonio Montero, identified as a Portuguese, and says that he had built cabins on the Powder River for the Crow trade. This reference belongs to 1837. See *Journal of a Trapper*, 81. (6) In the Adams Papers in the Missouri Historical Society is a letter in Antonio Montero's handwriting from Independence, August 5, 1838, to David Adams, one of Bonneville's former employees. Montero signed himself "Your Best friend." (7) That same year, on September 2, 1838, an order went out from Joshua Pilcher, Indian agent, to Papin, Picotte and Chardon forbidding Antonio Montero to remain in the Indian country without a license and ordering him to leave because of other offenses. Chouteau Collections, Missouri Historical Society.

Irving's next sentence is sufficient evidence to show that Montero did not winter on the Arkansas in 1834–35; see p. 301.

which war was making in his tribe, and that it was declining in force, and must eventually be destroyed, unless some signal blow could be struck to retrieve its fortunes. In a pitched battle of the two tribes, he made a speech to his warriors, urging them to set everything at hazard in one furious charge; which done, he led the way into the thickest of the foe. He was soon separated from his men, and fell covered with wounds,[2] but his self-devotion was not in vain. The Blackfeet were defeated; and from that time the Crows plucked up fresh heart, and were frequently successful.

Montero had not been long encamped among them, when he discovered that the Blackfeet were hovering about the neighborhood. One day the hunters came galloping into the camp, and proclaimed that a band of the enemy was at hand. The Crows flew to arms, leaped on their horses, and dashed out in squadrons in pursuit. They overtook the retreating enemy in the midst of a plain. A desperate fight ensued. The Crows had the advantage of numbers, and of fighting on horseback. The greater part of the Blackfeet were slain; the remnant took shelter in a close thicket of willows, where the horse could not enter; whence they plied their bows vigorously.

The Crows drew off out of bow shot, and endeavored, by taunts and bravadoes, to draw the warriors out of their retreat. A few of the best mounted among them, rode apart from the rest. One of their number then advanced alone, with that martial air and equestrian grace for which the tribe is noted. When within an arrow's flight of the thicket, he loosened his rein, urged his horse to full speed, threw his body on the opposite side, so as to hang by but one leg, and present no mark to the foe; in this way, he swept along in front of the thicket, launching his arrows from under the neck of his steed. Then regaining his seat in the saddle, he wheeled round, and returned whooping and scoffing to his companions, who received him with yells of applause.

Another and another horseman repeated this exploit; but the Blackfeet were not to be taunted out of their safe shelter. The victors feared to drive desperate men to extremities, so they forbore to attempt the thicket. Toward night they gave over the attack, and

[2] See Beckwourth, *Life and Adventures*, 173–75.

returned all-glorious with the scalps of the slain. Then came on the usual feasts and triumphs, the scalp-dance of warriors round the ghastly trophies, and all the other fierce revelry of barbarous warfare. When the braves had finished with the scalps, they were, as usual, given up to the women and children, and made the objects of new parades and dances. They were then treasured up as invaluable trophies and decorations by the braves who had won them.[3]

It is worthy of note, that the scalp of a white man, either through policy or fear, is treated with more charity than that of an Indian. The warrior who won it is entitled to his triumph if he demands it. In such case, the war party alone dance round the scalp. It is then taken down, and the shagged frontlet of a buffalo substituted in its place, and abandoned to the triumph and insults of the million.

To avoid being involved in these guerillas, as well as to escape from the extremely social intercourse of the Crows, which began to be oppressive, Montero moved to the distance of several miles from their camps, and there formed a winter cantonment of huts. He now maintained a vigilant watch at night. Their horses, which were turned loose to graze during the day, under heedful eyes, were brought in at night, and shut up in strong pens, built of large logs of cotton-wood.

The snows, during a portion of the winter, were so deep that the poor animals could find but little sustenance. Here and there a tuft of grass would peer above the snow; but they were in general driven to browse the twigs and tender branches of the trees. When they were turned out in the morning, the first moments of freedom from the confinement of the pen were spent in frisking and gambolling. This done, they went soberly and sadly to work, to glean their scanty subsistence for the day. In the meantime, the men stripped the bark of the cotton-wood tree for the evening fodder. As the poor horses would return toward night, with sluggish and dispirited air, the moment they saw their owners approaching them with blankets filled with cotton-wood bark, their whole demeanor underwent a change. A universal neighing and capering took place; they would

[3] This may be the battle between the Crows and Blackfeet narrated by Leonard, *Adventures*, 145–50, and by Beckwourth, *Life and Adventures*, 125–30.

rush forward, smell to the blankets, paw the earth, snort, whinny and prance round with head and tail erect, until the blankets were opened, and the welcome provender spread before them. These evidences of intelligence and gladness were frequently recounted by the trappers as proving the sagacity of the animal.

These veteran rovers of the mountains look upon their horses as in some respects gifted with almost human intellect. An old and experienced trapper, when mounting guard upon the camp in dark nights and times of peril, gives heedful attention to all the sounds and signs of the horses. No enemy enters nor approaches the camp without attracting their notice, and their movements not only give a vague alarm, but it is said, will even indicate to the knowing trapper the very quarter whence danger threatens.

In the daytime, too, while a hunter is engaged on the prairie, cutting up the deer or buffalo he has slain, he depends upon his faithful horse as a sentinel. The sagacious animal sees and smells all round him, and by his starting and whinnying, gives notice of the approach of strangers. There seems to be a dumb communion and fellowship, a sort of fraternal sympathy, between the hunter and his horse. They mutually rely upon each other for company and protection; and nothing is more difficult, it is said, than to surprise an experienced hunter on the prairie, while his old and favorite steed is at his side.

Montero had not long removed his camp from the vicinity of the Crows, and fixed himself in his new quarters, when the Blackfeet marauders discovered his cantonment, and began to haunt the vicinity. He kept up a vigilant watch, however, and foiled every attempt of the enemy, who, at length, seemed to have given up in despair, and abandoned the neighborhood. The trappers relaxed their vigilance, therefore, and one night, after a day of severe labor, no guards were posted, and the whole camp was soon asleep. Toward midnight, however, the lightest sleepers were roused by the trampling of hoofs; and, giving the alarm, the whole party were immediately on their legs, and hastened to the pens. The bars were down; but no enemy was to be seen or heard, and the horses being all found hard by, it was supposed the bars had been left down through negligence.

The ADVENTURES *of* CAPTAIN BONNEVILLE

All were once more asleep, when, in about an hour, there was a second alarm, and it was discovered that several horses were missing. The rest were mounted, and so spirited a pursuit took place, that eighteen of the number carried off were regained, and but three remained in possession of the enemy. Traps, for wolves, had been set about the camp the preceding day. In the morning, it was discovered that a Blackfoot was entrapped by one of them, but had succeeded in dragging it off. His trail was followed for a long distance, which he must have limped alone. At length, he appeared to have fallen in with some of his comrades, who had relieved him from his painful encumbrance.

These were the leading incidents of Montero's campaign in the Crow country. The united parties now celebrated the 4th of July, in rough hunters' style, with hearty conviviality; after which, Captain Bonneville made his final arrangements. Leaving Montero with a brigade of trappers to open another campaign, he put himself at the head of the residue of his men, and set off on his return to civilized life.[4] We shall not detail his journey along the course of the Nebraska, and so, from point to point of the wilderness, until he and his band reached the frontier settlements on the 22d of August.[5]

[4] Leonard wrote:
"Captain Walker, with fifty-nine men, was to continue trapping in this country for one year from this time, and Captain Bonneville, with the remainder, taking all the peltries we had collected, and which were packed on horses and mules, was to go to the States and return in the summer of 1836, with as strong a force as he could collect, and a large supply of merchandise, and meet Captain Walker in this neighborhood." *Adventures,* 160. But Bonneville's plans for continued operations in 1836 were not to materialize.

[5] Leonard was with the returning party and wrote of the trip back:
"As we traveled along we killed all the game we could, this being necessary, as provision is very scarce on the course we intended to pursue between the village of the Pawnee Indians [south of the Platte River and east of Grand Island] and the white settlements. About the 25th of July we arrived on the Platte River, which we followed down until we arrived at the Pawnee Village. . . . After trading with these Indians for some corn, we left them and traveled rapidly every day until we arrived in Independence (Mo.) . . . on the 29th of August, 1835. . . . *Adventures,* 161.

Here, according to his own account, his cavalcade might have been taken for a procession of tatterdemalion savages; for the men were ragged almost to nakedness, and had contracted a wildness of aspect during three years of wandering in the wilderness. A few hours in a populous town, however, produced a magical metamorphosis. Hats of the most ample brim and longest nap; coats with buttons that shone like mirrors, and pantaloons of the most ample plentitude, took place of the well-worn trapper's equipments; and the happy wearers might be seen strolling about in all directions, scattering their silver like sailors just from a cruise.

The worthy captain, however, seems by no means to have shared the excitement of his men, on finding himself once more in the thronged resorts of civilized life, but, on the contrary, to have looked back to the wilderness with regret. "Though the prospect," says he, "of once more tasting the blessings of peaceful society, and passing days and nights under the calm guardianship of the laws, was not without its attractions; yet to those of us whose whole lives had been spent in the stirring excitement and perpetual watchfulness of adventures in the wilderness, the change was far from promising an increase of that contentment and inward satisfaction most conducive to happiness. He who, like myself, has roved almost from boyhood among the children of the forest, and over the unfurrowed plains and rugged heights of the western wastes, will not be startled to learn, that notwithstanding all the fascinations of the world on this civilized side of the mountains, I would fain make my bow to the splendors and gayeties of the metropolis, and plunge again amidst the hardships and perils of the wilderness."

We have only to add, that the affairs of the captain have been satisfactorily arranged with the War Department,[6] and that he is actually in service at Fort Gibson, on our western frontier; where we hope he may meet with further opportunities of indulging his peculiar tastes, and of collecting graphic and characteristic details of the great western wilds and their motley inhabitants.

[6] Bonneville's leave was to have expired in October, 1833. He was dropped from army rolls on May 31, 1834, and subsequently reinstated on April 19, 1836.

We here close our picturings of the Rocky Mountains and their wild inhabitants, and of the wild life that prevails there; which we have been anxious to fix on record, because we are aware that this singular state of things is full of mutation, and must soon undergo great changes, if not entirely pass away. The fur trade, itself, which has given life to all this portraiture, is essentially evanescent. Rival parties of trappers soon exhaust the streams, especially when competition renders them heedless and wasteful of the beaver. The fur-bearing animals extinct, a complete change will come over the scene: the gay free trapper and his steed, decked out in wild array, and tinkling with bells and trinketry; the savage war chief, plumed and painted, and ever on the prowl; the traders' cavalcade, winding through defiles or over naked plains, with the stealthy war party lurking on its trail; the buffalo chase, the hunting camp, the mad carouse in the midst of danger, the night attack, the stampado, the scamper, the fierce skirmish among rocks and cliffs,—all this romance of savage life, which yet exists among the mountains, will then exist but in frontier story, and seem like the fictions of chivalry or fairy tale.

Some new system of things, or rather some new modification, will succeed among the roving people of this vast wilderness; but just as opposite, perhaps, to the habitudes of civilization. The great Chippewyan chain of mountains, and the sandy and volcanic plains which extend on either side, are represented as incapable of cultivation. The pasturage which prevails there during a certain portion of the year, soon withers under the aridity of the atmosphere, and leaves nothing but dreary wastes. An immense belt of rocky mountains and volcanic plains, several hundred miles in width, must ever remain an irreclaimable wilderness, intervening between the abodes of civilization, and affording a last refuge to the Indian. Here roving tribes of hunters, living in tents or lodges, and following the migrations of the game, may lead a life of savage independence, where there is nothing to tempt the cupidity of the white man. The amalgamation of various tribes, and of white men of every nation, will in time produce hybrid races like the mountain Tartars of the Caucasus. Possessed as they are of immense droves of horses, should they continue their present predatory and warlike habits, they may, in time, become a scourge to the civilized frontiers on either side of the mountains; as they are at present a terror to the traveller and trader.

The facts disclosed in the present work, clearly manifest the policy of establishing military posts and a mounted force to protect our traders in their journeys across the great western wilds, and of pushing the outposts into the very heart of the singular wilderness we have laid open, so as to maintain some degree of sway over the country, and to put an end to the kind of "blackmail," levied on all occasions by the savage "chivalry of the mountains."

Appendix A

Nathaniel J. Wyeth, and the Trade
of the Far West

WE HAVE BROUGHT Captain Bonneville to the end of his western campaigning; yet we cannot close this work without subjoining some particulars concerning the fortunes of his contemporary, Mr. Wyeth; anecdotes of whose enterprise have, occasionally, been interwoven in the party-colored web of our narrative. Wyeth effected his intention of establishing a trading post on the Portneuf, which he named Fort Hall. Here, for the first time, the American flag was unfurled to the breeze that sweeps the great naked wastes of the central wilderness. Leaving twelve men here, with a stock of goods, to trade with the neighboring tribes, he prosecuted his journey to the Columbia; where he established another post, called Fort Williams, on Wappatoo Island,[1] at the mouth of the Wallamut. This was to be the head factory of his company; whence they were to carry on their fishing and trapping operations, and their trade with the interior; and where they were to receive and dispatch their annual ship.

The plan of Mr. Wyeth appears to have been well concerted. He had observed that the Rocky Mountain Fur Company, the bands of free trappers, as well as the Indians west of the mountains, depended for their supplies upon goods brought from St. Louis; which, in consequence of the expenses and risks of a long land carriage, were furnished them at an immense advance on first cost. He had an idea

[1] Sauvie Island.

Appendix A

that they might be much more cheaply supplied from the Pacific side. Horses would cost much less on the borders of the Columbia than at St. Louis: the transportation by land was much shorter; and through a country much more safe from the hostility of savage tribes; which, on the route from and to St. Louis, annually cost the lives of many men. On this idea, he grounded his plan. He combined the salmon fishery with the fur trade. A fortified trading post was to be established on the Columbia, to carry on a trade with the natives for salmon and peltries, and to fish and trap on their own account. Once a year, a ship was to come from the United States, to bring out goods for the interior trade, and to take home the salmon and furs which had been collected. Part of the goods, thus brought out, were to be dispatched to the mountains, to supply the trapping companies and the Indian tribes, in exchange for their furs; which were to be brought down to the Columbia, to be sent home in the next annual ship: and thus an annual round was to be kept up. The profits on the salmon, it was expected, would cover all the expenses of the ship; so that the goods brought out, and the furs carried home, would cost nothing as to freight.

His enterprise was prosecuted with a spirit, intelligence, and perseverance, that merited success. All the details that we have met with, prove him to be no ordinary man. He appears to have the mind to conceive, and the energy to execute extensive and striking plans. He had once more reared the American flag in the lost domains of Astoria; and had he been enabled to maintain the footing he had so gallantly effected, he might have regained for his country the opulent trade of the Columbia, of which our statesmen have negligently suffered us to be dispossessed.[2]

It is needless to go into a detail of the variety of accidents and cross-purposes, which caused the failure of his scheme. They were such as all undertakings of the kind, involving combined operations by sea and land, are liable to. What he most wanted, was sufficient capital to enable him to endure incipient obstacles and losses; and

[2] For a brief, general survey of American interest in Oregon, see Ray Allen Billington, *The Far Western Frontier*, 69–73, 79–90.

to hold on until success had time to spring up from the midst of disastrous experiments.

It is with extreme regret we learn that he has recently been compelled to dispose of his establishment at Wappatoo Island, to the Hudson's Bay Company; who, it is but justice to say, have, according to his own account, treated him throughout the whole of his enterprise, with great fairness, friendship, and liberality.[3] That company, therefore, still maintains an unrivalled sway over the whole country washed by the Columbia and its tributaries. It has, in fact, as far as its chartered powers permit, followed out the splendid scheme contemplated by Mr. Astor, when he founded his establishment at the mouth of the Columbia. From their emporium of Vancouver, companies are sent forth in every direction, to supply the interior posts, to trade with the natives, and to trap upon the various streams. These thread the rivers, traverse the plains, penetrate to the heart of the mountains, extend their enterprises northward, to the Russian possessions, and southward, to the confines of California. Their yearly supplies are received by sea, at Vancouver; and thence their furs and peltries are shipped to London. They likewise maintain a considerable commerce, in wheat and lumber, with the Pacific islands, and to the north, with the Russian settlements.

Though the company, by treaty,[4] have a right to a participation only, in the trade of these regions, and are, in fact, but tenants on sufferance; yet have they quietly availed themselves of the original oversight, and subsequent supineness of the American government, to establish a monopoly of the trade of the river and its dependencies; and are adroitly proceeding to fortify themselves in their usurpation, by securing all the strong points of the country.

Fort George, originally Astoria, which was abandoned on the removal of the main factory to Vancouver, was renewed in 1830; and is now kept up as a fortified post and trading house. All the places

---

[3] Not entirely—"We opposed him as much as was Necessary," wrote Dr. John McLoughlin. Quoted in Billington, *Far Western Frontier*, 73.

[4] The Treaty of Joint Occupation, originally signed in 1818 and renewed in 1827, between the United States and Great Britain.

Appendix A

accessible to shipping have been taken possession of, and posts recently established at them by the company.

The great capital of this association; their long established system; their hereditary influence over the Indian tribes; their internal organization, which makes every thing go on with the regularity of a machine; and the low wages of their people, who are mostly Canadians, give them great advantages over the American traders: nor is it likely the latter will ever be able to maintain any footing in the land, until the question of territorial right is adjusted between the two countries. The sooner that takes place, the better. It is a question too serious to national pride, if not to national interests, to be slurred over; and every year is adding to the difficulties which environ it.[5]

The fur trade, which is now the main object of enterprise west of the Rocky Mountains, forms but a part of the real resources of the country. Beside the salmon fishery of the Columbia, which is capable of being rendered a considerable source of profit; the great valleys of the lower country, below the elevated volcanic plateau, are calculated to give sustenance to countless flocks and herds, and to sustain a great population of graziers and agriculturists.

Such, for instance, is the beautiful valley of the Wallamut; from which the establishment at Vancouver draws most of its supplies. Here, the company holds mills and farms; and has provided for some of its superannuated officers and servants. This valley, above the falls, is about fifty miles wide, and extends a great distance to the south. The climate is mild, being sheltered by lateral ranges of mountains; while the soil, for richness, has been equalled to the best of the Missouri lands. The valley of the river Des Chutes,[6] is also admirably calculated for a great grazing country. All the best horses used by the company for the mountains are raised there. The valley is of such happy temperature, that grass grows there throughout the year, and cattle may be left out to pasture during the winter.

---

[5] It is noteworthy that Irving adds his voice to the increasing number of propagandists for American settlement of Oregon.

[6] The first important river east of the Cascade Range. It flows north into the Columbia, joining it east of the Dalles.

These valleys must form the grand points of commencement of the future settlement of the country; but there must be many such, enfolded in the embraces of these lower ranges of mountains; which, though at present they lie waste and uninhabited, and to the eye of the trader and trapper, present but barren wastes, would, in the hands of skilful agriculturists and husbandmen, soon assume a different aspect, and teem with waving crops, or be covered with flocks and herds.

The resources of the country, too, while in the hands of a company restricted in its trade, can be but partially called forth; but in the hands of Americans, enjoying a direct trade with the East Indies, would be brought into quickening activity; and might soon realize the dream of Mr. Astor, in giving rise to a flourishing commercial empire.

Wreck of a Japanese Junk on the Northwest Coast

The following extract of a letter which we received, lately, from Mr. Wyeth, may be interesting, as throwing some light upon the question as to the manner in which America has been peopled.

"Are you aware of the fact, that in the winter of 1833, a Japanese junk was wrecked on the northwest coast, in the neighborhood of Queen Charlotte's Island; and that all but two of the crew, then much reduced by starvation and disease, during a long drift across the Pacific, were killed by the natives? The two fell into the hands of the Hudson's Bay Company, and were sent to England. I saw them, on my arrival at Vancouver, in 1834."

Appendix A

Instructions to Captain Bonneville
from the Major-General Commanding
the Army of the United States.[7]

Copy   Head Quarters of the Army.
                                    Washington 29th July 1831.
Sir,

    The leave of absence which you have asked for the purpose of enabling you to carry into execution your designs of exploring the country to the Rocky Mountains, and beyond with a view of assertaining the nature and character of the various tribes of Indians inhabiting those regions; the trade which might be profitably carried on with them, the quality of the soil, the productions, the minerals, the natural history, the climate, the Geography, and Topography, as well as Geology of the various parts of the Country within the limits of the Territories belonging to the United States, between our frontier, and the Pacific;—has been duly considered, and submitted to the War Department, for approval, and has been sanctioned.

    You are therefore authorised to be absent from the Army untill October 1833.

    It is understood that the Government is to be at no expence, in reference to your proposed expedition, it having originated with yourself, and all that you required was the permission from the proper authority to undertake the enterprise. You will naturally in providing your self for the expedition, provide suitable instruments, and especially the best Maps of the interior to be found. It is desirable besides what is enumerated as the object of enterprise that you note particularly the number of Warriors that may belong to each tribe, or nation that you may meet with: their alliances with other tribes and their relative position as to a state of peace or war, and whether their friendly or warlike dispositions towards each other are recent or of long standing. You will gratify us by describing their [changed to "the"] manner of ["their" inserted] making War, of the mode of

---

[7] The following letter is printed here in conformity with the copy on file in the National Archives, including three changes in a different hand. It deviates in numerous minor ways from the letter as published by Irving.

subsisting themselves during a state of war, and a state of peace, their Arms, and the effect of them, whether they act on foot or on horse back, detailing the discription [changed to "discipline"], and manuvers of the war parties, the power of their horses, size and general discription; in short any information which you may conceive would be useful to the Government. You will avail yourself of every opportunity of informing us of your position and progress, and at the expiration of your leave of absence will join your proper station.

    I have the honor to be Sir,
      Your O^t S^t
      (Signed) Alex^r Macomb Maj Genl Com^g

To Cap: B. L E Bonneville
7th Reg^t Infantry
New York

Appendix B

Copy   Crow Country,
                                 Wind River July 29, 1833

General

    This country I find is much more extensive than I could have expected, as yet I may say I have actually visited, only, the heart of the Rocky Mountains, or in other words the head waters of the Yellow Stone, Platte, the Coloredo of the west, and the Columbia,— I have therefore remained. I hope I have not trespassed too much upon your goodness, to explore the North of the Columbia in Cottonais Country and New Caledonia to winter on the lower Columbia, and going to the South West towards Calefornia on my return, which will certainly be in the course of next fall. I would not have presumed this much were I not aware how desirous you are of collecting certain information respecting the Country, and my return at present would have afforded but half a story which would have been laughable in the extreme. I have constantly kept a journal, making daily observations of courses, country, Indians &c: in fine of every thing I supposed could be interesting. The information I have already obtained authorizes me to say this much; that if our Government ever intend taking possession of Origon the sooner it shall be done the better, and at present I deem a sub-alterns command equal to enforce all the views of our Government; altho a sub-alter[n]s command is equal to the task, yet I would recommend a full company, which by bringing provision to last till June could then live upon the salmon which abounds there during the summer and fall and farming [?] for themselves for the next year could subsist themselves well. Five men then could be as safe as an hundred, either from the Indians who are extremely peacble [*sic*], and honest, or from the establishments of the Hudson Bay Company who are themselves too much exposed by their numerous small posts even to offer the least violence to the smallest force. They have a trading Post at the mouth of three or four men to appose all trading vessels, another above, *Vancouver,* which is strongly built, & capable of a Garrison of one hundred and eighty men; here they have farms[,] mills[,] &c. &c. & every convenience of old settlements, manned by half breeds, Indians, and some Canadians; but they are generally distributed in trapping companies who frequently remain absent a year. Wallawallah a post still higher up on the left bank of Columbia, handsomely built, but garrisoned by only 3 to 5 men, may be easily reduced by fire, or want of wood, which they obtained from the drift. Colville another fort upon the north Fork, is also feeble, 3 to 5 men there to keep up a connexion and trade. The returns from Vancouver[,] Wallawallah & Colville, do not exceed 3000 skins, which may be considered trifling for their expence, but from New Caledonia to the North of Columbia, and from towards the Calefornias their returns are immence; these are the Countries I have not yet examined, and am now so anxious to visit. As to the cultivation of the bottoms of the Columbia, the lands are of the best, the timber abundant, but it is deluged at the rise of the river, but the Multnomah or as it is named here the Wallamet, runs through one of the most beautiful, furtile and extensive vallies in the world, wheat, corn & tobacco country. The Hudson Bay at present have every advantage over the Americans. Woolens at half price, flour and tobacco they raise, Horses they obtain from their indians at $1 prime cost, shells they fish for, and their other articles of trade reaching them by water in the greatest abundance and at trifling expence compared to the land carriage of the Americans, that the latter have to avoid their recontre by every means in their power, not on the Columbia, but even on the Colorado, the head waters of the Arkansas, the Platte, the Missouri; they even speak of making a fort on the Big Horn to appose the American fur company. So you see the Americans have to as it were to steal their own fur, making secret rendezvous, and trading by stealth. The history of the Country is this, first the Hudson Bay entered it in 1810 trapping and trading, generally employing between 80 & 100 men, gradually increasing to their present number of about 280 men. The A M company about 1816 sent Imel & Jones with about 30 men who remained about 5 years, then totally defeated by the Blackfoot indians on the Yellow Stone. Mr. Henry also entered it about the same time of Imel and

Appendix B

Jones with about 80 men, built forts on the Big Horn[,] on Lewis River, and on the three forks of the Missouri, was also defeated by the Black foot indians on three forks. In 1825 Genl. Ashley came in with about 50 men met the Hudson Bay on Lewis River, on the point of fighting with them, however took from them the Iroquois & their furs, & subsequently himself was defeated by the Arrepehoes on the head waters of the Coloredo, and lost all his Horses, 120 head. Ashley then sold out to his clerks, Smith, Jackson and Sublette who raised their number to 130 men, who in 1830 themselves sold out to their clerks, and best trappers, Fitzpatrick[,] younger Sublette, Bridgers, Frap & Jarvis who now remain in the Country with about 80 or 90 men[.] Drips[,] Fontenelle, Pilcher, Vandaburg & Benjamin came in a firm in 1827 with about 75 men, reached the head of the Platte, then lost all their horses by the Arepehoes, there tacking [*sic*] the greater part of their merchandise and packing. Their men in the winter got lost in the deep snow, finally dispersed[.] Drips Fontenelle and Vendeburg, offering their services to the A M C, increased their number to 160 men. Gantt came up in 1831 with about 50 men, mostly a foot, done little, then returned to the head waters of the Arkansas, where I understand he has opened a trade with the Comanche, the Arrepehoes, & Shians. The above I think will give you a tolerable correct idea of the great quantities of Furs [which] must have been taken from the country in order to keep alive so many companies at such great expences in men & horses. The Country may be said at present to be poor, but beaver increases so rapidly that any part permitted to rest three years, is said to be as rich as at first[.] the companies therefore endeavor to assertain each others hunting grounds and to conceal theirs, and even their successes or disasters. Last year Fitzpatricks company in two years trapping sent down about 150 packs, 60 skins per pack; A. M. C. last year, one years work sent about 31 packs. This year A. M. C. and Fitzpatricks appear to have each about 44 packs, and sustained great loss in horses taken by the Aurickeries; again the same party lost 17 men by desertion taking each 2 Horses & Six traps. As to the indians, that the Paunees reside on the lower Platte in several bands, amounting to about 1200 warriors, they are well mounted and at war with the Crows. The Sioux, Shians and Auricurees make their hunting grounds in the Black Hills, 2500 Sioux, 400 Shaans, 160 Auricuries, they reside on the

Missouri, and wage war upon the Crows, and Pawnees. They are extremely warlike, and well mounted. The Crow Indians range upon the Yellow Stone, and head waters of the Platte about 1500 strong in three villages, fight with the black foot, and the Arrepehoes—the crows have good Horses, and I believe the best Buffaloe Country in the world. The Arrepehoes range upon the heads of the Arkansas and Canadian are very numerous, fight also with the Shoshones. The Shoshones a poor unwarlike race, some few who have arms & horses venture to desend into the plains in Villages, but they are generally dispursed by two & three into the Mountains without Horses, without arms, but the stone point arrow, and depending upon their numerous dogs to take the mountain sheep, they are met with in almost every Mountain running from every body, and are termed *Degne* [*Digne*] *de Pitie* ie, worthy of pitty, They will steal and kill whenever a good opportunity offers. Their villages are generally more friendly, tho. dangerous to be met alone. They range about the Salt lake. The Bannecks in villages, about 400 warriors mostly afoot, live about the falls of Lewis River, then during the summer months, catching & drying Salmon, and in the fall move up that river to the Great Plain, and hunt the Buffaloe which they dry and return to their falls, unwarlike defend themselves from the Blackfoot. The Flatheads 100 warriors with about 150 Nez Percey warriors detached from the lower Columbia range upon the Salmon River, the Racine Amere, and towards the three forks of the Missouri. The Flat-heads are said to be the only indians here, who have never killed a white man, they and the Nez Percey are extremely brave in defence, but never go to war, are the most honest and religious people I ever saw, observing every festival of the Roman Church, avoiding changing their camp on Sundays tho: in distress for provisions. Polegamy so usual among all Indians is strictly forbidden by them. I do not believe that three nights passes in the year without religious meetings—They defend themselves from the Black foot. Desend the Columbia waters, The great body of the Nez Percey and the large bands of the Pands orerrills [Pend d'Oreilles]—here horses may be said to abound, some individuals having from 2 to 3,000 head upon which they live, together with roots. The Cottenais 700 warriors, having the other day commenced a war with the Blackfoot have been driven from their original

Appendix B

grounds upon the Northern Branches of the Columbia, and have now joined the Flatheads[.] The numerous hords of Indians upon the head waters of the Missouri and its Northern branches are in one term the Black foot Indians. The Blood, the Surcies, the Piedgans and the Gros Ventres of the Praires are those most troublesome in these Mountains—They are well mounted, abundantly supplied by the richness of their Country in excellent shot guns and ammunition. They are extremely numerous. When the snow begins to fall, bands from 3 to 400 men move with their families, all afoot & packing dogs, locate them selves, some bands in the Shoshone Country, some towards the Nez Percey &c built stone forts, then dispatch their most active men to steal horses and to kill their nearest tribe, and as the snow melts in the Spring, gradually retreat with their spoils to their own Country. When the Grass is found sufficient, bands of about the same size leave their families and move to the plains in all directions to kill & steal. The only security against these Indians is to fight from the bushes[;] in the plains 'tis most certain destruction. The whites are unsafe with any tribe except the Nez Percey & Flat-heads, true[,] parties of size are unmolested, save by the Black foot, but individuals must be careful of the Bannecks, the Shoshones, the Arrepehoes, the Shians, the Pawnees, & the Crow—As to the whites they have their leaders, a trader, his hired men also what is termed free men, men who join, or runaway from other companies, & going to the next, remains with it in the following manner; if they have horses & traps of their own, they agree to sell all the furs caught at $4 per pound, purchasing all their supplies from that company, if they have no horses, & do not wish to hire, they are then loaned horses and traps, and are to sell their beaver unskinned at $4 to $5 each paying for their supplies and loss of traps. And the great object of Companies is to catch their men on their way to their rendezvous and trade all their credits, with whiskey, tobacco &c—

In the Winter, the parts of the same company meet and pass the winter together, seperating in the Spring and again meeting at some other place for their Summer rendezvous, where the supplies from S Louis are expected, each company, generally, having a place of its own-Rendezvous are certainly the scenes of the most extreme debauchery & dissipation

The ADVENTURES *of* CAPTAIN BONNEVILLE

Prices–at the Ms

Furs vary from		$3 to 5 per lb
Skin trapping do		4 to 5 per p. [?]
Blankets coloured		18 to 20 each
Tobacco		2 to 3 p. [? illegible]
Alcohol		32 pr gal
Coffee		2 pr tin cup or pint
Sugar		2 do
Flour		1 do
Shot Guns, prime best	4$	40 each
Rifles "	10$	60 each
Horses	20 to 25	120 to 250 each

The customary price as a years wages from $250 to $400. As to the prices and regulations of the Hudson Bay I know but little; but this Summer fall and Spring I believe I shall be able to explain all their regulations of trade &c. On the 30th of April I left Independence with 120 men and 20 wagons, On the 12th May crossed the Kansas, Kept up the left bank, move[d] up the Republican, which I headed, having at first gone through a rolling country upon the Republican. I marched upon an elevated plain, then struck it a little west and in one day fell on the Platte, the 2d June, here I found the River ¾ mile wide, the banks 2 to 3 feet high, river about 4 feet deep, but full of quicksands; the plains upon the banks of the Platte are from 3 to 5 miles wide, and I marched to the forks 130 miles without a break or creek, At the forks I first found Buffaloe—45 days from the settlements, having gone up the south fork about 10 miles I crossed this fork, the river below I measured 1¾ mile wide in two places, general width 1¼ mile, cut the tongue of land and fell upon the north fork, here the river plain is small, bluffs of immense size putting into the river, finally reached the main branches of the north fork, crossed this south, Laramies Fork, then begin one of the most broken countries I ever beheld, frequently letting my wagons down the bluffs with long ropes 80 men to each wagon. At last we came to the main forks of the north forks, having cut the tongue of land to the north, and in two days came to Sweet water, which we assended on the right bank to Wind river Mountains—having turned the mountains we struck a large sand plain, upon which we slept without grass or

Appendix B

water, having travelled from Sun-Rise till nine o'clock at night, next morning started again at day light & at twelve o'clock had the satisfaction to fall upon the water of the Coloredo of the West; having assended this river on the right bank forty miles, we built a picket work, fell in with the Gros Vantres of the Prairies, Black foot about 900 warriors, had no difficulty with them here we remained to recruit our horses, then went a north west course, and on the 10th November fell upon Salmon river, where I again built two log cabins, and waited for my men. One of my parties 21 men among the Crows was entirely lost, another of my parties of 21 men by the Shoshones lost 7 Horses & 4 men, and another of my parties on the rout through Lone prairie of 28 men lost all their horses, but fighting from 8 A M untill sun set, recovered all but one, taken by the Black foot & four badly wounded—On the 28th November some of my parties had returned. I then proceeded to the Flat-heads & Nez Perceys where I intended to wait the arrival of the remainder of my parties. At last on the 25th December I started with twelve men in search around the great Shoshone plains in the deep snow—lost one animal frozen to death, reached Lewis river on the 18th January, here I found one of my men from Shoshone parties, finding that not only the Mountains was loaded with snow, and that my animals were weak, I determined to send for that party to join me immediately, which they did, having increased another of my parties in the Shoshone valley, I started on the 19th of Feb.y with 18 men to join Mr. Cerré who I had left at the Flat-head town, there I again reached on the 14 March and on the 18th proceeded with 23 *engagees* and 14 indians, Nez Percey & Flat heads towards the Comanche Prairies, laying on the rout to the lower Columbia. On the 6th April came to the mountain which I found impassable, and remained at its base till the 27 May at which time I succeeded in passing, losing 4 horses and two mules, then continued to the west fell upon Rosy, Malade, Camanche, Boisey and La Payette rivers—as last found that living upon fish, horses and roots would not do—I then tried to cross the mountain to the North, (1st July [June])—the great debth of snow forced me to seek another pass, at last reached the forks of Salmon [?] river on the 15th of July [June], here I waited 4 days for my parties, having found their path, I took it, and on the 29th found them, much to my surprise with the Pends, Orrielles & the

Cottonains, the Flat heads & Nez Percey, having been driven from the country by the Black foots, who that Spring consolidated for that purpose, here I remained with these people till the 5th July, the Black foot being at that time quite near made me fear to cross the Prairies with my small party of 23 men, I therefore induced these friendly Indians by presents to march upon the Black Foot towns, and pretend to War while I pushed across the plains, and on the 23d [13th] reached the valley of the Coloredo, here I found so many Buffaloe carcases, and these only skinned that I actually feared to approach the rendezvous, and at night sent two men to examin it, had the satisfaction to hear all was well. I then continued, and next day met all the whites in the country, and on the 25th started with Mr Cerré to escort him to the Big-horn, which I expect will take me till the 10th August—I will then proceed to the north west towards the north of the Columbia. The country upon the lower Republican is rolling, becoming a high level plain as you assend, the country gradually rising to the West—The Platte runs through one of the most beautiful, and level plains in the world. Upon the north fork the country becomes much broken, from Laramies Fork to Sweet water is most terribly broken and difficult to pass,—this Country is termed the Black Hills; Upon Sweet Water high hills are constantly in view but easily passed, travilling generally on the bank of the river in the sand—The Sweet water heads into the Wind river Mountains, said to be the highest in the Country, about 2500 feet elevated above the plains, and constantly covered with snow. I have not measured these mountains, 'tis mere supposition. In this same bed of Mountains rises the Yellow Stone, the Columbia, the Coloredo, and the northern Platte[.] They are extensive and extremely difficult to be gone through, and are always turned. The general course I travelled to head Sweet Water was about west north west, and estimated by me at 1050 [miles] by the windings of the route. From the forks of Horse Creek of the Colorado to the head of Salmon River, the route lays generally through a country easily passed, with the exception of two Mountains which must be gone over—One is low, the other must be passed upon the river, and upon a cornice of the Mountain from which horses fell from every party, descent perpendicular 270 feet high—Course to Salmon N W 350 miles—here again begins a bed of Mountains lying North and South from the extreme north,

Appendix B

to a great distance to the south, about the Big-Salt Lake, then again from the Southern bank, to no person knows where, however this much is known that every river, even all the creeks run through the Cannions or [?] Calumnar blocks of lime stone. Greenston trap [sic], to the north, a little east lays immense plains; to the South a little east are the great Shoshone plains. To the South a little west lyes immense plains of sand, without water, without grass— To the West is a rough broken country, and west of North is the Cottonais Country remarkable for the great quantity of wood, and its difficulty of passage.—The Black Hills are the primitive clay of Minerals, Granite, mica slate, Hornblend & lime rock, without organic relics, occationally I would observe immense beds of red sand-rock, some plains saw slate, coal, iron ore, in one place I only found quantities of greasy quarts and Talcose slate—As we assended the sand Rock and Clay prevailed, which yielded upon the heads of Sweet Water, where began an immense region of lime rock, filling every mountain, and Lava every plain, In one of which, sixty by forty miles is filled up with large crevices about 15 feet wide and debth unknown, without a drop of water or the smallest bunch of grass to be found—The rivers to the East of the Mountains increase their size but slowly, upon the Banks we find no wood to the north fork of the Platte, having to cook with buffaloe dung, dried weeds, occationally, however we find the yellow or bitter cotton wood, above this, and through the Black Hills we have the Sweet Cotton wood, upon which we feed our horses in the Winter, and become extremely fat, above this and upon the Western waters the bitter cotton wood prevails,—upon the Mountains the Pine & ceder are abundant—The thermometer with me ranged at Sun rise through summer at about $47°$ at 2 P.M $72°$ once I saw it as high as $91°$. During the Winter months, in the valleys where we ventured it stood generally about 12 P M $26°$. I left it and travelled across the plains when the cold was much more severe. I find that at $25°$ my feelings were much as they would be in the States at $13°$—but the heat of $72°$ as oppressive as that of the States at $100°$—Soil of the Platte and other rivers to the east are entirely unfit for cultivation—Those of the West much the same till we reach the Boisy or Branch of Lewis' river— The soils here are excellent but not extensive—The Buffaloe range from North to South, begining about the Forks of the Platte and extending to the line running from about the forks of Salmon river to the east of Big Salt or Eutaw Lake, then running so as to strike a little north of Tous. West & south of this line not a Buffaloe can be seen—Elk Deer sheep and bear can there be had for a small party to subsist, excepting some large sand plains where nothing can be found—The Big Salt Lake I have never seen, but am told that it has never been travelled around; five trappers once attempted to coast it, and were near dying from hunger & thirst—Thus much General, I have been able to collect in compliance with my promises, and I hope will be satisfactory when you consider, how extensive this country is—An individual in the States goes his 40 to 50 miles easily, but here, where we have to feed our Horses on grass and being closely tied up every night, require time to feed morning noon and night makes our travelling very slow. I omitted to state that the Horses here are generally about 14 to 14½ hands high, stout built and upon which the Indians will gallop all day. The mode of travelling here is this; The Indians in villages at 8 A M raise camp, the chief leads upon a fast walking Horse, the whole, men, women and children follow, the women with their lodges, poles & baggage, while the men ride totally unincumbered —At 10 or 11 A M the chief pitches his lodge, the camp is then formed, extending along the river or creek, making for each lodge a small brush pen to secure their horses from their enemies; besides planting an 18 inch stake into the ground with a cord attached to the horses fore foot.—In the morning the Horses are turned out at clear day light; making their camps or journies about 8 miles long—The whites travel much in the same way, making however longer journies.—

In the course of a few days I shall be on my rout to the Cottonais Country, and round by the lower Columbia to the South— On my return about the last of June I shall meet Mr M. S. Cerré, and if you shall have any instructions for me, shall be glad to receive them; either to join any party that might be sent, to comply with any other commands in this Country, or to return to the States[.]

        I have the honor
           to be, General

To Maj. Genl with every consideration
  Alex^r Macomb   Your M^t O^b S^t
  Genl in chief   B. L. E. Bonneville
  U. S. Army.

Appendix B

Washington City
September 30, 1835

To the Honorable Lewis Cass.
Secretary of War.

Sir,

In obedience to your orders I have the honor to report, that in August 1831, I received a furlough from the Commanding General of the Army, to expire in October 1833, with a view of proceeding to the mouth of the Columbia River, and exploring the tract of Country between the settlements of the United States and the ultimate point of destination. I here beg leave to remark that the lateness of the season, when my furlough was granted, absolutely precluded my leaving the Settlements until 1st May 1832—thus in the very onset nine months of my furlough were consumed.—The plan of operations presented to the Commanding General was submitted to the Department of War, and approved & with my furlough received instructions to collect all the information in my power, touching the relative positions of the various tribes of Indians in my route, their numbers, manners and customs, together with a general history of the country through which I was destined to pass—On the 1st of May 1832 I departed from the Frontiers of Missouri with a number of men I had hired for that purpose—My route lay up the Kansas, the main Platte, its northern branches and Sweet Water, and reached the waters of the Colorado of the West, in the latter part of August 1832—Finding that this long journey had very much weakened my horses and that my men were yet badly qualified to feed themselves on small game, when they could scarcely do it among the buffaloe, I determined to travel north into the lands of the Nez-Percez's Flat-Heads, Cottonnains and Pend'Orreilles, where I would find game for my men, and plenty of grass and bark for my horses, and at the same time to become particularly acquainted with these several tribes.—As soon as the snow had disappeared in the Spring 1833 I proceeded to the Big Horn River, by the South point of Wind River Mountains and continued down that river to where it became navigable—here I halted made boats & having engaged a Mr Cerré with several men to proceed to the States and gave him a report for the Commanding General, stating that the shortness of my leave of absence made it impossible for me to accomplish the object contemplated at starting, within its limits, therefore

The ADVENTURES *of* CAPTAIN BONNEVILLE

requested its extension—at the same time reporting the progress I had made. This report cannot now be found in the Office of the Adjutant General; but Captain Cooper recollects such an one was received.—As the application for an extention [*sic*] was made several months anterior to the expiration of the furlough already obtained—having scarcely commenced collecting the information desired and believing there would not be the least difficulty in obtaining a further extension of furlough, I determined to prosecute the object originally intended and proceeded down the Big Horn which runs nearly north giving the advantage of latitudes so high, that I could easily cross over the heads of the Yellow Stone, to the Northern branches of the Columbia, and winter near the Sea—and that in the Spring I could return upon its Southern branches.—which plan I attempted to execute; but finding so much hostility on the part of the Black-Foot, that it was impossible to advance without continual fighting, and severe loss in men and Horses[.] As several battles had already been fought with these Northern tribes I found it absolutely necessary for me to retreat by the south point of the Wind River Mountains, by doing which I reached the Banneck's late in the winter 1833, and my men passed the remainder of that season with them. Constantly intent upon getting to the lower Columbia, I left my party with the Bannecks tribe and on the 25 December, 1833 started with three men down Snake river in order to ascertain the best manner of entering the vast wilderness still to the west, leaving instructions with the party in my rear to descend Snake River the moment the winter broke up and meet me in my ascent. In obedience to these instructions the party started, but finding that I did not arrive at the point proposed, after tarying until they had exhausted every means of subsistence, they determined to abandon the route, and returned above the Banneck tribe, to the buffaloe ground, where I overtook them the 16th June, 1834—and when I learned they had relinquished the prosecution of their route under the belief that my party of three men and self had been killed & they had so reported. Knowing that Buffaloe were generally plenty upon the heads of Black-Foot and Portneuf rivers I determined to go there and make meat sufficient to subsist my party on its descending the Columbia.— Upon this route I fell in with Mr. Cerré 28th June 1834, the gentleman to whom I had eleven months before entrusted my com-

Appendix B

munications to the General in Chief, which he informed me, he had delivered, and that the General appeared perfectly satisfied with my Report and also with my determination to persevere in the course I had adopted and persued; that owing to his remaining longer in New York, than he had originally contemplated, he was prevented returning to Washington and consequently had left the former city without bringing an extension of my furlough or any communication whatever from the Dept. of War—Highly gratified at the verbal report of Mr Cerré of the flattering expressions made by the General in Chief, I was inspired with renovated ardor for the enterprise I had undertaken[,] being now determined to accomplish it at all hazards. Previous to putting this intention into practice I had prevailed upon Mr. Cerré to take charge of my letters and reports to the General in Chief, General Eustes and other Gentlemen, which although he had now become attached to the American Fur Company: and felt some delicacy in doing, he did promise to forward them to their various addresses, upon his reaching Council Bluffs— These letters owing to causes impossible for me to explain, I regret to state, never reached their destination, which appears to have been the fate of most of the communications made to the States & which it was next to an impossibility to accomplish without employing persons expressly for that purpose.—

Having supplied my party & self each with a load of dried meat, I proceeded West, West North West over the Portneuf and Cassia Mountains and fell upon Snake River early in July 1834—Kept down the valley of that river for several days, then left it taking a course West South West over the Wyee and Gun River Mountains, so as to fall low down upon the Columbia, which I did about thirty miles below Walla Wallah a trading post of the Hudson Bay Company: to which place I repaired in order to procure provisions. On my arrival aid of every species was not only refused, but the settlers used all their influence, with the Indians, not only not to trade with us but to hold no intercourse whatever. Here I became acquainted with the Sho sho coes, the Lower Nez Percez, or Salmon eaters, the Skynses, the Walla-wallah and Tovellican [*sic*] tribes—Notwithstanding the unkind reception of the traders I continued down the Columbia, subsisting on horses, dogs, roots & occasionally a salmon, until I reached the vecinity of Mounts Hood & Baker [*sic*], both of which are visible from the Pacific Ocean. I now discovered that if I advanced much further, the snow that was then falling in the mountains, would soon prevent my retreat from this impoverished country and that in the spring I would not have a horse left—as it would become indispensably necessary to slaughter them for subsistence.—I consequently took a South course and entered the mountains of John Day's River, gradually turning my course towards the mountains of the upper Country [Portneuf R.], which I reached the 15 November 1834. My men and Horses [were] completely exhausted. Shortly after this moving slowly up Bear River, I fell in with a Village of Sho Shones and determined to unite with them to pass the Winter.—About the 10th January 1835 we came upon a Village of Eutaw Indians, that had been caught there by the snow, as the two tribes were at War, I used all my influence and a treaty of peace was made between these two tribes—and all united for greater safety from the Black Foot, tribes continually prowling for plunder & delighting in bloodshed.

Believing now that I had fully executed the order of the General in Chief and that from my maps, charts and Diary I would be able to furnish the department of War, with every information desired, respecting the Rocky Mountains and the Oregon Territory—I therefore congratulated myself with the pleasing anticipation that in the spring I should be able to leave this cold and solitary region for the more genial one of Society & civilization.—Accordingly, so soon as the snows had melted away I moved eastwardly to the Popo Asie river, where I lay to give my horses flesh and good hoofs for the long rout of returning home.—which I did by the heads of Powder River and its mountains arriving at Independence Missouri the 22d August 1835—.Judge then, upon my return to the settlements, what must have been my mortification, when instead [of] the approbation I expected for my exertions and enterprise, I learned my name had been dropped from the rolls of the Army and the consiquent loss of my commission which I held dearer that [than] life.

Trained at the Military Academy, I became as it were identified with the Army; 'twas my soul, my existence, my only happiness[,] and at a time, that I was exerting every nerve to win the approbation of my superiors—I find myself branded as a culprit—'tis mortifying indeed—My character as a soldier has been fair too

Appendix B

long—to believe my superiors will hesitate one moment, to restore me my character, and my rank.—
        I have the honor to be, Sir,
          very respectfully
        your Most Obdt. Svt.
        B. L. E. Bonneville
                  Late Capt. 7. Regt. U.S. Infantry

BONNEVILLE'S ITINERARY AND CHRONOLOGY

May 1, 1832	Bonneville departs from Fort Osage, Missouri.
May 12	Reaches Kansas River.
May 13	Fords Kansas River.
June 2	Reaches Platte River twenty-five miles below Grand Island.
June 11	Reaches forks of the Platte River.
June 13	Crosses South Platte River to North Platte.
June 26	Reaches Laramie River.
July 12	Leaves North Platte and angles off southwest to the Sweetwater River.
July 14	Reaches the Sweetwater.
July 20	Sights the Wind River Mountains; sees the Utah (Uintah) Mountains to the south.
July 24	Crosses the Continental Divide at South Pass.
July 26	Fontenelle overtakes Bonneville.
July 27	Bonneville reaches Green River.
Early August	Builds Fort Bonneville between Green River and Horse Creek.
August 22	Leaves Fort Bonneville and starts for Salmon River via Jackson Hole.
September 3	Crosses Teton Pass and descends into Pierre's Hole. Camps on site of recent battle of Pierre's Hole.
September 4	Resumes march toward Salmon River.
September 19	Reaches upper waters (Lemhi River?) of the Salmon River.
September 26	Establishes first winter camp on Salmon River five miles below junction of Lemhi River.
November 20	Leaves first winter camp after sending fifty men under Walker south to the Snake River sometime after November 7.
November 21 to December 9	Bonneville establishes second winter camp on North Fork of the Salmon among Nez Percé and Flathead Indians.
December 9	Raises camp and with Indians presumably moves up the main stream of the Salmon.
December 26	Leaves with thirteen trappers to search for Matthieu.

Appendix B

	Travels south along Salmon River to the Pahsimeroi River; ascends this and crosses over to Little Lost River via John Day's Defile.
January 12, 1833	Reaches Snake River after crossing Big Lost River (Godin's River) and the Snake River Plain.
January 13	Finds two of Matthieu's men on Snake River. Camps on Snake the remainder of January and during early February in neighborhood of Bannack Indians.
February 3	Matthieu and several trappers reach Bonneville's Snake River camp.
February 19	Bonneville sets out north with sixteen men to return to *caches* on Salmon River.
February 28	Reaches Big Lost River (Godin's River) after struggling across Snake River Plain in deep snow. Camps on Big Lost River and hunts buffalo.
March 6	Resumes march.
March 11	Meets Flathead Indians.
March 13	Meets the Nez Percés.
March 14	Reaches *caches* on Salmon River.
March 18	Leaves Salmon River *caches* with trappers and Indians and starts south along Salmon River for Big Wood River (Malade River).
About April 6	Camps on Big Lost River (Godin's River). Here runs into band of trappers led by Milton Sublette and J. B. Gervais. The two parties camp near each other, prevented from reaching the Malade by deep snow on mountain pass.
April 25	Bonneville's and Sublette's companies raise camp and succeed in crossing the pass to Malade River.
April 26	Reaches the Big Wood River area and begins spring trapping.
Early June	Sets out for Salmon River *caches* to meet Cerré.
June 15	Reaches Salmon River *caches*. Prepares to move back toward Snake River.
June 24	Meets his clerk Hodgkiss somewhere between Salmon River *caches* and Snake Plain, and soon thereafter camps on the Snake.
July 2	Nathaniel Wyeth overtakes Bonneville.

July 6	Bonneville and Wyeth set out for Green River and the rendezvous of 1833.
July 7	Bonneville and Wyeth camp at Henry's Fork.
July 13	Bonneville arrives at Green River rendezvous being held near his fort.
July 24	Walker party leaves Green River for Great Salt Lake and California.
July 25	Bonneville and Cerré leave rendezvous with furs for Big Horn River.
July 29	Bonneville camps on Wind River. Writes letter to Major General Macomb.
August 4	Campbell, Fitzpatrick, Stewart, and Wyeth overtake Bonneville. Bonneville soon sends parties ahead to trap west of Big Horn River.
August 29	Arrives at Medicine Lodge Creek to meet his trappers.
September 1	Withdraws from Big Horn area because of Indian danger and sets out for Wind River. Soon begins ascent of Wind River Mountains seeking a shorter route to Fort Bonneville.
September 17	Returns to Fort Bonneville after using Popo Agie and South Pass route.
September 18	Leaves Fort Bonneville and follows Green River north toward Union Pass.
September 25	Rejoins his main party on east side of Wind River Mountains after descending Wind River. Camps for two or three days; then moves south toward Sweetwater River and South Pass.
About Sept. 30	Reaches Sweetwater River.
October 14	Returns to *caches* at Fort Bonneville.
October 25	Having moved south through Green River valley, Bonneville strikes LaBarge Creek.
October 26	Reaches Hams Fork; finds Fitzpatrick and trappers with Shoshonie Indians.
November 6	Encamped on Bear Lake after moving west from Hams Fork.
November 10	At Soda Springs (Beer Springs).
November 11	Bonneville sets out north via Portneuf River to locate Hodgkiss trapping on headwaters of Salmon River.
November 20	Meets Hodgkiss in mountains north of Snake River.

Appendix B

December 4	Rejoins his men at a spot north of Beer Springs where he had left them. Shortly thereafter establishes winter camp near the Portneuf River.
December 25	Sets out on reconnoitering expedition along the Snake and through Blue Mountains into Hudson's Bay Company territory.
January 12, 1834	Bonneville reaches Bruneau River (Powder River) three miles above its mouth.
January 13	Moves down Bruneau to the Snake.
February 15	Reaches Imnaha River after traveling along west bank of Snake River.
February 16	Continues down Imnaha River and camps on it.
Later	Comes to Way-lee-way River (Grande Ronde River) and travels down it to Snake River.
March 4	Reaches Fort Walla Walla on the Columbia.
March 6	Rebuffed at Fort Walla Walla, Bonneville begins return trip to the Portneuf over approximately the same route.
May 12	Reaches Portneuf River two months late.
May 18	Shortly after this date camps above American Falls.
June 1	Joins main party on Blackfoot River.
June 3	Sets out up the Blackfoot River to rendezvous with his company on Bear Lake.
June 13	Reaches Little Snake Lake (Bear Lake).
June 16 (?)	Walker party from California rejoins Bonneville on Bear River.
June 28	Cerré rejoins Bonneville on Bear River.
July 3	Bonneville leaves Bear River for the Columbia, traveling first along Bear and Blackfoot rivers.
July 10 or 11	Wyeth overtakes Bonneville.
July 12 (?)	Bonneville moves west to Portneuf River.
July and August	Moves along left side of Snake River. Reaches Gun Creek (Powder River) and ascends it to headwaters of the Grande Ronde River. Moves into Grande Ronde Valley.
August 31	Wyeth, having built Fort Hall, overtakes Bonneville and joins him in Grande Ronde Valley for part of one day.
September	Bonneville is again rebuffed at Fort Walla Walla;

The Adventures of Captain Bonneville

	moves west to Ottolais River (Umatilla River) and continues west on the Columbia to John Day River.
October 1	Begins his retreat along John Day River and turns back toward Blue Mountains.
October 20	Reaches the Snake again.
November 15 (?)	Camps on headwaters of Portneuf River.
November 17	Reaches *caches* on Bear River. Arranges for winter camp on upper Bear River with the Shoshonie Indians.
April 1, 1835	Breaks up Bear River winter camp. Starts east towards Hams Fork and Green River.
June 10	Camps east of Wind River Mountains on the Popo Agie.
June 22	Meets Walker and Montero with their trappers at mouth of the Popo Agie. Shortly thereafter begins return journey to Missouri settlements.
August 22	Reaches Independence, Missouri.

Editor's Bibliography

I. Manuscripts

A. *National Archives*

Letter from B. L. E. Bonneville to Major General Alexander Macomb, Washington, May 21, 1831.

Letter from B. L. E. Bonneville to Major General Alexander Macomb, New York City, July 18, 1831.

Letter from Major General Alexander Macomb to B. L. E. Bonneville, Washington, July 29, 1831.

Letter from B. L. E. Bonneville to Colonel Roger Jones, adjutant general, St. Louis, September 10, 1831.

Letter from B. L. E. Bonneville to Colonel Roger Jones, adjutant general, Cantonment Leavenworth, October 10, 1831.

Letter from B. L. E. Bonneville to Colonel Roger Jones, adjutant general, Franklin, Missouri, December 5, 1831.

Letter from B. L. E. Bonneville to Major General Alexander Macomb, Crow Country, Wind River, July 29, 1833.

Report of Major General Alexander Macomb, Washington, May 28, 1834.

Order No. 42. Adjutant General's Office, May 31, 1834.

Letter of Washington Irving to Major General Alexander Macomb, New York, September 20, 1835.

Letter of B. L. E. Bonneville to Lewis Cass, secretary of war, Washington, September 26, 1835.

Report of the case of Captain Bonneville to Lewis Cass, secretary of war; Adjutant General's Office, September 29, 1835.

Letter of B. L. E. Bonneville to Lewis Cass, secretary of war, Washington, September 30, 1835.

Letter from officers of Fort Gibson to Lewis Cass, secretary of war, Fort Gibson, November 3, 1835.
Letter of Brigadier General Matthew Arbuckle to Brigadier General Roger Jones, Fort Gibson, November 4, 1835.
Report in the case of the late Captain Bonneville from Major General Alexander Macomb to the Secretary of War, Washington, November 17, 1835.
Letter of B. L. E. Bonneville to Lewis Cass, secretary of war, Washington, November 25, 1835.
Letter from B. L. E. Bonneville to Lewis Cass, secretary of war, Washington, December 7, 1835.
Letter from M. S. Cerré to B. L. E. Bonneville, St. Louis, December 9, 1835.
Letter from Major General Alexander Macomb to Lewis Cass, secretary of war, Washington, December 12, 1835.
Letter from R. Jones, adjutant general to the secretary of war, Washington, January 4, 1836.
Letter of Lewis Cass, secretary of war, to the President of the United States, January 5, 1836.
Andrew Jackson to the Senate of the United States, Washington, January 6, 1836.
Letter of B. L. E. Bonneville to Lewis Cass, secretary of war, Washington, March 11, 1836.
General Order No. 25, by Roger Jones, adjutant general, Washington, April 22, 1836.
Letter from B. L. E. Bonneville to Brigadier General Roger Jones, adjutant general, Fort Leavenworth, August 7, 1836.
Letter from B. L. E. Bonneville to Brigadier General Matthew Arbuckle, Fort Gibson, October 20, 1836.
Letter from Robert G. Campbell on behalf of Mrs. Sue Bonneville to General E. D. Townsend, adjutant general, St. Louis, June 16, 1878.
Statement of the Military Service of Benjamin L. E. Bonneville, Major General Robert C. Davis, adjutant general, June 25, 1926.

B. *Missouri Historical Society*

Letter from B. L. E. Bonneville to David Adams, mouth of Horse River, August 17, 1832.
Letter from L. Fontenelle to Wm. Laidlaw, Green River rendezvous, July 20, 1833. Chouteau-Maffitt Collection.

Editor's Bibliography

Contract between Nathaniel Wyeth, Thomas Fitzpatrick, and Milton Sublette, Big Horn River, August 14, 1833. Sublette Papers.

Letter from Zenas Leonard for Bonneville and Company to Antonio Montaro, Wind River, January 11, 1835.

Letter from B. L. E. Bonneville to David Adams, Fort Gibson, June 23, 1837.

Letter from Antonio Montero to David Adams, Independence, Missouri, August 5, 1838.

Joshua Pilcher to Papin, Picotte and Chardon, Upper Missouri, September 2, 1838.

II. BOOKS AND PAMPHLETS

Alter, J. Cecil. *James Bridger*. Salt Lake City, Shepard Book Company, 1925. Reprinted Columbus, Long's College Book Company, 1951.

Ball, John. *Autobiography of John Ball*. Grand Rapids, The Dean-Hicks Company, 1925.

Bancroft, Hubert Howe. *History of the Northwest Coast*. Vol. XXVIII in *The Works of Hubert Howe Bancroft*. San Francisco, The History Company, 1886.

Beal, M. D. *A History of Southeastern Idaho*. Caldwell, The Caxton Printers, 1942.

Beckwourth, James P. *The Life and Adventures of James P. Beckwourth*. Ed. by Bernard DeVoto. New York, Alfred A. Knopf, 1931.

Billington, Ray Allen. *The Far Western Frontier*. New York, Harper and Brothers, 1956.

Bonneville, Benjamin L. "Captain Bonneville's Letter," *Contributions to the Historical Society of Montana*, Vol. I, 105–10. Helena, Rocky Mountain Publishing Company, 1876.

Brooks, Van Wyck. *The World of Washington Irving*. New York, E. P. Dutton and Company, 1944.

Campbell, Robert. *The Rocky Mountain Letters of Robert Campbell*. New York, printed for Frederick W. Beinecke, 1955.

Chardon, Francis A. *Journal at Fort Clark, 1834–1839*. Ed. by Annie Heloise Abel. Pierre, Department of History, State of South Dakota, 1932.

Chittenden, Hiram M. *A History of the American Fur Trade of the Far West.* 3 vols. New York, Francis P. Harper, 1902. Reprinted Stanford, Academic Reprints, 1954.

Cleland, Robert G. *This Reckless Breed of Men.* New York, Alfred A. Knopf, 1952.

Conner, Daniel E. *Joseph Reddeford Walker and the Arizona Adventure.* Ed. by Donald J. Berthrong and Odessa Davenport. Norman, University of Oklahoma Press, 1956.

Coutant, C. G. *The History of Wyoming.* Laramie, Chaplin, Spafford and Mathison, Printers, 1899.

Dale, Harrison C. *The Ashley-Smith Explorations and the Discovery of a Central Route to the Pacific.* Glendale, Arthur H. Clark Company, 1941.

DeVoto, Bernard. *Across the Wide Missouri.* Cambridge, Houghton Mifflin Company, 1947.

Farquhar, Francis P. *Exploration of the Sierra Nevada.* San Francisco, California Historical Society, 1925.

Ferris, W. A. *Life in the Rocky Mountains.* Ed. by Paul C. Phillips. Denver, Old West Publishing Company, 1940.

Field, Matthew C. *Prairie and Mountain Sketches.* Ed. by Kate L. Gregg and John F. McDermott. Norman, University of Oklahoma Press, 1957.

Foreman, Grant. *Pioneer Days in the Early Southwest.* Cleveland, Arthur H. Clark Company, 1926.

Frémont, John C. *The Exploring Expedition to the Rocky Mountains, Oregon and California.* Buffalo, Geo. H. Derby and Company, 1849.

Frost, Donald McKay. *Notes on General Ashley, the Overland Trail, and South Pass.* Worcester, American Antiquarian Society, 1945.

Hafen, LeRoy R., and Carl C. Rister. *Western America.* New York, Prentice-Hall, Inc., 1941.

―――, and Francis M. Young. *Fort Laramie and the Pageant of the West.* Glendale, Arthur H. Clark Company, 1938.

―――, and W. J. Ghent. *Broken Hand, the Life Story of Thomas Fitzpatrick.* Denver, Old West Publishing Company, 1931.

Harris, Burton. *John Colter.* New York, Charles Scribner's Sons, 1952.

Hodge, Frederick W. *Handbook of American Indians.* 2 vols. Washington, Government Printing Office, 1907-10. (Smithsonian Institution, Bureau of American Ethnology, Bulletin 30.)

Editor's Bibliography

Irving, Pierre Munroe. *The Life and Letters of Washington Irving*. 4 vols. New York, G. P. Putnam, 1863.

Irving, Washington. *Astoria, or Anecdotes of an Enterprise beyond the Rocky Mountains*. 2 vols. Philadelphia, Carey, Lea, and Blanchard, 1836.

———. *The Rocky Mountains; or Scenes, Incidents, and Adventures in the Far West, digested from the Journal of Captain B. L. E. Bonneville, U.S.A., and Illustrated from various other sources*. 2 vols. Philadelphia, Carey, Lea, and Blanchard, 1837.

———. *A Tour on the Prairies. The Crayon Miscellany*. Philadelphia, Carey, Lea, and Blanchard, 1835.

———. *A Tour on the Prairies*. Ed. by John F. McDermott. Norman, University of Oklahoma Press, 1956.

———. *The Western Journals of Washington Irving*. Ed. by John F. McDermott. Norman, University of Oklahoma Press, 1944.

Langfeld, William R. *Washington Irving, a Bibliography*. New York, New York Public Library, 1933.

Larpenteur, Charles. *Forty Years a Fur Trader on the Upper Missouri*. Ed. by Milo M. Quaife. Chicago, R. R. Donnelley and Sons, 1933.

Latrobe, Charles J. *The Rambler in North America*. 2 vols. New York, Harper and Brothers, 1835.

Leonard, Zenas. *Adventures of Zenas Leonard, Fur Trader and Trapper, 1831–1836*. Ed. by W. F. Wagner. Cleveland, The Burrows Brothers Company, 1904.

———. *Adventures of Zenas Leonard, Fur Trader*. Ed. by John C. Ewers. Norman, University of Oklahoma Press, 1959.

Lewis, Meriwether, and William Clark. *Original Journals of the Lewis and Clark Expedition*. Ed. by Reuben Gold Thwaites. 8 vols. New York, Dodd, Mead and Company, 1904–05.

McArthur, Lewis A. *Oregon Geographic Names*. Portland, Binfords and Mort, 1944.

Marsh, James B. *Four Years in the Rockies; or, the Adventures of Isaac P. Rose*. New Castle, Pa., W. B. Thomas, 1884. Reprinted Columbus, Long's College Book Company, n.d.

Meek, Stephen Hall. *The Autobiography of a Mountain Man, 1805–1889*. Ed. by Arthur Woodward. Pasadena, Glen Dawson, 1948.

Miller, Alfred Jacob. *The West of Alfred Jacob Miller*. Ed. by Marvin C. Ross. Norman, University of Oklahoma Press, 1951.

Morgan, Dale. *The Great Salt Lake.* Indianapolis and New York, The Bobbs-Merrill Company, 1947.

———. *Jedediah Smith and the Opening of the West.* Indianapolis and New York, The Bobbs-Merrill Company, 1953.

Newell, Robert. *Robert Newell's Memoranda.* Ed. by Dorothy O. Johansen. Portland, Champoeg Press, 1959.

Nidever, George. *The Life and Adventures of George Nidever.* Ed. by William H. Ellison. Berkeley, University of California Press, 1937.

Parker, Samuel. *Journal of an Exploring Tour beyond the Rocky Mountains.* Ithaca, published by the author, 1838.

Porter, Kenneth W. *John Jacob Astor, Business Man.* 2 vols. Cambridge, Harvard University Press, 1931.

Ross, Alexander. *Fur Hunters of the Far West.* Ed. by Kenneth A. Spaulding. Norman, University of Oklahoma Press, 1956.

Russell, Isaac K., and Howard R. Driggs. *Hidden Heroes of the Rockies.* Yonkers-on-Hudson, World Book Company, 1927.

Russell, Osborne. *Journal of a Trapper.* Ed. by Aubrey L. Haines. Portland, Oregon Historical Society, 1955.

Ruxton, George F. *Life in the Far West.* Ed. by LeRoy R. Hafen. Norman, University of Oklahoma Press, 1951.

Stewart, Sir William George Drummond. *Altowan.* 2 vols. New York, Harper and Brothers, 1846.

———. *Edward Warren.* 2 vols. London, G. Walker, 1854.

Stuart, Robert. *The Discovery of the Oregon Trail: Robert Stuart's Narratives.* Ed. by Phillip A. Rollins. New York, Charles Scribner's Sons, 1935.

———. *On the Oregon Trail: Robert Stuart's Journey of Discovery,* Ed. by Kenneth A. Spaulding. Norman, University of Oklahoma Press, 1953.

Sunder, John E. *Bill Sublette, Mountain Man.* Norman, University of Oklahoma Press, 1959.

Swanton, John R. *The Indian Tribes of North America.* Washington, Government Printing Office, 1952 (Smithsonian Institution, Bureau of American Ethnology, Bulletin 145.)

Townsend, John K. *Narrative of a Journey across the Rocky Mountains to the Columbia River.* Philadelphia, Henry Perkins, 1839. Also in *Early Western Travels,* Vol. XXI. Ed. by R. G. Thwaites. Cleveland, Arthur H. Clark Company, 1905.

Editor's Bibliography

Victor, Francis Fuller. *The River of the West.* Hartford, Columbian Book Company, 1870.

Warren, Gouverneur. *Memoir to Accompany the Map of the Territory of the United States from the Mississippi River to the Pacific Ocean* in *Reports of Explorations and Surveys . . . in 1853–56.* 36 Cong., 2 sess., Sen. Exec. Doc. [unnumbered], Vol. XI. Washington, George W. Bowman, Printer, 1861.

Watson, Douglas S. *West Wind: the Life Story of Joseph Reddeford Walker.* Los Angeles, privately printed, 1934.

Wetmore, Alphonso. *Gazetteer of the State of Missouri.* St. Louis, C. Keemle, 1837.

Wheat, Carl I. *Mapping the Transmississippi West, 1540–1861,* Vol. II. San Francisco, Institute of Historical Cartography, 1958.

Williams, Stanley T. *The Life of Washington Irving.* 2 vols. New York, Oxford University Press, 1935.

Wyeth, John B. *Oregon; or a Short History of a Long Journey.* Cambridge, printed for John B. Wyeth, 1833. Also in *Early Western Travels,* Vol. XI. Ed. by R. G. Thwaites. Cleveland, Arthur H. Clark Company, 1905.

Wyeth, Nathaniel J. *The Correspondence and Journals of Captain Nathaniel J. Wyeth, 1831–6.* Ed. by F. G. Young. *Sources of the History of Oregon,* Vol. I. Eugene, University Press, 1899.

III. PERIODICALS

Anonymous. "The Rocky Mountains," *New York Review,* Vol. I (October, 1837), 439–40.

Ashley, William H. "The Diary of William H. Ashley," ed. by Dale L. Morgan, *Bulletin of the Missouri Historical Society,* Vol. XI (October, 1954), 9–40; (January, 1955, 158–86; (April, 1955), 279–302.

Ball, John. "Across the Continent Seventy Years Ago," *Oregon Historical Quarterly,* Vol. III (March, 1902), 82–106.

Beall, Thomas J. "Recollections of Wm. Craig," Lewiston, Idaho, *Morning Tribune,* March 3, 1918.

Bonneville, Benjamin L. [Contract between B. L. E. Bonneville and David Adams], St. Louis, February 22, 1832. *Midwest Review,* Vol. VIII (July–August, 1927), frontispiece.

Campbell, Robert. "Correspondence of Robert Campbell, 1834–1845," ed. by Stella M. Drumm and Isaac H. Lionberger, *Glimpses of the Past,* Missouri Historical Society, Vol. VIII (January–June, 1941), 3–65.

Hafen, LeRoy. "The Bean-Sinclair Party of Rocky Mountain Trappers, 1830–32," *Colorado Magazine,* Vol. XXI (July, 1954), 161–71.

Holmes, Reuben. "The Five Scalps," ed. by Stella M. Drumm, *Glimpses of the Past,* Missouri Historical Society, Vol. V (January–March, 1938), 3–54.

Lindsley, Margaret Hawkes. "Major Andrew Henry," *Scenic Idaho,* Vol. X (Summer, 1955), 6–28.

McDermott, John F. "Washington Irving and the Journal of Captain Bonneville," *Mississippi Valley Historical Review,* Vol. XLIII (December, 1956), 459–67.

Mattes, Merrill. "Hiram Scott, Fur Trader," *Nebraska History,* Vol. XXVI (September, 1945), 127–62.

Niles Register, Vol. XLIII (October 27, 1832), 131; Vol. LI (September 3, 1836), 16; Vol. LII (March 25, 1837), 50.

Overmyer, Philip Henry. "Members of the First Wyeth Expedition," *Oregon Historical Quarterly,* Vol. XXXVI (March, 1935), 95–101.

Parton, James. "John Jacob Astor," *Harper's Monthly,* Vol. XXX (February, 1865), 308–23.

Perrine, Fred S. "Early Days on the Willamette," *Oregon Historical Quarterly,* Vol. XXV (December, 1924), 295–312.

Seton, Alfred. "Life on the Oregon," ed. by Fred S. Perrine, *Oregon Historical Quarterly,* Vol. XXXVI (June, 1935), 185–204. Originally published in *American Monthly Magazine* (May–June, 1835).

Sublette, William L. [Letter to William H. Ashley], Lexington, Mo., September 21, 1832; *Missouri Republican* (October 16, 1832).

Todd, Edgeley W. "John Colter, Mountain Man," *Colorado Quarterly,* Vol. II (Summer, 1953), 79–91.

———. "Scotsman in Buckskin," *Colorado Quarterly,* Vol. IV (Winter, 1956), 309–36.

———. "Washington Irving Discovers the Frontier," *Western Humanities Review,* Vol. XI (Winter, 1957), 27–39.

Index

Adams, David: xxvii, xxvii n., xxix, xxxviii, 366n.; contract with Bonneville, xxvii–xxviii; losses in Crow country, 150–52, 387; trouble with Arickara Indians, 151–52.
Adventures of Captain Bonneville, The: vii, xvii, xliii–xlvi, xliv, xliv n., xlvi, 53n., 64n., 90n., 93n., 260n.; critical reception, xliv, xlv; decline in reputation, xlvii
Alcova, Wyo.: 40n.
Allen, Paul: xxvi n.
American Falls, Idaho: 221 & n., 276.
American Fur Company: xxx n., xxiv, xlix n., 5n., 7 & n., 17, 47 & n., 50, 51, 56n., 74 & n., 90 & n., 93, 96, 151n., 305, 308 & n., 309, 314, 315n., 320n., 356, 365n., 382, 383, 393; competes with Rocky Mountain Fur Company, 8; at Green River rendezvous (1833), 154 & n., 155n., 209n.; divides territory with Rocky Mountain Fur Company, 326
Antelope: Indian method of killing, 225–26; surround, 353
Antelope Hills: 43n.
Arapaho Indians: 51, 383, 384, 385
Arapooish (Crow chief): 164n., 169–70; 306, 366; account of Crow country, 164–65; death, 367
Arbuckle, Brig. Gen. Matthew: xxxv, xxxvi n., xxxviii
Arickara Indians: 29, 151–52, 317, 383
Arkansas River: 26, 27, 301, 350, 382, 384

Ashley, William H.: xxiii, 5 & n., 7, 31n., 74n., 88, 166, 383
Astor, John Jacob: xvii, xix, xlix & n., li, 3, 4, 7, 259
Astoria: xlix & n., li n., 3, 4, 159, 219, 233, 251, 259, 326, 328, 375, 376, 378; expedition to, 5n.; *see also* Fort Astoria
Astoria: vii, xviii & n., xxi, xlii, xliii, xliv, xlvi, xlix n., li n., lii n., 3n., 5n., 135n., 148n., 166n., 174n., 229n., 248n., 260n., 326n., 328n.; origin of, xix; map, xii & n.; decline in reputation, xlvii; cited, 348n.
Atkinson, General Henry: 167–68

"Bad Pass": 177, 183
Ball, John: cited, 64n.
Bancroft, Hubert Howe: disservice to Bonneville, xlvii
Bannock (Banneck) Indians: 51, 121, 123, 124, 127, 212, 213, 214, 216, 219, 337, 338, 384, 385, 391
Baptiste (Nez Percé Indian): 304, 307, 321, 321n.
Barren River: *see* Humboldt River
Battle Lakes: *see* Humboldt Sink *and* Carson Sink
Battle of Pierre's Hole: *see* Pierre's Hole, Battle of
Beall, Thomas J.: 281n.
Bear Lake: xxxiii, xxxiv, 74n., 99n., 210 & n., 279 & n.
Bear River: xxxiv, 74 & n., 99n., 101, 125, 161 n., 210 & n., 275, 276, 277

409

n., 278, 279, 282, 302, 322, 348n., 349n., 350, 352, 394
Bear-baiting: 293, 297
Beaver: food of, 196n.; habits, 195–97
Beaverhead River, "Gates" of: 81n.
Becknell, William: xxiii, 17n.
Beckwourth, James: xxx n., 5n., 150n., 164n., 209n., 367n., 368n.
Bee hunters: 22–24, 22n.
Beer Spring: 211 & n., 216, 277–78; *see also* Soda Springs
Benton, Senator Thomas Hart: xxxviii
Big Horn Mountains: 39n., 172, 177, 178, 181
Big Horn River: 4n., 15in., 163, 171, 172 & n., 173n., 177n., 178 & n., 183n., 207, 301 & n., 303, 305n., 308, 312, 382, 383, 391
Bighorn sheep: 31, 32n.
Big Lost River: 99n., 119n., 128n., 133n.
Big Porcupine River: 365n.
Big Southern Butte: 120n.
Big Wood River: 128n., 131n., 136n.
Big Wyre River: 249 & n.; *see also* Owyhee River
Biscuit root: 260
Bitterroot Range: 81n., 88n., 104n.
Bitterroot River: 88n.
Black Hills: 36 & n., 37, 39, 164, 190, 301, 350, 383, 388, 389
Blackfoot Indians: xxxii, 4n., 10, 35, 50, 56, 67, 68, 74n., 75, 85, 86 & n., 87, 93, 94, 96 & n., 102–108, 111, 119, 123, 124, 127, 129, 130, 139–41, 144–46, 166, 179, 200, 213, 215, 216, 217, 275–77, 297, 308–10, 314 & n., 317, 345, 363, 366, 369, 374, 385, 387, 388, 393; oppose Bonneville on Big Horn River, xxxii, 185, 392; in Battle of Pierre's Hole, 57ff.; ambush party from Pierre's Hole, 65; ambush Vanderburgh, 92; conflict with Bonneville's men, 182–85, 298–99; defeated by Crow Indians, 367–68, 368n.; kill Immel and Jones, 382; *see also* Surcie, Piegan, Blood, *and* Gros Ventre Indians
Blackfoot River: 99n., 123, 275, 276, 325n., 327, 329, 349n., 392
Blacksnake Hills: 320n.
Blood Indians: 51, 385; *see also* Blackfoot Indians
Blue John (Nez Percé chief): 140–41
Blue Mountains: 175, 219 & n., 232, 261, 348, 349n., 393
Blue River (Kan.): 27n.
"Bluffs," The: 172
Bodega Bay: 290 & n.
Boise (Boisée) River: 123, 136 & n., 216, 229, 249n., 337, 387, 389
Bondago, port of: *see* Bodega Bay
Bondurant, Wyo.: 314n.
Bonneville, Benjamin L. E.: xxiv n., xxvii n., xxix, xxx n., xxxiin., xxxviii, xxxix n., xlii–xliii, xlii n., xlvii n., xlixn., 16n., 17n., 20n., 22, 25, 27n., 30n., 33 & n., 35–38, 39n., 40 & n., 41, 43, 44, 46, 48 & n., 51, 64n., 67, 68, 70, 72–79, 81 & n., 82, 85, 86, 97, 99n., 101, 103, 104 & n., 105–11, 112, 113, 115, 117, 118, 120 & n., 122, 123, 125, 126–28, 132, 133, 135–38, 139n., 142–48, 151, 154, 155n., 157, 159 & n., 161n., 163n., 172n., 174, 176, 182, 185, 186, 200, 204–207, 210 & n., 211, 212, 213–17, 219 & n., 220–21, 223–25, 227–29, 237, 240, 242, 245–47, 249, 251, 252, 254, 263, 265–67, 269, 271n., 274–77, 279, 280, 282, 284 & n., 285 & n., 296n., 297, 300 & n., 302, 303, 307, 315, 322, 326–28, 330, 332, 333, 335, 336, 338, 343–45, 347, 352, 355, 361, 362, 366n.; financial aspects of expedition, vii, xxiv, xxvi, li; army status, xix, xxv, xxxi, xxxiii–xxxiv, xxxv–xxxvi, xxxvii, 371n., 379–80; "Journal of a March . . . to Fort Clark," xx, xxi n.; maps, xx–xxii, xli–xliii; submits journal to War Department, xx, lxi; at U. S. Military

Index

Academy, xxii, 1; contributes essay to *Astoria*, xxii n.; Mexican passports, xxv, xxvii, 163n.; employees of, xxvii n.; letters to David Adams, xxix–xxxi, xxxviii, 150n.; letter to Macomb, xxx–xxxi, xxxiii, xxxv, xxxix, 26n., 381–90; recommendations concerning Oregon country, xxxi, 381; first expedition to Columbia River, xxxii, 219ff., 230ff., 237ff., 258–61, 271–73; second expedition to Columbia River, xxxiv–xxxv, xli, 301, 323–25, 329n., 339n., 340n., 347 & n., 370 & n., 393; letters to Lewis Cass, xxxv; xxxvii, xl, xli, 391–95; sells manuscript to Irving, xxxvii; returns to mountains (1836), xxxvii; later career, xxxviii–ix; death, xxxix; appraisal of expedition, xxxix–xliii; takes first wagons across South Pass, xliii, 5n., 16n., 46; relations with Lucien Fontenelle, 49, 71; route to Jackson Hole, 76n., 77n.; winter camps of 79n., 80 & n., 81, 99n., 100, 122–27, 218–20, 274, 350–60, 387; learns of Vanderburgh's death, 93n.; search for Matthieu, 101, 116 ff.; as physician to Indians, 101–102, 248, 256; returns to Salmon River *caches*, 131, 137; competes with Milton Sublette, 133–36; at Green River rendezvous (1833), 148ff.; losses for 1822–23, 150n.; plan to explore Great Salt Lake, 162 & n.; climbs Wind River Mountains, 187–99, 192 n.; pursued by Indians, 202–203; attitude toward Walker expedition, 296; holds rendezvous on Bear River (1834), 299–300; Townsend's impressions of, 340 n.; chronology and itinerary, 396–400
Bonneville, Mrs. Sue: xxxix n.
Bonneville's Folly: *see* Fort Bonneville
Boone, Daniel: 65
Bourdalone, B.: xxvii n., 366n.
Bradshaw, Capt. John: 286n., 296n.

Bridger, James: 5n., 7 & n., 54n., 64n., 74 & n., 75, 90, 90n., 91 & n., 93–95, 96n., 134n., 150n., 154n., 366n., 383; arrowhead removed from, 95n.; discovery of Great Salt Lake, 159n.
British Columbia: xxxii, 381, 382
Bruneau River: 222 & n., 223n.
Buckeye: 76–77, 78, 296–99
Buenaventura River: xlii & n.
Buffalo: 29, 81, 137, 313, 361–62, 386; buffalo hunting, 186, 212–14, 279, 327, 350–52; range, 389–90
Bull boats: 315 & n.; construction, 177 & n., 303 & n.
Bull fighting: 294, 297
Burning Mountain: 172
Burnt Rocks: 128

Cache Valley: 99n.
Cain, Tom: 41–42
California missions: San Juan Bautista, 286n., 291n.; Jesuit, 287, 288; Dominican, 289; Franciscan, 288, 289; San Carlos Borroméo de Carmelo, 291n.
Camas Creek: 138n.
Camash: *see* camass plant
Camass plant: 231 & n., 261 & n., 342
Camp Henry (1810): stones of, 4–5n.; 148n.
Campbell, Robert: 5n., 7, 36n., 37, 52, 54n., 55, 59, 60 & n., 61, 64n., 66, 154n., 160n., 163, 164, 171, 172n., 174, 176, 178, 303, 308n., 315n.; letter reporting Bonneville's death, xxxix n.; partnership with Wm. Sublette, 7n.; with Arapooish, 169–70; letter to Hugh Campbell, 308n.
Canadian River: 384
Carmen, Idaho: 80n.
Carson, Kit: 150n.
Carson Sink: 285n.
Cascade Range: 377n.
Casper, Wyo.: 39n.
Cass, Lewis: xxxv, xxxvi, xxxvii, xl, xli; letter from Bonneville (Sept. 30,

411

1835), 391–95
Cassié River: 282; *see also* Raft River
Cather, L.: 5n.
Cayuse Indians: 339n., 340
Cerré, Michel Sylvestre: xxx, xxxi, xxxii, xxxiv, 16 & n., 17 & n., 79, 80 n., 86, 131, 137n., 154n., 163, 171, 178, 300, 300n., 363n., 385, 388, 390–92; delivers Bonneville's first report to Maj. Gen. Macomb, xxxi, xxxiii; rejoins Bonneville at Bear River, xxxiii; letter to Bonneville, xxxiii–xxxiv; brings supplies to Bonneville, 299
Che-ku-kaats: *see* Edward Rose
Cheyenne Indians: 383, 385
Chimney Rock: 29, 29n., 33n.
Chippewyan Mountains: *see* Rocky Mountains
Chittenden, Hiram M.: appraisal of Bonneville's expedition: xl ff.
Chouteau, A. P.: xxiii
Chouteau, Pierre: 325n.
Christy, Edmund: 154n.
Clark Fork: 88n., 365
Clark(e), Gen. Marston G.: 20
Clark(e), Gen. William: 13n., 51
Clay River: 230n.; *see also* Grande Ronde River
Cody, Wyo.: 173n.
Colorado of the West: *see* Green River
Colter, John: 4n., 173 & n.; race from Blackfeet, 174 n.
"Colter's Hell": 173 & n.
Columbia River: xix, xxxii, xxxiv, xlix n., 4n., 44, 53, 72n., 159, 176, 190, 251, 301, 322, 347, 348, 375, 376, 377n., 382, 384, 385, 387, 388, 390, 391, 393
Comanche Indians: 27, 383
Comanche Prairies: 387
Comanche River: 387
Commissary Ridge: 46n.
Continental Divide: xxiii, 4n., 16n., 46n., 81n., 200n.
Cooper, Capt.: 392
Cornice, the: *see* Teton Pass

Cottonois Indians: *see* Kutenais Indians
Council Bluffs: xxxiv, 320n., 393
Coutant, C. G.: quoted, 172–73n., 192n.
Cowish plant: 260 & n.
Craig, William: xxvii n., 282n.
Craters of the Moon National Monument: 136n.
Crooks, Ramsay: 5 & n., 8, 219
Crow country: 164–65
Crow Indians: xxx n., 10, 29, 33–36, 38, 68, 75, 94, 109n., 151, 166, 167, 168n., 200, 205, 206, 305, 309, 317, 366 & n., 369, 383–85, 387; rob Fitzpatrick, 207–208; molest N. Wyeth, 305–307; defeat Blackfeet, 366–68 & n.

Daily, Nathan: xxviii n.
Dalles, The: 377n.
Daniel, Wyo.: 49n.
Days Creek: 99n.; *see also* Little Lost River
Delaware Indians: 19
Deschutes River: 377
DeVoto, Bernard: xlvii, 143n.
Digger Indians (Root Riggers): *see* Shoshokoes
Dillon, Mont.: 81n.
Dripps, Andrew: 47n., 56n., 74 & n., 90 & n., 91 n., 99n., 154n., 383
Drummond, Idaho: 5n.
Dubois, Wyo.: 200n.

Eaton, Gen. John H.: xxxv
Edible plants: 25 & n., 231 & n., 260 & n.
Eneeshur Indians: *see* Skin Indians
Ermatinger, Francis: 65n., 138n., 139n., 143n., 351n.
Eustis, Gen. Scott: xl, 393
Eutaw Indians: 352, 355–57, 360, 394
Eutaw Mountains: *see* Uinta Mountains

Fellows, Dr.: 321
Ferris, Warren Angus: xlvi, 81n., 91n., 92n., 99n., 154n.; cited, 64n., 65n.,

412

Index

74–75n., 81n., 86n., 90n., 92n., 126n., 157n.; quoted, 80n., 92n., 160n.; relates Vanderburgh's death to Bonneville, 93n.
Fifteenmile Creek: 177n.
Fink, Mike: 5n.
Fishing Falls: 221
Fitzpatrick, Thomas: 5n., 7 & n., 54n., 74, 75, 90 & n., 91, 93, 99n., 134n., 135n., 154n., 166, 167, 174, 176, 178, 206, 307, 326n., 383; pursued by Blackfeet, 54–56; robbed by Crows, 207–208, 209n.
Flathead House: 88n.
Flathead Indians: 51, 56n., 57, 86, 88, 90n., 97, 98, 100–103, 128, 143, 144, 343, 344, 346, 384, 385, 387, 388, 391
Fontenelle Creek: 47n.
Fontenelle, Lucien: 46, 47n., 48 & n., 67, 68, 71, 74, 75, 90n., 154n., 325n., 365n., 383; entices men from Bonneville, 49
Fort Astoria: xix; *see also* Astoria
Fort Bonneville: xxix, 49, 99n., 207n.; location, 49n.; described by W. A. Ferris, 49n.; *caches*, 73; Stewart's description of, 149n.
Fort Bridger: 74n.
Fort Cass: 151, 151n., 305, 308, 309 & n.
Fort Clark: xxxix, 320n.
Fort Clatsop: xix
Fort Colville: 382
Fort Fillmore: xxxix
Fort George: 376
Fort Gibson: xxii, xxiii, xxxv, xxxvi n., xxxvii, xxxviii, 17n., 371
Fort Hall: 325n., 326n., 374
Fort Kearny: xxxix
Fort Laramie: 36n.; *see also* Fort William (on Laramie River)
Fort Leavenworth: xxvii, xxxvii, xxxviii, 320n., 321 & n.
Fort Lisa: 4n.
Fort McKenzie: 50n.

Fort Marcy: xxxix
Fort Nonsense: *see* Fort Bonneville
Fort Osage: xxv, xxvii, 13 & n.
Fort Piegan: 50n.
Fort Pierre: 320n., 365n.
Fort Smith: xxii, xxiii, xxxix n.
Fort Union: 47n., 90n., 314, 315
Fort Vancouver: xxiii, xxxii, 4 & n., 175, 258, 328n., 376, 377, 382
Fort Walla Walla (Fort Wallah-Wallah): xxxiv, 243, 249, 257, 258, 259, 340n., 347 & n., 382, 393; desribed by N. J. Wyeth, 258n.
Fort William (on Laramie River): 37; *see also* Fort Laramie
Fort William (on Upper Missouri River): 7n., 308n., 315n.
Fort Williams (on Wappatoo Island, Columbia River): 374
Fourche de Glace: see Grande Ronde River
Fowler, Jacob: xxiii
Foy, John: 65 & n., 77 & n.
Fraeb, Henry: 7n., 54n., 134n., 383
Frémont, Lieut. John C.: 26n., 135, 211n.
Fur trade: 372, 377

Gale, Joseph: xxvii n., 281n.
Gallatin, Albert: xlii & n.
Gallatin River: 365n.
Gamble, Archibald: 13n.
Gantt, John: 383
Gantt and Blackwell: 54n., 65n.
Gervais, Jean Baptiste: 7n., 54n., 134 & n., 154n., 383
Glass, Hugh: 5n.
Glenn, Col. Hugh: xxiii
Glenns Ferry, Idaho: 222n.
Goddin's River: *see* Godin's River
Godey, Alexis: xxvii, 281n.
Godin, Antoine: 58, 120
Godin, Thyery: 119n.
Godin's Defile: 134
Godin's River: 119 & n., 120, 124, 127–

413

28 & n., 133 & n., 134, 135; *see also* Big Lost River
Gordiez River: *see* Big Lost River
Grand Island: 26 & n., 27n.
Grand Rond: *see* Grande Ronde River
Grande Ronde River: 230 & n., 244n., 338, 339 & n.
Grande Ronde Valley: 230n., 340n.
Graybull River: 183
Great Island: *see* Grand Island
Great Salt Lake: xxii n., xxx, xlii, 74n., 160n., 161n., 162–63n., 210, 280–82, 294n., 296, 384, 389, 390; discovery and circumnavigation, 74n., 159–62
Green River: xxix, 5n., 6 & n., 16n., 40n., 44 & n., 46 & n., 47 & n., 48, 49n., 54, 55, 67, 72, 76, 99n., 146, 149, 171, 185, 187, 191, 199–201, 207, 215, 281, 287, 360, 381–83, 387, 388, 391
Greybull River: 177n., 183n.
Gros Ventre River: 99n.
Gros Ventres du Baum: 309n.
Gros Ventres of the Missouri: 51; *see also* Blackfoot Indians
Gros Ventres of the Prairies: 51, 385, 387; *see also* Blackfoot Indians
Gulf of California: 44, 191, 287, 288
Gun Creek: 229, 230n., 274, 338; *see also* Powder River (Oregon)
Gun River Mountains: *see* Blue Mountains

Hamilton, James A.: 366n.
Ham's Fork: 207 & n., 210n., 299 n., 328n., 360 & n.; rendezvous of 1834, 326n.
Hand game: 331–32 & n.
Hane's Fork: *see* Ham's Fork
Hanging Ears: *see* Pends Oreille Indians
Hardister, Benjamin: xxvii n.
Harrison, Dr. Benjamin: 154n., 172n.
Hay-she-in-cow-cow (Lower Nez Percé Indian): 253, 256

Head, Mark: xxvii n., 282n.
He-mim-el-pilp (Lower Nez Percé chief): 258
Henry, Andrew: 4–5 & n., 6, 148n., 382
Henry's Fork: 138 n., 139 n., 148 & n., 150n.
Henry's Fort: xxi, 88, 99n., 148n.
Hoback, J.: 5n.
Hoback River: 65n., 314n.
Hodgkiss, E. (?): xxvii n., 132, 138 & n., 145, 146, 212, 215, 216
Holmes, George: 154n.; victim of mad wolf, 157n.
Holmes, Capt. Reuben: 167–68n.
Hook, Maj. James Harvey: xxxvii; dedication, liv
Horn Mountains: 190
Horn River: 172, 174, 176, 183; *see also* Big Horn River
Horse Creek: xxix, 49n., 99 & n., 144, 149, 150 & n., 167, 388
Horse Prairie: 81 & n., 85, 86 & n., 104, 139, 142
Horse racing: 343
Hudson's Bay Company: xxiii, xxx, xxxi, xxxii, xlv n., 4 & n., 50, 87, 88, 138 n., 144, 175, 219, 247, 258–61, 283, 323, 325n., 327, 331, 340n., 342, 343, 347, 348, 377, 381, 386, 393; competitive advantage, 143, 382
Humboldt, Baron Alexander von: xxvi n.
Humboldt River: 162n., 163n., 283 & n., 284, 285, 294 & n., 296n.
Humboldt Sink: 283n., 285 & n.
Hunt, Wilson Price: xxi, 5 & n., 148 n., 166, 167, 219 & n., 348n.

Ice River: *see* Grande Ronde River
Immahah River: *see* Imnahah River
Immel and Jones: 382
Imnahaha River: 230 & n., 234 & n., 242, 259, 265, 271 & n.
Independence, Mo.: 9n., 16n., 17n.,

414

Index

53, 322n., 370n., 386, 394; described, 19n.
Indian dogs: 38
Indian potato: 25, 25n.
Indian religion: 229, 259, 356, 384; Christian beliefs of Nez Percés, 83; among Pends Oreilles and Flatheads, 88–89; among Skins, 343–46
Indians: in California, 295
Iroquois Indians: 87, 383
Irving, Pierre M.: xx
Irving, Washington: xix, xix n., xxxvii, xliii, xlviii, li n., lii n., 5n., 7n., 30n., 36n., 53n., 54n., 88n., 135n., 175n., 176 n., 209 n., 222 n., 223 n., 277n., 296n., 300n., 377 n., 379n.; uses Nathaniel Wyeth's manuscript journal, viii, 53n., 303–12 n.; and the West, xvii, xlvi, 19n.; meets Bonneville, xvii, xix, xxi, lii; visits Bonneville, Washington, D. C., xix, xxxvi, liii; buys Bonneville's manuscript, xx, xxxvii; visits Canada (1803), xviii; requests copies of Bonneville's maps, xx–xxi; correspondence with N. J. Wyeth, xlv n.; friendship with Astor, xlix n.; meets William Sublette, 64n., 66 & n.

Jackson, President Andrew: xxxvi
Jackson, B.: 5n.
Jackson, David: 5n., 7n., 383
Jackson, Wyo.: 77n.
Jackson('s) Hole: 18n., 57n., 65 & n., 77, 149, 174n., 314
Jackson's Little Hole: 314n.
Janisse, Antoine: xxvii n., 281n.
Jarvie, ———: see Jean Baptiste Gervais
Jarvis, Leonard: 139n.
Jefferson Barracks: xxii, xxxix
Jenkins, Perry W.: quoted, 49n.
Jennings, ———: xxvii n., 126
Jesuits: 287, 288
John Day River: 348 & n., 349, 393

John Day's Creek: 118; see also Little Lost River
John Day's Defile: 116 & n.
Jones, Col. (later Maj. Gen.) Roger: xxvii n., xxxiv
Jordan River: 161n.

Kansas Indians: 13n., 20
Kansas River: 20 & n., 26n., 386, 391
Kees Kees Kee River: 261n.
Kemerer, Wyo.: 210
Kern River: 294n.
Kiowa (Kioway) Indians: 27
Kipp, James: 50n., 320n.
Kooskoos River: 261n.
Kosato: 108–10, 129, 130, 139, 140, 142, 146
Kowsoter (Nez Percé chief): 112, 115
Kutenai Indians: xxxii, 143 & n., 144, 384, 388, 391

LaBarge, Wyo.: 47n.
LaBarge Creek: 207 & n.
Lagoda, The: 286n.
Laidlow, William: 320n., 365n.
Lake Bonneville: xxii n.; see also Great Salt Lake
Laramie Mountains: 36n., 39n.
Laramie River: 30, 36 & n., 37, 54n., 386
Laramie's Fork: see Laramie River
Larpenteur, Charles: 154n., 157–58n., 171n., 172n., 176n., 308n.
Latrobe, Charles: 19–20n., 66n.
Leavenworth, Col. Henry: 321n.
Lee, Daniel: 322n.
Lee, Jason: 322n., 339n.
Lemhi River: 79n.
Leonard, Zenas: xxvii n., xlvi, 65n., 154n., 292n.; quoted, 17n., 162–63 n., 283n., 284n., 285n., 294n., 296n., 365n., 370n.; cited, 54n., 64n., 281n., 283n., 285n., 286n., 299n., 300n., 301n., 365–66n., 368n.
LeRoy, ———: xxvii n., 126
"*Les dignes de pitié*": 193, 217, 384

415

Lewis, Meriwether: 20, 51
Lewis and Clark Expedition: xix, xxii, 5 1n., 173
Lewis River: *see* Snake River
Lexington, Mo.: xxvii, 16n.
Liberge's Ford: *see* LaBarge Creek
Liberty, Mo.: xxvii
Lisa, Manuel: xxiii, 173n.
Little Blue River: 27n.
"Little Hole": 86n.
Little Horn Mountains: 172, 179, 185
Little Horn River: 178
Little Lake: *see* Bear Lake
Little Lost River: 99n., 116n., 118 & n.
Little Lost River Sinks: 119 & n.
Little Missouri River: 164
Little Popo Agie: 173n.
Little Porcupine River: 365n.
Little Salmon River: 99n.; *see also* Pahsimeroi River
Little Sandy Creek: 46n.
Little Snake Lake: *see* Bear Lake
Little Vermillion River: 322n.
Little Wyer: 229; *see also* Malheur River
Logan, Utah: 99n.
London, England: 376
Long, Maj. Stephen: expedition, xxiii
Loreto, Lower Calif.: 287n.
Loretto: 94–96 & n.
Louisiana Territory: xxiii
Lovelock, Nevada: 285n.
Lower California: 287
Lower Nez Percé Indians: 103, 106, 123, 229, 235, 239, 242, 243, 245, 247, 248, 250, 253, 257, 259, 260, 265, 267, 393

McBride, P.: 5n.
McKay, Alexander: 328n.
McKay, Thomas: 328 & n., 331n.
M'Kenzie: *see* Kenneth McKenzie
Mackenzie, Sir Alexander: xxvi n.
McKenzie, Kenneth: 314 & n.
McLoughlin, Dr. John: 4n., 139n., 328 n., 376n.

Macomb, Maj. Gen. Alexander: xx, xxi, xxv, xxvi, xxxiii–xxxvi, xxxix n., xl, 393, 394; letter to Lewis Cass, Nov. 17, 1835, xli; letter authorizing Bonneville's leave of absence, 379–80
M'Tulloch: *see* Samuel Tulloch
Mad wolves: at rendezvous of 1833, 157 & n.
Madison River: 91n.
Malade River: 128 & n., 131 & n., 132–36, 387; *see also* Big Wood River
Malheur River: 229; *see also* Little Wyer River
Mandan Indians: 320n.
Mangeurs de lard: 70
Marias River: 50, 51n.
Mary's River: *see* Humboldt River
Matthieu, ———: xxvii n., xxix, 74 & n., 99n., 101, 116, 122, 125–27
May Dacres: 322, 340n.
Medicine Lodge Creek: 177 & n., 178, 180, 183n.
Meek, Joseph: xxvii n., 91n., 96n., 150n., 154n., 162n., 281n., 366n.
Meek, Stephen: xxvii n., 162n., 281n.
Meldrum, Robert: xxx n.
Menard, Pierre: xxiii, 4n.
Mexican horsemen in California: 293
Minnetaree Indians: 168n.
Mississippi River: 320
Missoula, Montana: 88n.
Missouri Fur Company: 74n.
Missouri River: xxi, 5, 13n., 20n., 44, 47n., 88, 91, 163, 167, 190, 312, 314, 315 & n., 316, 320, 382, 384, 385
Mitchell, Robert: xxvii n., 281n.
Mojave Desert: 294n.
Monterey, Calif.: 286 & n., 290, 292, 294, 296, 296n.
Montero, Antonio: xxvii n., 150 n., 360 n., 367–70; leads Bonneville trapping party into Crow country, 300–301n.; sends express to Bonneville, 350; joins Bonneville on Wind

Index

River, 365; evidence of his existence, 365-66n.; letter from Leonard, 365-66n.; Powder River camp, 366n.; Letter to David Adams, August 5, 1838, 366n.; ordered to leave Indian country, 366n.
More, Joseph: 65 & n., 77 & n., 314; Wyeth finds powder flask of, 314-15n.
Mount Baker: 393
Mount Bonneville: 192n.
Mount Hood: 393
Mountaineer: *see* trappers
Multnomah River: *see* Willamette River
Multnomah (Willamette) valley: 159

Nebraska River: *see* Platte River
New Caledonia: *see* British Columbia
New York Review: xliv n.
Newell, Robert: xxvii n., 154n.
Nez Percé Indians: xxx, 51, 56 n., 57, 61, 78, 79 n., 81, 85, 88, 97, 98, 100, 102-105, 107, 108, 111, 127-30, 138-40, 143-45, 237, 331, 343-46, 384, 385, 387, 388, 391; Christian beliefs of, 83; disastrous battle with Blackfeet, 140-42; *see also* Lower Nez Percé Indians *and* Upper Nez Percé Indians
Nidever, George: xxvii n.; cited, 64 n., 281n., 285n.; quoted, 163n.
Niles Register: xliii, 66n., 281n.
North Platte, Neb.: 27n.
North Platte River: 27n., 28, 33n., 36n., 39, 40 & n., 54
Northwest Company: xxiii, xxvi n., 3, 4, 10, 143, 191, 259; Irving meets members of, xviii
Nuttall, Thomas: 322n., 326

O'Fallon, Maj. Benjamin: 154n., 167 & n.
Ogden, Peter Skene: 283 & n.
Ogden's River: *see* Humboldt River
Oil Spring: 172-73 & n.

O-push-y-e-cut (Lower Nez Percé chief): 255-57
Oregon River: *see* Columbia River
Oregon Territory: xlv, 394
Oregon Trail: xxix, 29n., 36n., 40n.
Osage Indians: 13n., 20, 217
Otter River: 365n.
Ottolais River: 347; *see also* Umatilla River
Owl Creek: 177n.
Owyhee River: 249n.

Pacific Fur Company: xix, xlix, 5n.
Pahsimeroi River: 99n., 116n.
Pambrun, Pierre C.: 258 & n., 259; refuses to supply Bonneville, 261
Pambrune: *see* Pierre C. Pambrun
Parker, Samuel: 64n.
Patten, ———: 314n.
Pawnee Indians: 20, 370n., 383-85
Payette, Francis: 143n., 261 & n.
Payette River: 123, 228n., 337, 387
Pends Oreille Indians: 88, 93, 98, 100, 146, 384, 387, 391
Piegan (Peagan) Indians: 51, 385; *see also* Blackfoot Indians
Pierced-nose Indians: *see* Nez Percé Indians
Pierre (Indian chief): 87
Pierre's Hole: 18 & n., 52, 56 & n., 67, 68, 74, 87, 95, 99n., 145, 146, 149, 175; 1832 rendezvous, 54n., 56ff.
Pierre's Hole, Battle of: 18n., 57-63, 63-64n., 120, 309 & n., 315; casualties, 63 & n.; eyewitness accounts listed, 64n.
Pike, Lieut. Zebulon M.: xxiii
Pilcher, Joshua: 74n., 320n., 366 n., 383
Pirogue: 315n.
Platte River: 20n., 26 & n., 33n., 37, 164, 370 & n., 381-84, 386, 388, 389, 391; forks of, 27
Pocatello, Idaho: 99n.
Ponca Indian village: 320n.
Ponca Post: 320n.

417

Poordevil Indians: 217
Popo Agie: 46n., 172, 173n., 174, 186, 187, 208, 300n., 301n., 360n., 365n., 394; pronunciation, 172n.
Portland, Ore.: 258n.
Portneuf River: 99n., 123, 150n., 212, 214, 223, 260, 274, 275, 325, 327, 330, 349, 374, 392, 393
Portuguese Houses: 366n.
Powder River (Idaho): 223–25; *see also* Bruneau River
Powder River (Ore.): 229, 338n.; *see also* Gun Creek
Powder River (Wyo.): xxxviii, 39n., 151, 164, 178, 207, 365n., 394; Montero's camp, 366n.
Powder River Mountains: 39 & n.
Prairie Chicken River: *see* Green River
Prairie fire: 338–41
Prairie Hen River: *see* Green River
Prairie tomato: 25 & n.
Priors (Pryors) Fork: 365n.
Provot, Etienne: 47n.
Pryor, Nathaniel: xxiii

Racine Amère: 88, 384
Raft River (Cassié River): 220 & n., 282 & n.
Raynolds, Capt. W. F.: xxx n.
Red River: *see* Vermillion River
"Red root": 25, 25n.
Ree Indians: *see* Arickara Indians
Rendezvous, trappers': 5n., 8–9; in Pierre's Hole (1832), 17–18 & n., 52, 56ff.; on Popo Agie (1830), 46n.; on Green River (1833), 99n., 144, 145, 149ff., 154–57, 163n., 388; Bonneville's on Bear River (1834), 299–300, 299n.; on Ham's Fork (1834), 326n.; debauchery, 385; prices of goods, 386
Renwick, James: 191n.
Republican River: 26–27n., 386, 388
Riverton, Wyo.: 172n., 186n.
Robidoux, Joseph: 320n.
Rocky Mountain Fur Company: 7 & n., 17, 46, 52, 54n., 56n., 57, 74, 75, 90, 91n., 93, 96, 99n., 134n., 150, 174, 308, 374; competition with American Fur Company, 8; at 1833 rendezvous, 154 & n., 155n., 163 & n.; repudiates contract with Nathaniel Wyeth, 326 & n.; divides territory with American Fur Company, 326
Rocky Mountains: 4, 8, 31, 36n., 43, 45, 46, 51, 164, 188, 189, 181, 191 & n., 251, 301, 320, 371, 377, 379, 381, 394
Rocky Mountains, The: xvii, xliv n.; maps in, xxii, xlii; *see also The Adventures of Captain Bonneville*
Root Diggers: 224, 225, 226, 227, 228, 283, 352; *see also* Shoshokoes
Rose, Edward: 166–68 & n., 306; death, 168
Rose, Isaac P.: cited, 322n.
Rosebud River: 365n.
Ross, ———: xxvii n., 126
Ross, Alexander: 119n.
Rosy River: 387
Russell, Osborne: 172n., 322n., 325n., 366n.
Russian settlements: in California, 290, 376
Ruxton, George F.: 211n.

St. Anthony, Idaho: 148n.
St. Joseph, Mo.: 320n.
St. Louis, Mo.: xxvii, xxx n., 5n., 9n., 17n., 50, 301, 374, 375, 385
St. Louis Missouri Fur Company: 4n.
Salmon: 72–73; 332
Salmon, Idaho: 79n.
Salmon River: 72 & n., 74, 76, 78, 79n., 88, 125, 127, 128, 132, 133n., 137n., 145, 150, 212, 216, 276, 384, 387, 388, 390; north fork, 111 & n.
Salmon River Mountains: 135n., 220
Salt River: 99n.
Salt River Range: 46n., 99n., 121–22, 360n.
Salt weed: 128

Index

San Antonio, Texas: xxii
San Carlos Borroméo de Carmelo Mission: 292n.
San Diego, California: 290
San Francisco Bay: 287n., 290
San Gabriel, plain of: 288
San Joaquin Valley: 286n., 294n., 296n.
San Juan Bautista Mission: 286n. 292n., 294n.
Sandwich Islands: 175-76
Sandy Creek: 46n.
Santa Barbara, Calif.: 290
Santa Fé, N. M.: 28n.
Santa Fé trade: xxiii, 13n., 17n., 28n.
Santa Fé Trail: 20n.
Sauvie Island: 374n., 376
Sawtooth Mountains: 131n., 136n.
Scott, Hiram: 29-30, 30-31n.
Scott's Bluff: 29
Seeds-ke-dee Agie: *see* Green River
Seton, Alfred: xxvi, li & n.
Sheep Rock: xxvii n., 125, 126n., 277n.
She-wee-she-ouaiter: 264-70
Shoshokoes: 224, 245, 283, 342, 342n., 352, 393; *see also* Root Diggers
Shoshone (Shoshonie) Indians: 51, 74 & n., 125, 176, 207, 274, 350, 355-58, 360, 384, 385, 387, 394; at 1833 rendezvous, 156
Shoshone River: 173n.
Sibley, George C.: 13n.
Sierra Nevada Mountains: 285 & n., 289, 294n.
Sinclair, Alexander: 57 & n., 60, 65n.; killed in Battle of Pierre's Hole, 60-61
Sinclair, Pruett: 61n.
Sioux Indians: 383
Skin Indians: 259 & n., 339, 342, 393; religious practices, 343-46
Skynses: *see* Skin Indians
Smith, Jedediah Strong: xxiii, xlii n., 5n., 6n., 7 & n., 166, 167, 282n., 383
Smith's Fork: 365n.
Snake Indians: 154n., 156n.
Snake River: xxi, 4n., 72n., 98, 99n., 120, 122, 123, 135 & n., 148, 175, 212, 214, 216, 219-25, 228-31, 234, 242, 244, 251, 263, 273, 275, 295n., 332, 336, 338, 349, 383, 384, 387, 392, 393; Grand Canyon of, 232n.; *see also* Lewis River
Snake River Plain: 101, 119n., 127, 128 n., 135, 136, 138, 142
Soda Spring(s): 211; described, 277n.; *see also* Beer Spring
South Pass: 40n., 174n., 360n.; rediscovery of, 5n.; Bonneville takes first wagons over, 16n.
South Platte River: 27 & n.
Stephens, Alfred K.: 65 & n.
Stevens: *see* Alfred K. Stephens
Stewart, Sir William George Drummond: 149, 154n., 158n., 174-75, 178, 208, 328 & n., 329n., 339n.
Stinking River: 173, 365n.; *see also* Shoshone River
Stuart, Robert: 5 & n.
Sublette, Milton: 7n., 54n., 57, 59, 63, 134n., 154n., 175, 177, 315n., 322n., 383; competes against Bonneville, 134-36; with Nathaniel Wyeth, 304; leaves Wyeth on Missouri River, 315; contract with Wyeth, 326n.
Sublette, William: 5n., 7, 52 & n., 53 & n., 54n., 55 & n., 56, 57, 59, 60, 64, 65, 75, 154n., 167, 308 & n., 326, 383; partnership with Robert Campbell, 7n., 36n., 37; takes wagons to rendezvous, 46 & n.; wounded at Pierre's Hole, 61; exploration of Great Salt Lake, 161; opposes American Fur Company, 315 & n.; meets Wyeth on Missouri River, 315
Surcie Indians: 51, 385; *see also* Blackfoot Indians
Sweetwater River: 40 & n., 45 & n., 54, 171, 174 & n., 176, 190, 206, 386, 388, 389, 391

Taos, N. M.: 28n.
Tar spring: *see* oil spring

Teton Basin: 18n.
Teton Pass: 18n., 57n., 77n., 99n.; the Cornice, 149, 388
Teton Range: 4n., 57n., 65n., 174n.
The Horse (Bannock chief): 123, 124
Thermopolis, Wyo.: 177n.
Thing, Capt. Joseph: 322n.
Thompson, David (?): 191
Three Buttes: xliii, 120, 122; *see also* Twin Buttes *and* Big Southern Butte
Three Forks: 4n., 91n., 384
Three Tetons: 56, 122, 136, 191, 309n.
Tongue River: 178, 208, 365n.
Tonquin: 328
Too-el-ican Indians: 342, 342n., 393
Topeka, Kan.: 20n.
Tour on the Prairies, A: vii, xvii, xliv, 19n., 22n.
Townsend, John K.: 325n., 326; cited, 53n., 322n., 331n.; quoted, 119n., 156-57, 329n., 340n.
Trappers: characterized, 10-12; French, 11, 145; American and French contrasted, 19; definition of free, 68-69; hired, 69; atavism of, 69-70; *mangeurs de lard,* 70; marriage to Indian girl, 112-13; Indian wife of, described, 113-14; at Beer Spring, 277-78; outfit of, 336; and Indian wives, 357, 363; wages, 386
Trapping: method of, 197-98, 336; dangers of, 336-37
Treaty of Joint Occupation: xxxi, 376n.
Tulloch, Samuel: 151n., 309 & n., 366n.
Tulloch's Fort: *see* Fort Cass
Twin Buttes: 120n.
Twin Falls: 221n.

Uintah Mountains: 43 & n., 125
Umatilla River: 347 & n.
Union Pass: 200n.
United States Military Academy: xxii, xxvii, l, 394
Upper California: 289

Upper Nez Percé Indians: 238, 243, 244, 248, 249

Vanderburgh, William H.: 56n., 74 & n., 75, 90n., 91n., 373; pursues Fitzpatrick and Bridger, 90ff.; death, 92n., 93 & n.
Vaqueros: 293
Vasquez, Louis: 154n.
Vermilion Sea: *see* Gulf of California
Vermillion River: 26 & n., 27n.
Victor, Frances F.: 90n., 96n., 150n., 209n., 281n., 366n.

Walker expedition to California: xxvii, xxx, xxxii, xlv, 16-17n., 282n.; exploration of Great Salt Lake, 162-63 n.; Mexican passports, 163n.; kills Root Digger Indians on Humboldt River, 283, 284 & n.; first organized party to cross Great Basin, 285n.; crosses Sierra Nevada Mountains, 286-87 & n.; discovers Yosemite Valley, 286n.; leaves California, 294n.; kills Root Digger Indians, 295; rejoins Bonneville after California expedition, 295n.; Bonneville's attitude toward, 296; inaccuracy of Irving's account, 296n.
Walker, Joseph Reddeford: viii, xxiii, xxiii-xxiv n., xxvii, xxx, 16-17 & n., 80n., 86 & n., 98-99n., 120n., 122n., 126n., 150n., 154n., 162-63n., 286n., 296n., 300 & n., 360n., 365n., 366n.; exploration of Great Salt Lake, 162; rejoins Bonneville, 280; expedition to California, 281-96; as an explorer, 296n.; in Crow country (1834-35), 301n.
Walker Lake: 285n.
Walker Pass: 294n.
Wallamut River: *see* Willamette River
Walla-Walla (Wallah-Wallah) Indians: 259, 393
Walla Walla River: 348

420

Index

Wallowa Mountains: 230n., 271n.
Wappatoo Island: 374, 376; *see also* Sauvie Island
War of 1812: xlix n.
Warren, Lieut. Gouverneur: xlii; *Memoir* cited, xlii n., xliii n., 160n.
Way-lee-way River: 244 & n., 245, 250, 251, 259, 339, 342; *see also* Grande Ronde River
Weber River: 161n.
West Point: *see* United States Military Academy
Wetmore, Alphonso: 13-16n.
Wheat, Carl I.: xlii
Wheatley, Col.: *see* Col. William Whitley
White Plume (Kansas Indian chief): 21 & n., 22, 24
Whitley, Col William: 7 & n.
Whitman, Dr. Marcus: 64n.; removes arrowhead from Bridger, 95n.
Wild onion: 25, 25n.
Willamette River: xlv n., 258 & n., 301 & n., 328, 340, 348 & n., 374, 377, 382
Williams, William S.: xxvii n., 281n.
Wind River Mountains: xxi, 40n., 43- 203, 205, 207, 350, 361, 365 & n.
Wind River Mountain: xxi, 40n., 43- 46, 55, 76, 172, 173n., 185, 187, 194, 199, 200, 204, 386, 388, 391
Woody (or Wood) River: *see* Boise River
"Woolly sheep": 31
Worland, Wyo.: 177n.
Wyeth, Charles: 138n.

Wyeth, John B.: cited, 53n.
Wyeth, Nathaniel J.: viii, xxxii n., xlv n., xlvi, 52-53 & n., 55, 56n., 57 & n., 59, 61, 63, 77n., 163n., 175 & n., 176, 177, 223, 301, 309, 312, 314, 315, 320, 321, 326, 327, 330, 344, 345, 348n., 351, 375, 378; quoted, 54n., 138n., 139n., 143n., 150n., 154n., 177n., 220n., 223n., 258n., 277n., 300n., 303-305n., 307-12n., 314- 21n., 325n., 326n., 328n., 329n., 339n., 340n., 351n.; cited, 65n., 155n., 163n., 171n., 176n., 332n., 342n.; journey down Big Horn, Yellowstone, and Missouri rivers, 303-22; organizes Columbia River Fishing and Trading Company in Boston, 322; leaves Independence on second expedition, 322n.; overtakes Bonneville, 323, 339n.; Fort Hall, 325 & n., 326n.; Rocky Mountain Fur Company repudiates contract with, 326 & n.; correspondence with Bonneville, September 1, 1834, 340n.; plans to combine Salmon fishing and fur trade, 374-75

Yellowstone National Park: 251n.
Yellowstone River: xxx n., 4n., 5, 6, 47n., 150, 163n., 164, 172, 174n.; 178n., 190, 308, 312, 314, 365n., 381, 382, 384, 388, 391
Yenghies River: 260 & n.
Yo-mus-ro-y-e-cut (Lower Nez Percé Indian chief): 242, 250, 252, 254
Yosemite Valley: 286n.

THE AMERICAN EXPLORATION AND TRAVEL SERIES

of which *The Adventures of Captain Bonneville* is Number 34, was started in 1939 by the University of Oklahoma Press. It follows rather logically the Press's program of regional exploration. Behind the story of the gradual and inevitable recession of the American frontier lie the accounts of explorers, traders, and travelers, which individually and in the aggregate present one of the most romantic and fascinating chapters in the development of the American domain. The following list is complete as of the date of publication of this volume.

1. Captain Randolph B. Marcy and Captain George B. McClellan. *Adventure on Red River*: Report on the Exploration of the Headwaters of the Red River. Edited by Grant Foreman. Out of print.
2. Grant Foreman. *Marcy and the Gold Seekers*: The Journal of Captain R. B. Marcy, with an account of the Gold Rush over the Southern Route. Out of print.
3. Pierre-Antoine Tabeau. *Tabeau's Narrative of Loisel's Expedition to the Upper Missouri*. Edited by Annie Heloise Abel. Translated from the French by Rose Abel Wright. Out of print.
4. Victor Tixier. *Tixier's Travels on the Osage Prairies*. Edited by John Francis McDermott. Translated from the French by Albert J. Salvan.
5. Teodoro de Croix. *Teodoro de Croix and the Northern Frontier of New Spain, 1776–1783*. Translated from the Spanish and edited by Alfred Barnaby Thomas. Out of print.
6. A. W. Whipple. *A Pathfinder in the Southwest*: The Itinerary of Lieutenant A. W. Whipple During His Exploration for a Railway Route from Fort Smith to Los Angeles in the Years 1853 & 1854. Edited and annotated by Grant Foreman. Out of print.
7. Josiah Gregg. *Diary & Letters*. Two volumes. Edited by Maurice Garland Fulton. Introductions by Paul Horgan.
8. Washington Irving. *The Western Journals of Washington Irv-*

ing. Edited and annotated by John Francis McDermott. Out of print.
9. Edward Dumbauld. *Thomas Jefferson, American Tourist*: Being an Account of His Journeys in the United States of America, England, France, Italy, the Low Countries, and Germany.
10. Victor Wolfgang von Hagen. *Maya Explorer*: John Lloyd Stephens and the Lost Cities of Central America and Yucatán.
11. E. Merton Coulter. *Travels in the Confederate States*: A Bibliography. Out of print.
12. W. Eugene Hollon. *The Lost Pathfinder*: Zebulon Montgomery Pike.
13. George Frederick Ruxton. *Ruxton of the Rockies*. Collected by Clyde and Mae Reed Porter. Edited by LeRoy R. Hafen.
14. George Frederick Ruxton. *Life in the Far West*. Edited by LeRoy R. Hafen. Foreword by Mae Reed Porter.
15. Edward Harris. *Up the Missouri with Audubon*: The Journal of Edward Harris. Edited by John Francis McDermott.
16. Robert Stuart. *On the Oregon Trail*: Robert Stuart's Journey of Discovery (1812–1831). Edited by Kenneth A. Spaulding.
17. Josiah Gregg. *Commerce of the Prairies*. Edited by Max L. Moorhead.
18. John Treat Irving, Jr. *Indian Sketches*, Taken During an Expedition to the Pawnee Tribes (1833). Edited and annotated by John Francis McDermott.
19. Thomas D. Clark (ed.). *Travels in the Old South, 1527–1860*: A Bibliography. Three volumes. Volume One and Two issued as a set (1956); Volume Three (1959).
20. Alexander Ross. *The Fur Hunters of the Far West*. Edited by Kenneth A. Spaulding.
21. William Bollaert. *William Bollaert's Texas*. Edited by W. Eugene Hollon and Ruth Lapham Butler.
22. Daniel Ellis Conner. *Joseph Reddeford Walker and the Arizona Adventure*. Edited by Donald J. Berthrong and Odessa Davenport.
23. Matthew C. Field. *Prairie and Mountain Sketches*. Collected by

Clyde and Mae Reed Porter. Edited by Kate L. Gregg and John Francis McDermott.
24. Ross Cox. *The Columbia River*: Scenes and Adventures During a Residence of Six Years on the Western Side of the Rocky Mountains Among Various Tribes of Indians Hitherto Unknown; Together with a Journey Across the American Continent. Edited by Edgar I. and Jane R. Stewart.
25. Noel M. Loomis. *The Texan–Santa Fé Pioneers*.
26. Charles Preuss. *Exploring With Frémont*: The Private Diaries of Charles Preuss, Cartographer for John C. Frémont on His First, Second, and Fourth Expeditions to the Far West. Translated and edited by Erwin G. and Elisabeth K. Gudde.
27. Jacob H. Schiel. *Journey Through the Rocky Mountains and the Humboldt Mountains to the Pacific Ocean*. Translated from the German and edited by Thomas N. Bonner.
28. Zenas Leonard. *Adventurers of Zenas Leonard, Fur Trader*. Edited by John C. Ewers.
29. Matthew C. Field. *Matt Field on the Santa Fe Trail*. Collected by Clyde and Mae Reed Porter. Edited and with an introduction and notes by John E. Sunder.
30. James Knox Polk Miller. *The Road to Virginia City*: The Diary of James Knox Polk Miller. Edited by Andrew F. Rolle.
31. Benjamin Butler Harris. *The Gila Trail*: The Texas Argonauts and the California Gold Rush. Edited and annotated by Richard H. Dillon.
32. Captain James H. Bradley. *The March of the Montana Column*: A prelude to the Custer Disaster. Edited by Edgar I. Stewart.
33. Heinrich Lienhard. *From St. Louis to Sutter's Fort, 1846*. Translated and edited by Erwin G. and Elisabeth K. Gudde.
34. Washington Irving. *The Adventures of Captain Bonneville*. Edited and with an introduction by Edgeley W. Todd.

The most enduring type face in American typography, from the Colonial period to the present century, has been Caslon, which was originated by William Caslon in England in the eighteenth century and was early exported to American type shops. Appropriate because of the historical link with American literature, Linotype Caslon Old Face was chosen for this edition of *The Adventures of Captain Bonneville*, with handset display in larger sizes of Caslon.

NORMAN

UNIVERSITY OF OKLAHOMA PRESS